NEVER MIND THE MOON

NEVER MIND THE MOON

Jeremy Isaacs

BANTAM PRESS

LONDON • NEW YORK • TORONTO • SYDNEY • AUCKLAND

TRANSWORLD PUBLISHERS
61–63 Uxbridge Road, London W5 5SA
a division of The Random House Group Ltd

RANDOM HOUSE AUSTRALIA (PTY) LTD
20 Alfred Street, Milsons Point, Sydney
New South Wales 2061, Australia

RANDOM HOUSE NEW ZEALAND
18 Poland Road, Glenfield, Auckland 10, New Zealand

RANDOM HOUSE SOUTH AFRICA (PTY) LTD
Endulini, 5a Jubilee Road, Parktown 2193, South Africa

Published 1999 by Bantam Press
a division of Transworld Publishers

A catalogue record for this book is available from the British Library.
ISBN 0593 043553

Typeset in 11/14pt Ehrhardt by Falcon Oast Graphic Art

Printed in Great Britain
by Clays Ltd, Bungay, Suffolk

1 3 5 7 9 10 8 6 4 2

For all who work for, or care for,
the Royal Opera House

CONTENTS

LIST OF ILLUSTRATIONS

HRH Princess Margaret, Darcey Bussell and Plácido Domingo, Farewell Gala, 14 July 1997. © *Bill Cooper*

Richard Jones's *Ring*: *Rheingold*, Act One, Scene One, 1994. © *Clive Barda/Performing Arts Library*.

Poul Elming and Ulla Gustafsson in *Die Walküre*, 1994. © *Clive Barda/Performing Arts Library*

Nigel Lowery's front-cloth for *Götterdämmerung*, 1995. © *Clive Barda/Performing Arts Library*

John Gunter's set for *Der Fliegende Holländer*, 1992. © *Clive Barda/Performing Arts Library*

Gwynne Howell and Nancy Gustafson in Graham Vick's production of *Die Meistersinger von Nürnberg*, 1993. © *Clive Barda/Performing Arts Library*

between pages 292 – 293

The auditorium, Royal Opera House. © *Bill Cooper*

The Royal Opera House photographed in 1990: the scene-painting room, ballet running wardrobe, ballet shoe storeroom and wig studio. *National Monuments Record*

Presenting the lottery application, 4 January 1995. © *Bill Cooper*

Lottery winners: JI and Angus Stirling, Floral Hall, 25 July 1995. © *News Group Newspapers/Andre Camara*

Vivien Duffield. © *Bill Cooper*

Redevelopment: JI in the Floral Hall. © *Times Newspapers Limited/Tim Bishop*

Computer-generated view of the restored Floral Hall. © *Hayes Davidson – Bill Cooper*

A Chance to Dance. JI addresses parents, 23 September 1993. © *Keith Saunders Photography*

A Chance to Dance, 1997. © *Kristyna Kashvili*

Project by the education department at St Clement Danes Primary School. © *Kristyna Kashvili*

Cricket match: ROH vs ENO. *Author's collection*

JI and Gillian Widdicombe, 14 July 1997. *James Peltekian*

The publishers have made every effort to contact the owners of illustrations reproduced in this book. In the few cases where they have been unsuccessful they invite copyright holders to contact them direct.

Line drawings: 6: cartoon by Marc © Anna Ford; 24, 36, 66, 83, 140, 205, 227, 309: from Mel Calman, *Calman at the Royal Opera House*, 1990 © S & C Calman; 38/9, 45, 62, 100, 147, 321: courtesy the Royal Opera House; 62: *Samuel Beckett*, lithograph by Tom Phillips, 1984; 77: costume design for *Cunning Little Vixen* by Bill Dudley © William Dudley; 91: cartoon by Matt © Telegraph Group Ltd, 1999; 106: '1989/90 at a glance' redrawn from the ROH annual report; 113: autograph manuscript for *Gawain* by Harrison Birtwistle © 1990 Universal Edition (London) Ltd. Reproduction by permission; 122: cartoon by McTrusty / © Evening Standard/Solo Syndication; 173: © Dixon Jones BDP; 234: headlines from *The Stage*, by kind permission of *The Stage / Evening Standard & Daily Mail* © Solo Syndication / *Sunday Times* © Times Newspapers Ltd 1996 / *Daily Express* © Express Newspapers; 286: drawing by David Driver, © *The Times*, 1994; 295: 295: cartoon by Trog, © Wally Fawkes; 308, front-cloth design for Jones/Lowery *Ring*: © Nigel Lowery; 321: front cover of *upROHr*, cartoon © Sarah Lenton.

PREFACE

This is a personal account of my time at the Royal Opera House, not an official history. I have put down here what I remember, stated what I believe. There is an Old Testament saying: 'If I am not for me, who is for me?' I am for me, and for the Royal Opera House too.

I owe gratitude to the many colleagues I have consulted. Stephen Mead shared with me his memories of nine seasons in the amphitheatre, Stella Chitty her show reports. Francesca Franchi and Jane Jackson have been their usual helpful and professional selves in the Archive, as has Gina Boaks in the Music Library. Helen Anderson has racked her memory to help clarify mine. Alison Latham has been good enough to read the entire typescript. So has Denis Forman. Martin Ward, of Building Design Partnership, kindly read the chapter on the development, Christopher Nourse the chapters on ballet and several others. The chapter on education owes a great deal to Pauline Tambling. All these made helpful criticisms. Richard Wright, Judith Vickers, Joyce Ryley, Jenny Sunderland, Tessa Forsey and, especially, Siri Fischer-Hansen helped me check facts. For the years before my arrival at Covent Garden, I have referred to Frances Donaldson's *The Royal Opera House in the Twentieth Century*. Michael Kaiser has permitted me to use Royal Opera House papers. I thank him, and also all those whose more casual utterances appear here.

Fiona Maddocks has read these pages more than once, and markedly improved them. Nini Aldridge has coped, super-efficiently as ever, with repeated versions of the text, as well as eliminating howlers. Any errors left are mine.

My wife, Gillian Widdicombe, dearest and sternest critic, wielded the sharpest pencil and left the whole better ordered than she found it. Having supported me through thick and thin at Covent Garden, she has kept me at this till it was completed. She has my gratitude, and my love. Sally Gaminara, at Transworld, has been patient, supportive, encouraging, and Brenda Updegraff's copy-editing logical and meticulous. Katrina Whone was there at the finish.

For everything in these pages only I am responsible.

Jeremy Isaacs
Plakias/Market Weston
May 1998–August 1999

1

VERY HEAVEN

In September 1988, after the first opera production of my time at the Royal Opera House, a revival of Puccini's *Turandot*, I attended a supper party for the cast in the Crush Bar. The Calaf was Franco Bonisolli, an idiosyncratic tenor who once missed a high C in a performance and gave it instead, without warning, at the curtain call. As Bonisolli left, I went to say goodbye to him. He was wearing a yellow-and-red tartan oilskin raincoat – he had spent some time in Scotland – and was crooning to himself. His American wife stood beside him. Mustering my Italian, I pointed at the tartan and said, '*Scozzese.*' 'Yes,' said his wife, 'but listen to what he is singing.' I listened. He was singing:

> Never mind the moon;
> Get yer knickers doon.

For this rarefied air, I asked myself, I have left the rich pastures of commercial television?

My love of music and of opera I owe to my parents, who encouraged it in every way they could. I was not musically gifted, could never sing a note in tune; I was even asked at school to keep silent so as not to untune the others. I gave up piano lessons almost as soon as they started – my teacher complained not just of the clumsiness of my fingering, but of my grubby schoolboy's fingers. I cannot, to this day, play an instrument or read a note of music. But how I loved to hear it. I longed to listen to more and more, to get to know it all.

My mother was much more of a musician and music-lover than my father. Isidore Isaacs' passion was for books rather than for music. After Sunday lunch, when I listened to Beethoven on the radio, he slept through it. But his small Glasgow jeweller's shop, together with my mother's earnings as a general practitioner, paid for my and my brothers' education, and, in tickets for concerts and opera, for our musical education. My mother, Sally Jacobs, had sung in cabaret at Glasgow University when she studied medicine there immediately after the First World War. Half the intake to the medical school in her year were women, so many men had been slaughtered in France. In synagogue, she sang out loud and clear, holding the note half a beat longer than anyone else, to make sure we knew she was there and enjoying herself. She practised as a family doctor on Glasgow's South Side, in the Gorbals where she was brought up, climbing flights of tenement stairs to reach tubercular patients at the top and, latterly, driving herself from visit to visit in a little grey car, a Standard, CWP 617. On Sunday she cooked and served a huge lunch: Scotch broth so thick you could stand the spoon up in it; roast beef; Eve's pudding. Then she drove my two brothers and me to Sunday matinée concerts by the Scottish Orchestra in Green's Playhouse. There, couched on golden divans, and struggling sometimes to keep awake, I was enthused by J. Wight Henderson playing a Beethoven piano concerto, and jolted upright by the loudest bits of Tchaikovsky 4, 5 or 6. At home, we had a gramophone and a few 78s: Chabrier's *España*; Dennis Noble singing 'Largo al Factotum' from the *Barber of Seville*, and Amelita Galli-Curci throwing off her highest notes in 'Lo Hear the Gentle Lark'. Later we acquired Sir Thomas Beecham conducting *La bohème* with Victoria de Los Angeles as Mimi. An austere friend, offered a choice one evening, asked if we didn't have anything a little less cloying.

But concerts were the thing. Beecham came to Green's Playhouse too. When he conducted the waltz from *Eugene Onegin*, he abandoned the rostrum and swirled with the melody from one desk of strings to another. The tune stuck in my head for years. Offering an encore not in the programme, Beecham challenged the distinguished Glasgow audience to 'recognize this familiar masterpiece'. He would send word in advance, through the *Glasgow Herald*, of his marked displeasure should coughing, spluttering, wheezing or any form of bronchial spasm mar his performances. (I little thought then that I should stand on the stage of an opera house, in front of the curtain, appealing to an audience on a conductor's behalf not to cough and spoil a recording. But I did.)

In our early teens my parents provided season tickets for the Saturday-night subscription series in St Andrew's Halls, one of the symbols of Glasgow's Victorian prosperity. It had perfect sight-lines and, cigarbox-shaped, an excellent acoustic. The Scottish Orchestra was conducted then by Walter Susskind, to whom I still owe gratitude; he opened my ears to much. The form of concert the audience expected was simple: overture, concerto, symphony. The order might be reversed if the concerto was, say, Brahms No. 2. A long succession of great pianists came to play Mozart, Beethoven, Schumann, Liszt, Tchaikovsky, Dvořák, Grieg, Rachmaninov. These evenings were events in people's lives; in those days you might get only one chance to hear a favourite piece each year. I remember a dear friend of my mother's almost salivating at the prospect of hearing the 'Eroica'. Rarely, in those days, did someone offer Bach. More rarely still, anything from the twentieth century. After Mahler's Ninth Symphony – the first performance in Glasgow – I remember a long hushed silence. 'A good concert tonight,' the subscriber in front of me muttered once, studying the programme, 'if it weren't for this piece by this, em, Vaughan Williams.' But Ralph Vaughan Williams's Sixth Symphony, given at the first opportunity by Susskind, was the audience's choice by ballot for the piece they'd most like to hear again in the plebiscite concert at the season's end.

The most perfect concert I ever heard was given by Peter Pears and the horn-player Dennis Brain: Mozart's 'Haffner' Symphony, Don Ottavio's arias from *Don Giovanni*, and Mozart's 4th Horn Concerto before the interval; after it, the 'Sea Interludes' from *Peter Grimes*, and the Serenade for Tenor, Horn and Strings. That high tenor and those horn calls sound to me still, down the long years since. I so loved the music I heard that, in the sixth form at Glasgow Academy, I dragged schoolmates with me to share my joy. St Andrew's Halls are no more. After a boxing promotion in 1962, they burned to the ground.

What drew me on from symphonic music to a lifelong love of opera was the Edinburgh International Festival in its early heyday, under Rudolf Bing and George Harewood. It was my specific good fortune to hear, in the early 1950s, performances by Glyndebourne Festival Opera in the tiny King's Theatre, which, in my memory, have never been bettered.

In Glasgow's own King's Theatre I heard the Royal Opera on tour: *The Magic Flute*, Britten's *Billy Budd* and Vaughan Williams's *The Pilgrim's Progress*; I best remember Pilgrim enquiring, 'Whose Delectable Mountains are these?' But it was the work I heard in Edinburgh, at an impressionable age, that formed my taste. Grandiose staging at the King's was impossible; musicality and understated acting *de rigueur*. It was Mozart, Rossini and Strauss who delighted my ear, rather than Puccini who tugged at my heartstrings. I heard and saw – what should we say when describing our experience of opera? 'I heard *Parsifal*?' or 'I saw *Carmen*?' – anyway, I saw *and* heard Glyndebourne give *Don Giovanni*, with George London as Giovanni and Léopold Simoneau as Ottavio, and *Così fan tutte*, my first. I heard Vittorio Gui conduct Carl Ebert's production of Rossini's comic gem *Le Comte Ory*, with Oliver Messel's sets from *Les très riches heures du Duc de Berry*. In the prologue to *Ariadne auf Naxos*, when Sena Jurinac sang 'Musik ist eine heilige Kunst', I was enslaved for life. I still judge Mozart, Rossini and Strauss by those Edinburgh nights.

Those trips were the climax to long-protracted pleasures, which began when the Festival programme arrived at our Glasgow home in spring. We booked early, not just for the opera but, each year, for entire days in Edinburgh. We bought cheap day rail returns, 5/- from Glasgow Queen Street to Edinburgh Waverley. With sandwiches wrapped and packed, my brothers and I caught an early train to our triple whammy of a day: 11am, chamber music in the Freemasons' Hall; 2.30pm, a theatre matinée at the Lyceum – John Gielgud and Diana Wynyard in *The Winter's Tale;* 7.30pm, the Usher Hall – Kathleen Ferrier in *Das Lied von der Erde* under Bruno Walter – or opera at the King's. As soon as the curtain fell we ran down the hill to the Haymarket station to catch the last train home. Bliss was it in that dawn to be living in Glasgow; to be young was very heaven.

At Oxford in the early 1950s, never without a book or a film or a concert, this great happiness continued. Opera was part of it. The Chelsea Opera Group gave Mozart, under Colin Davis, in the Town Hall. The University Opera Society also performed there, creditably. I heard Mozart's *La clemenza di Tito* and Verdi's *Macbeth* and Marschner's *Hans Heiling*. Sir Thomas Beecham, in the New Theatre, gave the world première of Delius's *Irmelin*. I was there. What I most vividly remember of it – I found it afterwards in Neville Cardus's review, anthologized in *A Bedside Guardian* – is Irmelin's outright dismissal of her suitors:

These knights mean nothing to me;
Some are young, and some are old,
Some are meek, and some are bold,
But they all leave me cold.

The finest operatic evening I spent while at Oxford was at Covent Garden. The Opera Society organized a coach trip to London to hear Alban Berg's *Wozzeck*, Erich Kleiber conducting. We came home overwhelmed. I had never heard such music before, nor an orchestra play as they did that night for Kleiber. Throughout my life, pleasure in performance, and sharing that pleasure with others, has counted for me above much else.

After Oxford, the army: two years' national service. There was no opera or ballet at Maryhill Barracks, Glasgow, or Churchill Barracks, Ayr, though I did dress in scarlet regimentals from the depot museum for mess dinner on St Andrew's night. A fellow officer, excited by atholbrose – the appearance, not the taste – propositioned a mess waiter; after a decorous interval, he resigned his commission and took holy orders instead.

After drawing the dole at Lisson Grove while applying for jobs, in May 1958 I got a start as a researcher with Granada Television in Manchester. There I worked under Denis Forman, who years later would help me to Covent Garden. In the Opera House in Manchester I saw a *Fidelio*, in which Leonore, rushing between the murderer Pizzaro and her husband, could not draw her pistol from its holster. Pizzaro could have cut Florestan to pieces before she could stop him. Leonore, improvising, pretended to be about to fire from the hip. The trumpet sounded for rescue. Husband and wife – 'O namenlose Freude' – were in each other's arms. The Royal Ballet came to perform *The Sleeping Beauty*, with Margot Fonteyn as Aurora. Just a day or two before her performance, Fonteyn's husband, Roberto Arias, was involved in Panama in a botched political *coup d'état*. I was sent down to London to travel back with her on the plane to Manchester to beg for an interview, citing a claimed friendship with Granada's owner Sidney Bernstein. Margot would not talk to anyone. She danced that night. Leaping high, she floated and, I thought, remained suspended in mid-air. When I moved to London, Granada provided theatre tickets. As these stretched to opera and ballet, I was able to use them to go to Covent Garden till an economy drive cut off that supply. A high point for me of those London years was La Scala's visit to Covent

Garden in 1976. I missed Giorgio Strehler's production of *Simon Boccanegra*, to my lasting regret, but caught Teresa Berganza in *La Cenerentola*.

After making *The World at War* for Thames Television, I was appointed Director of Programmes in 1974 with responsibility not just for documentaries and current affairs but for light entertainment and drama recorded at our Teddington studios. The Technical Director welcomed me with a plea: 'Jeremy, promise me one thing: whatever you do, never give us drama that takes more than two days in Studio One!' I gave no such promise. Of course ambitious work would upset a smooth routine. I was being asked to settle for the ordinary, in this case for the guaranteed popular success of *Callan* and *Public Eye*, and not to risk the system bearing the weight of *Edward and Mrs Simpson*, or *Bill Brand* or *Rock Follies*. I refused to be ruled by a norm so undemanding. Happily, Thames was rich and ambitious enough to live with my plans; I had the Board's support in what I did.

ITV had room for only a modest offering in opera. In a partnership with Southern Television, it took one production a year from

Glyndebourne; these included *Le nozze di Figaro* with Kiri Te Kanawa, and Janet Baker in Monteverdi's *Il ritorno d'Ulisse in patria*. Laurence Olivier left a commentary-recording of *The World at War* early to be there in time for that. He was, he told me, overwhelmed at the end.

In November 1982 I launched Channel 4 as founding Chief Executive. Channel 4 was obliged by Act of Parliament to encourage 'innovation and experiment in the form and content of programmes' and to provide 'a distinctive service'. But it was left to me to determine in what lay distinctiveness. Denis Forman had written, urging me to be an impresario. There was scope to capture high ground in the arts left unoccupied by BBC2, including straight performance. Channel 4 should satisfy music-lovers neglected by the other channels. Broadcasting a testcard, in the run-up to our opening, we played classical music over it. This gave pleasure; viewers wrote, begging us not to stop. I had to answer: 'When we go on air the music, and the testcard, will stop; there will be programmes instead.' This pleased no one.

Channel 4 had only a limited programme budget, but was free to import: buying programmes is much cheaper than making them. The world was our operatic oyster. At its peak Channel 4 broadcast a dozen operas a year, a boon to opera-lovers in Wick or Worcester, living at a distance from theatre performances. We raided the back catalogues and on a few occasions could afford to make our own recordings. I could not resist forking out for English National Opera's *Giulio Cesare*, with Janet Baker. Such a triumph should, I felt, be recorded on video. I so loved Berganza in *La Cenerentola* that I scheduled the recording three times. However, my commissioning editors shunned predictability; their taste ran the gamut: Philip Glass's *Satyagraha* for a winter Sunday afternoon – opera in Sanskrit seemed very Channel 4. For Good Friday I purchased Hans-Jürgen Syberberg's film of Wagner's *Parsifal*. These offerings might reach no more than 200,000 viewers – a zero rating – but that was as many as might catch the piece in over 100 performances in a conventional theatre. At Christmas, Plácido Domingo as Don José in Francesco Rosi's film of *Carmen* held 2.5 million viewers.

We had *Carmen* coming out of our ears. At the Bouffes du Nord in Paris, Peter Brook staged it pared down with a text by Jean-Claude Carrière. He used three casts. In that small bare space, the show made a fierce impact. When we offered to film it, Brook posed one absurd condition: he valued each cast equally, he said, and they were to be filmed separately – *Carmen* in triplicate. Meekly, I accepted. When it came to it, one singer did not take part, so two of the recordings had the same Carmen. Only a little put out ourselves, we put out all three, as well as *Carmen Jones*, Rosi's *Carmen* and a stunning flamenco *Carmen* filmed by Carlos Saura. This may be a little more exposure than *Carmen* can easily stand.

In May 1982, a few months before Channel 4 went on air, I agreed at Cannes to join with Leo Kirch's Unitel in relaying to Europe via satellite two performances a year from the Metropolitan Opera House, New York. In Germany and Austria New York's Saturday matinée would be seen live on Saturday night. First up would be Luciano Pavarotti in *Idomeneo*. I preferred to broadcast on Sunday afternoon, and lumbered my colleagues, busy with so much else, with recording the performance on only our fifth evening on air, subtitling overnight and broadcasting it the next day. On the Saturday evening, I went into our offices in Charlotte Street. As I crossed the floor towards the machines recording the feed, I heard not Mozart but what sounded like a sports commentary. It was exactly that. Someone at White Plains, outside New York, had thrown a switch and sent to Europe not *Idomeneo* but American football, live. This lasted several minutes. We asked the Met's TV unit to satellite us Act One again, after the rest of the opera. Viewers in Germany and Austria, live, got the football until *Idomeneo* came on again. No one complained; some rang to ask the final score.

Channel 4 took six pieces from the Met over three years, as well as an eclectic range of productions from elsewhere. I took particular pleasure in screening the minimalist Jean-Marie Straub's film of Schoenberg's *Moses und Aron*. The Welsh composer William Matthias told me that at breakfast in a Cardiff hotel he was greeted by a farmer: 'Did you see that wonderful opera last night? Not just beautiful music, but theology too.'

From the TV archive where it had been hidden for years, I dug up a 1964 recording for ATV's *Golden Hour* of Callas and Gobbi in Act Two of *Tosca* from Covent Garden. Clearing the rights took others years of work. Now, on video, it is available to all.

Channel 4 got a huge audience, mainly perhaps of gays, for a film by Peter Weigl of Debussy's *Le martyre de St Sébastien*. We showed Trevor Nunn's *Nicholas Nickleby* in the stage version by David Edgar, and Peter Hall's masked *Oresteia*, and, most ambitious and perhaps most wonderful of all, Peter Brook's staging of the *Mahabharata*. I saw this Hindu epic in a shipbuilding hangar outside Zurich all one summer night. The hangar was aligned east–west and, as the eight hours of drama ended, the eastern shuttered wall of the hangar was raised and dawn came up behind the players. Brook is a true magician of the stage, who has not forgotten his early baptism in opera at Covent Garden in the 1940s. In the *Carmen* he then directed, the officer Zuniga, furious that Don José, a mere private soldier, has allowed his prisoner Carmen to escape, was to slap his face as the Act One curtain fell. Zuniga is a baritone. Don José protested: 'He can't slap me, I'm the tenor ' After that, Brook was inclined to put conventional opera behind him.

Dance on Channel 4 enjoyed less prominence, but was not forgotten. To mark her eightieth birthday we recorded Dame Ninette de Valois rehearsing productions of two of her own ballets, *The Rake's Progress* and *Checkmate*. Very spry and forceful she was too. Modern dance was a particular feature on Channel 4. During one performance by Pina Bausch's dance company from Wuppertal, a man rang the duty officer and enquired angrily: 'What is this rubbish I am watching? And why, after an hour and a half, am I still watching it?' That man was my favourite Channel 4 viewer. Arts performance, uncut, unmediated, should have its place on public TV. Producers don't like it much because it cuts out some of their skills; commissioning editors don't like it because it denies them creative input; schedulers don't like it because it comes in awkward lengths. But audiences welcome it. Broadcasting is for audiences, not for broadcasters, after all.

It did not escape attention that Channel 4 offered a feast in the arts, nor that, after a rough start during which the tabloids howled daily for my blood, we came through smoothly to gain the audience share we needed without compromising our stated ends. In the summer of 1985 Sir Claus Moser, Chairman of the Royal Opera House, Covent Garden, came unheralded to see me in Charlotte Street and invited me to join his Board. I said yes at once, though I knew very little about the Royal Opera House (ROH). I suspected no further motive behind the invitation. I joined in November, becoming a member of the Opera Committee chaired by Isaiah Berlin. At the first Main Board meeting I attended, the House appeared to be in a difficult, indeed a critical, financial situation. My neighbour, a former Governor of the Bank of England I seem to remember, assured me that it always was.

In January the next year, the Board spent part of a weekend at Wadham College, Oxford, of which Claus Moser was Warden. A matter for quiet consideration was the retirement of the then General Director, Sir John Tooley, planned for two and a half years away. This, if the Board insisted, would be a little earlier than he wanted to go. John Tooley had been at Covent Garden since 1955, first as assistant to David Webster, the first General Director, eventually becoming General Director himself in 1970. By his projected retirement date of 1988, he would have served in that role for eighteen years – long enough, the Board thought. The recently appointed Music Director, Bernard Haitink, had written urging that Tooley stay on; his letter was read out to our meeting. Tooley, though much criticized at that time in the press, was widely admired and respected in the profession; his experience would be missed. The Board, however, reaffirmed its intention to begin the search for a successor. They would also be seeking a successor to Claus Moser as Chairman; he had held that position for a dozen seasons. So, all change it was to be. Posing for the casual group photograph outside the Warden's lodging, driving back to London, I thought little of all this. Channel 4 occupied all my working hours.

At this time, in any case, I was racked by anxiety and gloom because my wife, Tamara, was dying. She had undergone a mastectomy ten years before; then, in the summer of 1984, scans had revealed that secondary cancers, showing up only as tiny specks, had spread widely through her body. In January 1986, exercising a Board member's occasional privilege, we sat together in the Royal Box at Covent Garden and enjoyed the evening. Calm, brave, she remained in good spirits for several weeks more. In March, she died. We had been married for twenty-eight years. A long, happy part of my life was over.

Later that year, Claus Moser took me to lunch. He and other Board members hoped I would allow my name to go forward as John Tooley's possible successor. The post would be advertised; they wanted me to apply. I was genuinely taken aback – the thought had never crossed my mind. It was only just over five years since I had taken up my post at Channel 4, less than four since we had gone on air. But I had tried to make it a rule at Channel 4 that none of us dispensing public funds should wield that patronage for life. We should do a stint – two contracts, say – at the most, then leave and hand over to someone else. I was beginning to put this into effect; if the rule applied to others, it applied also to me.

Then again, I had started work in television in 1958; by 1988, I would have lasted thirty years in broadcasting. Launching Channel 4 had been the most challenging job of my life; merely keeping it on air would be less satisfying. I was now fifty-four years old. Before retiring I had wanted to tackle one further major task, preferably, like Monty Python, something completely different. And Tamara was dead. It was time, I thought, for change. When, towards the end of the year, the Covent Garden job was advertised, I applied for it.

These considerations were personal. None related directly to the Royal Opera House. Leading a great artistic house through a difficult period of redevelopment and closure was plainly a demanding task. But I did not weigh up the problems or how they could be overcome. No difficulty, I used to think then, was insuperable. I simply decided it was a job I wanted to do, and could do, and went for it. I did discuss it, quietly, with Gillian Widdicombe, who had been Opera Consultant to Channel 4. We were close. A music critic and arts journalist for twenty years, Gillian knew far more about the Royal Opera House, its cast of characters, its nature, than I did. She had enjoyed a close friendship with a previous Chairman, Lord Drogheda. She had also been on the staff of Glyndebourne for two years. Gillian never took a starry-eyed view of my abilities; indeed, she was scathingly aware of my deficiencies. But she did not urge me *not* to apply. Perhaps she thought that, with hurdles still to leap, and stiff competition, I would not be selected.

There were two rounds of interview, by a committee of the Board and by the full Board. I sent in a paper outlining my understanding of the role and my aims for the House. Claus Moser chaired the meetings. A formidable presence across the table was Sir John Sainsbury, who was to succeed Moser as Chairman. The Board of the ROH was then still a wholly self-perpetuating body: they chose their fellow members and they also appointed their Chairman, only as a matter of courtesy informing the Arts Council and the Prime Minister of their choice. The Leaders of the Opposition and of the Liberal Democrats were also told. As a Board member, I had been deputed to tell David Owen of our intention to appoint John Sainsbury Chairman. Accosting him smartly on some public occasion, I mentioned Sainsbury and one alternative. 'I suppose, in the circumstances, you had better have the businessman,' said Owen. Mrs Thatcher was notified at 10 Downing Street; Neil Kinnock was seen by Denis Forman. They were content. A new General Director's name would be passed before the Chairman of the Arts Council and the Minister for the Arts; but he, or she, would be the Board's choice. Buckingham Palace would be sounded on both Chairman and General Director; we were, after all, the *Royal* Opera House.

The interviews seemed to go reasonably well. Leadership of creative institutions, I implied as forcibly as I could, was just my forte. And I had always kept to budgets. There were not too many questions about house-keeping, more about artistic ambition. John Sainsbury did ask me what I thought of the Priestley Report of 1983, a thorough inquiry into the Royal Opera House's, and the Royal Shakespeare Company's (RSC's), management and finances, set up by Thatcher in response to persistent pleas of underfunding. 'An interesting document,' I said, not having read it cover to cover. Sainsbury gave me a look.

These were exceptional times. The Board was looking for someone who could raise artistic standards, but also lead the House through the un-certainties of a major redevelopment scheme, closure and re-opening. In January 1987 Claus Moser told me I was the preferred candidate; he offered me the job, subject to one further test. John Sainsbury wanted to assure himself that he and I could work together. We had never spoken tête-à-tête. There would have to be a meeting and a satisfactory conversation before I could be appointed. It was agreed I would go to his house in The Boltons for a drink one evening after work. On that afternoon, I was sitting with my Chairman Edmund Dell in his office at Channel 4. The door opened, a head came round it, and a colleague informed us that the Director General of the BBC, Alasdair Milne, had suddenly resigned – brutally pushed out we now know by the BBC's Chairman, Marmaduke Hussey. I went to John Sainsbury's home. We spoke plainly to each other and found we agreed on much of joint concern. Clutching a generous whisky, I looked him in the eye and undertook to keep him fully informed in all crucial matters – what any Chairman wants to hear from a respon-sible Chief Executive. He relaxed; we shook hands on it. The job was mine.

At home that evening, my telephone rang and rang as friends urged me to apply for the vacancy at the BBC. Milne's dismissal had left an instant gaping hole. The Director General's job was the pinnacle of the British broadcasting profession, head of the corporation which sets, or should set, standards for all British broadcasters. I tried hard to resist as, through the weekend, from outside the BBC and within, pressures on me grew to apply. Nothing was known publicly of the Opera House's choice. The BBC announced that it would make its selection within a month. I decided that, after all my years as a broadcaster, I would not forgive myself if I did not try for it. I asked Claus Moser for a month's grace before saying whether I would accept his offer. Graciously, he allowed it. I sent in my application to the BBC.

After a preliminary chat in his flat with 'Duke' Hussey and his deputy Joel Barnett (my only supporter among the BBC Governors), I was summoned for formal interview. I had submitted a brief policy paper on the BBC's future and the DG's role. When I arrived at Broadcasting House, the Head of Public Relations advised me, before the interview, to be at home by my telephone by 5pm or 6pm, in case of a summons. 'If it's my voice,' he told me, 'you've been unsuccessful. If it's the Chairman, you've been appointed.' He suggested I reserve time the following morning to meet the press. The commissionaire, as I left the side entrance, hoped to see me back. He must have said that to all the candidates. All very friendly. The Governors were quite otherwise. Their most urgent concern seemed to be how to keep the BBC out of trouble with the press and politicians. They were not sure that had been the largest preoccupation of my broadcasting life. It had not. One tough questioner, with an intelligence background, could not forgive me for a tendentious short series on Channel 4 which had attacked political partisanship in Britain's wartime activity in German-occupied Greece and in the bitter civil war that followed. (Britain was, of course, partisan, but the programmes had been more one-sided than I had expected or had liked.)

The *coup de grâce* was delivered by an ex-Salvation Army Scottish trade unionist, President of the Amalgamated Engineering Union, Sir John Boyd. 'You don't seem to me, Mr Isaacs,' he said, in a broad Glasgow accent, 'to be a man who takes kindly to discipline. Now I see by the smile on your face that you take that as a compliment. But I can assure you that some of us here see it as a criticism.' That was, decidedly, that. At home that evening, with my brother Raphael (Ralph) and sister-in-law Ruth, with old friends Tony and Carol Howard and Gillian, I waited for the telephone to ring. It did not ring at 7pm, at 8pm, at 9pm or at 10pm. Then the PR chap rang. I had not got the job. 'Who has?' I asked. 'I can't tell you that,' he said, 'the Chairman will ring presently to tell you himself.' A Channel 4 colleague, Paul Bonner, rang to tell me that Michael

Checkland, the BBC's Director of Administration, had been appointed. Paul had seen it on the television news.

Duke Hussey rang, very courteously. 'Jeremy, I expect you've gathered we have not appointed you. We were all very impressed, though, with what you had to say. But, then, we were very impressed with what everyone had to say. Fact is, I'm slightly surprised at what we've actually done. But there it is.' Hussey had wanted David Dimbleby. He had spent hours that evening arguing that if the Governors could not make an editorial appointment as Director General, then they should at least appoint Dimbleby as his Deputy. The Governors would not have this. They would allow Michael Checkland to make his own appointment. After a few months he chose John Birt, who later succeeded him as DG without any open selection process at all.

I had another drink and, late as it was, rang Claus Moser at the Hotel Dolder in Zurich and, in a mood of anticlimax mixed with anticipation, told him I would come to the Royal Opera House. I left Channel 4 on 31 December 1987, shadowing John Tooley at Covent Garden, very informally, from January. This season, 1987/88, was my chance, as General Director Designate, to learn all I could about the ways of the House before taking over. John Tooley was gracious in his welcome, inviting me to management meetings he chaired and encouraging me to chair those which dealt with forward planning beyond his time.

In April 1988, I married Gillian Widdicombe. We spent three honeymoon weeks in Turkey. Kemal Atatürk, founder of the modern Turkish state, had decided that opera was an essential civilizing force. The new Turkey would have opera houses. There were now three, Ankara, Izmir and Istanbul, just beginning, sensibly, to exchange productions. Subsidy was high: tickets cost about £1. In Ankara, we could not avoid meeting the General Director and later, in London, all three intendants called on me. 'What do you sing?' they asked. All three were baritones: two Rigolettos and a Macbeth. They were shocked to find I did not sing at all.

We returned from Turkish delights in time to catch the final performance of a new *Salome*, produced by Peter Hall, rented from Los Angeles. The theatre was sold out, as it had been from the moment the first-night notices appeared. Salome was played by the slim and sensuous Maria Ewing – Peter Hall's ex-wife. At the end of the Dance of the Seven Veils, Salome, her veils draped like angels' wings over outstretched arms, briefly showed herself to the audience nude, full frontal, without the

G-string she had worn in Los Angeles. Box-office boomed. The most disappointed man in the theatre was the tenor Robert Tear, playing Herod. For too many *Salome* performances, he complained, he had been obliged to contemplate expanses of flesh-coloured body-stocking worn by ampler sopranos. Now that the seductive Ewing was performing, she showed herself not to him but to the audience, who had no power to grant her any favours, let alone the head of John the Baptist on a silver platter. Ted Downes, who conducted a later revival, has very bad eyesight and normally can hardly see the stage. But he claimed, standing just in front and below the action, to discern sequins spangling Maria Ewing's pubic hair. Bob Tear, who must have managed a peek, informs me that they were not sequins, but silver dust. His wife Hilary reports Kiri Te Kanawa's comment: 'Anyone can look slim, with her arms stretched up like that.'

In May 1988, as General Director Designate, I came on the payroll. On 1 September I took over as General Director of the Royal Opera House, Covent Garden – one of the five great houses of the world. Two friends, Richard Eyre in charge of the National Theatre and Nicholas Serota at the Tate Gallery, took up their tasks on the same day. I faxed them the suggestion that we form the 1st of September Club and dine once a year. This was agreed, though never acted on. Nicholas Serota made two conditions: no breakfast meetings; no premature retirements.

2

WARM UP

1985–1988

On the Opera House payroll, I took a cut in my Channel 4 salary and expectations to serve in this impoverished corner of the public sector. I agreed to drop the entitlement in my contract to a fixed expense allowance. With no protest on my part, and only a little on hers, I said we would do without a modest dress allowance for my wife – formerly provided, I suppose, to ensure she was properly dressed, particularly in the presence of Royalty. Gillian got by, for nine years, on two formal frocks and a steady supply of Thai silk jackets from Mr Harryson in Bangkok.

Gillian already knew how to curtsey. I was instructed in how to bow by a friend, that courteous Grenadier Lieutenant-Colonel Sir Eric Penn, lately Comptroller of the Lord Chamberlain's Office at Buckingham Palace. Upright stance, heels together, short sharp inclination forward and downward of the head. I did this quite well. What I did not always manage later on was to be in position to greet a royal visitor. Once, having changed into black tie for the evening, I was putting my day clothes into the boot of the car, parked beside the Bow Street entrance, when a helpful security man remarked, 'Sir, he's here, you know.' The Prince of Wales had arrived a moment or two early. I dived through the goods entrance, dashed into the foyer and jumped the silken rope enclosing the welcome area in time to see our unflappable House Manager, Trevor Jones, greeting His Royal Highness in Bow Street. 'Come on the wrong night, have I?' Prince Charles enquired.

Royal visits could be formal or informal. One Monday morning in 1987, my final year as Chief Executive of Channel 4, I had had a mild disagreement with a colleague, Gillian Braithwaite-Exley, Head of Programme Planning. To make up for my intemperance, I asked her to join me that evening for the performance at Covent Garden, for which I had a spare ticket. At 7.25pm we took our seats. At 7.28pm two women took their seats, quietly and without fuss, in front of us. They were escorted by Anthony Dowell, Director of the Royal Ballet, and the Administrative Director, Anthony Russell-Roberts. In the interval Gillian asked, 'Who are those two women sitting in front of us?' 'Don't you know your own monarch?' I replied. Princess Margaret had brought her sister to see Anthony Dowell's new production of *Swan Lake*. Before the next act, the Queen acknowledged my presence. Ignoring protocol, which required me not to speak till spoken to, I dared present Gillian Braithwaite-Exley as the colleague who had shifted Channel 4 Racing on Saturdays to a time that suited the Queen better. Princess Margaret, President of the Royal Ballet, assiduous in her interest, said it was time she and I, General Director Designate, talked. In later years I wished this informal royal visit had been more often repeated.

My contract provided I should have a car and chauffeur, but I never did; I have never relished keeping a driver hanging about through a working day. The Royal Opera House's premises were scattered – there were scenery workshops in Mile End, a props workshop in King's Cross, the ballet companies in Barons Court and Islington – but, whatever the inconvenience of getting about London, I would do without a chauffeur, and use taxis and the tube instead. John Tooley had done the same. Foreign intendants found this amazing. But, facing hard protracted annual negotiations over a half or quarter per cent on wages, and needing to scrape together every pound and penny we could to enhance production, it made no sense to add to staff numbers even by one. John Tooley had lived in a flat in Mart Street, above the shop. I would get myself to work from Bermondsey. The crucial perk was the car-parking space. Could that but be defended from predators – Board members' wives were the most shameless in their piracy – Gillian could drive us home after the performance. This had a disadvantage, though. I too often had to listen to a brutally frank assault on a performance from a former music critic of the *Financial Times* and the then Arts Editor of the *Observer*. A chauffeur would have kept silent.

Channel 4 I had built, with my colleagues, from nothing; a new construct on a greenfield site. The Royal Opera House was the opposite. Although only brought into being in 1946, it was an institution with an ethos of its own – close, companionable, set in its ways. I was new, and an outsider. It would take me time to understand fully what made the House tick. It would take those who belonged there time to accept me. The Royal Opera House saw itself as a family, a community of people working together to achieve one end. In nooks, crannies and pockets of the House thriving cottage industries, cut off from each other, each got on with its task and its own craft-skill: wardrobe, jewellery, millinery, costumes, wigs, lighting, stage, music staff, production, front of house, cleaners, maintenance, firemen, stage door, box-office, finance and wages, and, offsite, scenery-construction and props. Each was separate, yet all belonged to the whole. There were two ballet companies, one based in Islington, with a remit to tour, the other based at Barons Court, performing alongside the opera. The dancers gloried in the Covent Garden stage, but wondered sometimes, a little resentfully, why it was called the Opera House. The chorus struggled, on their modest earnings, to make ends meet at home. The orchestra thought of itself, though no one else did, as an élite within the House and a little apart. The musicians jealously guarded their freelance schedule D tax status; they were not, they claimed, staff employees, but worked on contract – in spite of which they always assumed they'd be back next season. ROH musicians did not earn as much as other London orchestras, supplementing concert fees by racing from one recording session to another, but they had security, and had chosen the reticence of the theatre pit against the glare of the concert platform.

In spite of dire working conditions and annual disagreements over pay, most rejoiced in being at Covent Garden. Many had worked there for years; some all their lives. Clerks and cost accountants were imbued with a love of the place and a passion for the lyric art forms given in it. Their wages were low but they had the chance to attend a rehearsal, and a head start, perhaps, in purchasing a cheap seat for an otherwise inaccessible performance. The tannoy carried orchestra and voice to their desks; more fun than a bank or a factory. In the lowliest jobs, cleaning and maintenance and kitchen staff had more than a statutory share of the disabled among them, carrying out menial routines without saying much. They were sheltered and cared for by all. The cleaning ladies always had a cheerful greeting for me and a smile; Margaret, not quite all there, but determined to make her presence felt, would step aside with a flourish and a loud 'Good morning, Sir' as I passed. Two of them wore identical dyed frizzy perms, so that it was hard to tell them apart; I thought, mistakenly, that they were twins. Jean Flower, married to Bill, a House carpenter, kept greyhounds with him and raced them at Catford. Bill Flower used to put a fiver on for me when he judged his chances favourable and would come to the office with my winnings. There was never a reckoning, but I made a profit over the years. He and Jean entertained Gillian and me one evening at the track. The manager of the stadium, we learned, was a Wagnerite. A bookmaker approached me between races, holding *The Times* open at the arts pages and asked, 'Is this *Walküre* worth coming to?' (Both Bill and Jean have, alas, raced their last.)

When I arrived at the Royal Opera House, personnel practice was antique and creaking. There was no fixed staff retirement age. The House pension scheme, started in 1959 for administration staff only, had been extended in 1978, but very few of the 1050 employees belonged to it. Dancers forced to end their careers, for the most part, in their thirties and musicians had their own pension arrangements. The result for the rest, with nothing but the state pension to rely on, was that no one could afford, or would willingly agree, to retire. For years no fixed age was agreed on. Eventually it was conceded that retirement should be at sixty-five, provided every group in the House was party to it. The orchestra refused. Musicians did not retire, they claimed, at sixty-five, or at any other age; like old soldiers, they only faded away, and stopped playing when they were no longer able. It took Richard Wright, Director of Administration, further years of persuasion to bring them into line. Meanwhile, when standards of performance flagged, all we had in place for dancers were protracted systems of warnings; and for musicians and chorus members, warnings, auditions and further trials before it was possible to terminate a contract.

In 1986, I sat above the pit at a concert performance of Rossini's *Semiramide*; the overture's exposed woodwind runs suggested to me that one player's services should instantly be dispensed with. Bernard Haitink is a kind soul. It took years to get that fluffing fellow out. A few years later, we embarked on the drastic course of losing sixteen members of the chorus, partly for economy, partly to weed out older and weaker members. A doughty and diminutive Scot, Ignatius McFadyen, a tenor, could still manage a high C at nearly seventy-five. 'How old are you, Iggy?' I asked, 'Eighty-five?' 'Och no, Jeremy,' he said, 'coming up seventy-five!' I offered to give a party for his seventy-fifth birthday if he went immediately afterwards. He agreed, and assured me he'd be all right as he had interests buying and selling modest properties in Scotland.

On the stage, the hinge of the House's entire operation, a powerful fellow-feeling and almost clan-like loyalty prevailed. Here, although some practices had been eradicated and some economies found, much remained to be achieved. In September 1987, as Chief Executive of Channel 4, I attended a seminar on broadcasting at 10 Downing Street. Mrs Thatcher was in formidable form, assailing ITV's representatives as 'the last bastion of restrictive practices left in Britain'. Suddenly, she caught my eye and added, 'And you, Mr Isaacs, at the Royal Opera House, are just as bad.' I protested that I was used to answering for matters for which I was responsible, but not for what I was not yet in charge of. It was principally performers' attitudes to rights, then an issue for companies seeking exploitation in perpetuity, that the Prime Minister had in mind, but also perhaps the ROH stage.

The Covent Garden stage was a law unto itself. In this key area the House had no open employment policy implemented; vacancies were not advertised, selection procedures were not in use. In the days of the fruit and vegetable market, porters picked up extra earnings for carrying a spear, and even bulking out a chorus, on the Opera House stage. The stage crew traditionally was recruited locally. Families – the Holborn mafia – looked after their own. Brothers worked together on the day crew, or in the flies; sons and nephews were sent along to get a start. Once the youngster had done a few weeks' casual work, it was only natural that he should, without further test, recruitment or training, step into a vacancy that had just arisen. There were no jobs for the uninitiated, for blacks, for women. Covent Garden's stage crew never approached in greed or in-genuity the Spanish practices of Fleet Street, or the Trotskyite luddism of the union members who for years bedevilled the start of the National Theatre. But for them some parts of the agreement were more lucrative than others; they knew it, and took advantage. With performances six evenings a week, Sunday was the only day we could get in a full technical rehearsal. It cost more to run the stage on Sundays than it should have done. And, seven days a week, the union agreement provided for fixed-number crewing and automatic crew-member replacement. This was particularly costly. A crewman would phone in sick. He had no need to send a sick note till his third day off; there was no penalty for missing two days' work. By union agreement, he must be replaced; in practice this meant by a colleague on the other shift volunteering to work on his day off. He would be paid at time and a half, a nice little earner. Overtime ran at a high percentage of total earnings. It was hard to police the reality of reported sickness, though we did send round to some homes. It took determined managerial effort to end automatic replacement. In that matter, Mrs Thatcher had a point. Unskilled labourers, paid more than skilled craftsmen in other areas, the stage crew kept the show on the road. Day after day, working against the clock, they got the curtain up each night. That gave them considerable clout.

The Royal Opera House was highly productive. Its three companies, the Royal Opera, the Royal Ballet and Sadler's Wells Royal Ballet (SWRB), gave more performances than any other house in the UK, in Europe, in the world: 476 performances in the 1987/88 season against 211 at English National Opera (ENO), or compared to 329 in Munich, 300 in Vienna, 275 in Paris; this on less than half the subsidy obtaining in those three cities. Some performances were given on tour, particularly by SWRB, but up to 300 were given at Covent Garden. And all of those were rehearsed, by no means the case in Berlin, Munich or Vienna, where on a repertory system 100 productions were rotated so that forty or more were given each season.

Until quite recently Vienna prided itself on performing a different opera every night of the month. On this system nothing could be rehearsed. The Vienna Philharmonic, in the pit, knew the works anyway; conductors did too, or had a score to hand; singers were presumed to do so. Sets were changed once a day, put up on stage, used for the performance, then sent back to store by lorry. On the afternoon of the performance singers were taken on stage and told, you enter here, you exit there. 'What am I supposed to do in between?' inquired Anne Evans, guesting as Brünnhilde. 'Do what you usually do,' was the answer. 'If in doubt, go down to the front and sing.' So much for production values in old Vienna. It is somewhat different now; Claudio Abbado, in his time as Music Director there, insisted on adequate rehearsal at least for his three or four new productions a season. Revivals still go without.

La Scala in Milan and La Monnaie in Brussels practise the very different *stagione* system in its purest form. In this singers come together to rehearse one production at a time. The producer has unfettered use of the stage for entire weeks before a run of performances; the scenery stays in place. Until the first night, the theatre is dark; no other performance is given, so there is no need to strike the set and clear the stage. Nor need the set be removed between performances: it is in nobody's way – *La traviata* shares the stage with no other production. On this system the theatre gives only, say, ninety performances a season, though it may receive more state grant than do the Royal Opera and the Royal Ballet, which give 150 performances each. In London's West End the sets for *Les Misérables* and *Miss Saigon* are massive; but the Paris barricades and a US helicopter can be accommodated on stage and in the wings at the Cambridge and the Theatre Royal Drury Lane. These long-running fixtures have each occupied stage and scene-dock uninterrupted for years. The curtain rises and falls. A decade passes. The ageing blockbusters have it all to themselves.

At Covent Garden, however, the only constant is change. Two or three, sometimes four, different shows are seen in the theatre in a week. Opera alternates with ballet, and two operas with each other. All share the same stage, and the stage is used both for performance and for rehearsal. Covent Garden combines the *stagione* system, in which each production, whether new or revival, is adequately rehearsed, with the repertory system's frequency of performance. Dark nights are rare. Both opera and ballet also use dedicated rehearsal studios, but these meet only a partial need. There is only one space in which it is possible to rehearse with scenery, costume, lighting and the orchestra: that space is the main stage. Each opera production will have stage rehearsals with orchestra; a piano dress rehearsal for the producer, with sets, lighting, costumes; a pre-general and a general rehearsal. The ballet company perhaps gets less stage time than it really needs. Certainly they think so. But any new piece or major revival will have stage rehearsals before the piano dress, and then the orchestra in the pit for the general (dress) rehearsal before the opening night. So if the opera company is playing *Aida* and rehearsing *Fidelio*, and the ballet company is ending a run of *Swan Lake* and working up a new triple bill, all these productions are accommodated in the theatre, as near to the stage as possible, at one time. Rehearsals are at 10.30 in the morning; performances at 7.30 in the evening. Between each morning rehearsal and each evening performance comes the crunch – the sets must be struck, stored, changed over, reconstructed and reset, the lighting rehung and refocused before the curtain swings up and open.

Modern theatres, equipped with sophisticated stage machinery, can effect these crucial routine transitions quickly, smoothly, cheaply. Covent Garden, for year after year, has achieved them only by working against the clock to get the curtain up on time. Some changeovers are easier than others. If one show is all built scenery and the next all cloths, then, provided the cloths are well clear of the lighting rig, the crew will finish comfortably on time. If both shows involved are heavy – problems. If there's no room at the side and rear of the stage for two sets, then one, dismantled and lowered by lift, has to be stashed in the Floral Hall. For a

STAGEHAND:

"Anyone who designs these sets should be made to fucking work here for two years and have to move them around. That would teach them"...

'OTELLO'

longer opera, the curtain goes up at 7pm or even at 6pm. Everyone still has to ensure that the show starts on time. The last train home must not be missed. If the crew is pressed, there's a delay in opening the auditorium; work is still being done, lighting cues run through and checked. Finally, the stage clears and the tabs close. The public may now be admitted. Sometimes, curtain-up is delayed. The House Manager will apologize for keeping the audience waiting. But for decades, in spite of occasional mishaps, the miracle has been that forty-nine times out of fifty the curtain went up on time. The stage crew worked this miracle; their pay, status, clout reflected that fact.

In the term that lay ahead of me, I was minded to push productivity still further, to put as many good things as possible on stage. In my time, too, I was expected to see the House through to closure, to the re-equipped stage that would for ever end the necessity for the clumsy, repetitive, manual labour on which we now depended. New technology could alter all, but only in a redeveloped House. We planned, John Sainsbury noted in his first Chairman's Statement, to close for redevelopment in 1993. All being well, I would take the House up to that point, then through a two-year closure period, see it re-open in 1995, and leave, after a seven-year stint. That is not how things turned out.

Recent Annual Reports had revealed the problems of coping with endemic underfunding. In February 1983, responding to annual pleas that funding be increased, Margaret Thatcher asked a valued adviser in the Cabinet Office, Clive Priestley, to report to her on the financial position of two of the great national companies, the Royal Opera House and the Royal Shakespeare Company, and on their management. She undertook to implement his findings, but in the end government reneged on its side of the bargain. For one year (1984/85), it implemented Priestley's recommendation substantially to increase the Arts Council's grant to the ROH, but failed to follow his further recommendations to sustain that increase and to index it for the future. Wages failed to keep pace with inflation; morale was sapped by niggling industrial conflict. All was again uncertainty. Paradoxically, John Tooley pointed out in his final Report as General Director that for the first time the House had been told what grant it would receive for three years ahead – a comfort to forward planning long sought; but in real terms the amounts promised represented cuts. This would take some ingenuity to live with, and to overcome.

One bright spot in this period had been the arrival of a new Chairman,

John Sainsbury, who took up his office a year before I began in mine. Chairman and Chief Executive of J. Sainsbury plc, John was one of Britain's most successful businessmen at the head of one of Britain's most profitable businesses; he would bring drive and vision to his task at Covent Garden, a quarter of a mile away from Drury Lane, where his family's first grocery store had opened in 1869. Married to the ballerina Anya Linden, John had long been a prop and mainstay of the House, serving for years on the Board, and chairing the Finance Committee. With Anya, through the Linbury Trust, he had contributed to the cost of ballet productions and of ballet touring. John Sainsbury has a dominant personality and a short fuse. He was thought not easy to work for. But he was determined to support excellence on the stage. With his brothers Simon and Timothy, he was giving to the nation the new Sainsbury Wing of the National Gallery. At Covent Garden he would demonstrate to Margaret Thatcher and to her government that the arts were capable of helping themselves, by increasing, steeply, self-generated income. In return, government would surely take a positive and sympathetic view of arts funding. With his heavy business commitments to consider, Sainsbury hesitated long before accepting the ROH chairmanship for a limited term. He saw the Chairman of the Arts Council, William Rees-Mogg, and was met with general expressions of goodwill, but he received no specific assurance that funding would be increased. The previous regime had chided, argued, pleaded, for a better deal; John Sainsbury would act.

When Claus Moser was Chairman, his Board had shrunk from any drastic increase in seat prices. They believed they had a duty to keep them low, whatever the impact of that on the House's work. John Sainsbury would put prices up, but would insist that the customer got value for money; good opera and ballet would cost more at Sainsbury's, but be worth it. For the 1987/88 season the Board (of which by then I was a member) approved increases in opera-ticket prices of up to 40 per cent. Box-office and attendances lifted. Traced back a decade, and compared to other items, it was clear that the Royal Opera House had held prices artificially low. The market would stand the uplift. And Sainsbury set out to increase private funding, income from sponsorship and from corporate supporters. To his surprise and delight he was able to persuade another successful businessman, Alex Alexander, Chairman of Allied Lyons, supplier to the retail trades, to leave Glyndebourne, where his fundraising activities had helped put finances on a new, securer footing, and to devote his energies to aiding Covent Garden instead. Sainsbury asked Alex's advice on whom he could recruit, adding wistfully, 'I don't suppose you would consider it yourself.' 'John,' said Alex, 'I have a big heart.' Sainsbury went round next day to clinch the move. These were favourable omens. But would the increased income the ROH could generate compensate for a still eroding Arts Council grant? And would it sustain us if we sought to raise standards? On that, the quality of opera and ballet depended.

The House's work, when I took over, was at a low ebb. Whatever the artistic achievements of the previous regime – and some of them scaled the highest peaks – the general quality of performance, in its last seasons, was too often mediocre. In opera, too many tired productions in ill-rehearsed revival; in new productions, more misses than hits. In ballet, high aspiration too seldom matched by dazzling performance; established talents fading, newcomers waiting to break through; excitement lacking. In the pit, an orchestra of great capability, and some weaknesses. On stage, a chorus long in the tooth, short on mobility, at times faltering of voice. I wanted improvement all round, and that would cost.

In the seasons that followed the Priestley Report, the Royal Opera had fought to keep up its courage and ambition. In 1983/84, for example, the Chairman could boast of eight new productions in the repertory, compared with only two the year before. Abbado conducted Andrei Tarkovsky's fine, sombre production of *Boris Godunov*, and Riccardo Muti conducted Bellini's *I Capuleti e i Montecchi*. Stravinsky's *The Nightingale* and Ravel's *L'enfant et les sortilèges*, with designs by David Hockney, were borrowed from the Met. For Joan Sutherland, Tooley brought in Massenet's *Esclarmonde* from San Francisco, though when Sutherland was ill and could not sing, there was no performance. But it was part of a brave display after all. Subsequent seasons faltered rather. Critical discontent grew, like the crescent moon.

A new *Der Rosenkavalier*, a twenty-fifth anniversary gift for Georg Solti, distinguished 1984/85. Otherwise, borrowing kept the production roster alive. The following year the House ventured into the modern from the word go: Karlheinz Stockhausen's *Donnerstag aus Licht* was given at the start of the season, the composer supervising the elaborate, part-synthesized sound-mix from centre stalls. To fill a gap, a too hastily mounted new production of *Der fliegende Holländer* was given, directed by Mike Ashman and designed by David Fielding. This had tremendous, provocative vitality. The spinning chorus was seen at work in a clothing factory; the Dutchman's ship was a submarine. Taken aback, the first-night audience booed. A new *Fidelio* produced by Andrei Serban, conducted by Colin Davis – his last new production as Music Director – also ran into a critical storm. On a bare stage symbolic cut-outs descended to frame the action; at the end, death-heads on stilts towered over the rejoicing crowd. Again, booing; sheer dislike, or a failure to comprehend. Covent Garden, prompted partly by innovatory work down the road at English National Opera, was stepping out tentatively into the new, and stepping back again. Bernard Haitink, appointed Music Director in Colin Davis's place, told the Board that nothing like the *Der fliegende Holländer* should ever be seen again. As a newcomer, I kept quiet and my powder dry, but I could not agree. Creative activity has a licence to fail. Design at Covent Garden should not stick in a groove.

A new *Otello*, conducted by Carlos Kleiber, with Plácido Domingo in the title role, finally made the stage. Elijah Moshinsky's production, with designs by Timothy O'Brien, was a deserved success. Domingo glowed, Kleiber triumphed. John Copley's production of *Norma*, with Margaret Price, and John Pritchard conducting, had the opposite effect, at least on me. Gillian and I watched this, together with our guests, from the Royal Box. There was something about the ancient Gauls' shaggy costumes which threatened to bring on a fit of the giggles. Then something else did. A spiderweb-like iris was meant to remove itself from front stage. It stuck. Stagehands could be seen pulling and tugging at the wretched device. It would not budge. Hoping they'd manage it, Pritchard's beat got slower and slower. Eventually he stopped, and put his baton down. The curtains closed. Gillian by now was on her back on the floor, drumming her heels and stifling hysterics. Thus she discovered that from this position in the Royal Box, thanks to a mirror on the side-wall, one may see everything that happens on stage, without being seen oneself. I decided then, perhaps too hastily, not to bring that *Norma* back.

The Royal Ballet was in transition – upwards. Anthony Dowell had been Director since 1986. Picked out and moulded by Sir Frederick Ashton, he had been one of the company's greatest classical dancers, of style and presence and charm, whose partnerships with Antoinette Sibley had given seasons of delight. He had succeeded Norman Morrice, a surprise choice as Director when Kenneth MacMillan had handed over responsibility in 1977. Morrice, though widely liked and respected, and with a caring touch, had not succeeded in lifting the company to the heights. He was diligent in giving every dancer his or her turn, disinclined to favour ambitious excellence. Star-glitter was, he believed, inimical to the company's general well-being. The Royal Ballet had needed new leadership. The search committee of the Board, passing over for the second time Peter Wright, Director of Sadler's Wells Royal Ballet, chose Dowell, a great dancer with a keen eye for costume and staging, to provide it. Dowell's production of *Swan Lake*, in Yolanda Sonnabend's handsome, autumnal designs, did not please everyone. Some thought it over-designed – costumes and sets in ballet should always show off the dancer, and never obscure or dominate – but I admired this *Swan Lake* and the public loved it. It was Anthony Dowell's first major achievement as Director, and a success. Dowell, attempting to find a new look for familiar classics, was always going to be judged against some almost mythical ideal, enshrined in memory and mindset, of how these nineteenth-century masterpieces should look: every limb clearly delineated against sets of shimmering gossamer. Oliver Messel, the great master of the 1940s and 1950s, was dead; his spirit lived on. But I was sympathetic to Dowell's aim to re-invigorate tradition from within, to find a new look for the great classics on which, he profoundly believed, the company's strengths were to be honed and modelled.

The principal task Anthony Dowell set himself was to improve the quality of dance. Here there was evidently much to achieve. The Royal Ballet, in 1987, had no Fonteyn and no Nureyev, nor ever would have again. It had no Dowell, at his peak, and no Sibley at hers. We badly needed to lift standards. Even to my untutored eye, it was obvious that some principal dancers were not the force they had been, the *corps de ballet* not as together as they should have been. In a *pas de quatre*, or a *pas de six*, unison was lacking; angles of gesture, carriage and attitude varied. The *corps de ballet* might never be as made to measure as the Kirov's was, every one handpicked for size – peas out of a perfect pod – but it must keep time and line together. Anthony Dowell, vigilant in his seat in the Grand Tier, never missed a performance – except when he was himself on stage. Nothing escaped his eye. He strengthened the teaching staff. Faults would be corrected, ability brought on, underperformers – if we could afford it – let go. Separated from the company's base in Barons Court by nine stops on the Piccadilly Line, I would find it hard to keep in daily touch with Anthony, but I believed I could rely on him, with a little prodding, to work the transformation we both sought. Cost would be a limiting factor: the Royal Ballet had fewer than eighty dancers; ideally it needed ninety-five.

The Royal Opera House's third company lent the House a regional dimension. At its North London headquarters in Islington, the Sadler's Wells Royal Ballet was in the safe hands of Peter Wright. Wright had begun as a dancer, then become a choreographer and a producer of high distinction. He had great all-round skills. As Director, he shaped an evening's programme and a season's repertory with imagination and fine judgement. He was a leader of real quality. His company's problems were its premises, its size and its role.

The Royal Ballet shared the stage at Covent Garden with the opera company, dividing performances there. SWRB toured classical ballet in Britain and abroad. Wherever it danced, it gave as many as seven or eight performances a week on variable surfaces. But the company had only fifty-five dancers. At any time half a dozen or more might be injured, succumbing to the hard pounding of bone and muscle that performance after performance, without interruption, necessarily caused. Normally, a ballet dancer in a demanding leading role might expect the next night off. In SWRB such a dancer could easily find herself on again the following night, sometimes just to make up numbers in the *corps*, or to help fill the ranks of peasants, courtiers, suitors that dressed the stage. In emergency, some went on again, in another role, the same evening. The company had long needed and pleaded for, but had never been afforded, five more dancers to help alleviate strain, compensate for injury and reduce it. I immediately responded to this plea.

But what was to be SWRB's function? My first thought was that the sister ballet companies should have quite disparate roles and repertories. Perhaps, reverting to past models in its history, SWRB, the smaller company, should put emphasis on new choreography and smaller-scale work, offering ballet-lovers a wider diversity of style and subject. Such a company might cost less to run. But this was not how Peter Wright and his colleagues saw things. Peter wanted his company to keep performing the classics, the backbone of its repertory. SWRB's principal task was to tour the United Kingdom, taking classical ballet out of London. SWRB played *Swan Lake* and *The Sleeping Beauty* and *Giselle* and *Coppélia* in Bristol and Plymouth, in Sunderland and Bradford. That meant a company of a size to do those pieces justice. For the Royal Ballet to tour the classics at full strength to the few theatres, in Birmingham and Manchester, whose stages were big enough, made no sense. It cost too much and earned too little. The Arts Council grant was limited. Spending a substantial chunk of it on travel, hotels and boarding houses, and away-from-base *per diem* allowances, seemed and still seems wasteful – the more so if the second company could fill just that role economically. The Royal Opera House was criticized as too metropolitan; in fact, funded from its unitary grant, one company, SWRB, toured the UK.

Peter Wright was eager to get his hands on other three-act crowd-pullers in the Royal Ballet's repertory, Kenneth MacMillan's *Romeo and Juliet* for one. Meanwhile, he had commissioned David Bintley, most promising of choreographers, to make for SWRB his second full-length narrative ballet, *The Snow Queen*. It was an instant success, filling houses wherever it went. Not just its qualities, but the very title seems to exert a powerful appeal. Bintley, a showman to his toenails, understands about titles.

Based at Sadler's Wells, SWRB could never grow, develop or even long survive. The stage and the rehearsal studios were cramped, the facilities inadequate. Slimmer then than I am now, I still could not flatten myself against the wall of the main rehearsal studio and keep out of the dancers' way; entry from the wings, either stately or precipitate, was impossible; there was no wing-space. Tied by sentiment to the Wells, the company needed more spacious premises. If an opportunity came up to move, we should seize it.

The Royal Opera House's Annual Report for 1987/88, Tooley's last season, pointed to some good things on stage. Bernard Haitink had led, as a Music Director should, a Stravinsky ballet triple bill, *The Firebird*, *Scènes de ballet*, *The Rite of Spring*. One of the glories of ballet is the great music to which it is danced – Tchaikovsky giving us one masterpiece after another. It is right that it should be played to the full potential of the score, but not every ballet conductor achieves that. Haitink did. That season, too, saw the world première of *Pursuit*, a new ballet by Ashley Page, promising a major choreographic talent, with a score by Colin Matthews. David Bintley gave us an inventive crowd-pleaser, *Still Life at the Penguin Café*. It ended the evening with a flourish; this one would run and run. The Royal Ballet revived Frederick Ashton's *Ondine* with its score by Hans Werner Henze. Ashton was there. In August, early one morning, I took the call from Eye in Suffolk that told me that Britain's greatest choreographer had died. Happily, Gillian and I had had him to supper in our home some months earlier. He would not make a new ballet or, clutching a huge vodka, appear in the Crush Bar again.

A new *Le nozze de Figaro* was given, appropriately for the retiring chairman, Claus Moser: *Figaro* is his first love. Bernard Haitink, expertly at home in Mozart, conducted; Johannes Schaaf, an experienced German theatre director, produced it very well in handsome, slightly off-beat sets. Covent Garden had flirted with engaging a new generation of producers and designers, but was hesitant about taking on the young Turks who were inventively carrying all before them at ENO. It is easier to try new talent in a brand-new work; the public has no preconceived idea of the piece. John Tooley invited Nicholas Hytner to stage a new opera, *The King Goes Forth to France* by the Finnish composer Aulis Sallinen. Covent Garden had shared in the commissioning and honoured its commitment to new work by putting it on. The staging was deft, in vivid colours, but the piece was not quite strong enough to carry all before it.

Elijah Moshinsky directed *Die Entführung aus dem Serail*, conducted by Georg Solti and with sets designed by Timothy O'Brien. Sidney Nolan, who had been meant to design them, did not deliver. Instead, at the last moment, he provided the front cloth, which did not really match the sets. The confection was visually a muddle. Solti, I gathered, had had a veto on the choice of director and designer. I was amused, but not impressed, to hear that when John Tooley sent Moshinsky to see Solti to discover whom he would accept as designer, Moshinsky had come away with a longish list of names; all on it were famous, several were dead. Solti, a masterly Music Director of the Royal Opera House, had helped lift it to world rank, but I did not think that conductors should decide on staging.

When I gave him dinner, tête à tête, in my apartment in Bermondsey – I overcooked the calves' liver – Bernard Haitink trustingly confided that as I came from television and obviously enjoyed paintings – my walls were crowded – he was sure I would know how productions should look. I was not so confident. Haitink was, if we could afford it, to conduct a new production of *Parsifal*; Bill Bryden would direct. This was the whole point of his coming to Covent Garden as Music Director. Great conductors, masters of the symphonic repertory, long to conduct Wagner. Music Directors get to conduct Wagner. But the House was carrying forward a deficit, and there was no sponsor for *Parsifal* in sight, so for indecisive months there were no funds to put it on. Eventually, however, the go-ahead was given. One morning early in 1988 I sat in the stalls to hear Haitink rehearse the orchestra alone in *Parsifal*. As the broad phrases of the prelude sounded from the pit in the empty auditorium, a feeling of bliss stole over me. This was great music, marvellously played. After years in television, with its nightly flow of the good, bad and indifferent, I could scarcely believe my good fortune in being part of an enterprise whose daily task was to realize works of genius.

The Annual Report for 1987/88 praised work on stage, but John Sainsbury reported a trading loss of £522,000 – less than the £1.2 million that had been anticipated, but a deficit all the same. He warned government of the consequences of continued underfunding. The Arts Council grant had now fallen from 54 per cent of total revenue in 1983/84 to 46 per cent, compared with state funding of 83 per cent in Paris. Blithely, I refused to allow harsh facts to cloud my optimism or shade my determination to succeed. I forgot too that a year earlier, as he folded his Board papers away for the last time, the composer Alexander Goehr had looked at me with large eyes and said, matter of factly, 'It is impossible, you know. You will never achieve anything here.'

In August 1988, on a visit to Israel, I called on the director Yuri Lyubimov in his airy house in Yemin Moshe, across the Sultan's Pool from the walls of the Old City of Jerusalem. He was due in London shortly to direct *Das Rheingold*, one of the prime attractions of my first season. I had enjoyed Lyubimov's bare, taut *Jenufa*. What were his thoughts on the *Ring*? 'The music', he said, 'is all right, I suppose, or bits of it; I quite like some of it. But great parts of the libretto are terrible nonsense.' I gulped, and my heart sank. Could John Tooley really have entrusted Wagner's massive masterpiece to someone who neither admired nor understood the work? I hoped no other such surprises lurked ahead.

3

BEGINNER

1988

Turandot opened my first full season, the great part of it planned well before. Andrei Serban's production, with its dark galleries, and colourful *commedia dell'arte* costumes and masks designed by Sally Jacobs (my mother's name), had been mounted first in Los Angeles in 1984, with Colin Davis conducting – a British cultural salute for the Olympic Games. (There, accompanying Gwyneth Jones, Eva Turner, the great early Turandot, then nearly ninety-two, had got stuck in the hotel lift.) Tonight Gwyneth Jones would sing Princess Turandot, in a voice that could summon an army to battle, and Franco Bonisolli would hit his high C. At 7.30pm on 12 September, the masked chorus took their places in the wooden gallery that framed the action; Ping, Pang, Pong, in parti-coloured silks, ran forward and struck their staffs together, cueing the conductor and the opera's opening chord. Red banners striping the stage fell. *Turandot* began. The first of my nine seasons was under way.

It was a strong performance. At the end, as the curtain calls continued, the stage manager, Stella Chitty, in total command as usual, pushed me out on to the stage to present Gwyneth Jones with a medal, given for long service – twenty-five years – at Covent Garden. Not every singer cares to be reminded that she has sung that long, but Gwyneth was unabashed. 'This medal comes to you, dear Gwyneth,' I said, 'with our gratitude, our admiration, our love.' 'I have enjoyed singing for you for twenty-five years,' Dame Gwyneth told the audience. 'And, now that Jeremy is here as General Director' – as she said this she put an arm round my neck in

Large masks with RED silks ↓coming out of mouths.

Turandot

a half–Nelson wrestling hold – 'now that Jeremy is here, I look forward to singing for you for another twenty-five years.' She meant it too. In the prompt corner as I came off, 'You passed your audition,' said Stella Chitty.

At ten every morning I passed through the door of 45 Floral Street (across from the stage door), along the corridor hung with posters advising safety at work, the Music Library and occupational health on the right; up the narrow stair; turned right past the ladies' loo and the clutter of rehearsal in Studio 45; avoided hampers of costumes and props, fire and safety hazards themselves, and the glass case holding a model of the auditorium as it was in the nineteenth century; up three steps and through heavy metal fire doors, which clanged shut at night; then left and right again, until finally I arrived in the spacious office which David Webster and John Tooley had inhabited before me, right at the back of the building, on the corner of Hanover Place, running between No. 45 and the box-office in 51, and Long Acre. The desk had been Webster's and Tooley's. At the long table, they too had met their colleagues. It had served also as a table for Board meetings till a new, lighter Boardroom was created beneath. Seated at this desk, I had to my right my secretary's office, with room for two, and off that, a tiny space for my assistant, where I had perched while shadowing Tooley. Years later, as privation gripped and we rented out the Long Acre ground-floor frontage for shops, the Boardroom moved back to my office. Because other meetings filled the Boardroom daily, I moved into what had been my secretary's space.

As well as the upright chairs at the long table, I had a cheap, black imitation-leather sofa, and two armchairs. In honour of my arrival, two or three of the most dishevelled of the uprights were re-upholstered. The table and sofa were in good condition; the carpet ancient and threadbare. I reported an asthma attack to a chest specialist in Harley Street; he had been involved in a charitable function at the Royal Opera House and, to my surprise, knew that carpet well. He nodded understandingly, only raising an eyebrow when I added that, an asthmatic, I lived in London in a converted grain warehouse, in Suffolk in a hayfield, and was married to a woman who, until recently, had kept exotic birds.

No. 45 Floral Street housed crewmen's showers beneath; opera-company management on my floor, the archive and the plotting room down along; accounts and personnel on the floor above, and wardrobe. There, cutters and seamstresses created costumes for ballet and for opera, and gave artists fittings. There too were millinery and jewellery. At the top were wigs, where, much later, I discovered I could have my hair cut free by Juan and enjoy a gossip with his boss Ron Freeman. At the top of the next-door rabbit warren over the box-office, above music rehearsal rooms, was the model room where designers took advantage of direct roof lighting. Prince Charles had called these conditions 'Dickensian squalor'. The people I talked to were happy at their work.

Every morning on my desk I found the Stage Manager's show report on the previous evening's performance, written up immediately afterwards and pushed under the door in time for my arrival. In nine seasons, it never once failed to be there to greet me. From it, whether I had been 'in' last night, or not, I learned what had happened on stage. 'Nothing to report' was good news. But sometimes I read of missed cues, forgotten props, scenery that had got stuck and the other accidents that attend live performance. This tenor had forgotten to take his sword on with him, another his hat. And always the time of curtain down, correct to the second: 10.28pm exactly, diligently checked in the old days by speaking clock.

ROYAL OPERA – EXTRACTS FROM SHOW REPORTS

Season 1988/89

13th Dec	Rigoletto	ACT III: The water connector blew off & had to be forced back on again, resulting in a variation of rainfall & a wet Stage Manager.
24th May	Turandot	ACT I: When Mr Lloyd collapsed onto the floor, his hat & wig came off. He covered his head with his hands & deftly replaced the wig.
13th June	Trovatore	There is a smoke saga going right through this performance. Complaints of insufficient smoke, but as the temperature increased, the smoke effects became disastrous. The dry ice in ACT IV rose in seconds & enveloped the Principals. The temperature was in the eighties.
19th June	Trovatore	Curtain calls: Mr Faggioni made a totally unexpected appearance towards the end of the 1st call from the mezzanine level. He was booed immediately.
12th July	Pagliacci	Prologue: There was excellent applause for Mr Cappuccilli, but after he came back through the House Curtain, the applause stopped – but Mr Cappuccilli did not! He went out again & the audience resumed clapping.
26th July	Pagliacci	Mr Cappuccilli substituted a real egg and Miss Soviero was not pleased.

Season 1989/90

28th Oct	P. Grimes	It was an eventful evening:- End of the Pub Scene – the front cloth caught on the prompt side curtain pole & had to be lifted again. 1st interval – The hoist for the plastic failed to operate. Trip lines from the eye pick-up were put onto the plastic but when it was lifted it caught the MEDEA window unit parked upstage. This opened a shackle on one of its two chain hoists. The window moved violently and was left suspended by only one chain hoist. This was dangerous & had to be brought down to stage level. After about 45 minutes, JI spoke to the audience, explaining our technical problems etc. The interval was 1 hour 16 minutes & JI spoke again 5 minutes before the start of Act II.

The scene change into the Hut could not be completed in time & a prior arrangement had been made with Mr Norrington to stop, but he unexpectedly kept a quiet timpani roll going (1½ minutes). At the end of the Curtain Calls, JI presented Miss Bainbridge with the 25 years medal & talked to the audience. There was a splendid response from the audience & artists despite the late hour – 11.29 pm.

Season 1990/91		
21st Feb	Samson & Dalila	JI made an announcement before the performance concerning the death of Dame Margot Fonteyn.
3rd May	Carmen	At 7 o'clock Maestro Mehta realised that he did not have a bow tie. The Wardrobe Staff came to the rescue, but there was a problem over the size and the performance started late – 7.07 pm.
Season 1991/92		
14th Oct	Siegfried	ACT I: The sparking hammer did not produce sparks.
17th Oct	Götterd.	During Mr Haitink's solo call, JI spoke very briefly concerning the tremendous achievement of the RING performances & presented a laurel wreath to him.
11th Nov	Huguenots	(Performance No. 3) During both scenes of ACT II loud comments on the production were heard from the auditorium.
18th Dec	Figaro	ACT III – The audience were amused when a set of antlers came off the prompt side truck when the doors were used violently by Mr Allen.
11th Jan	Così	Act 1: The scene change during Dorabella's aria was excessively noisy when the inner box was raised. Maestro Rizzi was most displeased & his comments were noteworthy.
24th Feb	Hoffmann	Giulietta Scene: Mr Hadley's trousers split during the scene & despite attempts to repair them, they remained split for the rest of the Act.
14th April	Fiery Angel	At the end of the opera, JI joined the Company to make a presentation to Sir Edward Downes, commemorating his 40 years of association with Covent Garden.
Season 1992/93		
8th Mar	Damnation	At the end of the performance, there was enthusiastic applause and some enthusiastic booing for the Production Team.
5th July	Vixen	Act III: The poacher's gun fell down into the Clock/Saw slot. The other gun (unloaded) was slid onto him onstage. The stand-by gun was not fired in the confusion.
Season 1993/94		
15th Oct	Mitridate	ACT 1: The buzzard came off its perch & fell into the grave at the end of the first Aspasia aria. The handler had to go onstage & remove it. Concern was expressed in the form of some shouting from the audience.
4th Mar	Katya	There was a tremendous reception at the end of the performance & the Orchestra unfurled a banner in the pit to wish Mr Haitink a happy 65th Birthday.
19th April	Carmen	The Maestro inadvertently cut a page of music in Act 1 during the children's scene, which confused both stage & pit for a short while.
20th May	Carmen	The performance was shown on the Big Screen in the Piazza. Miss Graves missed an entrance with several lines of singing after the ACT III fight – she was being interviewed by Double Exposure.

That was a relief: 10.28 and ten seconds, after a 7.30 start, meant half an hour's overtime.

In my first weeks I invited groups of my new colleagues to the office for a drink and asked one stage veteran what was the funniest thing that had happened to him in his time at the Opera House. 'Well,' he said, 'it's got to be Peter Hall's *Moses und Aron*, hasn't it?' 'Really? Why?' 'I was standing at the side of the stage one night,' he said, 'with my smoke-gun ready, and just at the end of the orgy scene, after the animal sacrifice, I saw a fella coming towards me carrying a bucket of that muck they were using as blood for the sacrifice, and just as I saw him he tripped and threw the bucket over me, me wearing a clean white shirt and newly pressed trousers. I slipped in the muck and fell and hit my head, and as I did so, the smoke-gun went off at the wrong time and pointing in the wrong direction. When I came to, for I'd given my head quite a bang, the Technical Director Mr Bundy – he'd run right round the back of the set – was standing over me and he gave me such a look I was sure I'd get my cards and lose my job. Next day he summoned me to his office and asked, "Do you know when you let that smoke-gun off last night?" I said I did, 'cos it was just after the animal sacrifice. And he said, "Good. Keep it in. Peter Hall thinks it's just right."' This brought the unpredictability of live theatre home to me as vividly as anything could. The Hall–Solti *Moses und Aron* was in 1965. In New York the Met finally got round to giving the piece in 1999.

After the show report, I would study the print-out of last night's attendance and takings: the percentage of seats sold against capacity, the total sum realized – any advance on budget particularly welcome – and the itemized list of recipients of comps (artists, critics, company members, guests). And then the post. Anyone can write, and daily someone does, to tell the General Director what he or she thinks of the tenor, the ballerina, the sets and costumes, the price of coffee or champagne, the lack of leg-room in the stalls circle or of air-conditioning anywhere, the impossibility of seeing anything at all from certain restricted-view seats – this last coupled with a request for a refund. One amphitheatre patron had had his knee fondled by his neighbour; what was I going to do about it? All these required an answer. In good times I could distribute some letters to colleagues to deal with. Up against it, I answered them all myself, as pleasantly as I could. Once, I hit back. A Mr David Green wrote to me on the notepaper of the Banking Supervision Division of the

Bank of England – after the BCCI affair, before the collapse of Barings – to complain that a Russian Otello had sung 'neither in tune, nor in tempo nor in Italian . . . I want a straight answer to a straight question, Mr Isaacs. How can you allow this?' I wrote that the conductor agreed with him, but that the real answer was simple: we aspired to excellence, but did not always achieve it – rather, I added, as may be said of the Banking Supervision Division of the Bank of England. I got back the reply I wanted: 'Touché!' An old television colleague wrote commending his son's ability as a singer, the best young bass-baritone in England, he said, whom we should certainly engage at Covent Garden. A fine chump I should look, I thought, pushing artists at my skilled colleagues in the old-pals act. But John Miles had spoken up for his son Alastair, and he was right.

As the day went on, I would see the Director of Finance and his Chief Accountant. They came every day; the news they brought was never cheerful, but we made a point of remaining so. I also saw the Director of Administration, with news of wage claims; the Directors of the opera company and of each of the two ballet companies; the Orchestra Director; the Technical Director – this usually meant trouble; the Directors of the Royal Opera House Trust, the fundraising arm, and of the Friends of Covent Garden; the Marketing Director and the Head of Press and Public Relations. Most of these came to senior management meetings. To get the feel of things, I also attended, in the plotting room, the 'small' planning meeting at which details of the schedule were final-ized. Everyone concerned in getting a production on stage came to plead for an extra rehearsal here, an extra hour there. At that meeting, which did not deal with larger strategic planning issues, you could feel the House's pulse throbbing. Judith Vickers, on any practical labour-relations point, and Royal Opera Artistic Administrator Peter Katona on the finely meshed schedule he had written, were mistress and master of their briefs. And I went to opera-production post-mortems to pick over what had gone wrong.

If I had too many managers reporting to me, I had too many Boards to report to. In my time at Covent Garden I attended more Board meetings than management meetings. The Royal Opera House had Boards like the Circle Line has trains; the meetings came round again and again. There was the Main Board, the Ballet Board and later the Birmingham Royal Ballet Board, the Opera Board, the Development Board; the Royal Opera

House Trust; the Friends of Covent Garden, both the Executive Committee and the Council; the American Friends of Covent Garden; the Royal Ballet Governors; the Royal Ballet School Governors. There were Educational Advisory Committees for opera and ballet, and for the House jointly. The Royal Opera House Benevolent Fund met in the Boardroom, as did other charitable trusts on which I sat. All of these I was expected to attend. I occasionally sent apologies to some; I unfailingly turned up to others. Some weeks, Opera, Ballet and Main Board meetings were on successive days.

The Opera and Ballet Boards were set up in 1987 by John Sainsbury to replace the committees which had overseen repertory and performance before that. These had talked a lot and decided nothing. John Tooley kept his calm and, giving little away, got on with the job. The committees had their use as an internal audit of performance quality; the change to subsidiary Board status slightly widened their responsibilities. John Sainsbury required them to take account of financial realities in their comments; we reported production cost and box-office results to each. But Sainsbury held back from delegating budgetary approval to the subsidiaries; that he reserved for the Main Board. With the Ballet Board chaired by Sainsbury, and the Opera Board by Denis Forman, I, and the Artistic and Administrative Directors, were subjected monthly to thorough scrutiny by an informed and extremely beady-eyed bunch. Little escaped either of them. They stiffened our backbone and lightened the Main Board's load, enabling that body in turn to concentrate on finance and development. I was concerned at first that the Directors of the opera and ballet companies would report to those Boards and their Chairmen rather than to me, and occasionally had to be nippy on my feet to ensure they did not; but all worked out sensibly. For each monthly meeting a meticulously prepared, clearly presented set of accounts was circulated, or, at a pinch, tabled. There was no absence of financial information. On the contrary, trees were felled to provide it fully. An Arts Council representative sat at each of those three Board tables.

In the past, the Main Board of the Royal Opera House had intervened in artistic decisions, vetoing a proposed new production, allowing *Moses und Aron* only after considerable debate, seeing a role for itself in choosing producers and designers, appointing a distinguished art critic, Bryan Robertson, to advise on design. There was none of that in my day: John Sainsbury was adamant that artistic decisions were a matter solely for the executive, though he took an acute interest in other quite minor matters – his business motto was 'Retail is Detail'. The subsidiary Boards' prospective review of proposed repertory was general, encouraging, supportive. I can think of one exception: in 1996/97 Tessa Blackstone forced a change in the season's plans. She insisted on one fewer three-act ballet and one more triple bill. Even then, it was left for Anthony Dowell to decide precisely what to do. Retrospective criticism, of course, was frank and free. I never received what Osbert Lancaster described as the artist's due – 'not criticism, but constructive praise'; but with knowledgeable colleagues round the table – Antoinette Sibley, Colin Nears and Deborah MacMillan, Ted Downes, Janet Baker, John Manduell, Michael Berkeley and Norman Rosenthal – these meetings were pleasant and stimulating. Encouragingly, they kept us on track.

From 1946 to 1987 just over fifty people served as ROH Directors. The list, beginning with John Maynard Keynes, is a distinguished one. It includes William Walton, Thomas Armstrong, Arthur Bliss, Viscount Waverley in earlier years; Noel Annan, Isaiah Berlin, Lionel Robbins later on. Only one was a woman, Colette Clark, daughter of the art historian Sir Kenneth Clark. Some had very long terms of service. Annan served twelve years, Garrett Drogheda twenty, Claus Moser twenty-two, Isaiah Berlin two separate terms of ten and thirteen years. John Sainsbury, when he retired as Chairman, had served twenty in all. A place on the Covent Garden Board was much coveted and, once obtained, elegantly clung on to. Angus Stirling served as Chairman of the Friends for a decade. Colette Clark owed her continuing place for nearly fifteen years to her informed passion for ballet and to her friendships with those among whom she found herself. John Sainsbury altered this, limiting members to a five-year term renewable only for three years, with exceptions for Committee Chairmen. He recruited, with a fresh emphasis on City expertise, new wise heads to join: Sir Martin Jacomb and Sir James Spooner. He also brought in Tessa Blackstone, Master of Birkbeck College, extremely able, a thinking balletomane, and Labour to boot. New blood was all new strength.

In a good year, the Royal Opera House Trust might come up with a tenth or more of the House's income. A General Director must therefore attend the ROH Trust monthly meeting. It was both polite and politic to go to the Friends Executive Committee; the surplus earned by nearly 20,000 subscriptions, and the Friends' other activities, rose over my years well above the £500,000 mark. I would go to claim my share of it, to express my gratitude, to explain what I proposed to spend it on. Each body, Trust and Friends, had its own existence. Each kept itself – to the indignation of management consultants invited to run a rule over us – at arm's length from the Opera House. The Royal Opera House's fundraising and support agencies have only this logic: like Topsy, 'they just growed'. Having charitable status, they are not easy to do away with. They have each lasted and will last a while longer, their work co-ordinated, their identities retained.

As General Director, ROH, I represented the House's interest in the development and its construction. In theory the Main Board was the client; in practice, I was. The architects saw me as such, reporting, through me, to the Development Board. This had a major task to perform, and a clear supervisory role and purpose: securing planning permission for a scheme to redevelop that would meet the House's need; and putting in place the managerial systems and controls that would see the job safely through to completion. Under Christopher Benson, Martin Jacomb, Kit McMahon, Angus Stirling and, now, Stuart Lipton, this has been accomplished. Expert advisers in construction and property played their part. Trevor Osborne took the key role in planning matters.

Without making immediate major changes, I still wanted to signal, as soon as I had taken over at Covent Garden, that a new regime was in place. I made a gesture, and altered the format and design of Royal Opera House programmes. The old programme was much loved; it bore on the front cover the Royal coat-of-arms in black on the House's traditional red. It was handy in size and format, it would fit neatly in your pocket. It contained a cast list for the very performance you were attending, a synopsis of the plot, timings of the acts and intervals, information about the performers – postage-stamp pictures and biographies in very small print – some facts about the House and its Boards, lists of company members, orchestra and chorus, lists of sponsors from way back, a few advertisements and not much else. On the title page inside, 'The 249th performance of *Tosca*', or 'the 300th performance of *The Sleeping Beauty* at the Royal Opera House', and the date. The programme was a record of an event. It served to remind us we were at that performance, as does an entry in a diary. Some regular attenders collected them over the years and could point to shelf on shelf of them, crammed tight. Change would not be to their liking.

I thought the programme should say more, and earn more. There was more we could tell audiences about the works they were to see and hear, even if they only read it after they got home. If the programme carried more text and coloured illustrations, it could carry more advertising and bring in income. I decided that the programme's regal look was too sober and that, since the format was to be enlarged anyway, the appearance should alter too. With an eye to the season's opening in September, a new Marketing Director, John Paine, and I asked design consultants for proposals for change, and settled on something lighter and brighter. Our cover was creamy white, not red. In addition to the royal coat-of-arms, it had a Dufyish sketch of the façade of the House, impressionistic, light-hearted, friendly – and feeble.

The Board, consulted after the event, hated it. And they said so. They wanted, at all costs, to return to the traditional red. By now I knew I had made a mistake: a major change in programming would have caused less upset. As gracefully as I could, I beat a retreat. The revised format, which increased page size, was accepted; the change of colour was not. Lesson: change substance if you must, but do not mess about with symbols which people hold dear. The red was restored, with the coat-of-arms, and has lasted well. Under Alison Latham's distinguished editorship, the new programmes soon became a byword for intelligent writing and well-chosen illustration. (At £3 they are also a bargain buy; at La Scala or Bologna or Brussels the programme will cost £10.) A cast list is offered, free.

That summer of 1988 I decided to try to improve the auditorium's acoustic for singers and orchestra. We wanted to hear more string tone. We took up the carpet on the stalls floor. Absorbent textile soaks up sound, whereas polished wood reflects it, keeps it in play. Beneath the carpet, laid on the very decent wood flooring, we uncovered several layers of super-absorbent fibrous underlay. Up it all came. The acoustic marginally, but noticeably, improved. There was a drawback: the new, heavier programmes, when dropped on the wooden floor, made a momentary clatter. But I never regretted the change. Except for the week of the annual Midland Bank Proms, when the stalls audience sits on the floor, no one ever suggested putting the carpet back.

The old question *'Chi canta?'* ('Who is singing?') was once all you needed to know before deciding to go to the opera. Isaiah Berlin used to challenge anyone to show him the producer's name on a nineteenth-century playbill. It was not there. Now, some said, we suffered from the disease of 'produceritis'. The producer, not the conductor, was king; his concept of what the piece was really about prevailed and was imposed on it. I was not a committed fan of 'concept opera', any more than I am an unqualified admirer of Turner Prize-winning conceptual art, but I did think that the producer was there to interpret the piece and that the choice of producer mattered immensely. I wanted to employ the brightest new talents in English theatre and to contract designers aware that modern painting had altered the way we see things. I wanted to make it possible to change the look of opera at Covent Garden. And, as I had tried to do at Channel 4, I wanted to take the public with me. If a producer chose a controversial reading, I welcomed a debate as to what he or she was on about.

European opera houses employ a mediator between theatre and public who brings an understanding of text to the choice of a piece, and then works with its interpreters to explain it and enrich audiences' enjoyment. In Germany they call this person a *Dramaturg*. I decided Covent Garden should have a 'Dramaturg'. English National Opera already had one, Edmund Tracey, and then Nicholas John; their role consisted both in editing their programmes, and, crucially, in commissioning the English translations they sang. I saw our Dramaturg in a different role and supposed that the right person would find it possible, as we embarked on a *Ring* cycle, or on a new opera, or on a controversial new production of a core piece, both to offer guidance to a producer, if that was needed, and also to interpret his work and the text's meaning to an attentive public. I offered the post to the senior editor of music books at Faber, Patrick Carnegy. When I had doubts, he insisted that the title of 'Dramaturg' was right and he was sure there was a job that could be done on the lines I sketched. Patrick Carnegy organized a series of events and study days; he introduced a series of lunchtime Crush Bar recitals; he helped create a genuine buzz, but not as a true Dramaturg.

On the public's part there was avid interest. Places for study days were always taken up; the lectures, questions and answers, and panel discussions were hugely enjoyed. If I got to them, I learned something. And the Opera House benefited in other ways. At one Wagnerian occasion, John Tomlinson, giving up free time to discuss the *Ring* and his part in it, in the Baylis Theatre at Sadler's Wells, was asked how he set about studying a part. 'I look at it whenever I can,' he said. 'In the train coming up today I was looking at *Meistersinger*.' At the session's end, I ran to him. 'John, when you do sing Hans Sachs, sing it first for us.' He did. For *Gawain*, Harrison Birtwistle attended a crowded Sunday at the Royal Academy of Music; it was heartening to be one of the 200 there, preparing for a new operatic experience. There was no problem in involving the audience.

What Patrick Carnegy did find difficult was to involve the producer in his work. He had no ground to stand on, no leverage. In a German opera house, the music director's office, or suite of offices, is next to the Intendant's, and the Dramaturg's is next to the music director's. The Dramaturg is that important, with a say in the choice of repertory and in the house's publications – he is one of the triumvirate that runs the theatre. (What about the finance director? There is none. There may be a general manager, but a finance director is not needed. Funds from the state are adequate for their purpose. The opera-house budget is supplied, and overseen, by civil servants in the finance ministry.) In Germany a Dramaturg is in a powerful position and the producer, therefore, must pay him attention. But producers at Covent Garden owed nothing to the Dramaturg. They regarded themselves as too experienced to need advice and were disinclined to take it. And whereas mediation may be needed for 'concept' opera, it can readily be dispensed with in a less didactic theatre. Carnegy never succeeded in carving out that mediatory role for himself. We had plenty of work for him to do – in a rational world, he would still be at Covent Garden – but in the next financial crisis I had to find economies by cutting staff numbers and I told him he had to go. It was unduly hard on him. An experiment ended before it had truly begun.

Another innovation was more successful: surtitles. In *Power House*, a three-cheers-for-us account of their stint at English National Opera, David Pountney, Peter Jonas and Mark Elder describe the use of surtitles in the opera house as 'like making love with a condom on'. But the introduction of surtitles is opera's greatest success story of the 1990s. The Royal Opera House first used them to explain the plot at a schools' matinée of *Die Fledermaus* in December 1983. They made their appearances, at first irregularly, at Covent Garden evening performances from the 1986/87 season, causing some controversy. Purists argued that, whatever language a piece was sung in, communication in the theatre was

intended to be by voice and facial expression across the footlights. For work given in a native language this was, in theory, incontrovertible: Italian audiences could understand opera sung in Italian, and so should English audiences opera sung in English. ENO gives all opera in English, commissioning excellent translations to ensure singable words. Whether in practice you can easily hear all the words is another matter; it varies from performance to performance, composer to composer.

But how could English audiences, subscribing for a Covent Garden season, be expected to hear and fully understand the words of different operas sung one night in Italian, another in German, a third in French, a fourth in Russian, a fifth, perhaps, in Czech? They could not. Oh yes, they could, stern voices rejoined, if only they would do their 'homework'. Let opera-goers apply themselves properly, before visiting the theatre, to a study of the text, with a translation beside them – librettos in several languages printed in CD packs come in handy here. Then, if they thought hard and remembered hard and listened hard and, above all, never took their eyes off the expressive features of the singer, however far away they sat, they would have no difficulty in following closely what was going on. But no one, except a music critic with days to prepare, or men and women completely at leisure, can manage that: it simply is not reasonable to expect anyone to mug up, line by line, *Parsifal* and *From the House of the Dead* and *Prince Igor* in that way. People who go to the opera lead crowded, busy lives. Hence the old absurd scramble to read the synopsis before the house lights darkened.

But a synopsis is not a libretto. There is far more text, detail and nuance in the librettos of Da Ponte or Hofmannsthal, or Boito or Wagner, than any summary can provide. Who writes and sends exactly what letters to whom in *Le nozze di Figaro*, and why? The playwright Michael Frayn, at *L'elisir d'amore* one night, asked me why all the girls had fallen in love with Nemorino. He hadn't picked up from the text, or from the action, that Nemorino's uncle had died, left everything to him and made him a rich man. Nemorino's uncle dies offstage. And that is another difficulty. It is not hard to infer from the action that a couple are falling in love, or are about to fight a duel. But how, without the language, is one ever to work out what is conveyed when someone launches into a long monologue about events of the past – Siegmund in *Die Walküre*, say, or Mime in *Siegfried*? The audiences' understanding and enjoyment would be enhanced if they could follow not just the plot, but the argument.

Subtitles made foreign-language films, in the cinema and on television, intelligible. Subtitles, beginning in the 1970s, made opera on television intelligible too. Who can forget first seeing them on relays and recordings from Glyndebourne or Covent Garden, or on the revelatory *Ring* from Bayreuth by Patrice Chéreau, brilliantly scheduled by Brian Wenham on BBC2 an act at a time over ten weeks? Those broadcasts made conquests for opera, winning over hundreds of thousands to a new experience.

As soon as the technology offered, it made sense to introduce surtitles into the theatre, on a board in Covent Garden's case, high up within the proscenium. Their curiosity value at first distracted. A few complained that the necessity to raise the eyes to read them, or their inability to avoid glancing at them, detracted from their pleasure in the performance. In the early days the quick-fire dialogues of the Da Ponte operas posed problems: the titles came up too soon, the laughs too early. But at least there were laughs. When I took charge at Covent Garden, we gave some performances with English titles, others without. This was to allow the public to avoid them if they wished. But it was apparent where the demand lay. Bernard Haitink reported that, without looking, he could tell from the audiences' appreciation behind him whether or not the titles were in use for *Figaro*. In an essay for a Glyndebourne programme, Isaiah Berlin made an elegant case for their use. Jonathan Miller pointed out an evident epistemological truth: the brain took in the translation through the eye far more quickly than the words were sung, or the action unfolded.

To be sure of our ground, we asked audiences to fill in a questionnaire. The overwhelming majority, over 90 per cent, said they wanted surtitles. The Chairman was enthusiastic and would brook no delay. We moved instantly to supply their need – and never regretted it. Surtitles appeared at every opera performance from May 1988. From then on, in my seat in the Grand Tier, B33, my concerns were only that the system should not fail (it sometimes did), that legibility be improved, that spelling be accurate, that the sense be clear. It was not long before my postbag included complaints from those who could not easily read the surtitles. Not one patron wrote to complain that they were in use. Surtitles have brought a sea-change in opera-going. In New York, in its towering auditorium, the Met has installed them, for use at discretion, in a strip affixed to the back of the seat in front of you. You decide whether to use them or not. The technology will only get better. The demand will grow. Now, in London, audiences at both opera houses, in theory at any rate, can understand pretty well every syllable they pay to hear. No one has to pretend any more. The programme at Covent Garden can devote less space to plot, more to context and meaning. Some composers write music for the female voice, high above the stave, that makes it hard to hear precisely what is being sung. When we came to present Harry Birtwistle's *Gawain*, the issue arose of whether we should surtitle opera in English. Second time round, we did.

When my appointment was announced, I received a telegram from the French opera producer Jean-Louis Martinoty who had recently directed *Ariadne auf Naxos* in our theatre, expressing delight that Covent Garden was to be ruled by '*un moderne*'. My reputation at Channel 4 was for new ideas, but actually what I offered was a mix of innovation and the secure popularity of golden oldies. Bearing in mind that, for both opera and ballet, the great preponderance of the productions we would stage in my early years would be revivals taken from store, and anyway wishing to proceed with proper caution, I thought it wrong to proclaim a total commitment to a challenging modernity. In any case, uncompromising 'challenge' could never be the right watchword for Covent Garden. At my first press conference I expressed respect for my predecessor's achievements and stressed continuity in my intentions. But, looking ahead, I did seek change, and intended some of the new work the companies would perform to be both innovatory and demanding. Magda Alexander, forthright wife of our principal fundraiser, Alex Alexander, said to me one evening, as she took her seat in the stalls, that if I only ever put on *Swan Lake* and *La bohème* she would be content. But I thought I could do better than that. In any case, I knew how much others hoped I could lift the House from a creative slough, caused partly by financial stringency, partly by weariness, into which it was perceived to have fallen.

In those first few weeks I wrote papers for the Board setting out my aspirations. The principal end we served, I argued, and perhaps the only justification for our existence, was to put work of true excellence on the stage, to perform to the highest international standard. But what work?

The Royal Ballet is born of and dedicated to classical ballet. It is not a modern dance company but, building on classical technique, much may be attempted. Anthony Dowell was quite clear in his mind: it was the great nineteenth-century masterpieces of the Russian court tradition that stretched young dancers, tuned their technique, tested their strengths, taught them carriage, formed their style, shaped and promoted their artistry. If men and women could master Marius Petipa's choreography, they would continue, as they must, the tradition from which they sprang. They would also be able to dance anything else he was likely to set them to. So *The Sleeping Beauty*, the company's signature ballet, *Swan Lake* and *The Nutcracker* formed the backbone of the company's repertory, together with other ever-popular classics. Next in importance came the work of Ashton, the English creative genius who helped bring the company into well-being and advanced it on the world stage. With Ninette de Valois and Constant Lambert, Ashton had made the Royal Ballet not just a great company, but a distinctive one. The elegant fluency of his choreography, lyrical and reticent, gave the company an English look all its own. Ashton had made his ballets for the company, working with the dancers, creating dance on their bodies. Now he was gone. His work, however, was part of the company's heritage; they must cherish it, keep it alive. But who would ensure that they could do so? There were great dancers, now teachers, on whom this work had been created. They would not be around much longer.

An early visitor to my office was the other great Royal Ballet choreographer, another genius, Kenneth MacMillan. We had never met. He had succeeded Frederick Ashton as Director, but never enjoyed the directorship as much as he enjoyed making ballets. He came now, accompanied by his formidable wife Deborah. They sat together on the sofa, Kenneth saying scarcely a word while she let me have it. In the past Kenneth's work had been scorned by the Board and neglected by the House. I must ensure that he was properly treated, see to it that more of his ballets were given. Kenneth MacMillan's early *Romeo and Juliet* nobly, touchingly, extends the language of love in dance; his *Manon*, not universally well received at first, seethes with sexual energy. Today both masterpieces command audiences' loyalty and figure regularly in the repertory. Deborah MacMillan pointed out to me how many other works Kenneth had created for the company, some highly controversial at their premières, and urged that those should be revived. Such a commitment to our greatest living choreographer would, Anthony Dowell knew, be a main charge on his necessarily limited range of programming and resource. But it was a proper one. Ashton was dead; MacMillan was able to create new ballets and we would be celebrating his sixtieth birthday soon. Revivals of both men's work would contend for place.

Isidore and Sally Isaacs sent three sons to Glasgow Academy, Oxford and Cambridge.

My brother Raphael (*left*) served the British Council with distinction; Michael (*centre*) moved to Israel and was killed, with his wife Ribbie, by a PLO bomb in Jerusalem in 1975.

1980, appointed founding Chief Executive of Channel Four.

The Royal Box at the end of the previous regime; from left, Claus Moser,
Anya Sainsbury, John and Patsy Tooley, John Sainsbury and Garrett Drogheda.
Ninette de Valois is next door.

Rheingold, October 1988, directed by Yuri Lyubimov. Alberich's curse struck early.
We switched to a *Ring* cycle by Götz Friedrich.

General Director and Chairman: 'Don't talk while I'm interrupting.'

Gwyneth Jones as Princess Turandot, September 1988; after all those forfeited severed heads, a long service medal.

Luciano Pavarotti, in *Ballo in maschera*.
'For you, I will come back to
Covent Garden . . .'

José Carreras in *Stiffelio*. After
leukaemia, 'God gave him back the
strength that once he had.'

Plácido Domingo, in Verdi's *Otello*;
always growing in artistry, he never
surpassed this.

Kiri Te Kanawa, the Countess
in *Capriccio*, dressed by Versace;
beautiful as her voice.

Ruth-Ann Swenson as Handel's and Congreve's
Semele; 'Endless pleasure . . .'

Karita Mattila as Elisabeth, in Verdi's *Don Carlos*,
touched greatness.

Bernard Haitink in rehearsal. The orchestra loved him because he gave his all.

Jeffrey Tate, a positive force in the German repertory.

Edward Downes, determined advocate of all of Verdi.

Georg Solti celebrates his eightieth birthday, accepting the silver rose from *Der Rosenkavalier*, his debut piece at Covent Garden, and the title Music Director Laureate.

Elijah Moshinsky at *Stiffelio* rehearsals; he worked always to keep the action moving.

Simon Rattle and Bill Bryden rehearse Janáček's *Cunning Little Vixen*. Rattle, choosy about the operas he conducts, made every shimmering note of *Vixen* tell.

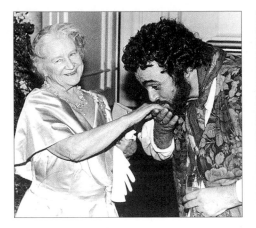

The Queen Mother and Luciano
Pavarotti; *L'Elisir d'amore*.

Floral Street; greeting the Majors. The
Gorbachevs came too.

14 July 1997; on stage as the House closes, Princess Margaret, Plácido Domingo,
Darcey Bussell and back-stage staff.

The next priority, the Board, Anthony Dowell and I might agree, would be new work by new choreographers, ideally resident in the company. Dance is shaped on individual physiques; the choreographer needs to know the bodies he or she will work with. The first thing a visiting choreographer does is to see the company at work, at morning class, at studio rehearsal, on stage. The fresh eye spots not just ability, but potential. It often takes the visitor to pick out talent from the rank and file, and to offer the young a chance of stardom. But the Principal Choreographer has the inside track. That post then was already Kenneth MacMillan's; he would make new commissioned works each year. Would there be room for others? Ashley Page, with *Pursuit* behind him, his talent burgeoning, itching to work, would hope so. So would the prolific David Bintley, bidding impatiently to make it to the very top. Bintley had been choreographing non-stop at SWRB and was now with the Royal Ballet, creating work for both our companies. Adept in a classical mode, as his *Galanteries* showed, Bintley was also very much an entertainer, a showman with an instinct for touching the audience's pleasure zones. He was assured, self-confident, arrogant even. The problem would never be to get work from him, only to find room in the schedule for half he could do.

The nineteenth-century classics, the heritage of Ashton and MacMillan, new work from MacMillan and Bintley and others – I charted these as objectives in my note to the Board. Embroidering, I added other goals: past British choreographers like Anthony Tudor; living choreographers of world class like Jerome Robbins, George Balanchine, Jiří Kylian; new foreign choreography – Neumeier, Tetley, Forsythe. This statement of aims, I now think, was too diffuse. Programmers, putting together repertory, will select from a wide range of work, but no company can easily be faithful to all the lyric gods at one time. In any case, the Royal Ballet might dance only a dozen different programmes a year, or fewer. It would have to concentrate on what it did best. Anthony Dowell, with a notably smaller company than those of New York or Paris, Moscow or Leningrad, and rehearsal space divided between Barons Court and Covent Garden, was going to have to choose.

The Royal Opera, meanwhile, had the sets and costumes of more than 100 productions in store, in Morden in Kent and scattered round London. Rolled-up cloths were buried in heaps in a dark hole below the stage; this was called The Cut, and stage crew were paid danger money to work in it. The company, in theory, had an extensive repertory, but the cloths, and the productions, were mostly moth-eaten. And in repertory I wanted to cast a wide net. We would perform, I suggested, as of un-questioned right, the core repertory of Verdi and Puccini, Mozart and Wagner (including the *Ring*), Rossini, Donizetti, Bellini and Strauss. Russian and French opera should have their place. To British opera we owed a special duty, as we did to work made in this century, to con-temporary composers, and particularly to new work we ourselves commissioned. Opera was not a museum exhibit, but a living art form.

The opera company, offering twenty or so productions a season, could touch several of these bases. I wanted a repertory of broad appeal, with as much freshness and variety as was practicable. And I wanted it to look new. There was little chance of that if we relied solely on reviving pro-ductions we already owned. Two-thirds of the shows we held in store were more than thirty years old; some had disintegrated, and all showed their age. A handsome masterpiece like the 1958 Visconti *Don Carlos* was still worth performing. The famous Zeffirelli *Tosca* of 1964, designed by Mongiardino, in which Callas and Gobbi had sung, lasted longer than any other. Re-made three times, it still served, a comfortable vehicle for changing casts of great singers, a bold, grand, period rendition of Puccini's melodrama. The church of Sant' Andrea della Valle, the Palazzo Farnese and the Castel Sant'Angelo are in turn convincingly spread before you. By 1997, when the House closed, this famous production had done duty 210 times. I hope it may appear again.

With very few exceptions, the productions of the 1950s, 1960s and 1970s were dated. There were patrons who relished the common style of heightened naturalism that these designs exhibited and would not be comfortable with anything else. For some of them, Zeffirelli's *Tosca* WAS *Tosca*; it had formed their image of the piece, and always would. To change it was a sort of sacrilege. But marvellously as any good design may show an opera to advantage, none can claim to capture and embody its only conceivable form. Producers and designers invent and re-invent the look of an opera by their own lights, for their own time, our time. When a run of performances is over, and the production, if successful, has been revived for a few seasons, its fabric begins to wear, its structures creak, it ceases to exert the fascination it did when first staged. Time, then, if the House can afford it, to replace it and move on.

In the late 1970s and early 1980s, English National Opera at the Coliseum, under George Harewood and Peter Jonas, had given Covent

Garden a fright. Productions there were livelier, fresher, more exciting; the finest of them, using the best available talent, came up new minted, teaching boldness and invention not just to other opera houses but to theatre itself. The foundation of all great performance in opera is music-making of the highest standard; without that, no sets and costumes or producers' tricks and concepts can satisfy. *Prima la musica, poi le parole* – first the music, then the words. But opera must reach both eye and ear, and through them mind and heart. Opera is music drama, and knocks you out by the way the piece looks and through singers who can act. At ENO, David Pountney's *Rusalka*, Nicholas Hytner's *Xerxes*, Jonathan Miller's *Rigoletto* brought this off. Other productions – Pountney's *Macbeth*, David Alden's *Simon Boccanegra* and *A Masked Ball* – used a vivid, expressionist brutalism to make their effect. Audience reaction was mixed; first-nighters booed vigorously, though someone suggested this was encouraged by ENO's press office. There was a serious consequence later: productions which used shock tactics to make their effect turned out to be less capable of revival. Shocks wear off; worth lasts. Peter Jonas, when he left ENO in 1993 for Munich, left behind a substantial deficit and a store of exciting productions, several of which failed second time round. All the same, under Jonas ENO fizzed with an enviable creative energy. Covent Garden appeared staid and drab by comparison. That had to end.

I wanted first to raise musical standards to the highest and then to employ, as soon as we could, the producers and designers and lighting designers who were making waves in their profession, preferably in Britain. I had nothing against Germans or Italians, Frenchmen or Spaniards. But if the British were best, why not employ them in the first instance, rather than soldier on with distinguished continental imports and watch the young Brits steal our thunder in St Martin's Lane? I told the Board it was my intention to engage Hytner, Vick, Albery, Freeman, and as soon as possible. (And David Pountney, whose ENO commitment at first prevented it. When eventually he was free, we were booked solid too far ahead.) One Opera Board member, John Manduell, Principal of the Royal Northern College of Music, urged me to include on my list the young Richard Jones, who had produced a *Manon* he rated highly at the Royal Northern and who would work next with Opera North. Richard Jones soon after directed Judith Weir's *A Night at the Chinese Opera* for Kent Opera, which I much admired. In the end, he came to us too.

Not everyone accepted that a bold new look to our work was needed. A tussle was in process; I would need allies. The Priestley report had called for both artistic and financial responsibilities to be devolved from the centre to the opera and ballet companies. John Tooley, somewhat reluctantly I suspect, had accepted this in the case of opera, and agreed to the appointment of Eva Wagner-Pasquier as Director of the opera company. Some fruit came of this – the collaborations with Johannes Schaaf and Carlos Kleiber – but it did not work out. Either Tooley was not prepared to delegate authority, or Wagner failed to seize and implement it. Eva Wagner is a woman of sharp artistic sensibilities and considerable strengths, yet she did not find it easy to win acceptance at Covent Garden, which seemed to her hidebound and stuffy. A tall blonde with a fine figure, someone instructed her not to appear for work wearing trousers. This, in a theatre! In any case, decisively, Bernard Haitink took against her and declared he could not and would not work with her. He never spelled out why. Eva hoped, I think, that on my appointment I would reverse this and keep her on. But well before I took over Claus Moser had told her she would have to go. She is by far the best-qualified Wagner to succeed her father Wolfgang at Bayreuth. But he does not speak to her. His second wife Gudrun will freeze out Eva, and Wolfgang's other children, if she can.

Eva Wagner's departure was, I thought, my opportunity to see an Opera Director in post who might share my artistic vision for the House. I contacted Brian McMaster at Welsh National Opera (WNO) and tried to reach Nicholas Payne at Opera North to see if either was interested in working under a novice General Director in overall charge. Neither was. Each preferred being in sole command in his own theatre. In this brief uncertainty, Paul Findlay, John Tooley's chief assistant, seized his moment. Bernard Haitink warmly embraced him in the key role and together they moved to reinforce the axis by proposing we engage John Cox, whom Haitink knew from Glyndebourne, as Production Director. They made a strong team, if more than a shade conservative. There was never any conflict between them and me, or even serious disagreement over decisions down the line. But I still wanted change. I told Paul Findlay I reserved the right to approve all repertory and the engagement of producers. Given commitments made and in the pipeline, it would take a season or two at least to move things forward. Johannes Schaaf had been contracted, after *Figaro*, to do the other two Mozart–Da Ponte operas, *Don Giovanni* and *Così fan tutte*. Piero Faggioni, who had already produced at Covent Garden a gigantic *La fanciulla del West*, with designs by Ken Adam of Bond movie fame, would do *Il trovatore* in my first season. If that worked, it was intended he would go on to the three other Verdi operas set in Spain. John Cox would, as well as supervising revivals, make one new production a season. There would be nothing garishly modernist about any of those.

A key musical appointment in the opera company was made before I arrived. Jeffrey Tate is a fine musician, an excellent conductor and an exceptional man. He graduated from Cambridge in medicine and qualified as a doctor, but preferred to make his career in music. After working as a repetiteur at Bayreuth and Covent Garden, he seized his chance as a conductor and has not looked back. What makes this the more remarkable is that Jeffrey Tate has a deformed spine, which means he needs a stick to put his weight on as he walks, and he lies down to rest from time to time through the day. In 1986 John Tooley announced Tate's appointment as Principal Conductor at the Royal Opera, to work with Bernard Haitink, conscious that Haitink would be absent half the year. To have input from so articulate a musician could only benefit the company. But there was a snag. German music was Tate's first love, as it was Haitink's. Italian music – Verdi, Puccini, Rossini, Donizetti – is at the heart of opera's repertory and popularity, and of what Covent Garden stood for. But neither Haitink nor Tate was particularly at home there. Jeffrey Tate gave us some fine performances, but his appointment left us much chasing still to do to find the right conductors for part of the season. The answer to our problem, Edward Downes, was in Manchester all along, with the BBC Philharmonic. When he joined in 1991, Tate's appointment was not renewed and, with Daniele Gatti, Carlo Rizzi and Evelino Pido also in the frame, the balance began to right itself.

The Music Director approved the engagement of any conductor for the opera. (He would also approve the appointment of a Music Director for the ballet.) Here, Bernard Haitink's generosity stood the House in excellent stead. Given his commitments to orchestras abroad – the Boston Symphony, the Berlin Philharmonic – he could not be Music Director full time. He gave about a third of his time to his duties at Covent Garden, conducting three or four productions a season, giving us up to twenty weeks and, at most, up to thirty performances. Some music directors – James Levine at the Met was one – conduct everything they can. Levine thinks nothing of conducting both the Saturday matinée and the evening performance. But Bernard Haitink is wholly absorbed by any one piece he is conducting: he gives his mind to that and to nothing else. He might insist on reserving certain operas for himself – the Music Director's most prized prerogative – but he never jibbed at our engaging the finest talents we could recruit to the pit and would, if necessary, pick up the telephone to Kleiber or Solti to add his persuasions to ours. And he welcomed women to the pit: Jane Glover, Sîan Edwards, Simone Young. Since everything musical in opera stems from the score and the conductor, this confidence of his, this lack of jealousy of others' talents, this opportunity he offered them to perform on his patch, made a singular contribution to the quality and ambition of our work. Not every music director takes a similarly generous stance.

An abiding image for me is of Bernard expressive, urgent in the pit, shaping the music. Another is of him in his box above it, watching – as I think few other conductors can easily bear to do – others occupying his place, working on his orchestra, reaping their applause. I saw him there for Carlos Kleiber, Georg Solti, Colin Davis, Christoph von Dohnányi, Christian Thielemann, Esa Pekka-Salonen, and honoured him for it.

Engaging the finest conductors in the world, however, is easier said than done; their engagement books are full, for years ahead, and they are expensive. We had several ominous gaps to fill in the very next season.

Whenever I meet the publisher John Calder at the opera, or anywhere else, I ask the same question: 'How many?' He answers instantly: 489, or 526, or whatever, this being the total number of different operas he has, by then, in a lifelong quest, seen in performance. As I write, his total is 825. He does well to keep score, reminding us that the opera repertory is larger than we think. And it is growing all the time. The great joy of the nineteenth century was that opera, a newish art form, brought newly composed works into the opera house each year. Verdi was sung in the street in Italy as Mozart had been in Vienna. Verdi wrote thirty-two operas; Rossini thirty-nine; Donizetti nearly seventy. Their output was prodigious; much is now neglected but all is worth hearing. The great joy of the twentieth century is that we can exploit our knowledge of the past to give it a present, and a future. We can choose from the cornucopia of the world's operatic creation to arrange our feast. Before Mozart, Handel; before him Purcell; before Purcell, Monteverdi and Cavalli.

The twentieth century has a claim to be opera's most varied and one of its most productive. Puccini wrote masterpieces in it, as did Strauss. Janáček, for me the century's greatest operatic composer, gave us half a dozen masterworks. Debussy and Poulenc, Prokofiev and Shostakovich, Berg and Stravinsky, Britten and Tippett, Glass and Adams contribute. In Britain, Judith Weir and Mark-Anthony Turnage – to name two of several – exhibit great talent; Birtwistle is a giant; Thomas Adès may surprise us all. But the bulk of the work John Calder collects was written centuries ago and is now rarely played. Even Mozart has suffered neglect. Thought too frivolous for Victorian taste, *Così fan tutte* was not performed; Jonathan Miller's Covent Garden production of 1995, dressed by Armani, was only the third given of that masterpiece at the Royal Opera House – partly perhaps because it was thought not best suited to a largish house; partly because the piece itself was distrusted and undervalued. *Jenufa* was the only opera by Janáček to have been given at Covent Garden before my time. No opera by Prokofiev had been staged. John Tooley had brought us Shostakovich's *Katerina Ismailova*; he had part-commissioned and staged Hans Werner Henze's *We Come to the River*, with a libretto by Edward Bond. (It was before a performance of this, walking into the empty Grand Tier one summer evening in 1976, that I heard someone in the stalls call out: 'British troops out of Ireland.') Tooley had helped commission Luciano Berio's *Un re in ascolto*, which would reach our stage in my time. He had made his own trawl through the riches of opera's past. All the same, there were many unfamiliar works we could bring to music-lovers. The House would close, we thought, in 1993, and the new stage, equipped with machinery we did not now possess, would enable easier handling of more complex sets. It seemed to me sensible, rather than embark singlemindedly on renewing the core repertory, to complement it by adding pieces not usually given, some of them by great masters, Mozart, Rossini, Verdi. What I was not prepared to do was rout out yet again all the tired old productions gathering dust in the warehouse.

The staple of any season's offering is bound to be the revivals. One complaint laid to the House's charge was that ours were lazily presented, carelessly thrown on stage, without adequate rehearsal. Staff producers were adamant: it was not their fault, the reason was inadequate rehearsal time: not enough allocated, not enough productively used. We lost valuable time every morning because the stage was not ready; conductor and orchestra, director and cast were, wastefully, kept waiting. A prompt start, with scenery and props in place, and lighting hung and focused, was not in Paul Findlay's or John Cox's gift to guarantee. Other action was required.

Stage crews were divided into two teams, working day and day about. They worked long days of fifteen hours, from 8am till 11pm, and took the next day off. This system was less than ideal: much of the fifteen hours was spent hanging about and, at their end, the stagehands' work was not yet done. The next day, at 10.30am sharp, a different producer and a new conductor would start rehearsal of another production, expecting all their scenery to be in place. This could not always be achieved in the time available – an hour late at night, two more in the morning – particularly if two fairly heavy shows followed each other. If the work took longer, morning rehearsals started late. To avert this we sometimes worked nights; volunteers from the same crew that had already worked fifteen hours now went on, past midnight and into the early hours, to prepare for the next day's rehearsal. They were guaranteed a minimum eight-hour call at double time. But they were not meant to work all night – how could they be? Their task was defined as 'job and finish'. They went home as soon as they could. Those were not productive hours.

Now I intended to increase the proportion of new work. Production and technical staff warned me that this would require productive use of every minute for stage rehearsal. The system could not deliver that. We needed a dedicated night crew, who would work a full eight-hour shift, five nights a week. That way we could expect fruitful rehearsal and cater for the heavy load that more new productions in the repertory would entail.

Pondering the problems that faced me in running the House as a whole, wondering how I could square the circle, raise quality *and* balance the books, I had thought at first to reduce the staff. There were 1050 on the payroll. Not excessive for three companies, but there must be economies we could make. Surely, I thought, I could reduce staff numbers by some fifty posts. Yet here I was, immediately proposing not to lose people but to add them. Problems ahead, for sure. With hindsight, I see now that I should have insisted on reducing the size of the stage crew and on drastic alteration in their methods when, eventually, we added the night gang. But such an insistence could well have resulted in disruption of performances by industrial action. And that we could ill afford.

One change was needed immediately: we could not, it was forcefully represented to me that summer, go on to an enhanced workload with the Technical Director then in post. A new appointment was required. At the end of my first week in the office, I sent for the incumbent and told him I intended to find someone else to do the job. Time now to ring up the curtain.

4

FAIL BETTER

Opera 1988–1991

In my retiring room in the theatre I hung a *Spectator* cartoon by John Glashan, watercolourist and humorist. In the nearly completed Sistine Chapel, Michelangelo can just be seen high in the top corner on the scaffolding, finishing his ceiling. Below, a Cardinal is telling the Pope, 'I don't like it either, but it's too late to get someone else.' Next to this I hung Tom Phillips's portrait of Samuel Beckett from the National Portrait Gallery. Beckett is seen from behind watching *Waiting for Godot*. Below, Tom has put these words:

No matter · Try again
Fail again · Fail better

In the performing arts, 'failing better' is all you can ever hope for. In any case, if you have failed, it is too late to get someone else.

Much depended on the new *Ring* cycle which Yuri Lyubimov would start directing in September 1988. The set for *Das Rheingold*, like his *Jenufa*, was simple, an arrangement of levels and flats of bare wood. The production was to be of modest cost and was meant to last. It was intended to be toured when the House closed in 1993, only five years away. Lyubimov had been director of the Taganka Theatre in Moscow, admired for the total theatrical experience – text, sets, sound effects, lighting – his productions achieved. He was very sure of himself, exhibiting no humility whatsoever in his attitude to the *Ring*. He saw the cycle

as four different dramas: *Das Rheingold* as comedy, *Götterdämmerung* as melodrama, *Die Walküre* and *Siegfried* as something indefinable in between. He spoke no German. Peter Hall had laboured under the same handicap in Bayreuth in 1983. I put my foot in it at that time with Georg Solti, remarking that he would conduct Peter Hall's *Ring*. 'Peter Hall will direct MY *Ring*,' the maestro replied. In the event, neither triumphed.

Lyubimov, with no German and very little English either, was seriously hampered in directing the singers. He spoke Russian, communicating through an interpreter. This was clumsy, time consuming and irritating. More important – though this did not prove an overriding difficulty with *Das Rheingold*, where action keeps the story on the move – he could give no guidance on the meaning of the text; to do so effectively, surely, every syllable must be understood. The cast assembled was a strong one; Ekkehard Wlaschiha as Alberich was happy enough at the antics Lyubimov proposed, James Morris as Wotan was less amenable to direction. In the end, *Das Rheingold* was a fair success. Musically it was more than that. As Haitink immersed himself in the score, he drew playing of real quality from the orchestra, and the singers, whatever their differences with the producer, sang pretty well. The public could look forward to the rest of the cycle. At the end of *Das Rheingold*, as the gods processed across the rainbow bridge into Valhalla, Loge warned us that they were going, blindly, to their doom.

Could we go on with the Lyubimov *Ring*? Most did not doubt it. They had enjoyed *Das Rheingold*, in Lyubimov's hands clear, adroit, amusing; his gods were less than heroic, but appropriately so. The problems had been in the rehearsal room where some of the cast had been in a state of near rebellion; they felt they knew the piece very much better than he did. Haitink was unhappy about what had gone on there, and fearful of what was to come. In Jerusalem, Lyubimov had told me, in all seriousness, that he thought Wagner's text was mostly rubbish. If that was so, how could he possibly direct the singers in the long monologues and duologues of *Die Walküre* and *Siegfried*? Had he anything meaningful to convey to James Morris as Wotan, or to Gwyneth Jones's experienced Brünnhilde? This concern swung it for me. By Christmas, Bernard Haitink, Paul Findlay and I were agreed that we had to call a halt. But what could we do instead? We could not, lightly, cancel the *Ring*. The expensive cast was contracted to sing *Die Walküre* the following season, and *Siegfried* and *Götterdämmerung* in 1990/91, and dates were pencilled in for complete cycles the season after that. The *Ring* is the biggest forward commitment any opera house can make: four complete operas, three of them long, nearly eighteen hours in total duration. The *Ring* takes more rehearsals, occupies more stage time, causes more dark nights in the theatre than anything else. There was no time to bring another production into being to fill the huge gaps cancellation would leave in our schedules. Financially, with so many singers contracted, cancellation would be a wasteful disaster we could not possibly afford.

At just this point, something turned up. Götz Friedrich had famously produced the *Ring* at Covent Garden in the 1970s. Now he had created a new production for the Deutsche Oper, his theatre in West Berlin, built to rival the East's Staatsoper on Unter den Linden, then cut off politically and physically from the West. This production had been invited to Washington DC. Friedrich's designer, Peter Sykora, had devised an amazing set, a tunnel stretching to infinity (inspired, it was said, by the Washington underground system). In Berlin, Sykora used the stage, the rear-stage and half a stage behind that. Seen front on, the tunnel went on for ever. (At Bayreuth, Hans Schavernoch and Harry Kupfer had devised a 'highway of history', also using nearly three depths of stage, to set the puny gods against infinity.) Paul Findlay, however, spotted that the extraordinary Berlin production had fitted the Washington stage. To do so, it must have been drastically cut down. Could we rent it? If Friedrich were free, or could make himself free, we could give that *Ring* in London. Would it fit our stage? Technical staff were dispatched to Washington and reported that it would. Haitink welcomed working with an acknowledged master, who knew the piece inside out. We took the decision: Sykora's set was crated up in Washington when it finished there and came straight to London. The *Ring* was saved: we could honour our contracts with artists, and keep faith with the public. Haitink would master all four operas, and rise to the marathon challenge of two complete cycles at the end. All this was pure gain.

There was a loss, the full force of which I did not comprehend until I saw *Götterdämmerung* in Berlin at the Deutsche Oper, with its pristine, original set. In that theatre, the 'time tunnel' was stunningly effective; it not only took the eye away, past the singers towards infinity, but when, closed off, it brought the action to the front of the stage, the contrast (as from wide shot to close-up in the cinema) took the breath away. But the touring version, confined to one stage's depth, provided a mere *trompe-l'œil* effect. It worked fairly well, but the eye was confined to a box. Now the walls of the set, receding from either side of the proscenium, had a prominence they never had in Berlin, so that every sign, slogan, daub, graffito was liable to distract from singers, action and music. Götz Friedrich's *Ring* cycle, not as revelatory as his earlier achievement at Covent Garden, lent solid substance to our programme for the next three years. It was serious and moving; it told the story well; it provided a vehicle for great music-making. But some in the audience listened with their eyes shut.

We learned another lesson before the cycle was complete. The rehearsal schedule, as was usual with the *Ring*, left little space for other productions. Financially, we could not live with that. Again, it looked as if we might have to cancel. With Friedrich's agreement, we curtailed his rehearsals and inserted in the schedule performances of *La bohème* and *Rigoletto*, almost ad lib, to fill box-office coffers. The stage crew worked harder than ever to serve up these double helpings. The important thing was that the *Ring*, by one improvisatory device after another, had survived in the schedules. No other *Ring* was created in Britain until the next began at Covent Garden in 1994. Yet without a *Ring*, opera repertory is incomplete. Opera-goers are entitled to find one on offer, at not too prolonged intervals.

'Mr Isaacs,' a chorus member asked at my first House meeting, all welcome, 'why are we doing this modern music? We can't learn the piece, and, even if we do, the public won't want to hear it.' Wrong, on both counts. With my back to the pit-railing, I had talked for thirty minutes about funding, the development, closure and all that, and this was one of the first points put to me. I insisted that Luciano Berio's *Un re in ascolto* was work of a sort that, at least every couple of years, we should be presenting. Opera was a living art form. A few weeks later my questioner was suspended by a wire, with two dozen other chorus members, high above the stage, as the production of *Un re in ascolto* demanded. With prices steeply reduced, the house was full for the event of the season.

Un re in ascolto is a piece about theatre, 'a reflection', as Antony Peattie puts it in the new *Kobbé*, 'on the complex nature of opera itself, the encounter (conflict or collaboration) between words, music, singers, production, chorus, stage, theatre and drama'. It had been given first at Salzburg in 1984. We gave the UK première and I doubt if Graham Vick's deft rendering has been bettered; Chicago, and other houses, rented it from us. Donald McIntyre sang Prospero, the old impresario at the end of his life; Kathryn Harries the Protagonista, the singer with the mind of her own (like Berio's late wife Cathy Berberian, for whom he wrote some of his best music). A manic Bob Tear enjoyed himself as the Director, bringing the show within the show to life and causing the chorus, at his command, to rise halfway to the flies. Chris Dyer's set served its multiple purposes effectively. On it, top right, there sat, throughout the ninety minutes of unbroken action, a tame golden eagle, bored, not stirring. I asked if it was stuffed. No, it was a real live eagle. In that case, I wanted to know, why didn't it move? What were we paying for? Could not someone give it a gentle poke? Graham Vick, I was to discover, had a thing about birds. Peter Hall wrote me a postcard after *Un re in ascolto*: he had no idea we could put on such a show at Covent Garden. Berio was pleased too.

Not too proud to borrow from other British houses, we rented from Scottish Opera that season a new *Madama Butterfly*, and also hired in

'Un re in Ascolto'.

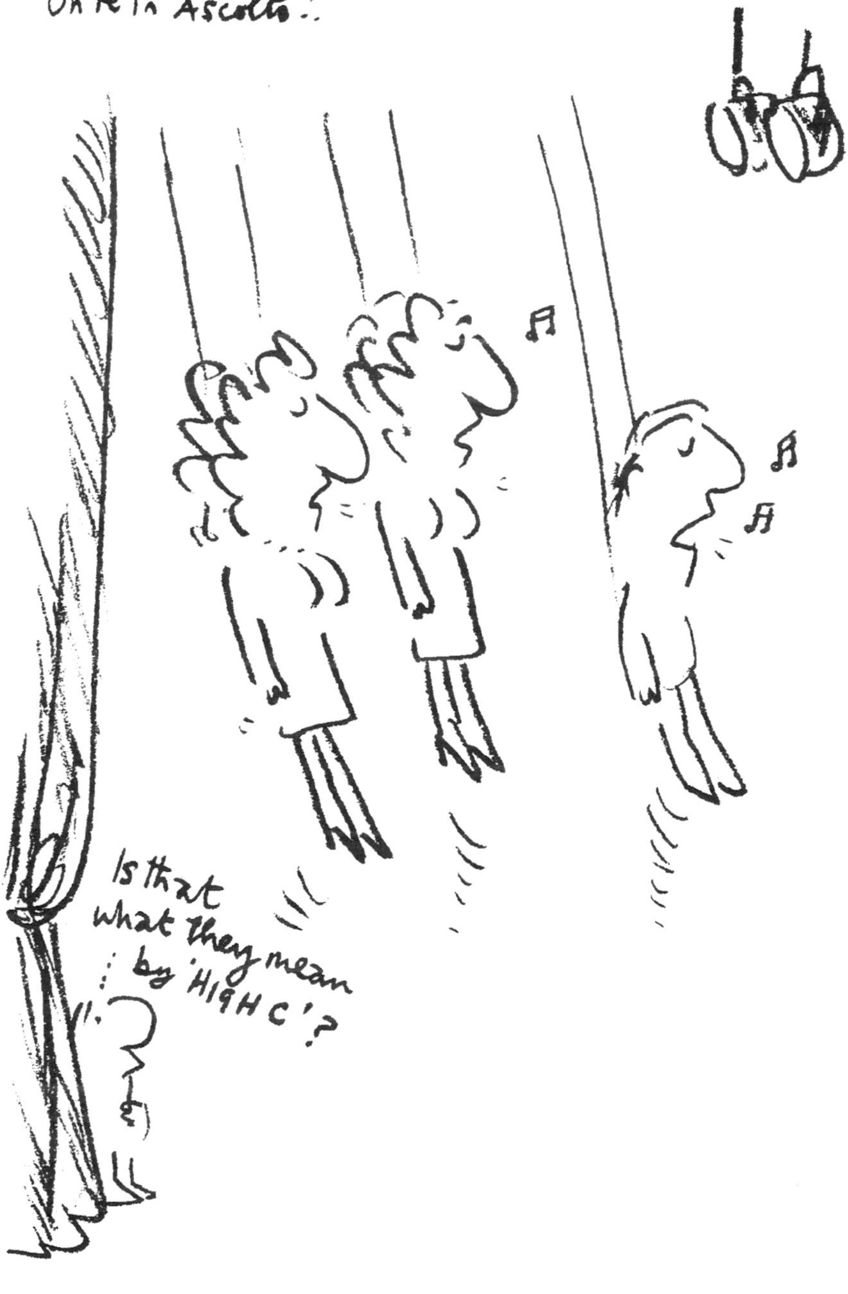

from Glyndebourne an *Albert Herring*, hitherto unseen at Covent Garden, produced by Peter Hall. *Herring* played well in the larger house; the thirteen-piece orchestra was clearly heard in Britten's pellucid score. Peter Hall gave notes to the cast: 'Remember this is a comedy. Do not laugh or smile.' John Cox, Production Director, levelled up the quality of revivals. Leontina Vaduva, all smiles, won a Laurence Olivier Award for her outstanding debut performance in *Manon*.

A major event, with Bernard Haitink conducting, was a revival of Luchino Visconti's production of Verdi's *Don Carlos*, first seen in 1958. No production of ours, other than perhaps Zeffirelli's *Tosca*, has lasted better; none was more warmly anticipated. The Irish wolfhounds that came on with King Philip were not, someone told me, the exact same shade of black as in 1958, but the painted canvas sets looked well. We had a fine cast and gave *Don Carlos* in French, complete with the Fontainebleau act. Opera-lovers came from all over the world to revel in the piece and in the beauty of the sets on perhaps their last outing. The first two performances went well. Then disaster struck.

On the afternoon of the third performance, 31 March 1989, sitting at my desk in Floral Street wondering how the crew was doing setting the show, I glanced up at the television monitor opposite. Suddenly I saw figures running urgently, diagonally across the stage, to the prompt-side rear, and huddling there. I went down immediately. A man was dying. Greg Bellamy, a stagehand, had been pushing a heavily loaded A-frame trolley across the back of the stage. He had too many flats on it and it was loaded unevenly, lopsidedly, weighted to one side of the frame – his fault. A wheel had stuck in a depression, a groove on the stage surface that should not have been there – our fault. The A-frame canted to one side. Bellamy, unable to move it, began to unload it. The heavy load slipped and came down on top of him, crushing his skull and his chest cavity. He was given first aid, an ambulance was sent for. His friends were calling out to him, 'Stay in there, Greg,' but he was pumping out his life blood. There are three hospitals within a mile of Covent Garden; in the traffic it took half an hour to get an ambulance to us. He died in hospital, shortly after being brought there. Earlier arrival, the doctors said, could not have saved him.

The crew was shattered, silent, dazed. It was mid-afternoon. The performance was due to start earlier than normal; the audience was on its way to the theatre. After a pause, and believing that if we could we should, I began to try to find out if we were able to get the curtain up. Two thousand people would be disappointed if we did not. Some had come far. I could see the case for deciding immediately not to perform, but could not, unquestioningly, accept it. What did my management colleagues think? And chorus and orchestra, and the cast? The key was the stage crew: if they were prepared to work, the performance, as tradition would have it, could be given. In their rest space at the side, I asked as gently as I could if they would consider it. Gutted, they refused. The audience were allowed to take their seats. I went out to explain that we could not perform for them that evening, and why. Some few were angry, most accepted it. Whatever the legend, the show cannot always go on.

On the Sunday after the death, I went to Kennington to call on Greg Bellamy's family and offer my condolences. A sort of quiet wake was in progress; it was to last more than a week. My visit was noted. 'We liked you for that,' a stagehand said to me much later. The following Sunday, we gave the Verdi *Requiem* in Greg Bellamy's memory and to benefit his family. Haitink had concert engagements but Colin Davis, generously and unhesitatingly, came in to conduct. At the brief rehearsal, Katia Ricciarelli, our Elisabeth, kept asking for a quieter pianissimo over which she would float 'Libera me'. Before the performance, dancers of the Royal Ballet, with lit candles, lined the darkened stage; they and the stagehands were good friends. The singers received fees for the performance we cancelled. Agnes Baltsa, our Eboli, had once flashed a huge stone at us at supper and announced, 'I didn't earn this at Covent Garden'; now she gave her fee to the fund for Bellamy's family. The funeral was a truly amazing event; family and crew organized the service in St Peter's Church, Kennington. John Tooley and I went down together. The church was packed. Several crew members took part in the service. Twenty and more black limousines carried mourners to the committal afterwards, covered in enormous heaps of flowers. A community was burying one of its own.

This terrible accident exacerbated tensions between stage and management – we were seeking drastic changes in working practices at the time – and yet it also, somehow, brought us closer together. The stage crew had a bust made of Greg Bellamy and insisted it be placed just inside the stage door. Visitors asked who it was. Over the years, the stage doormen complained that it gave them the willies, it was depressing constantly to have to tell the story. But the bust stayed there till the House closed.

I had been fortunate to engage John Harrison, ex-ENO, ex-WNO, as Technical Director. Harrison reiterated, reinforced, toughened up safety procedures. In particular he gave clear instruction as to how and how not to load an A-frame. He made it mandatory to load correctly. Only weeks later, he found A-frames incorrectly loaded; crew members had disobeyed orders and were carrying on in the same old casual, dangerous ways. At a Health and Safety hearing months later, the House was fined £1000 for its partial responsibility for the accident.

Our stage crew always worked against the clock, manhandling pieces of scenery that grew heavier and potentially more lethal each year. In one interval, during a performance of *Peter Grimes*, I found that a heavy piece of *Medée*, stored in the flies, was swinging dangerously across the stage. We desperately needed stage mechanisms that would end the need for manual labour twice a day, every day. We needed modern, capital-intensive stage machinery and a trained, skilled stage crew to work it. Greg Bellamy's death called attention, as nothing else could, to the urgent need for the redeveloped Opera House.

Frank Johnson, lately editor of the *Spectator*, came closer to operatic glory than any of us when, as a child, he played one of Norma's children in Bellini's *bel canto* drama. Norma, furious at her lover Pollione's betrayal and contemplating infanticide, clutched her infant children to her bosom, coming near, Johnson assures us, to putting out his eyes with her breast. This Norma was Maria Callas. Johnson has been in thrall to opera ever since. In the autumn of 1989, in my second season, Rosalind Plowright was due to sing Norma at the Royal Opera House. But this was the *Norma* which had provoked critical derision and had Gillian rolling on the floor of the Royal Box. I had said then we should not bring it back. Plowright had sung Medea at the Buxton Festival in 1984 and made a great impression. Suppose, scrapping *Norma*, we persuaded Rosalind Plowright to repeat her Buxton success and sing Medea instead? If we could mount a production, this would be something of a coup. The lead role, following Callas, was a challenge to any soprano, and the piece had not been given at Covent Garden since 1959. Rosalind Plowright was willing. We made the change. Now all we had to do was find a conductor, cast and select a producer, all at very short notice: easier said than done.

Casting was not too difficult. Plowright was plainly up to the role, as Buxton had showed. We got that fine artist Robert Lloyd, still a member of the company, as Créon; Renée Fleming, a star in the ascendant, would make her House début as Dirce. She sang beautifully. Jason was harder; we cast a Russian tenor, who would find French strange to him. Hardest of all, at less than a year's notice, was to secure a conductor who knew the piece or was able to master it. No French conductor was available, nor were others from a longish list. Finally we engaged Mark Ermler, who had a wide opera repertory at the Bolshoi, and who was often in the House conducting ballet. It was not an ideal choice; Cherubini's was not an idiom in which he was comfortable.

More controversial was the choice of director. We did have a choice. Michael Rennison's name was put forward. He hastened, with a model all prepared, to show us his ideas – simple, classical, graceful even. Rennison had experience, was a safe pair of hands. The alternative was Mike Ashman, the staff director to whom John Tooley had entrusted *Der fliegende Holländer* which had caused an upset in 1986. Ashman was excited to be considered and buzzed with ideas for the piece; he wanted to set mythical Corinth in the visual world of the time of its composition, Second Empire France. The paintings of David were his inspiration. He presented his argument eloquently, but I needed little winning over. I saw this as a key choice for me. If, at the very first opportunity, I opted for safety, I thought I would always regret it and would find boldness harder next time. If, on the other hand, I chose to take a risk with Ashman, and we brought it off, an important step forward in revealing new possibilities would have been taken. We chose Mike Ashman. Rosalind Plowright, aware of our options, agreed to go forward.

The production was handsome in Bernard Culshaw's designs. Ashman was an invigorating presence in the rehearsal room, but on stage his comparative inexperience counted against him. Some aspects of the production did not seem fully worked out by the time of the general rehearsal; I was still not sure what one effect – a sort of clothesline dividing the set – was intended to convey on the first night. But the *coup de théâtre* that caused most concern was the apotheosis at the opera's climax: Medea, vindicated by the gods for asserting her just rights to pitiless vengeance, was to be carried up to heaven, resolute and triumphant, by wire attached to her waist. This ascent, not in the libretto, might make anyone nervous, let alone a soprano who had sung so demanding a role. And Rosalind Plowright, as I had begun to detect in *Il trovatore* the previous summer, was nervous and given to self-doubt. If she trembled, so might her voice. In the event, she kept her nerve, but was below her thrilling vocal best.

Medée was not a success. Most criticism centred on our choice of conductor; plainly this was our fault not his. The failure served to remind me, if I needed reminding, that from those who profess to offer the best, only the best will do. People often ask why, if a production was in any respect unsatisfactory, it was allowed to appear? Why not change it, or junk it? To ask this indignantly, as if there were an easy answer, is to misunderstand the production process. This, from start to finish, will last more than a year, yet the sole opportunity management has to intervene decisively is at the model-showing stage, months before the first night. Even then, time will be short to change it. Directors and designers describing their concept in the model room are always stimulating. If approval is given there, the model is costed and, if the sums add up, it goes to the workshop for construction. When rehearsals start, a director can modify a projected move, or a lighting effect, but the sets are now a given. All must live with them. The conductor, who will have seen the model, must cheerfully do his best with what is now in front of him. I liked the *Medée* Mike Ashman conceived, but could not wholly commend his execution of it. To my regret, he has not produced at Covent Garden since. He will one day, I hope. He did a lively *Paul Bunyan* at the Royal College of Music and his *Ring* in Oslo, which in 1997 came to Norwich, was admired as thoughtful and well judged. He knows his stuff. You cannot keep so good a man down.

Johannes Schaaf continued his Mozart cycle with a new *Idomeneo* and a new *Così fan tutte*. The latter banished John Copley's picture-postcard pretty Bay of Naples, designed by Henry Bardon in the familiar easy-on-the-eye mode. Designer Hans Schavernoch set *Così* first in a gentleman's club – far too much business, drunks falling off chairs, etc. – then in the adored sisters' apartment. In the second act, the lovers were transported on a fantasy picnic with carpets and cushions and silk draperies forming a tented caravanserai. These silks were elegant and handsome, when they did not get caught up in the flies. In *Idomeneo*, much fuss was made over Electra drinking a cup of tea while singing her aria. The monster, terrorizing Crete and demanding human sacrifice, was seen by Schaaf as a man-made catastrophe, polluting the landscape. Men in yellow plastic protective clothing vacuumed up contaminated matter. This contrasted sharply with the formal dances, in wedding-day white, with which Schaaf and the conductor Jeffrey Tate chose to end the opera, to music Mozart wrote but which is usually omitted. This was a distinguished *Idomeneo*, but a long one.

Hans Schavernoch, delightful as he is talented, would also that season design Götz Friedrich's *Elektra*, Solti conducting. Friedrich, surprisingly, had never produced *Elektra* on the stage, but had done it on film for Unitel. Schavernoch came to our home to see the video. When Gillian asked him in passing what flooring we should have in our warehouse loft in Bermondsey, he thought only for a second before answering: 'Pebbles.' He was ahead of his time. For *Elektra*, Schavernoch devised a vast, cloacal tunnel under the royal palace, grim and effective, the concave structure sending Elektra's voice ringingly out into the auditorium – a singer's dream aid. This was in sharp contrast to the House's previous production, a stately classical exterior by Isabel Lambert for Rudolf Hartmann, which had lasted at Covent Garden for nearly forty years. Gwyneth Jones was furious that Solti would not have her for the new Elektra. He chose the Hungarian Eva Marton instead. She had a triumph. So did Solti; it was masterly conducting. The cheers rang out, forcing me every night into my cautionary Olivier-in-*The Entertainer* routine: 'Don't clap too loud, it's a very old building.'

The Cold War was ending; we seized the operatic opportunity this offered. As *perestroika* undercut state communism and the Soviet Union crumbled, restrictions lifted. Russians, and singers from other Soviet republics, were free to travel to the West on their own and to keep what they could earn there. In 1987 the Kirov Opera came to Covent Garden and showed what they could do. The baritone Sergei Leiferkus had already sung with Scottish Opera. I said at once that we must engage him. Later Paul Findlay and Peter Katona went to Russia to hold auditions. In Moscow they heard twenty-seven singers in one day, all passable, many of genuine international standard, none known in the West. The Bolshoi and the Kirov companies sang only in Russian. Russian singers, with marvellous voices and sound techniques, were nevertheless exposed in Western opera houses performing in French, German, English and Italian. Correct accent and pronunciation came with difficulty. To take full advantage of the flood of Russian talent, the thing to do, surely, at this time, was Russian opera in Russian.

We decided on *Prince Igor*, a great melodious epic, not given at the theatre since 1935. Someone said *Igor* needs six great singers. We had six out of six for Andrei Serban's production. Anna Tomowa-Sintow, a Bulgarian, to whom Russian was a second language, sang Yaroslavna, heartmeltingly. Leiferkus, the tenor Andrei Steblianko, the bass Nicola Ghiuselev and the mezzo Elena Zaremba sang other leading roles. Khan Konchak was taken by the Georgian bass Paata Burchuladze. The Royal Ballet hesitated long but, in the end, agreed to dance in the opera. Serban's budget had been slashed, as we struggled to keep the House's finances in balance. The designer, Livia Cilieu, had to make one basic set work for all four acts; the costume budget was half of what was originally earmarked. A spectacular pageant of all the Russias, peoples on the move, each in ethnic costume, intended by Serban to refer to the nationalisms that were then tearing the Soviet Union apart, was reduced to mono-chromatic homogeneity. But the great piece, in all its spacious grandeur, worked its magic. Haitink conducted. The orchestral playing and singing were sublime, artist after artist capping what had gone before. Tomowa-Sintow's last falling phrase at the end of her lament reduced one seasoned critic to tears. We never could afford to bring back this *Prince Igor*; the revival planned for two seasons later – it makes sense to amortize cost – was to fall victim to cuts still to come. But if an opera house exists to give an opera-loving public what it yearns to hear, this *Prince Igor* vindicated that claim.

Igor had another legacy: a hangover. A couple of seasons later, Gillian and I took Paata Burchuladze and a girlfriend out to supper at the Ivy. (When his family was in town I ate an authentic and gigantic Georgian repast at their rented home.) After he had consumed two large malt whiskies, Burchuladze, with the ferocity of Konchak, pronounced 'I no drink.' I raised an eyebrow. 'I no drink', he resumed, 'except with friends. When I drink, if you my friend you drink too. If you drink, you drink whole glass. If you leave drink in glass, these are tears for our friendship.' This may make sense in Georgia, with vodka served in tiny glasses, knocked back in one gulp, at toast after toast. But it makes no sense when drinking a decent red from glasses dutiful waiters keep filling. Struggling to keep up, we toasted fathers, mothers, sons, daughters, my country, your country and anything you can think of. Supper ended. Real trouble began. 'You very kind buy supper. I buy champagne,' Khan Konchak insisted. He bought champagne, two bottles – not house champagne, but vintage Krug. This too we knocked back, a glassful at a time. Gillian retired to the ladies' loo, where, under the watchful eye of the girlfriend, plainly used to this routine, she left all our toasts to friendship and her supper too. When they returned, we were just starting the second bottle. It was good light Burgundy we drank, and very good champagne, which explains why I ended up with a severe hangover next morning, rather than lasting alcoholic poisoning. Gillian was fresh as a daisy. Khan Konchak remains my favourite character in *Prince Igor*.

The Royal Opera in 1990/91 put on what Paul Findlay described as the most ambitious programme it had ever mounted. It was not flawless. From the Salzburg Festival we rented a production of *La Cenerentola*, and discovered, a little late, how unwieldy were the sets. Scenery left in place on stage during festival performances does not necessarily handle easily when run in repertory. There was no lighting plot; the lighting designer had other commitments on the day set aside for a lighting rehearsal. To fit the rehearsal in on another day meant cancelling another *Cenerentola* stage and orchestra rehearsal. To this the conductor, Carlo Rizzi, took adamant exception. The harsh alternative was to cancel a ballet per-formance. I chose the latter. Ballet-lovers and the ballet company found this, understandably, hard to forgive. I found it hard to forgive Paul Findlay for helping to put us in this fix.

John Cox, as well as overseeing revivals, took happy charge of two other new productions: Richard Strauss's *Capriccio*, never given before in the House, and, by my particular command, Rossini's *Guillaume Tell*, not seen at Covent Garden for over 100 years. I had loved Rossini's music since first hearing it and I wanted to see this great masterpiece of grand opera given in London. Our production marked the 700th anniversary of the birth of the Swiss Confederation in 1291. Till Haberfeld, Gwyneth Jones's Swiss husband and a connoisseur of neckwear, gave me Switzerland's official commemoration tie, designed by Jean Tanguely. The first performance was the 103rd at the Royal Opera House, which shows how nineteenth-century audiences had loved *Guillaume Tell*. As with *Prince Igor*, this other epic suffered rather from swingeing cuts to its budget. The designer Robin Wagner had to make do with a final figure half what we had originally set aside. But John Cox did a skilled job in handling his forces. Three choruses enter famously at one point to represent the three cantons of Unterwalden, Schwyz and Uri, as Switzerland is born. The Swiss Ambassador, my guest, told me proudly that he was from Uri. Nestlé was a sponsor. Michel Plasson, from Toulouse, took charge of the orchestra impressively. The singing was pretty good – 'Sombre forêt', sung by Lella Cuberli as Mathilde, wonder-fully done. Chris Merritt, the tenor, tackled, expertly but not easily, the umpteen high Cs the role demands. A hostile claque came from Germany one night expressly to boo him. Justin Lavender, who sang the Boatman, gallantly stood in for Merritt at one performance and did well. In *Guillaume Tell* the sun that rises at the opera's end symbolizes Switzerland's dawning freedom and the bright future of our dreams. Wagner told Rossini it was all a work of genius, but that the second act was written by God. We touched, I felt, those heavenly heights.

But not without one serious mishap. To my chagrin, a system that had never failed proved not to be fail-safe. The Royal Opera does not engage full-time understudies for every role. By not doing so, we saved thousands of pounds annually. With European cities an hour or two away, and European time an hour ahead of us, we reckoned we could always fly in a substitute if a singer reported sick, provided he or she did so by the dead-line set, 10am on the day of the performance. If we knew the night before, so much the better, but the morning would do at a pinch.

We were singing *Tell* in French, not in the Italian I had heard at La Scala, and had no cover for Tell himself, who holds the piece together. When our baritone reported sick one morning, Peter Katona urgently consulted his black book of artists, agents, opera houses, and reached for the telephone. In Germany he found a baritone who could sing Tell, but only in Italian. Katona should have said instantly, 'Catch the next plane.' Instead he said, 'Stay by your phone, please, for an hour.' He rang Italy and found someone who could sing the role in French. 'Come,' he said, 'we'll meet the plane.' That singer missed his flight. When Katona heard and rang Germany again, that morning's Tell had gone out shopping and could not be found. The curtain was due up at 6pm. In my office we con-fronted the hard fact: we had no lead singer and could not now fill the role. I asked if someone could sing it from the pit or from the prompt corner from a score, however unsatisfactory that might be. I was told no, for this rare and demanding role it was simply not possible. The stage was not yet set for *Tell*. If I took the decision now, we could put on *La bohème* instead. Sick at heart, I agreed. A paper was prepared to give to the audience as it arrived; refunds were offered. Again, it fell to me to go out front when those who stayed had taken their seats and repeat our apologies. They were inadequate. In the old days, doing twenty different operas a month, a German house – Vienna, Munich, Berlin even –

thought little of changing the performance promised to subscribers on the day. But it is one thing to pull a war-horse *Bohème* and substitute *Tosca*. It is quite another to deny a paying public the enjoyment of a piece so rarely given as *Guillaume Tell* and offer instead a routine *Bohème*. There were opera-lovers in the House that evening who had come from San Francisco expressly for *Tell*; their schedules, they told us despairingly, could not be altered to take in another performance in two days' time. I was ashamed. Only 27 per cent of the audience chose to stay for our last-minute *Bohème*. We had rustled up a fine cast. The Bohemians, Rodolfo, Colline, Marcello and Schaunard, spend part of Act One horsing around, playing games. The unfeeling quartet who played that night worked up a take-off of Tell shooting the apple off his son's head, and sent us up rotten.

Covent Garden had never mounted Strauss's *Capriccio*. John Cox was directing it in San Francisco with Kiri Te Kanawa as the Countess, and sensibly suggested we bring this chamber piece, and her with it, to Covent Garden. If it worked there, a bigger house than ours, it should certainly work here. Kiri, as beautiful to look at as she is to listen to, would help sell the tickets. All was agreed. An afterthought: John, who allies his skills whenever he can to those of a signature designer – Hockney at Glyndebourne for *The Rake's Progress*, and Erté for *Der Rosenkavalier* – was using for *Capriccio* sets by Maurizio Pagano. Gianni Versace, he told me, would design the costumes. Was that all right? I said fine.

Capriccio dramatizes the perennial question about opera: which matters most, words or music? Our *Capriccio*, like others nowadays, was given in a contemporary setting. Versace dressed all the cast handsomely and put Kiri in a dazzling gown. This in itself need not have caused comment. But there was more. The opera begins with a musical prelude, six instruments of the orchestra, a sextet, in the pit. Versace leaned on John Cox. Could the players not perform on stage, in the Countess's salon, where the piece is set? Then he could costume them. John succumbed. The critics could not resist. This was a unique *Capriccio*, they said: a case of '*Prima i costumi . . . e poi la musica e le parole.*' The production never quite gelled, either.

When our long wooing of Simon Rattle at last bore fruit, Janáček's *The Cunning Little Vixen*, never given at Covent Garden, was the piece he chose to conduct. Bill Bryden directed; Bill Dudley created sets, costumes and meltingly beautiful scenic effects. Rattle wanted to give the piece, against our practice, in English translation. A little reluctantly, we

accepted. He did not warm to conducting singers in a language they did not understand, and particularly not a chorus of young boys, playing forest fauna. This chorus was recruited from local schools; Rattle's young son was among them.

With its mix of human and animal characters, *The Cunning Little Vixen* paints a picture of the cycles of life, of a nature that always renews itself, that is the greatest in music. *Vixen* celebrates living and lifts the heart. For all the fine singing, the show was stolen by an acrobat, and by Janáček. Imprisoned in the farmer's yard, the Vixen dreams of her freedom. As her hopes soared skyward, a lissom figure, Deborah Pope, climbed on a trapeze and swung high across and above the stage. The music soared also. George Harewood, in *Kobbé*, calls *Vixen* one of the great masterpieces of opera. I felt that, and that we had done it proud.

Attila is *not* one of the great masterpieces, but any work by a master as commanding as Verdi is worth hearing. With the centenary of his death due in 2001, a plan was formed by Paul Findlay, backed by Edward Downes, to give all Verdi's operas at Covent Garden – all thirty-two of them – by the anniversary date. A start was made with *Attila*, though at that stage the follow-through was only a hope and a prayer. We asked Elijah Moshinsky, most underrated of British opera producers, whom Bernard Haitink suspected of being 'clever', to do it for us. He chose to work with an American designer, Michael Yeargan; their earlier collaboration at Scottish Opera was the first step in a fruitful partnership. For *Attila*, Moshinsky and Yeargan showed us first rather grand and elaborate designs, matching the scope and content of the piece. Later, they scrapped them and went for something much simpler, whose essence was speed and ease of change. Instead of ponderous transitions from one grand set to another, we could go quickly from one scene to the next. For this Yeargan devised a very practicable set of meshing screens, livened by costumes and banners. The action never faltered. There was no time to wonder how good the music really was, or how convincing the plot.

Ted Downes conducted, a plus; no one lends more commitment and belief to early Verdi. *Attila* has four great roles, each a strong sing. Ruggero Raimondi, welcomed back, would sing Attila, the tenor Dennis O'Neill, Foresto. We lost two other singers before rehearsals started. The fine soprano unhappily suffered a car accident; the baritone withdrew. Giorgio Zancanaro had a gap in his engagements and could sing the Roman Ezio's meaty music. Josephine Barstow, who had never seen the score in her life, at three weeks' notice took on the chieftainess Odabella's electrifying role. When *Attila* opens the Huns are pillaging Aquileia. Attila is angry: against his orders some women have been left alive; what is this one on about? Odabella, entering high and with ferocious zing, tells him she represents Italian womanhood's desire for freedom and will fight for it. With this blast, only minutes into the opera, Jo Barstow set the place alight. We were off on a rollercoaster, with aria after glorious aria to come.

'Viva Verdi,' the crowds used to chant, an acronym for 'Vittorio Emanuele, Re d'Italia'. *Attila*'s high point for Risorgimento Italy, and for me, was the duet between the Hun and the Roman. Ezio offers Attila a deal: 'Avrai tu l'universo, resti l'Italia a me' ('You take the rest of the world, leave Italy to me'). Raimondi and Zancanaro sang this with trumpets; I could not hear it often enough. On nights off, I would steal back into the theatre, just to catch this number.

5

FIRST POSITION

Ballet 1988–1991

In 1990, 1 August was one of the hottest nights of the year. The audience sweltered. They were there to see the world première of David Bintley's ballet *The Planets*, to Gustav Holst's music. Ralph Koltai's set, which I had viewed in the model room with Anthony Dowell months earlier, showed a large orb and a separate metal band encircling it, occupying a fair area of centre stage. After two movements in which the dancers manœuvred round these obstacles, the orb would clear backwards to the rear stage, the ring lower into the stage surface. There were wires strung taut to hold the ring in place. Dowell was satisfied that the set would work; I raised no objection.

On the night, expectation was high. The ballet began. Two scenes or so in, it became apparent that something was wrong. The curtains closed. The orchestra stopped playing. The senior Stage Manager for ballet, Keith Gray, wearing the kilt as he did on important occasions, came out to tell the audience that something that should have gone down had not gone down, and was refusing to go down. We hoped to have it right shortly; meanwhile, apologies. Around me, temperatures rose. 'What a shambles,' I thought, sitting in B33, on the aisle, with Gillian and our guests. 'Who the hell is responsible for this?' After the briefest pause, I realized I was. I got up from my seat and ran round the back of the Grand Tier, down a flight of stairs and through the pass door on to the stage. Anthony Dowell was holding his brow; Anthony Russell-Roberts, Administrative Director, was in earnest consultation with technical management. Burly stage-crew members were, with force and deliberation and some semblance of rhythm, stamping on the metal ring, whose hydraulic mechanics had failed, to try to batter it down flush with the floor. They were not succeeding. I made an announcement to the audience, asking for their patience. Another quarter of an hour passed in the oven-like auditorium. There was no air-conditioning of any sort; windows, if opened on to Bow Street, admitted traffic noise, with sirens seemingly ever present. Eventually, after about half an hour, it looked as if we could start again. I went out front to promise a resumption in a few more minutes. Just before I did, as the tabs were being drawn back for me, someone on stage said, 'For heaven's sake, Jeremy, tell them something nice this time.' I added one short sentence: 'In the interval, drinks will be on the House.' That got a round of applause. My guest, Chairman of the Royal Shakespeare Company Sir Geoffrey Cass, turned to Gillian and asked, 'How on earth can the House afford that?' The same doubt must have occurred to my colleagues in house management. They ran round the bars and buffets warning the staff, 'Mr Isaacs said drinks, but he did not mean real drinks. He meant mineral water, and juices, and house wine.' This gesture cost £2000, all the same. *The Planets* was vivid and varied, humorous and sensuous, but perhaps over-designed.

Two years into my term, at the end of my second season, I was just about beginning to understand what I was doing, to get the feel of the House, to come to terms with the uncertainties of theatre. Lesson one: it is never all right on the night, except when you don't expect it to be. And I was learning to live with the financial ups and downs that go with any opera-house job, in the UK at any rate. In my first fiscal year, for part of which John Tooley was in charge, we had balanced the books for the first time since 1984/85. In my second year, 1989/90, we reported a substantial deficit. In spite of reverses, it was with the artistic output of the House that I tried principally to concern myself.

One Sunday afternoon the previous summer, I had found myself driving from Bermondsey to White Lodge, Richmond Park, to talk to the children of the Royal Ballet School in a series called, after Pevsner, *The Englishness of English Art*. Through Putney, I pondered what to say to them. I decided that, if only to provoke, I would question the whole notion of Englishness, in opera and ballet, reminding them that Covent Garden gave opera in the language in which it was written, and that the classical ballet, to which their lives were dedicated, was born in Imperial

Russia. Music and dance were universal in their appeal. Perhaps I was doubtful of my ability to explain precisely what it was that was English about, say, Frederick Ashton's choreography. In any case, I talked nonsense; or, at best, partial truths; I knew it, and I hoped they did too. Shortly after, I went to Birmingham to see a new ballet by David Bintley for SWRB, *Hobson's Choice*, based on the Harold Brighouse play about a bullying Lancashire patriarchal bootseller whose daughter gets the better of him. There's a clog dance; Lily of Laguna at the teatable; and, in Peel Park, Salford, on a Sunday afternoon, a ball or two of cricket, and the Salvation Army on parade. *Hobson's Choice* is classical ballet as popular entertainment, and as English as cricket and warm beer. The London critics took various views of its worth. Clement Crisp, sharpest of ballet-writers, found it vulgar. Clement would. But I shall not easily forget the old couple in front of me in Birmingham, seeing ballet perhaps for the first time; they loved every moment. Had I seen *Hobson's Choice* a week earlier, I should have given a very different talk to the children at White Lodge.

Kenneth MacMillan would reach his sixtieth birthday in 1989, and hoped to celebrate by creating a pure classical ballet, not an abstraction in the

K.M: When it's in your body, it'll be alright – it's not even in your HEAD yet!
Darcey: Oh (laughs) – it is – really!

All black sweater etc..

Kenneth Macmillan rehearsing 'Prince of the Pagodas'.

Bussell and Cope...

style of Balanchine, but a costumed narrative, a return to the nineteenth century, a homage to ballet's origins and to Petipa. The music would be Benjamin Britten's *Prince of the Pagodas*, a major score, commissioned by the Royal Ballet and first used by MacMillan's dear friend John Cranko. Kenneth intended by this a tribute to Ninette de Valois, who had given him his earliest opportunities. He wanted to present a work in which Margot Fonteyn might have revelled. Colin Thubron devised a narrative. This task was made difficult by the music itself; some passages sagged a little. Britten wrote marvellous music, rich in eastern timbres – a Balinese instrument, the gamelan, figures markedly. But, particularly in the middle act, there's too much music for a choreographer to set if the action is to keep moving. Kenneth wanted to cut; Donald Mitchell, for the Britten–Pears Foundation, would not allow it. *The Prince of the Pagodas*, in its original version by MacMillan, is too long. (Later, when the whole score had been recorded, some trims were permitted.) *Pagodas* was intended for the summer of 1989, but in Australia that winter, visiting Deborah's family, Kenneth suffered a heart attack. His life was saved; he recovered, returned to England, and gradually got to work, seizing every hour he could to build, brick by brick, the ample three-act structure. But Kenneth's illness meant we would have to have another three-acter first.

In 1988, Rudolf Nureyev had danced again at Covent Garden. 'How wonderful it will be to see him,' someone said to me before the performance of *Giselle*. 'Oh no, it won't,' I said, 'but do look at the ballerina he has brought with him.' Nureyev, though his electric presence still crackled, could do no more than go through the motions as Albrecht. Sylvie Guillem, *étoile* of the Paris Opera Ballet which Nureyev directed, danced Giselle. Almost as soon as she entered, she slipped, fell, recovered. Trained as a gymnast, rock steady on pointe, with the longest and highest extensions you ever saw – too high for the purist – she commanded the stage; Sylvie Guillem would surely dance here again. The Royal Ballet needed stars to dazzle us and encourage the others. It was fatal for a young dancer at class to think to herself, 'I am as good as anyone here.' Far better to have someone to gasp at, and to ask, 'Will I ever be as good?' I urged the ballet's directorate to engage guests, or invite outsiders to join us, until home-grown star talent appeared. Funds needed to be set aside to encourage fading stars to leave early; then, to engage new principals.

Each year, at the season's end, the Royal Ballet company gathered in a studio at Barons Court or Covent Garden for the Taglioni ceremony, named after the great nineteenth-century ballerina Maria Taglioni. A delicious cake was made to her recipe, with caraway seed in it, and the honour of cutting the cake went to the most loved and admired figure to leave the company that year. In 1988 Jennifer Penney cut the cake, and retired to her native Canada. With the youngest dancers all eyes and ears, Anthony Dowell paid tribute to a frequent partner. Jenny Penney, apparently, hated to discard a pair of shoes. Rather than throw them away, she repaired them; then she patched the patches. Dowell, shocking the youngest present, told how, holding his partner lightly round the waist and gazing out along the length of Penney's legendary leg, he would wrinkle his nose at a new purple patch. One day on stage, fighting to control himself, he saw that on the instep of the shoe, his tormentress had written 'Hullo Sailor'. In one way Jennifer Penney was irreplaceable – certainly for anyone who saw her in *Élite Syncopations* – but she and others would need to be replaced. Isabelle Guérin and Laurent Hilaire from Paris had already danced with the company. Then Sylvie Guillem decided to leave the Paris company and turn freelance. Anthony Russell-Roberts negotiated a contract, and Sylvie joined us as Principal Guest Artist.

When *Pagodas* had to be postponed because of MacMillan's illness, Anthony Dowell, who had spent a year with American Ballet Theater (ABT), invited Natalia Makarova to re-create in London her ABT production of *La Bayadère* (The Temple Dancer), to Léon Minkus's music, with designs by Pier Luigi Samaritani and new costumes by Yolanda Sonnabend. *La Bayadère* is hokum. It is also a wonderful vehicle for dance. The middle act contains a famous set-piece for the *corps de ballet*, 'The Entry of the Shades', in which each of thirty-two dancers, in white tutu, enters down a ramp, doing a series of arabesques in profile, every nuance of line individually exposed. This showpiece is often given on its own. *La Bayadère* is a feast with two dazzling female leads, two big roles for males and glorious opportunities for others. The sets and costumes on show were all colourful. The kitschiest moment in the prologue was when a tiger, hunted by the hero, is carried in, slung upside down on a pole. The Royal Opera House orchestra, in stroppy mood, seizing as an excuse on some poorly copied parts, refused to play it, saying it was not good enough. I let them know that it was good enough for the Kirov and the Bolshoi, and would they kindly get on with it. Natalia Makarova worked her powerful magic on the company, while Guillem, excelling alternately as lovely, doomed Nikiya and as nasty, spirited Gamzati, helped Darcey Bussell, Viviana Durante and Fiona Chadwick raise the roof. One critic denounced the piece before it got to us. He had seen it, did not admire the ABT production, and objected to our doing it. For this grouchy spoil-sport, Dowell could do nothing right. But London audiences grew to love *La Bayadère*, a crowd-pleaser which showcased virtuosity. Encouraged, the company took an upward path.

Ballet faced a programming dilemma. It was the familiar narrative, three-act ballets, absorbing all the company's resource, that most easily found audiences; tickets for triple bills, which allowed opportunity for new work, were harder to sell. *La Bayadère*, unfamiliar in London, would take a little time to sell out. *Swan Lake*, *Sleeping Beauty*, *Nutcracker* sold on the name alone. What did you call triple bills? They had no name, though it was possible sometimes to devise one – 'An Evening of Stravinsky', or of Ashton, or 'A Tribute to Fokine'. Worst of all to bill were ballets that were literally, till the last moment, nameless: 'New Ballet by . . .'. That served, no doubt, for Ashton or MacMillan or for Balanchine. It would be nice to think that a new piece by William Tuckett was itself an attraction; but it was not. Sometimes the name when it came was worse than no name at all. Balanchine's fame ensured an audience for *Violin Concerto* or *Symphony in C*. After a promising piece by Tuckett, *Enclosure*, I was told the music for his next would be from Schubert's last piano sonata. I said OK – a solo piano, well played by Philip Gammon, costs little. But the piece was not to be called 'Piano Sonata in B Flat Major, First Movement'. When the première came, Tuckett called it: *If this is still a Problem* – not much more appealing.

With Arts Council grant eroding, success at the box-office was imperative. When the company was dancing well, and *La Bayadère* boasted four fine Nikiyas, say, not just one, balletomanes would come to several performances, comparing different principal artists' interpretations, and assessing talent in the smaller parts. No one would dream of going to three 'Emperor' Concertos on successive evenings, or to three different *Hamlet*s, but plenty of ballet-lovers will see three *Swan Lake*s. As prices rose, audiences sought a guaranteed night's pleasure. A familiar title, with a starry name added, promised to fulfil their expectation. They flocked to *The Sleeping Beauty*. Familiar favourites did reach out to the new audiences we were always urged to attract. New work was harder to fit in.

In planning repertory, Anthony Dowell and his colleagues faced two severe constraints. The first was the company's limited size. The Royal Ballet, in 1988, had eighty dancers. It needed ninety-five. The New York companies, New York City Ballet and American Ballet Theater, each had 120. The Paris Opera Ballet had 150 on strength, though one *grande étoile* was reputed to send sick notes from Martinique. The Kirov and the Bolshoi had up to 300 dancers each. In the Soviet Union, the national companies never went short. With such numbers, and teaching staff and studios to match, wide-ranging repertory is no problem. For us, a three-act ballet in the schedule meant no spare capacity in the company to rehearse anything else. A *pas de deux* perhaps; soloists were coached separately. But if all were rehearsing *Swan Lake*, a choreographer, eager to get on with creating a new piece, could not easily steal away the dancers he needed to work with. This was the crucial difference between the ballet and the opera company: the ballet created all the new work it put on from within its own ranks; the opera simply said goodbye to one lot of visiting artists and brought in another. The opera could rehearse both new productions and old repertory at once; for the ballet it was one *or* the other.

The other constraint was space. The Royal Ballet then occupied only two rehearsal studios at Barons Court and, since 1982, two more at Covent Garden. Ballet rehearsals use half-hour blocks of time, and shorter, for artists to work out a scene, and so get ahead. But rehearsal space at Barons Court was soon occupied; and the studios at Covent Garden were a tube journey away. This set severe limits to the scope of the day's work. In the redeveloped Opera House, the ballet will at last come into its own. For the first time it will have the use of adequate, dedicated space at Covent Garden, five studios of its own under one roof. Company size will then be the issue. It will make no sense to keep the Royal Ballet's numbers down to eighty in the new House; the new, ampler space will be wasted and programming will remain unnecessarily narrow. The question will be whether the company can afford to grow, not whether it should.

In 1988, I moved at once to increase the company's strength from eighty. The ballet had educational obligations for which dancers were detached from rehearsals. I added two to numbers so that dancers could more easily be spared, and set eighty-five as the target strength to which we aspired. Crab-wise we crept towards it, taking one step forward in the budget estimates, and two backward, as economy bit before final figures were agreed for the year ahead. Meanwhile, we needed to lose dancers who had once excelled but whose bodies were no longer quite up to it, whose line and technique were letting them, and us, down. This was harsh; these were considerable artists, with fans who adored them. But it was a necessary harshness if opportunities were to be offered to a new generation. I was prepared to authorize modest sums to hasten the process. All dancers end their careers early in life. That is hard anyway, and tougher still if financial hardship is entailed. Some would choose to take a drop in salary and move sideways from principal to character artist. Others turned to teaching or administration. Others simply went. Anthony Dowell personally saw every dancer in the company each year to discuss progress, and the future. Not every duty the Director faces is on stage; lonely decisions in his office are the hardest. In my years, Anthony Dowell's strengths grew.

But his leadership, at any rate early on, was leadership by stealth. Quiet and reticent, Dowell spent too long shut up in his office, with his closest colleagues, the door guarded by a dragon, a caring personal assistant, jealously rationing admittance. And he went on dancing. It had been the whole of his life. He still gave good performances (though in very different roles), and still enjoyed it. Not sure that you could monitor the company's work from anywhere except out front, abruptly, one day, I suggested to Anthony that he should stop dancing. He blanched with shock; he could not do it, or even contemplate it. Perhaps I spoke too soon; perhaps no time would have been right. Dancing was in his blood. He continued to appear, leading the company, if you like, by example. He played the High Priest in *La Bayadère* and Carabosse, the wicked fairy, drawn in a sleigh in the prologue to *The Sleeping Beauty*. In this he bore, for me, a startling resemblance to Ninette de Valois. Kenneth MacMillan lovingly created new roles for him: the doddering old King, in another wheelchair, in *The Prince of the Pagodas*; and Kulugin, the kind, sad, bespectacled, cuckolded husband in *Winter Dreams*. In this he was marvellously touching; Dowell was an artist in all he did. If he was too often on stage, he was too seldom abroad. It was hard to persuade him to travel to see other companies at work, to compare standards, to explore other creative imaginations. Anthony responded most to the tradition in which he had been brought up from boyhood, which he had himself embodied, which he sought to enhance and to hand on one day, secure, vibrant, flourishing, to others.

Every year the Directors of the two companies, the Royal Ballet and the

Sadler's Wells (later to become Birmingham) Royal Ballet, run their eyes over the senior class of the Royal Ballet School at Barons Court. They will have followed the pupils' progress through the school. They are particularly alert if their company has room for new recruits to fill gaps left by retirement. The school staff will have marked their cards; some pupils will already have danced with the companies, making up numbers on tour perhaps, or in an emergency. In a fairer world, the two directors might take turns to pick, in alternate years each letting the other go first. Life is not like that. In practice, the Royal Ballet has first pick every year. Many – not all – young dancers wanting to tread in the footsteps of Fonteyn and Nureyev will prefer a company based at Covent Garden to a touring company based at Sadler's Wells, or now in Birmingham. That Anthony Dowell could take his pick stuck in Peter Wright's craw. He would remonstrate with me about it, but in the end there was nothing he could do. Anthony Dowell and Peter Wright, together with their ballet-masters and ballet-mistresses, would discuss each other's preferences, and those of the dancers, and take account of them if they could, before making a choice. But then the die was cast. In this routine, in 1987, they both saw a striking young dancer, very elegant, leggy, beautiful, of evident strengths, though perhaps an inch or two too tall for the *corps*, or for any likely partner. Dowell agreed that for two or three years she should go to SWRB. But after only one, Kenneth MacMillan was determined to get her back for *The Prince of the Pagodas*. He had seen her potential. He would create on her the role of Princess Rose. He had his way. Her name was Darcey Bussell.

The Prince of the Pagodas was due to open at a gala first night in December 1989. Nicholas Georgiadis, who had designed both *Romeo and Juliet* and *Manon*, had created the set and costumes. The first night nearly never happened, at least as planned. The ballet company was in dispute with management over pay and conditions. In 1988/89 we balanced the books; in 1989/90, we were struggling to do so. Wage offers to all were kept low. Ballet dancers felt particularly aggrieved. They resented the fact that a substantial flat-rate increase had been awarded to the chorus but not to them. The issue was complex. The chorus had been underpaid compared to ENO. They were all paid the same and we thought their case deserving. The dancers earned widely varied wages and salaries, from the corps at the bottom to principals on top. I thought any flat-rate percentage increase wrong; what was deserved and reasonable in the middle ranks was unaffordable at the top, and excessive for eighteen-year-olds newly joined from school. There were other resentments fuelling unease. I wanted the opera and ballet companies to collaborate, and had scheduled Borodin's opera *Prince Igor*, complete with the Polovtsian Dances, to show what they could do together. The Polovtsian Dances are spectacular but brief, so I did not propose to pay the dancers extra to appear in *Igor*. This did not go down well. Much as they loved performing at Covent Garden, the dancers felt, they told us, unloved, unwanted, second-class citizens.

These feelings were stirred by a few dissident voices, challenging leadership and testing the mettle, perhaps, of a new General Director. I hardly knew the dancers; it was hard for me, given problems piled high on my desk in Floral Street, to see more of them in Barons Court. I invited their committee to have supper with me in Bermondsey. Half a dozen came. They were frank about their concerns, in a free and friendly way. Their wish was the same as mine: to do the best work they could. They simply wanted conditions that would support them in it. I liked them very much. One senior figure took a different line. Whispering in my ear rather than pronouncing it openly, he brought bad news. The root of the matter, according to him, was that Anthony Dowell should never have been appointed Director. This was Wayne Eagling, a handsome, virile dancer of great abilities, much seen about London, a character – perhaps also a leader – in his own right, someone very much to be reckoned with. I could not listen to this, and regretted at once, though Dowell knew of the meeting, that I had laid myself open to disloyalty and apparent sub-version. The evening ended.

When a company of eighty meets to discuss a wage offer, senior figures like Eagling command attention. Twenty-year-olds are easily led. That autumn, wage negotiations dragged on. The dancers always took longer than anyone else to accept an increase, partly because it had once been agreed that their wages should be linked to those of the chorus. (Both groups are members of Actors' Equity.) They would never commit until the chorus settlement was known. To me this rather undermined the urgency of their case. It never seemed to matter to them to receive the increase; they were in no hurry. It would be backdated, in any case. Now, after months making no formal response, they voted for industrial action: they would work strictly to contract, for precisely the hours they could be required to work in a week. All overtime was voluntary. And they refused to dance in *Prince Igor*.

'They're a menace these
flying pickets'

Both of these were arrows to the heart. *Prince Igor* was a major undertaking for the Royal Opera and for the House. And the ban on overtime would, if we kept on normal course, inevitably pose a threat, as was intended, to the gala opening of *The Prince of the Pagodas*. This not only marked the sixtieth birthday offering of our Principal Choreographer but, importantly also, the gala would be a fundraiser for the House. Looking at the schedule a week away from the opening, a plain fact stared me in the face: all the hours we were contractually able to insist the dancers should work would be exhausted, in performance and rehearsal, before the curtain rose on the world premiere of *The Prince of the Pagodas*. If we kept to the published schedule they could refuse to dance that night. Given the loyalty they all felt to their art, and to the company, and to MacMillan, only dedicated mischief-makers could have planned such a scenario. They hoped we would concede their wage claim, of course. But I could not do that.

Kenneth, in frail health, had much more to do to ready this major work for performance. In similar circumstances, a West End musical would simply have postponed its opening; but we could not shift the gala, nor, with other work cramming our schedules, find another date. To cancel rehearsals would in itself threaten the show, as the leaders of the action well knew. We were already behind. Without the last stage and orchestra rehearsal, without the piano dress – the first chance to see all the costumes on stage – without meticulous care and attention applied, and confidence engendered, we could not do *The Prince of the Pagodas* justice. All tickets were sold. Up against it, I cancelled two performances of a ballet triple bill instead. With those hours saved, *The Prince of the Pagodas* was saved also.

This drastic, wholly unexpected move on my part provoked reactions. One of the performances cancelled at such short notice was on a Saturday. It was not possible to let all ticket-holders know in advance. We refunded the travel and hotel costs of those who had come to London to see it. I turned up at the theatre to attempt to explain why there would be no performance, and to apologize. Some dancers, the activists, also turned up, and again on the following Monday, to protest that they had never meant this to happen. They had not, of course – but they were disingenuous. What they had not intended for the triple bill, they had certainly intended – unless we conceded their claim – for *Pagodas*. The gala première went ahead. The company, perhaps with relief, gave only of their best. The new ballet was a glorious success. MacMillan, who had in the past pushed so hard at the frontiers of content in dance, now, in his mellow age, produced a classical showpiece. To Britten's music, one inventive number succeeded another. The salamander turned into a prince, discord was banished from the kingdom, and love, honesty and beauty triumphed. Anthony Dowell, an ageing monarch, careered about in his wheelchair. Jonathan Cope, horizontal, slithered on the floor as the lizard prince. Beautiful Darcey Bussell, the good princess – her bearing noble, her technique dazzling, her long legs eating up the stage – shone brightly, smiling on her prince and all of us, on her great night.

The dancers' dispute was settled shortly after. At the last possible moment, and only after their claim to be paid extra for dancing in opera was met, a troupe of them agreed to dance in *Prince Igor*. Bintley provided new steps to replace Fokine. We promised the dancers a charter to set out their rights and their role at ROH. It was drafted, circulated, and never responded to. The mood improved all the same.

The Royal Ballet took MacMillan's *The Prince of the Pagodas* to the Kennedy Center in Washington DC. The first night was a modest success, though marred by one of the longest intervals I remember. A member of the audience collapsed during it, in the auditorium, but no one, not even trained paramedic staff, would move him till the ambulance arrived. The ambulance took its time. The audience waited. No announcements were made. An already lengthy evening lengthened.

Wayne Eagling eventually retired in 1991. By now there probably was not room for him and Anthony Dowell in the same company. Eagling received an offer from the Dutch National Ballet to become director there, and accepted. He had been a striking and popular dancer with our company, unmatched in MacMillan's *Requiem* and in other demanding roles. As a choreographer, he had made *Frankenstein, the Modern Prometheus*, with costumes by Elizabeth Emmanuel, the Princess of Wales's wedding-dress designer, and music by Vangelis of *Chariots of Fire* fame. This made a bold visual impact, showing perhaps one direction in which the company's work could go – though in my view, the wrong one. I thought the choreography unoriginal, undistinguished. When Eagling went, I agreed to pay tribute to him, on stage, as custom would have it, at the end of his last performance. (Anthony Dowell was nowhere to be seen.) Gritting my teeth, I did so. Bashfully, at first he said he would say nothing. I never saw anyone take longer to say nothing. He had a following, and had given us and audiences much. When he went, morale in the company improved. Instead of incitement to discontent, the young dancers now had another role model. They could look up to, and take their cue from, a great artist at the height of his powers, whose only object was to give his all to dance: Irek Mukhamedov.

In June 1990, on the eve of an American tour, Irek Mukhamedov broke his contract with the Bolshoi and joined the Royal Ballet. This was awkward for the Bolshoi; Irek's picture, leaping high, was on all the posters for the USA. The Soviet Ambassador sent a representative to me to protest. The issue was not one of a defector's freedom to choose a way of life, as earlier in the Cold War it would have been, but merely of the breaking of a contract and an individual's choice of where to earn a living. I saw off the envoy. We made Irek and his wife Masha welcome. Saturnine, virile, tigerish, yet supremely classical, he made himself at home.

Kenneth MacMillan also gave us a little masterpiece, which began as a *pas de deux* for Irek Mukhamedov, first performed in 1990 before the Queen Mother at the Palladium. This was *Winter Dreams*, MacMillan's distillation of Chekhov's *Three Sisters*; a sense of fragile relationships growing, lovers breaking up, hopes dying. Pathos, and humour; marvellous parts to dance, and to act; sets and music lightly sketched in; a touching role for Dowell; a great duet for the lovers at parting; the autumn of life, for some who had never seen summer. Alongside it, William Tuckett's *Enclosure* and Ashley Page's *Bloodlines*, with a power set by Deana Petherbridge and a pulsing score by Bruce Gilbert, looked to the future.

The Royal Ballet companies are established by Royal Charter. The Royal Ballet exists as an entity, rather like a Platonic essence or ideal, over and above the companies themselves. Their affairs are managed by the Board and executive of the Royal Opera House, with powers delegated to them by a separate body, the Governors of the Royal Ballet, charged by statute with ensuring their long-term welfare. It was by the Governors that a crucial decision was ratified: my recommendation that Sadler's Wells Royal Ballet should move to Birmingham.

SWRB toured the United Kingdom, from Southampton to Sunderland. It found itself particularly welcomed in Birmingham, at the Hippodrome Theatre. The company suffered extremely in cramped conditions at Sadler's Wells. Now the City of Birmingham invited it to make a new home at the Hippodrome, offering to assist the move, contribute an annual grant and pay for new premises, with every facility, on a site adjoining the theatre. The Arts Council's strategy document, *The Glory of the Garden*, had urged devolving arts expenditure from London to the regions. Challenged to match the funds Birmingham would put up, the Arts Council agreed to set aside a six-figure sum. Birmingham already boasted a fine repertory theatre. The City of Birmingham Symphony Orchestra under Simon Rattle was making an international name for itself. Now the city offered a hospitable base to a classical ballet company, of small bulk, national stature and international repute. The Labour City Council had Conservative support throughout. The City of Birmingham, following Glasgow's lead, believed the arts could, by helping make it a better place to live, stimulate the local economy. Civic pride was the admirable motivating force. But would the Royal Ballet Governors, with their loyalties to Sadler's Wells, where the Royal Ballet was born, go along?

The Governors were chaired then by Mark Bonham-Carter, a Liberal peer, ex-Deputy Chairman of the BBC, and a balletomane. He was a sprightly seventy-plus. Other Governors, including Dame Alicia Markova, were older. The most formidable figure by far was Dame Ninette de Valois, founder and maker of the Royal Ballet, the lasting inspirational force of ballet in Britain. So powerful was her personality, and in such awe was she held, that I sometimes wondered whether the Artistic Director of either company would elect to go to the lavatory without asking himself if 'Madam', as she was known, would approve. 'Madam' was now over ninety, and hard of hearing. The Governors' business was conducted partly by ear trumpet. Peter Wright, like Dowell and me in attendance, would sometimes dash round the table to shout into her instrument what had just been remarked. Mark Bonham-Carter, on these occasions, would catch my eye and grin wryly. Thoughtfully, he proposed modest reform. The Governors observed no fixed retiring age. Bonham-Carter sought to introduce one, and took soundings. The mention of seventy brought gasps of horror. Finally, the Governors assented to retirement at seventy-five, provided that all present incumbents were exempt. This was gratefully accepted, and later, when John Sainsbury took over as Chair, Ninette de Valois was respectfully invited always to send her representative, Pamela May.

In that forum, we discussed SWRB's projected move to Birmingham, and the notion that the company, while remaining in the Royal Opera House family, should attain independence from it, rather like children growing up, leaving the fold and, without severing family ties, standing on their own feet. Peter Wright was always concerned that some dancers might not relish living in the Midlands, and that standards, therefore, would fall. In the end, though, he was, like me, solidly for the move. One or two of us – Jeffrey Sterling, Chairman of the Governors of the Royal Ballet School, was one – spoke strongly in favour of change. Madam did not hesitate. 'Of course it is right. It is something I have always wanted. We must do it.' That settled the matter.

SWRB had always toured Britain, though ridiculous demarcations meant it could not be funded to play in Wales, Scotland or Northern Ireland, which had Arts Councils of their own. The unitary Arts Council grant to the three Royal Opera House companies, of which more than a quarter went to SWRB, already enriched British cultural life outside the metropolis. This move would make explicit that commitment. As Birmingham Royal Ballet, the company would play not three weeks at the

Hippodrome but eight or nine. Its education officers would involve Birmingham inner-city schools in dance, so that thousands of children participated. And the company would carry Birmingham's name, in the best of contexts, around the world. Two distinguished Birmingham citizens, David Justham of Central Television, and Tim Morris of the *Birmingham Post*, successive Chairmen of the Hippodrome Trust, played leading roles in tempting the company to the city. They brought about costly improvements to sight-lines in the Hippodrome's auditorium, and late and unbudgeted improvement to the stage – it was too unyielding for the dancers' feet. British Rail, as it then was, named a locomotive engine for the company – *Birmingham Royal Ballet* – in the presence of Dame Ninette, who I believe would have driven it if given the chance. On that day, I introduced Madam to the Labour leader of the Council, Dick, later Sir Richard, Knowles. As a young man in Islington, a plumber by trade, he had many times paid his sixpence to see de Valois's ballet company at Sadler's Wells. She had been his idol, and now he was able to meet her. I never saw a politician more pleased. The works on the company's new base needed to be completed for the start of the 1990 season. When considering the application, Birmingham Council's Planning Committee adjourned its meeting to visit the site. They found the building already half built. This story may be apocryphal, but it embodies Birmingham's eager determination to see the job done.

A most capable trio, Peter Wright, Christopher Nourse, his Administrative Director and later my assistant, and General Manager Derek Purnell, oversaw the move. They took virtually every member of the company with them. This, the first important decision of my time, was taken early in my tenure. It was right for the company, right for Birmingham, and, with due acknowledgements for once to the Arts Council, right for the arts in Britain.

Birmingham Royal Ballet's new premises were opened in October 1990 by Princess Margaret, President of the Royal Ballet, and assiduous in her attendance on both its companies' great occasions. Dame Ninette de Valois was there too. That season, the company gave a new ballet by David Bintley, *Brahms / Handel Variations*, and its first performance of Balanchine's *Symphony in Three Movements*; Ashton's *Jazz Calendar* and MacMillan's *Fin du Jour* were also given. Peter Wright's new *Nutcracker* sold out the Hippodrome at Christmas. 'All doubts have been dispelled about the move,' Peter Wright reported.

Birmingham Royal Ballet (BRB) could not have fared better. Under Peter Wright, the company made a tremendous success of its move. By 1992/93 the company was dancing for eight weeks at the Hippodrome. Wright found the repertory to fill the house: Paul Taylor's *Airs*; Kenneth MacMillan's *The Burrow* – Anne Frank as a ballet; and David Bintley's *Galanteries*. Wright acquired MacMillan's *Romeo and Juliet*, which the company had coveted for years. Paul Andrews, spotted by Kenneth at Wimbledon College of Art, did the sets and costumes and, near the end of her career, Marion Tait shone movingly as Juliet. And BRB performed a ballet only Peter Wright would have wished on it: Leonid Massine's *Choreartium*, to Brahms' Fourth Symphony. This is a company piece, on a grand scale. BRB carried it off triumphantly. Wright attracted able guest teachers to Birmingham. The standard of dancing, male and female, under Desmond Kelly's keen eye, constantly improved. Miyako Yoshida, BRB's Japanese prima ballerina, grew in grace and accomplishment. She was named Dancer of the Year in 1991. The company manager Jay Jolley, Anthony Dowell's partner, had the wit to stage a competition for conductors wanting to conduct for ballet. Andrea Quinn won it. She is now Music Director of the Royal Ballet. At the end of their third year in Birmingham, Peter Wright welcomed moves towards BRB's total financial autonomy, but could never countenance its total artistic separation from the Royal Opera House, the Royal Ballet or the Royal Ballet School. In 1993 Peter Wright was knighted for services to ballet. He richly deserved it: Birmingham and ballet were each enriched by him.

6

HOUSEKEEPING

Between her breasts, framed by the lowest of *décolletages*, the pear-shaped diamond dangled and dazzled. The wearer was Mrs Nelson Peltz, wife of the Chairman of Mountleigh plc, sponsors for the evening. The occasion, on 21 March 1990, was a gala performance of *L'elisir d'amore,* starring Luciano Pavarotti on his return to the House. The gala was given in the gracious presence of Her Majesty Queen Elizabeth, the Queen Mother. Queen Elizabeth brought Princess Margaret with her. The sponsor's cup of pride brimmed over.

Alex Alexander, Chairman of the Royal Opera House Trust, was happy. Mrs Vivien Duffield, assisted by Mrs Gail Ronson, were happy: they had sold tickets for the evening and would raise more than £500,000 for the Royal Opera House. In earlier days, galas at Covent Garden had supported other charities, or been shared with them. Now, charity began at home.

The Queen Mother was happy. Her smile broadened as she crossed the threshold. She told me she was so looking forward to the evening. Princess Margaret was not happy. 'I hate opera,' she said, as I greeted her. She spent Act Two, a colleague reported, in the Royal Box ante-room, sipping whisky and chatting to Norman St John Stevas. Luciano Pavarotti was happy, he was in fine form and was flattered by royalty's presence.

Before the performance, on the pretext of thanking Gail Ronson for donating the lavish floral decorations, I went in front of the curtain and encouraged this rather grand audience to enjoy themselves and, by their

This is a very special revival of
L'elisir d'amore. We are extremely
grateful to Mountleigh Group plc
for their generous sponsorship
of it.

Jeremy I. Isaacs

Jeremy I. Isaacs

applause, to let the singers know it. They took the hint. John Copley's entertaining production, in Beni Montresor's deft, lighthearted sets, wore well. 'Una furtiva lagrima' brought roars of applause – not a dry eye, except Luciano's, in the house. Such a gala was a high point of the season, and furnished a key portion of our income. Without private funding we could not survive.

No one made a greater contribution than Alex Alexander to the re-energizing of Covent Garden under John Sainsbury's chairmanship. A refugee from the Nazis, he left Prague to come to Britain in the late 1930s, immediately displaying a formidable business aptitude. Earlier than most, he spotted the vast potential growth of the frozen-food industry, and made his company's fortune by it. A genial figure, wearing a mischievous grin and an amply tailored suit, he was easing up a bit in his duties as Chairman of Allied-Lyons when John Sainsbury wooed him away from Glyndebourne – very much, one imagines, to George Christie's discontent; Christie had recently lost his Music Director, Bernard Haitink, to Covent Garden too. In spite of surface politeness and personal friendships, there has never been much love lost between Glyndebourne and the Royal Opera House. George Christie's father John, who founded opera at Glyndebourne, argued to government that he should run opera at Covent

Garden too, but was not heeded. I am vastly fond of George and Mary Christie, whose warm hospitality Gillian and I have often enjoyed, but it was not easy to deal with George as Chairman of the Arts Council music panel advising on Covent Garden's grant. I still think it odd that I should have had to do so. Could he really be objective about our needs?

Alex Alexander accepted Sainsbury's invitation to boost private funding to the Royal Opera House. We had to do it: there was no sign of any increase in Arts Council funding. Cheerfully and determinedly, Alex went about things with a will, and soon had remarkable successes to report. In the summer of 1989, he reported that private subvention had increased from £3.4 million in 1986/87 to £5.5 million.

These funds, far in excess of those earned, or sought, by any other European houses, came from several sources. Membership of the Royal Opera House Trust cost companies and corporations, and some wealthy individuals, an annual subscription and brought booking privileges. The subscriptions ran at £2500, at £5000, or even £10,000; income might total £3 million. Then the guaranteed purchase of what were called Premium seats (four every Monday night, say) produced another income stream: well over £1 million. Premium seat-holders paid more than twice the stated price for their tickets. In doing so they subsidized other ticket-holders, and helped keep our prices down. Some individual wealthy subscribers joined our First Night Club, launched in October 1988 at a dinner hosted by Margaret Thatcher at 10 Downing Street. The Prime Minister was showing her support for 'centres of excellence' by encouraging private citizens to pay for them. They paid £10,000 annually for the privilege. These three revenue streams could be predicted for a year ahead with reasonable accuracy in a buoyant economy, since those leaving a scheme and those joining were likely to balance over the year.

The one-off fundraising gala, held only once a year, was an entirely different affair. Tickets sold were from £500 in the stalls to £1500 in the Grand Tier, the top the market would stand. To mount such an evening, and justify those prices, we needed a unique attraction. In opera, Pavarotti or Domingo would serve. More appealing was the specially devised event: bits and pieces of ballet and opera arranged into a glitzy evening. With royalty present, and supper afterwards – perhaps in a gallery or museum – patrons are paying over the odds, but for something special. But it is never easy to assemble the artists. The annual 'fundraiser' ought to be a regular occasion – ideally, as it is at the Met, the season-opener. But that does not fit London's social round. To cram in performances, the Covent Garden season starts in early September, when too many likely patrons are still out of town. Still, any fiscal year with a gala in it means the House will have an extra £0.5 million to spend.

Then there is sponsorship of individual new productions, or, at lesser cost, revivals. In raising funds for these, Alex excelled. For monthly meetings of the Royal Opera House Trust, agendas were circulated in advance, but they scarcely made a difference. Under Alex, the Chairman's Report occupied very nearly all the meeting. Alex was a one-man band, his report a monologue: to such and such a person he had paid assiduous court; with another he had had tea, a preliminary discussion; yet another he had nobbled in his office; one likely donor he had entertained in the Royal Box. He left nothing out. In approaching his prey, Alex always went to the top, Chairman to Chairman. He played on the sense of public responsibility that attended on wealth and success. And, I fancy, he called in the favours of a long business life: 'My company must have purchased goods worth millions of pounds from yours over the years. You owe me something in return.' To others he expounded on the House's dire need, his own promise to meet it, the unfortunate victim's duty to help. His words fell on sympathetic ears. In those heady years of the Thatcher–Lawson boomlet – high incomes, low taxes, healthy profits – it was hard for businesses to refuse.

Alex never took no for an answer; he did not give up till he had extracted a promise or pocketed a cheque. On our afternoons of stuffy confinement in the Boardroom, it was Alex's pleasure to show us what he'd got, like a cat bringing a fieldmouse into the farm kitchen. He would crown his uninterrupted presentations by reaching into his jacket and taking out a wallet. With a broad grin, he would extract a cheque and wave it in front of us, signed and dated. We would break into applause. I would be particularly pleased; another key piece of the season to come was now assured. Once, he did not bring the cheque to our meeting, only the good news. Alex had long laid siege to Asil Nadir, Chairman of Polly Peck. Over tea, he had at last obtained the gift he sought: a cheque for £500,000. He banked it at 9am the following morning. Not all that long after, Nadir hopped off to Cyprus.

Several times I myself solicited the wealthy, but to no avail. One man whom I waited on for a production sponsorship that we were led to believe was on offer, promised, temporized and procrastinated. I was assured he was serious; indeed I met him once at a reception at 10 Downing Street. But he was having us on. The money never came. His name was Roger Levitt. Shortly after, he was convicted of serious fraud. But sometimes manna fell from a clear blue sky. I once received a post-card, in the ordinary mail, with a cheque attached, made out to the ROH, for £250,000. The cheque was drawn on the Clore Foundation and the postcard said, 'Do what you like with this. Love, Vivien.' Vivien Duffield is daughter of Sir Charles Clore, donor of the Clore Turner Gallery at the Tate, and a later Chair of the Royal Opera House Trust. Her personality is said to be overbearing, and was hard for my successive successors to live with. I found her clear-sighted courage at all times inspiring, and her commitment to the Opera House, together with John Sainsbury's, reassuring above all things.

Alexander's confidence and energy never flagged. With him in that role, I could be sure of vital support. My colleagues Philip Jones, Director of Finance, and David Pilcher, Chief Accountant, had never known any-thing like it, as together we looked at the budget for the coming year. Budget-making acquired a new dimension. With Arts Council grant flat, and wages chasing inflation, we invariably faced a projected excess of expenditure over income. Artistic aspirations for both opera and ballet were, properly I would argue, high; plans for opera had been laid some three years before. But each November, with five months still to go before the budget was finalized, income would not match. This gap had to be closed. We pruned expenditure as savagely as we could, beginning with the variables of the artistic programme: production costs were trimmed, and entire shows postponed or cancelled. Our high fixed costs were also cut to the bone. Then we revisited repertory and tweaked income, taking in the maximum possible box-office revenue. Still a gap remained. If Alex could deliver more, that would do it. If he thought he could, he would commit. If he committed, he would be as good as his word. For 1988/89, aiming high, he reached £5.9 million which, together with £600,000 from the Friends of Covent Garden, took private funding up to 18 per cent of the House's total revenue. We balanced the books. For 1989/90 Alex accepted a target of over £7 million, and fell short. He raised far more than anyone ever had for any UK arts institution, but that year, it was not enough.

The main expenses in an opera house lie not in fees to artists, but in fixed costs – the wages bill eating up 50 per cent of our income. Opera and ballet are both labour intensive, dancers in one, a chorus in the other, and the orchestra for both. The Royal Opera House orchestra numbered 120. If the orchestra is to be any good, you need to double up principals: two principal oboes, flutes, clarinets, trumpets, horns, and two front desks for violins, violas and cellos. A conductor at the House, looking over the faces in the pit at his first rehearsal, could be sure that he would see the same ones at every rehearsal and performance to come. We gave that undertaking, though it cost a bit. We rostered orchestra members by the work. This simple pledge made for excellence, and was the most compelling incentive to some conductors to accept our invitation. Some would stipulate for one of the two leaders, or for a favourite cellist or horn-player.

The ballet, at full strength, had eighty dancers and thirty-five to forty staff, consisting of teachers, coaches, music staff, physiotherapists, a modest administrative core. The chorus, seventy-six strong when I arrived, came down to sixty, and then, after me, to thirty-six. For *Lohengrin* or *Meistersinger* extra chorus was added, at some expense. (For Verdi's *Macbeth* in 1981, Riccardo Muti had demanded 140. When I visited La Pergola, Florence's small-scale eighteenth-century opera house, Luciano Berio reminded me that it was there that *Macbeth* had received its première. 'How many in the chorus?' I asked. Berio said, 'Twenty-four.') I upped Sadler's Wells Royal Ballet's strength to sixty dancers, to lessen the strain of injuries. They too had their back-up and support.

The stage and lighting crew, working seven days a week, forty-eight weeks of the year, numbered over 100. It was difficult to get by with fewer in so antiquated a working environment. The opera company numbered over fifty, including a dozen company singers, half a dozen repetiteurs, staff producers, the artistic administrator in charge of casting – a prime key to vocal quality – staff who handled contracts, a surtitle unit, press and publicity. There were cooks, servers and cashiers in the staff canteen, and waiters and waitresses at public bars and buffets; we had firemen, security men, stage doormen, timekeepers. Dressers, for opera and ballet, looked after the artists, helping them on with their different costumes for each act of a performance, and quick changes at the side of the stage. Wardrobe fitted costumes to individual dancers, singers, actors, supers and chorus, and stored them neatly, numbered and named, to save precious minutes next time round. There were milliners for hats, and wig-makers for wigs. Ushers and usherettes, part-time only, sold pro-grammes and ice-cream, and showed people to their seats. The linkman, Ivell Arnold, resplendent in his dark-red coat, hurried along slowcoaches, looked after latecomers and personally attended to anyone in need of assistance. With a colleague, he carried wheelchairs up to the Grand Tier boxes. Two 'flunkeys' in wigs and court dress manipulated the tabs, hydraulically operated and weighing 3 tons, and presented bouquets on stage. (One of them, Jonathan Kustow, succeeded me as captain of our cricket team; we challenged ENO and defeated them three years run-ning.) Some sneered at these costumed lackeys as a relic of a more deferential age. I always felt their appearance in keeping with the tradi-tion of the place, and decided to retain them.

I looked for economies, and could not easily find them. Everyone worked hard. The three companies gave 450 performances a year. When I joined there were 1050 staff on the books, fewer than at La Scala, which gives ninety performances. Leanest of all was the administration; every spare penny we had went on the stage, never on ourselves. In the finance department, more vital as self-generated income grew, staff numbers were tight. If the auditors insisted, we would engage an internal auditor, though we could scarcely afford the post. The personnel department, handling labour relations too, consisted of only three. (This was to be criticized in the Warnock Report.) The opera and ballet companies had separate press officers, kept busy by separate packs of critics. Whoever took charge of corporate public relations was always snowed under. There was no Marketing Director, until John Sainsbury became Chairman. In the box-office there were too few staff, not too many. More were needed to cope with peak demand. For a Domingo performance there would be six unsuccessful applications for every ticket sold; each must be acknow-ledged. The Royal Opera House, in key areas, was understaffed, not overstaffed.

It is always possible to appear to reduce staff numbers by hiring contract staff, and 'outsourcing' some tasks to external businesses, but this is often a false economy; pennies gained in lower costs are outweighed by value lost in quality of service. In some cases, outsourcing costs more. Making scenery outside certainly does. You pay the mark-up, someone else's profit, on top of the cost. Wages always threatened to increase in line with inflation, which was then moderate to fierce each year, but our fixed income, the Arts Council grant, persistently fell behind it. Priestley

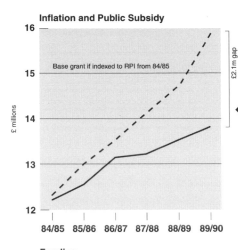

Inflation and Public Subsidy

Base grant if indexed to RPI from 84/85

£2.1m gap

£ millions

16 — 15 — 14 — 13 — 12 —

84/85 85/86 86/87 87/88 88/89 89/90

Funding
Percentage contributions from the three sources

Percentage

60 — 50 — 40 — 30 — 20 — 10 — 0

*

£14.4m £14.3m

£6.5m

85/86   86/87   87/88   88/89   89/90

Cost per performance
The international context

Average cost £ thousands

350 — 300 — 250 — 200 — 150 — 100 — 50 — 0

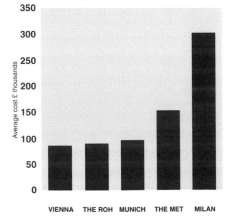

VIENNA   THE ROH   MUNICH   THE MET   MILAN

1989/90 at a Glance: the Annual Report

The Arts Council base grant has now fallen £2.1m below what it would be if it had been indexed to RPI from 84/85, when the base grant level set by the Priestley Report was adopted. The Report's further recommendation that the grant should be proofed against inflation has not been implemented. ◀

FINANCE
Record attendances: The Royal Ballet 91%
The Royal Opera 92%.
Record receipts: Royal Opera House up 35%.
Private funding: up 17%.
Public subsidy: up 1.7%, in real terms down 6%.

Deficit of £2.9m.

PERFORMANCES
459: more – on less subsidy – than any comparable European house.
The Royal Ballet: 148; 2 world premieres.
The Royal Opera: 139; 8 new productions.
Sadler's Wells Royal Ballet: 172; 2 world premieres, 2 overseas tours.

Over the past five years contribution from the public subsidy ■ has fallen from 53% to 41%, while box office ■ has gone up from 34% to 41%, and private funding ▨ from 12% to 18%. ◀

*Excludes an exceptional item of £2.1m income earned by The Royal Opera on a Far East Tour.

ROH SEAT PRICES
Average: £39.08 opera, £20.55 ballet.
Public subsidy per seat: £23.47 opera, £19.81 ballet.

800 seats at or under £24 opera, £16 ballet.

NEW AUDIENCES
Schools matinees saved for 3 years by £750,000 sponsorship.

4,000 prom for £5 in 18th Midland Bank Proms Week.

Big Screen brings opera free to thousands in Covent Garden Piazza.

10,000 enjoy open-air *Cav* and *Pag* at Kenwood.

12,000 new ballet-goers during Westminster Hamlyn Week.

THE FUTURE
The ROH Covent Garden Project receives planning consent.

Vienna (at £84k) and the ROH (£85k) put on performances at considerably less cost than Munich (£98k), The Met (£158k), and Milan (£302k). Compare with 'Subsidy per performance' chart on Page 3. (These figures are approximations based on a 3-year average, converted to 1990 sterling equivalents.) ◀

had seen the problem: he had recommended that the ROH's Arts Council base grant should be kept in touch with average earnings. Priestley was ignored. Balancing the books, as we did in 1988/89, was a constant struggle, and something of a miracle when we achieved it. In 1989/90, we incurred a deficit of £2.9 million. I saw it coming, but not its full extent.

In his statement in the Annual Report, John Sainsbury called it 'unavoidable, as the Arts Council grant fell even further behind Priestley's recommended level in real terms'. And he cited an actual increase, but a steep fall against an ambitious target, in private funding. The Board looked hard at me as I put forward plans for the following financial year, 1990/91. They were well advanced. Ballet companies, re-arranging internal resource, plan a season in advance; the peculiar difficulty in budgeting opera is that planning looks three years ahead, at least. Only on such a lead-time is it possible to book singers or conductors in an international market. Great conductors accept only precise engagements at the outset. Singers begin by pencilling in a period of weeks for the house seeking their services, but soon want to know what role to learn. So if a house aspires to international standard, repertory must be fixed three years ahead. Yet Arts Council funding is not known with certainty one year ahead, let alone three. And the more the Arts Council grant was eroded – in 1989/90 it declined in real terms by 6 per cent – the more dependent we became on sources of income not within our control. Demand for tickets was strong; we could predict box-office fairly accurately within 2 or 3 per cent. To predict the level of private support, dependent on economic imponderables and on the whims of individuals and of corporations, was much more difficult.

The question the Board faced in March 1990, as we finalized the budget for the next twelve months, was not whether we could cut into that £2.9 million deficit – I could see no prospect of that – but whether to allow a further deficit in 1990/91. In the months and weeks before the decision, I took millions out of the budget, cancelling productions to do so. But, without so decimating our work as to render hollow any claim to excellence, I could not, I argued, totally close the gap. The Board agreed the plans, and the further deficit they entailed. When this became known, all hell broke loose.

A few weeks earlier the Chairman of the Royal Opera House, John Sainsbury, met the new Chairman of the Arts Council, Peter Palumbo, at Stamford House, Sainsbury's south-of-the-river headquarters. I was present. Palumbo's was a key appointment, his attitude, we thought, crucial to our future. His predecessor, William Rees-Mogg, had believed that too high a proportion of limited Arts Council funds was spent on opera, and in London. His 1984 policy document, *The Glory of the Garden* (for us an ironic title), announced an intention to devolve resources away from both. There had been no hope for us there. And the newcomer? Margaret Thatcher had offered Peter Palumbo the Arts Council chairmanship after failing to persuade others to take it. Dapper, polished, a generous host, with a taste for fine wine, Palumbo was a property developer, and a contributor to Tory party funds. He was also, far more than Rees-Mogg, a genuine lover of the arts. He owned modern paintings, and houses designed by Frank Lloyd Wright. He sought to erect a tall tower by Mies van der Rohe at No. 1 Poultry, opposite the Mansion House, in the heart of the City. When that failed, he put up a building by James Stirling instead. Palumbo had eagerly accepted the Arts Council chairmanship. Had he received undertakings as to the level of funding at his disposal? At lunch, he assured us in categorical terms that he would help. In the most positive fashion, he expressed under-standing and support; the national companies would be his top priority. John Sainsbury and I took away the message that our grant would increase. But it all came to nothing. Peter Palumbo had never chaired a public body in his life. I think he imagined that as Arts Council Chairman his personal will would prevail. He had never reckoned with the harsh truth that would confront him: with static resource, to pay Paul you have to rob Peter. But Arts Council members came from all over Britain; they were against sacrificing regional claims to the needs of the national com-panies. If Palumbo had plans to divert funds, he could not carry them. If he had hopes of increased Treasury funds, they were, measured against what was needed, sorely disappointed. But in 1990, we were hopeful; so was he. Then he learned not just that we had incurred a deficit, but that we were budgeting to increase it.

As the annual press conference approached, the press was up in arms. Foolishly, seeking savings which would also bring home our plight, I attacked complimentary tickets for critics. I had already trimmed the list of great and good, and drastically pruned our regional press lists; the *Irish Times* and the *Glasgow Herald*, two of my favourite newspapers, surely did not need to be at every production as of right, but only on occasion. Now, meanly, I looked at the list remaining on first nights: about thirty pairs of tickets, in no way exceptional for an international house. But I decided to cut that. Critics were given two tickets, not one. I proposed to deprive them of the free second ticket; tickets for spouses, partners, pals, cost us, we estimated, some £15,000 a year, which we could ill afford. Gillian warned me what would happen; she was right. The heavens of reproach drowned me in complaint. Critic after critic wrote to say that it was essential he or she be accompanied. Apparently it took two to criticize: the job could not be done alone. I had attacked longstanding custom; deep offence was given. After the storm died down, I restored the second ticket to regulars, whose papers habitually gave us prominent notice, though I continued to allow only one ticket for all those performances (Domingo, Pavarotti) for which we could have sold the spare seat ten times over. We saved some money. But damage was done.

In this atmosphere of resentment, with a deficit looming, I prepared to announce opera plans for the 1990/91 season. I did a damn silly thing that morning. I accepted advice to make a statement but not to answer questions. But this was the opera press's principal opportunity each year to quiz me. I should not have denied it to them.

As soon as my statement was over, and details of the coming season given, I left the dais, mingled with the press and answered questions freely. What would happen, I was asked, if I was forced to cut back on next season's plans to avoid incurring a further deficit? The reluctant answer, rehearsed early that morning on the telephone to the *Evening Standard*, was 'Armageddon.' This single word, signifying global conflict at the end of the world, made little sense, but a lot of column inches. Next thing we knew, Palumbo was denouncing our attitude. To incur a deficit was one thing; to budget for a deficit put us wholly in the wrong. We must reverse ourselves. We shoe-horned in extra performances to increase revenue. I made further cuts in production, and got reluctant agreement on a wage freeze for all staff, including management. In addition I had to impose thirty job losses, losing posts and people I knew we really needed, and some of whom, a year later, we had to replace. Thanks to these firings, and to the remaining staff's sacrifice on wages – the cost of living rose that year – we came through the season on budget, and without evident diminution in quality making two years out of three so far.

By harsh economy, and unbroken success at the box-office, the House operated in the black. Opera paid attendance rose to a record 94 per cent – our best ever. Ballet was not far behind. We sold 88 per cent of the House's financial capacity across 254 performances, a rare feat. Yet, as the 1990/91 season ended, John Sainsbury announced that he was retiring from the post, 'having completed four years as Chairman (and nearly twenty years on the Board)'. It should have been a longer stint, to all our benefit. No one I ever worked with demonstrated such strength and determination for good. He gave a reason: 'Other responsibilities do not leave me with the time I believe is necessary to be Chairman of the Royal Opera House when it faces its present financial pressure.'

John Sainsbury was only a couple of years away from retirement as Chairman and Chief Executive of J. Sainsbury plc. In every year of his chairmanship so far, profits had risen; he was determined they should do so for the whole of his term. They did. He performed, to the utmost, his duties to shareholders and staff. He loved the Royal Opera House. I loved working for him. Later, in April 1992, when it was announced that he had been made Knight of the Garter, I spotted him sitting in row E of the stalls. From the stage, I invited the audience to salute the patron of the arts to whom we all owed so much. They gave him a rousing volley of applause. In 1991, no one could blame him for putting Sainsbury's first. It ought, all the same, to have been possible for him to continue a little longer in the chairmanship at Covent Garden. Had it not been such an uphill struggle, I am sure he would have done so. But government had remained aloof, even hostile. A new Minister for the Arts, David Mellor, barked at me across his office as I entered that there would be no more money for the Opera House. John Sainsbury, a week later, had just as hectoring a greeting.

Sainsbury made his reason for leaving plain in his last Annual Report, written in summer 1991: 'When I became Chairman in 1987, I believed that the Government and the Arts Council would recognize the real needs of the Royal Opera House, while expecting that a greater proportion of our revenue would come from the box-office and private sponsorship.' That 'recognition' of real needs never came. He had played his part; others had not played theirs. We had steeply increased box-office revenue and sponsorship income. In return, against Priestley's specific recommendation, government had allowed our grant to fall in real terms and drastically to diminish as a proportion of our total resource. The long-term underlying financial situation remained 'most critical'. It would continue to be a bumpy ride.

7

PEAKS AND TROUGHS

In the summer of 1990, I fulfilled a dream. High in the Spanish Pyrenees, in the Parc Nacional d'Aigues Tortes, I came at last to 'the Enchanted Mountains' I had read of long before, and ever since longed to see. Twin slender peaks, Los Encantados – or, in Catalan, Els Encantats – are not for scaling by mortals, but with Gillian I walked instead, breathed the mountain air, trekked the rocky paths up to the high plateaux, and rejoiced in the steep views down the narrow, watered valleys beneath. Glad to be away from it all in Espot, the simple resort village in which we had secured a bed, I had decided, nevertheless, to visit Harrison Birtwistle on the way home through France. He was writing an opera for us, *Gawain*, based on the pre-Chaucerian poem *Sir Gawain and the Green Knight*, to a libretto by David Harsent. It was due to be completed by midwinter, and delivered to us in full score early enough in 1991 for performance in May. Would it be ready in time? I proposed to call on Harry and see for myself. By message from London, I suggested we drop in. A cordial invitation resulted, but also, as I found out later, a flurry of anxious telephone calls. Would I be the bearer of bad tidings? Had we been compelled to cancel *Gawain*?

We crossed the Pyrenees and, by way of Foix and Albi, made our pilgrimage to Lunegarde in the Corrèze, a landscape of bare cropped grass over limestone, where the composer and his family were waiting for us in their home. Harry was relieved it was a social visit. There was moussaka and a salad dressed with walnut oil, and a delicious pear tart.

After lunch, Harry took me across the grounds to the specially designed outbuilding in which he worked, a handsome, airy dovecote. There I saw and fingered the tall, stiff quires he wrote on, making signs on paper to invent a new world of sound. On each sheet, building layers of noise from thirty or forty sources to create, say, half a minute of music, he had made a myriad tiny, meaningful marks. There was evident pride as he showed his handiwork, translating what he heard in his head to the score that would bring it into being. I was humbled, exhilarated, and very glad we had come.

There was no intention whatever, I assured him, of cancelling *Gawain*. But he knew, and I knew, there might easily have been. Any opera out of the ordinary tests the financial limits within which lyric theatre operates. Long pieces eat up extra days in rehearsal and time in performance overtime. Large choruses or a large orchestra – for Strauss, say, as compared to Mozart – dip deeper into tubs of resource. Strange repertory may drive away audiences; a challenging production style may fail to win the word of mouth that fills the house. Toughest of all to schedule is the completely new work. No one knows it; some may not want to. *Gawain* needed weeks of orchestral rehearsal, and we would use a special chorus, The Sixteen. *Gawain* would not have been easy to mount in any season, but in 1991 its demands – not in themselves immoderate – were harder to sustain, with deficit hovering over us. If we replaced six performances of Harry's opera with *Tosca*, the year's figures would certainly have improved by over £600,000. But Paul Findlay and I never doubted we must stay with it; John Tooley had commissioned it, and we had been there in the casting discussions that attended its conception. 'Shall I write Lady Hautdesert', Harry pondered, 'for high soprano or for counter-tenor?' He wrote the role for a mezzo-soprano in the end. We had found space for movement classes and costume trials long before the piece was ready for rehearsal, or even complete. We cut ticket prices to ensure a young audience, and prepared talks and study days to precede performance. We were committed to *Gawain*, affirming that opera lives, and that a great composer was in our midst.

Gawain received its première in May 1991. It is a mature masterpiece, containing at least one moment of pure theatrical magic. The Green Knight rides into Arthur's court and issues a challenge: anyone there may strike at his neck with an axe, but must be ready to have the same done to him, a year and a day on. Gawain accepts, and strikes off the Green

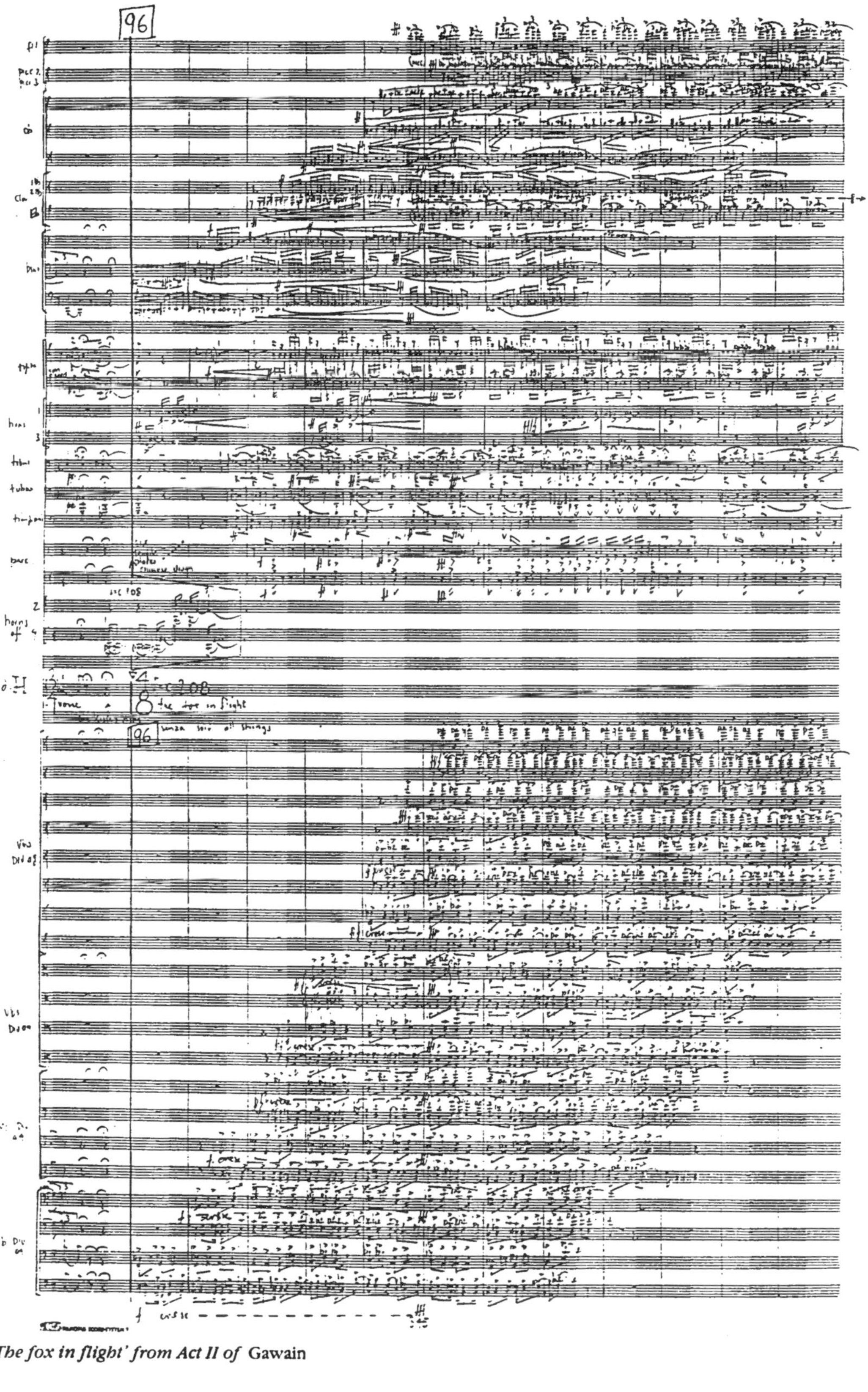

'The fox in flight' from Act II of Gawain

Knight's head. The Green Knight picks it up, and it continues to sing! Gawain goes on his journey of self-discovery, survives the axe blow he has engaged for, and returns 'not that hero' the court expects. Our life's journey, too, the libretto tells us, starts with a single step.

Elgar Howarth, conducting, realized it, never failing to keep the orchestra together, though sometimes, he warned them, the tempos he beat would change with every bar. John Tomlinson as the Green Knight and François le Roux as Gawain gave their testing roles life. Not everyone cared for Harsent's fine libretto. No one, I think, doubted the composer's genius. ENO had given his *Mask of Orpheus* in 1986 but had never been able to afford to revive it. I made up my mind we would, as we planned, bring back *Gawain* in April 1994. By scraping around, with others chipping in, we managed to have a recording made too. I take pleasure in all I know of Birtwistle's music; at Channel 4 we had given the television première of an earlier opera, *Yan Tan Tethera*, though it was commissioned by BBC2. But the high point I remember is what Harry Birtwistle said in the Crush Bar at Covent Garden after the first night of *Gawain*: 'No composer has ever been better served by an opera house than I have been by you here.'

'Isaacs, this is rubbish. Go back to television,' cried a voice from the balcony. After a grand new *Carmen*; after the astonishing male soprano Jochen Kowalski in Harry Kupfer's production of *Orfeo ed Euridice*; after two cycles of Friedrich's production of Wagner's *Ring*, conducted, with growing authority, by Haitink; we are, in October 1991, at a performance of Meyerbeer's *Les Huguenots*. The production by John Dew, a talented young Englishman working in Germany, is controversial, and heartily disliked. The orchestra is about to embark on industrial action in pursuit of a wage claim of 20 per cent.

A year or so before I had received a letter from a clergyman, a passionate Meyerbeer fan, beseeching me to say what we would do on the centenary of the master of French grand opera's birth. I told him, I hoped *Les Huguenots*. Paul Findlay had suggested that we take John Dew's staging from the Deutsche Oper in Berlin. It was famously successful there. Dew, who was in charge of opera at Bielefeld, a small town in Germany, was notorious for the outrageous inventiveness of his productions, and his daring choice of repertory. He had set *Les Huguenots* in a Berlin divided by the Wall between East and West, as sixteenth-century Paris was torn between Protestant and Catholic. The Wall was now down; our divided city would be Belfast, where for decades troops and barbed wire had been needed to keep Protestants and Catholics from each others' throats, and gangs of killers crossed the sectarian divide to maim and murder. The slaughter of St Bartholomew's Eve would speak to us of horrors nearer home.

Something of a coup, too, would be the restoration to the Covent Garden stage of a piece which opened the present theatre in 1858, was given there 250 times, but had not been seen since 1927. *Les Huguenots*, although it rises in the end to the seriousness of its subject, has been traditionally a showcase for great singing, particularly in the role of Marguerite de Valois, a favourite part of Joan Sutherland's. The work needed, it was thought, seven great singers: Les Sept Étoiles. We did not have seven stars, but nor had they in Berlin. Gottfried Pilz, Dew's designer, gave us a grim, modern city; the Catholic gentlemen celebrate their besting of the Protestants in an officers' club; Marguerite de Valois and her ladies prepare to bathe in a hotel swimming pool. The members of the Royal Opera chorus would wear bathing costumes. This caused a stir in the press, and a greater stir in the chorus. Some protested to the Wardrobe Mistress, Janice Pullen, that their costumes, a little too revealing, did not suit. 'Oh no,' said Janice. 'None of that. I have had to listen over too many years to your complaining that bulky costumes are unflattering. Now you complain these bathing costumes reveal too much. No arguments; get them on.' They did too and, with the help of a few wispy wraps, got away with it.

But we did not get away with the production. Many hoped for the greatest voices, and did not get them; most expected a conventional production, in period and costume, and it was not. We had touted the piece as a nineteenth-century grand opera; we did not prepare audiences for a contemporary stab at it. *Les Huguenots*, our programme noted, 'is a classic example of building up and resolving tension over a whole work'. It begins lightheartedly, frivolously even, and ends in determined, religiously motivated, slaughter. Dew decided that, since the music encompassed this transition in mode and feeling, so should the production. It would end in grim confrontation, but begin by playing for laughs. In Act Two, Marguerite dreams of a world without religious hatred and strife. Dew, responding to the soprano's coloratura, set her, in glittering costume, in a neon-lit booth, in front of the hotel. With serious intent, he was sending her up. Judith Howarth as Marguerite did bravely, but could not carry it off. Audience hostility mounted, and was never, on the first night anyway, assuaged. Booing at curtain call is less common in Britain than elsewhere; at *Les Huguenots* we caught up. Most of it was directed at John Dew. He did not need to take a solo call, but did. I was beside him behind the curtain as he decided to brave it; wearing a gaudy waistcoat and a bold smile, out, in a dignified way, he went. I admired him for that, enjoyed *Les Huguenots* myself, and was grateful for the show. I told him we looked forward to the next production he was to do for us, Halévy's *La Juive*. (If Jeremy Israel Isaacs could not put on *The Jewess* at Covent Garden, who could?) But *La Juive* never happened: the axe of economy forced cancellation, depriving us of a second look at Dew's work.

I had something else on my mind that night: disruptive industrial action by the orchestra, who in October still had not concluded wage negotiations begun in late spring. A few weeks earlier, courtesy of the film producer David Puttnam, we had invited our supporters in the Royal Opera House Trust to the première of his *Meeting Venus* at the Odeon, Leicester Square, and to dinner afterwards. I spoke, briefly. *Meeting Venus*, directed by István Szabó, is an account of a soprano's affair with a conductor, but also of the nightmare of putting on an opera, Wagner's *Tannhäuser*, at the Palais Garnier in Paris. Szabó had once attempted that, as part of a dream Hungarian trio – conductor Christoph von Dohnányi and, as designer, the painter Vasarely. They found the bureaucracy that ran the Garnier, and the unions who organized the workforce there, equally obdurate, self-interested and blind to artistic purpose. In the movie, *Tannhäuser* is given, but as a concert performance only, unstaged. The opera house has defeated art, even though music, the director seems to be saying, rises above all that. In my speech I recalled how, after a late-Victorian performance of *Antony and Cleopatra*, as Cleopatra clasps the asp to her bosom and dies, a woman in the audience commented to her neighbour, 'How unlike, how very unlike, the home life of our own dear Queen.' Life and work at Covent Garden, I assured my audience, bore no resemblance whatever to the film they were about to see. I should have kept my mouth shut. I had reckoned without the orchestra's shop steward, a violinist, Robert Trory.

Trory was a busy, self-important fellow, affable enough in private; he made his own wine, and brought me a bottle. I drank a glass. He had been a Labour town councillor and enjoyed the limelight. The Orchestra Committee, elected each year, always contained an activist or two, but was broadly representative of orchestral opinion. Trory was something else. On any pretext – it was too hot or too cold; there were people in the auditorium who should not be at a rehearsal – he would exercise his privilege and address the orchestra in the pit. Now, after years of minimal increases in salary and then a total freeze on earnings, Trory persuaded the orchestra that this year their turn had come; their worth, under his guidance, would be recognized monetarily as never previously. With the Opera House's finances rocky as ever, he convinced them of the justice, and the likely success, of a wage claim for 20 per cent.

Orchestra players at Covent Garden earned less than other London orchestras. Because we insisted that the same band should play for each opera and ballet, and did not permit deputies, they had fewer chances than other musicians of picking up lucrative session work. A rank-and-file musician at ROH in 1991 earned about £17,000 a year in basic pay, with more for extra sessions worked. It was hard to keep a family and meet a mortgage. And they worked 'unsociable hours'. No one could blame musicians for seeking to better their earnings; but within reason.

The Opera House, imposing a wage freeze, had balanced its books the previous fiscal year. The next year, 1991/92, would be as difficult. There was no fat, no reserve to call on, no possibility of meeting a claim that was not in low single figures. Trory's arguments to us fell on stony ground. We were seeking a concession or two from the orchestra. In the summer, when the pit was baking hot and they stripped to short sleeves, the glaring white shirts distracted. I wanted them to wear a black shirt, or lightweight jacket, instead. The orchestra did not fancy black shirts – memories perhaps of Mosley in the East End. They would not agree to provide a jacket at their own expense; the Opera House could not afford to either. Perhaps a sponsor would. When this became known, Mr David Moss of Moss Bros wanted to know if he could help; but it came to nothing. In any case, it was a side issue. At the negotiating table, a wide gap remained. The musicians threatened industrial action, stopping short of a strike. If they withdrew their labour, we would lose box-office income but they would lose their pay. In this impasse Trory devised a novel course: by remaining true to Meyerbeer's intentions, they would force management to pay up. *Les Huguenots* is in five acts, but we proposed to give the piece with only one interval. This was an affront, Trory suggested, to the musicians' sensibilities. Meyerbeer had intended intervals between the acts; the orchestra would leave the pit after each act ended. No, I said, it was for us to determine how the piece should be given. If you don't intend to work normally, stay at home. They stayed away, without pay. Attitudes hardened. We had to cancel three performances of *Les Huguenots*, and several of ballet too. The House was dark for more than a week. Lost box-office revenues came to over £500,000, though there were savings on orchestra pay to set against them.

A more serious threat was to the gala, to be attended by the Princess of Wales, on the opening night of a new production of *Simon Boccanegra*. The proceeds would be split with Help the Aged. Georg Solti was due to conduct; Elijah Moshinsky, again working with designer Michael Yeargan, would direct. There was a fine cast, headed by Kiri Te Kanawa.

Talks with the orchestra continued at ACAS, as the House remained dark. At a House meeting, I explained the gravity of the situation: management could not meet the orchestra's claim. The meeting could see how serious things were: many of those present were already losing income and some might soon be laid off. As I have mentioned, the orchestra thought of themselves as in the House, but not quite of it; to guard their tax status, they remained on contract, not on staff. Their aloofness was resented. Andy Warner, the nurse in charge of the occupational-health unit, a veteran who kept many secrets, got up to speak. Bluntly she told the orchestra to think of others, not just of themselves. 'We are all in this,' she said. 'Behave yourselves.' That turned it. Negotiations resumed; half the orchestra, we thought, wanted to end their action and get back to work. *Simon Boccanegra* was in the rehearsal room. The days were ticking away. Solti had to rehearse with the orchestra alone if we were to hold to the gala opening night. The day before the last possible start for those rehearsals, union and management sat down, in separate rooms, at ACAS. The afternoon and then the evening wore on. I was due, with Gillian, to have supper in Chelsea with Vivien Duffield and her partner Jocelyn Stevens. I kept telephoning to say I would be late, and then later. In the end, after 11pm, we had a deal. There was still something to eat in Chelsea, though Gillian, Vivien and Jocelyn were almost asleep round the table.

The wage settlement was within our limit: 5.5 per cent. We refused to repay wages lost. And for an extra £9 a week, we bought out payments for twelve radio relays a year. This was a major breakthrough; now Radio 3 could plan regular broadcasts. The union said they must put the agreement to the full orchestra. They would be in touch with them tomorrow, instructing them to come in for a meeting, and if that meeting agreed the settlement, work could resume the next day. 'Absolutely not,' I said. 'Unless the orchestra rehearses for Solti tomorrow afternoon, there will be no *Simon Boccanegra*, and therefore no deal.' We offered to bike to everyone through the night a summary of what had been agreed, and a summons to be in by lunchtime. Protocol, the union said, required that *they* summon the orchestra, not us, so they rang round. Next morning an orchestra member, John Woolf, a wise counsellor with whom I had kept in touch, came to my office. 'When the orchestra enters the pit this afternoon,' he told me, 'you must be there to welcome us back.' He was right. Leaning on the pitrail, I said as pleasantly as I could, 'We have missed you. Good to see you back.' Solti raised his baton.

The first night was a short ten days later. That morning I rang the director, Elijah Moshinsky. 'Elijah,' I said, 'tell me something. Why is it that in the recognition scene, when a father rediscovers a daughter he has not seen for twenty-five years, the singers do not look at each other? I know I should have brought this up earlier, but can you tell me?' 'Of course, you are right,' he said, 'it is a good idea: they should look at each other.' 'Elijah, don't tell *me* it's a good idea. You are the director of this show. Tell them. Tell them this afternoon, or even in their dressing rooms this evening, to look at each other.' 'Well, I will,' he said. 'But there is a problem. The problem is the conductor, Solti. He keeps saying "Elijah, vy are they looking at each other; they should be looking at *me*."' *Simon Boccanegra* was a considerable success, especially for Solti.

The summer of 1992 was long, and testing – artistically exhilarating, mentally and physically exhausting. Other houses have shorter seasons. The Met plays opera from late September to the end of April; La Scala opens on Sant' Ambrogio, 7 December, and runs on to early summer. In May, the intendants of American houses pay their annual visits to Europe, relaxed and in holiday mood. They find Covent Garden slogging on through the dog days of summer into August. This summer of 1992, misery lay ahead.

We had balanced the books in 1990/91, *mirabile dictu*. In 1991/92 we slipped again. Until mid-March 1991, we sold virtually every seat in the House, but then a stagnant economy, teetering into recession, began to take its toll. If box-office income comprises, as in European houses, only

20 per cent of total revenue, and the state grant is tailored to need, then an opera house is sheltered from wintry economic winds. But in the UK, if the Arts Council grant falls to 40 per cent of income, the house will struggle. The orchestral dispute had cost us nearly two weeks at the box-office. Paid attendance in fiscal 1991/92 was down to 83 per cent for ballet, 88 per cent for opera. We had sold 78 per cent of financial capacity; the National Theatre budgets to break even at 75 per cent. But for us this was not enough. In this year we incurred a deficit of £1.4 million, taking our cumulative deficit to £3.6 million. Alarm bells rang. The Arts Council, already privy to our every tremor, attending Board meetings and receiving minutes, now decided to set up an external appraisal of our affairs – one of several, they said, into the national arts companies.

For the last year and more the Arts Council had been, at the initiative of a new Secretary-General, Anthony Everitt, conducting a strategic review of arts and media in Britain. Everitt, a former journalist and previously Deputy Secretary-General, had been appointed by Peter Palumbo, and could scarcely believe his luck. Palumbo took us both one day to lunch at the Ritz, and ordered, after much scanning of the list, the finest claret they had – I believe it was Pétrus. Everitt's eyes popped. (I never saw him look so pleased again till, in his office, I once brought myself to use the jargon 'performance indicators'. A similar ecstasy resulted.) Strategic decisions, I pointed out to Everitt, would involve hard choices: encouraging some initiatives, denying others; spending more here, less there. This was wasted breath. The National Arts and Media Strategy Unit consulted every interest group in the land, and gave each equal priority. Their report cost £1 million. When it appeared, titled – hopefully – *Towards a National Arts and Media Strategy*, it listed eleven principles, and contained 153 conclusions and recommendations. It pointed towards everything, and led to nothing.

Incapable of arriving at a view of their own, or seeking confirmation of one they held but dared not utter, the Arts Council invited Baroness Warnock to chair an appraisal of the Royal Opera House. She had a keen mind, and a spry, tough persona. I had known Mary Warnock in television as a member of ITV's regulator, the Independent Broadcasting Authority (IBA). I liked her. She knew nothing of opera or ballet. Brian Ivory, a Scots whisky distiller, and Veronica Lewis, a livewire and leading figure in dance administration, joined her. Dennis Stevenson, a City whiz and, later, Chairman of the Tate Trustees, looked at our plans to redevelop the House. He spent two days over it. We kept hammering away at the need for higher funding. From their pursed lips as we passed each other in corridors, our impression grew that we were in for a pasting.

Meanwhile, the Royal Opera House Board, concerned about recurrent financial crisis, had commissioned a study of its own from Price Waterhouse. Their team was led by an engaging swashbuckler, Ian Beesley, who knew a headline when he saw one. His colleagues looked hard at labour practices on the stage. Both Warnock and Price Waterhouse were due to report by September. The Board, aware that well-rehearsed work of quality risked an annual deficit, earnestly canvassed solutions – some plain daft. One member half-seriously used to advocate 'wall to wall *Sound of Music*'. By this he meant *Tosca*, *La bohème*, *Butterfly* and *Carmen*, *Swan Lake* and *The Sleeping Beauty*, and nothing else. Another urged we do opera without scenery. I did not think opera-lovers would pay our prices for concert performances on a bare stage. Frivolities aside, either these new appraisals gave us a clean bill of health, in which case we had an unanswerable case for more funding; or, if weaknesses were detected, reform must ensue.

Lurking somewhere behind this, though I did not know it, was David Mellor, back as Arts Minister with the grand title Secretary of State for the National Heritage – Mellor nicknamed it the Ministry of Fun. Mellor was a lover of music and a supporter of the arts. He acted to enhance arts funding. He was determined, however, to decide for himself where any increase should go. As Chief Secretary, he had persuaded the Treasury to find £11 million for ENO to help them buy the freehold at the Coliseum. He made it clear to the new Chairman of the ROH, Angus Stirling, that he should get rid of me, implying that the Royal Opera House would get no more money while Jeremy Isaacs was General Director.

One incident at the Opera House drove Mellor to apoplectic fury. One night, in late 1990, when he and his wife Judith were Denis Forman's guests in the Royal Box, she arrived late and found the door of the Royal Box entrance in Floral Street open, but unguarded. (The attendant assumed all guests had arrived.) With some difficulty – she was partially sighted – she made her way round to Bow Street, and from there was escorted up to the Royal Box ante-room and her husband. Mellor blew his top; in front of others, in unrestrained language, he upbraided Denis Forman for the House's discourtesy to his wife. Forman apologized. In confidence, he reported to me, and to the Chairman, what had happened.

I told Gillian, then Arts Editor of the *Observer*. At the paper Gillian heard one journalist suggest that Mellor, with the Majors, had been at Covent Garden to celebrate their victory in the election. 'Not true,' said Gillian, and added, 'but he was there the other night and made the most tremendous fuss when his wife was shut out by mistake.' The *Observer* ran a short diary story, pointing out that Mellor of all people should have known that the Opera House could not afford idle flunkies. Mellor was furious and demanded apologies from Forman, from me, from Gillian. The Secretary of State, apparently, never lost his temper. It was, of course, a breach of his privacy, though he was there as Secretary of State. We wrote grovelling apologies, which were not acknowledged. Moni, Lady Forman, personally took flowers to Judith Mellor. Later, in Kyoto, a British Council officer told me of Mellor's tantrums at being seated less than ideally at a concert, and then at the officer's failure to secure a last-minute seat for him on the bullet train to Tokyo (fully booked) after a severe storm had cancelled all trains for a day. Mellor had a short fuse; his privacy, and his marriage, would soon be blown apart by the tabloid press, ending his tenure as Minister of Fun, and his political career. Whatever the provocation, bad blood between General Director and Secretary of State was unfortunate for the ROH.

Angus Stirling, twelve years on the Board, and Chairman of the Friends of Covent Garden, had succeeded John Sainsbury as Chairman. After Sainsbury's abrasive style had failed to deliver increased funding, the Board turned to the diplomatic skills of an ex-Arts Council officer; he had been Deputy Secretary-General in palmier days. Angus, a tall

THE LAURENCE OLIVIER AWARDS 1993

Outstanding Achievement in Opera
Edward Downes: *The Fiery Angel* and *Stiffelio*
Bernard Haitink: *Die Frau ohne Schatten*
Philip Langridge: *Death in Venice*
Julia Varaday: *Der Fliegende Holländer*

Best New Opera Production
Death in Venice
Der Fliegende Holländer
Stiffelio
The Fiery Angel

daddy-longlegs of a man, is diligent, fair minded, clear thinking, given to putting his view, lucidly and persuasively, on paper. He basked in our success on the stage; in 1992 we won Olivier and Evening Standard Awards for opera and ballet. But Angus was very worried about the financial picture, and with reason. Whatever Mellor said to him, Angus must certainly have thought about firing me and canvassed the Board. Should my contract be renewed? Denis Forman was one who pointed out that the Board had backed me, all the way. They continued to do so.

The House had been for years inured to an annual deficit. The seasons 1983/84, following Priestley's award, 1988/89 and 1990/91 were exceptions in which we managed to avoid one. In the past, a discreet approach, Chairman to Chairman at the Arts Council, or to the Arts Minister, or even directly to the Treasury, had usually identified a sum, in a back pocket somewhere, which could tide the House over. Those days were finished; a nexus had snapped. We had no reserves whatever and only limited borrowing powers. At £3.6 million, the deficit was a weighty burden to carry forward. Things were coming to a head.

In July, back from Tokyo with the opera company, I saw the start of a strong Royal Ballet season at Covent Garden. I attended, at Hampton Court, a celebration of our bankers Coutts' tercentenary; I showed Hayden Phillips, Permanent Secretary at the Department of National Heritage, over the stage, and briefed him on our situation and on our development plans. And, at Glyndebourne, I attended the last performance in the old theatre. Fireworks on the lawn. There I sensed again the fierceness of Cabinet hostility to Europe. With my dinner jacket, I was wearing, for the hell of it, a cummerbund and bow tie in the EC colours, blue with gold stars. Norman Lamont, Chancellor of the Exchequer, snarled at me, 'Why are you wearing that disgusting thing?' 'I am wearing it, Norman,' I said, 'to mark the United Kingdom's assumption of the Presidency of the European Commission.' 'It is in terrible taste,' he said. He was, I guess now, under some strain; Black Wednesday was two months away, and Europe rankled.

Leaving behind the remaining midsummer evenings of ballet, I went to Suffolk. Festivals at Salzburg, Bayreuth, Edinburgh – not exactly a holiday – lay ahead of me. I walked and rested, leaving Angus to greet the Queen Mother when she came to *La Bayadère* – Asylmuratova, Mukhamedov, Bussell – on her birthday. One languid summery day, Angus rang. Price Waterhouse had been in touch; they had found something very nasty, perhaps fraud, in one of the production departments. Early one morning at the end of the week, I heard the worst from Ian Beesley. A valued colleague had been paying out cash against forged receipts. After our own investigation, she had to go. In grim mood, Gillian and I set off on the festival circuit.

In Salzburg we took Ann Murray and Philip Langridge, who were singing respectively in *La clemenza di Tito* and *Moses und Aron*, to supper at the Goldener Hirsch; the restaurant changed our table to a better position when they saw our guests. The bill was horrendous; I could not possibly charge it to the ROH. We drove to Bayreuth; *Götterdämmerung* and *Der fliegende Holländer*. We drove back to Salzburg. On Sunday evening, Bob Tear came to take us out to supper, in an ancient tavern in the Steingasse, past the municipal brothel. Tom Allen came too, on a bike. We had ham and eggs, and the yellow, fermented grape juice called pre-Heuriger. The bill for four was less than £20.

At Tomaselli's Café, we bumped into Isaiah Berlin. 'Have you seen the English papers? Don't look. You won't like them.' At the kiosk opposite we bought the *Guardian* and the *Sunday Times*. Both had leaked and, as it later turned out, exaggerated accounts of Warnock's findings, ferociously critical of ROH management. They made sickening reading. One member of the inquiry, unnamed, was quoted: 'They could not run a girls' school choir.' Brian Ivory was in Salzburg. I saw him at the Österreichischer Hof. The Report would be critical, he said, 'but nothing in the paper was accurate or an actual quote from it'. Whoever leaked, or briefed, did harm and hurt. We went home and waited.

In September, both Warnock's Report and Price Waterhouse's were in our hands. Warnock suggested that the House faced an unprecedented crisis, whose key elements were 'a building crisis', 'a financial crisis' and a concern over 'quality of management'. There was 'an inadequacy of management, both executive and non-executive'. This broad charge, they went on, reflected a deep-seated problem; 'it would be simplistic and wrong to lay responsibility for it at the door of the General Director, who has clearly had to fight many battles on many sides'. It was Warnock's view that 'responsibility should be borne by the Board, senior ROH management, and to a lesser degree by the Arts Council itself'. This scattergun approach to blame bore the mark either of internal debate, or of reluctant acknowledgement that the House was in a peculiarly difficult position. Warnock found that the House was repertory-led – no surprise to me – and ought not to be. Instead of repertory being planned three years ahead, and final budgeting not completed till the month before a new financial year began, Warnock insisted that all planning should fit within fixed, cash-limited financial envelopes from the outset.

Warnock argued, as would Price Waterhouse, that the House was being run at too energetic a pace; there were, above all, too many new productions. Ambition should be lowered; in opera, four new productions a year should be the maximum. The House could then revert, Warnock thought, to the admirable calm of the period that preceded my arrival. What this ignored was immense; the end of John Tooley's era, also attended by deficit, had been years of dearth and artistic doldrums. We needed to recover. But Warnock insisted we should find equilibrium at a lower level of activity. The ROH board had concerns about the prices we charged. Warnock washed its hands; we must live with them. The Report made no suggestion that funds should be found to help reduce them – what we had principally hoped for. There was criticism of our personnel procedures: the absence of job descriptions and annual reports on management performance. We were urged to renegotiate house union agreements. Indeed, this had force. We had only one senior executive in Personnel, my wise and diligent colleague Richard Wright; he had charge of industrial relations too, itself more than a full-time job. The Report recommended that we should get no more money till we had, expensively, improved our personnel practice. One new executive's salary and a secretary might be worth half a point on the orchestra's wage bill; if you can afford that, the orchestra might say, you can afford our claim. However, we prepared to do as we were told. Warnock advised a move to full in-dependence for Birmingham Royal Ballet, which we had already envisaged. It recommended that the Royal Ballet should no longer tour the UK at full strength as a condition of funding. We eagerly accepted. The Birmingham company did that more economically.

Warnock and her colleagues made one sweeping recommendation: since they could not see how we could afford it, we should scrap plans for the redevelopment. This ill-judged pronunciamento delivered them into our hands. It was true that, at that point, no one could see clearly how to find all the funds we needed. Promised private funding, and property value to be realized on site, did not together add up to sufficient to complete the scheme. But a new government, John Major's, with a new mandate, was looking at the possibility of a National Lottery, urged on by its advocates. And we knew, and Warnock noted, that the House had to close very soon, or be shut down as unsafe; running repairs to the fabric and rewiring would cost £25 million. Did the Arts Council really want to pay that bill? We also knew that the House's principal supporters, our former Chairman, now Lord Sainsbury of Preston Candover, and Mrs Vivien Duffield, had pledged substantial sums towards a redevelopment, provided those sums were, somehow, matched from public funds; we would not rest till those matching funds were found. No one on the Board was ready to abort a scheme nurtured over twenty years. It turned out that Dennis Stevenson, drafted in to tackle this area of Warnock's inquiry, had spoken neither to Sir Kit McMahon, Chairman of the Development Board, nor to John Sainsbury, our principal donor.

The recommendation to abort development was immediately a dead letter. Much else of Warnock fell with it. The *coup de grâce* was admin-istered at the Arts Council when Mary Warnock presented her findings. There had been separate Arts Council appraisals of each of the companies. 'All the same, had she not noticed', a member asked, 'the vast improvement in the work of the House of recent years? Why did not her Report take proper note of the quality of artistic achievement?' 'We did not see our-selves', she replied, 'as qualified to be critics. So we said nothing.' Some Council members never came to the House; the questioner came often. He was Peter Gummer, and he determined at that moment to take up our cause as an intermediary with his colleagues. The Warnock Report lacked context; it showed little knowledge of our past, offered no positive track for the future. But its reproaches did prod us into internal change.

Price Waterhouse was another kettle of fish. In precise findings, they pointed out courses of action which should save us money. First of all, like Warnock, they urged we renegotiate the stage agreement. I had shied away from this, preferring to postpone it till closure; a new agreement to exploit new stage machinery in a new House. With closure scheduled for summer 1993 or 1995, this was perhaps defensible; if, as began to seem likely, closure would not now come till 1997, there was no case for delay. The other principal Price Waterhouse recommendation was simply to reduce overtime. This, too, given our parlous finances, I had to accept. Cutting Sunday technicals would mean fewer new productions and skimped preparation for revivals. Quality would suffer. Retrenchment, I wrote to the Board, has a price:

> We shall rigorously move to find economies, and to set up and implement systems which make economy more easily attainable. I would wish to eliminate waste wherever it is detected. But the Board should be under no illusion; what is being proposed, and what our financial plight dictates we must accept, is, regrettably, a reduction in the quality of what we do. With the exception of payments resulting from the framing of the stage agreement, virtually all the economies proposed to us will affect directly rehearsal and performance. Given the postponement of closure from 1992, when I arrived, to 1997 now, it is obviously sensible to renegotiate the stage agreement forthwith. I should have preferred to wait till closure and a new stage technology allowed us to tear up the current deal, and start again. Wapping made a new deal in print possible. But we cannot wait.
>
> In achieving other economies we shall try at all costs to avoid denying the possibility of excellence in our work. Warnock suggests longer runs of fewer, more popular pieces, Price Waterhouse a reduction of overtime costs and earnings; less emphasis on quality in some aspects of our work; more insistence on savings within tight budgets. Management's role is to say 'no' to excess, at all times. Well yes, but the trouble is that anyone who is any good in the arts wants to do the very best that can be done always, and will not easily settle for less. If directors, designers, conductors, choreographers are forced to, everyone's spirits sink.
>
> The House I came to in 1987/88 was dispirited. Our work was underfunded, under-budgeted, under-rehearsed, drab and unexciting.

Managers earned less than men. The then technical director was paid £20,000 a year.

I set out, with the Board's encouragement, to make this House the best in the world (see my policy papers on opera and ballet), and, by achieving excellence, to enable us to charge the prices, attract the sponsorship, claim the funding that would pay for it.

We have just about achieved that quality I sought, though we could always do better. We have, in two of my four years, failed, by a depressing margin, to pay for it.

And, of course, that quest for excellence has added to our cost-base.

We hired a night gang to service morning rehearsals; added dancers to the strength of an injury-hit SWRB; encouraged the Royal Ballet to slough off, and, if necessary, pay off fading principals, engage guest stars, liven up repertory; in opera, we engaged the great conductors, and cast good singers in all the roles; we widened the repertory, giving subscribers a chance to hear pieces they had long dreamed of hearing; we embarked on an ambitious – it can now be seen too ambitious – programme of new productions; we said yes to additional technical or orchestral rehearsals when they were needed; we found the funds to winkle out failing musicians from the orchestra (some inadequacies remain), and to make redundant eighteen ineffective choristers; we hired the best chorus director in Britain; we installed surtitling equipment and employed the staff to use it; we organized 'In Focus' events, and budgeted, albeit sparingly, to increase educational activities; we strengthened box-office and marketing, and engaged the catering staff to serve at new, profitable, sales points, e.g. in the bars.

In brief, we sought to improve our service to the public. My post-bag and our complaints monitoring system tell me that we have done so.

Charging the prices we do, dependent on box-office and private subvention to raise 60 per cent of our income, we should have been failing in our duty had we not attempted to give of our best at all times. The trick, for the future, is to cut back without destroying all that has been achieved.

In that spirit, I accept that cut-backs there must be.

I told the staff of harsh economies ahead. I advised the Board that I set a target of seventy, at a pinch fifty, job losses. I promised also to look at other options; in September 1992, the 'opera without scenery' scenario had already been tried. After Luciano Pavarotti, in fine form, had opened the opera season in *Tosca*, we had looked forward to Amanda Roocroft and Anne Sofie von Otter in *I Capuleti e i Montecchi*. On the afternoon of the first performance, a bomb scare forced us to empty the auditorium for some hours. The stage was not set. We gave the piece as a concert; very fine, but we could not do that every night.

The Board, after some discussion, renewed my contract. At my sixtieth birthday party at the end of September, at Flowers East in Hackney, Jocelyn Stevens, Vivien Duffield's partner, made a speech in which he darkly denounced 'snakes in the grass' who wished me harm. One or two present blushed. Back at work, performances reminded me of what I was there for; a good evening in the theatre took my mind off money troubles. They were there again on the desk next morning. This was a particularly grisly time. The nadir came when I went to the Department of National Heritage to a meeting chaired most civilly by the Permanent Secretary, Hayden Phillips, to explain how we proposed to try to dig ourselves out of the pit. A fellow Board member, Bamber Gascoigne, accompanied me. At one point he brashly informed the meeting that all was now bound to be well, because from now on Jeremy would be kept on a short leash, and not allowed to act on his own initiative. Those present did not know where to look. How I contained myself, I do not know. Afterwards, I told the Chairman and my colleague, by telephone and letter, what I thought of this conduct. Bamber apologized. Eventually, he and I made it up.

Could the ROH manage, under these new financial constraints? Perhaps because we had already begun to rein in, we managed very nicely. In the same fiscal year in which we underwent this agony, 1992/93, we balanced the books, again; the third time now, in five years, though when we succeeded we just scraped home and when we failed the loss was sizeable.

For the 1993/94 fiscal year, I reduced the cost base by cutting new productions and the cash budget for productions generally. We held the guest artists' budget, house overheads and expenses, all overtime, salaries and wages at 1992/93 levels. There had been a pay pause from September 1992. It would be necessary, if the wage bill for 1993/94 were to be held to the previous year's level, both to restrict overtime, that is earnings, and to identify jobs we could lose. Many of these posts were needed. Losing them might save £1.2 million in revenue, but would cost us £0.5 million in redundancy payments. But whatever agony was involved, I preferred this course to a total ban on new productions, and a season without any artistic challenge; or, worse, to reduced numbers of performances and seasonal opera only.

For our work in calendar 1992 we earned all eight nominations in opera for the Olivier Awards; four for best production, four for outstanding achievement. The Chairman wrote promptly to congratulate me. He also, at the end of the fiscal year, paid tribute to our stewardship. We had earned, by sacrifice all round, a tidy operating surplus. This was in a year in which Arts Council subsidy to the Royal Opera fell to a startling 26.7 per cent of income; the rest was earned or secured by us. The Chairman, in his Annual Report, also referred to a reduction we had been able to make to our accumulated deficit through 'an exceptionally generous private benefaction of £2.5 million (to be spread over three years)'.

Enter now a favourite character in the Opera House story: our exceptionally generous benefactor, Dr Stanley Ho OBE, Gr Cross OM, Chev Lég d'Hon. SPMP, D Soc Sc., C St J. Dr Ho has interests in Hong Kong and Macao. It was following a summer party at the Prime Minister's official weekend residence, Chequers, that Dr Ho first swam into our ken. Dr Ho was not at Chequers; Philip Harris was. Now Lord Harris of Peckham, Philip Harris is himself a generous benefactor of the arts and of medicine, and became Treasurer of the Conservative Party in 1993. On their business, he had been chasing up contributions in Hong Kong. There he discovered Dr Ho. He had given liberally to charity in Portugal and been decorated with every honour in the Portuguese government's gift. He had also made a modest donation to the British Conservative Party. Now he wished to make a substantial gift to 'a good cause' in the United Kingdom. But Dr Ho was not clear where most need was evident, or where such a donation might do him most good. Any suggestions? My understanding is that, when this was mentioned to him by Philip Harris, the Prime Minister, knowing our needs, and how unlikely it was that the Treasury would fund them, suggested that Dr Ho make his gift to the Opera House. At any rate, Philip Harris told Vivien Duffield that a gift was on offer. Eagerly we wooed Dr Ho. He confirmed his intention to give us £2.5 million over two and a half years. Avidly, I awaited the first instalment. After only the most delicate of reminders, the first cheque for £500,000 arrived. I was considerably cheered. With Dr Ho's help, we had a chance to clear the deficit; without it, none. In due course, at six-monthly intervals, four further cheques for £500,000 arrived. By such acts of almost random generosity was our fate determined.

In the aftermath of Warnock and Price Waterhouse, I lost two able colleagues. Philip Jones, Finance Director, and Richard Wright, Director of Administration, had both served the House loyally and well for a decade. Now, nearing retirement, they left. I acquiesced. I had always found them both pillars of strength. Philip Jones, with an able Chief Accountant, David Pilcher, under him, provided prompt, accurate information on income and expenditure on request. For every regular meeting of senior management, for the subsidiary and the Main Boards, he put the figures on the table. We knew how every hour of overtime was incurred, what the amphitheatre took last night, how many ice-creams we sold. We never succeeded in modelling a total costing system that would instantly predict, three years ahead, the impact of changing *La bohème* to *Butterfly*. But Philip Jones could tell me and the Board anything we needed to know about the present, and very patient in explaining it he was too. In mid-1997, people who should have known better suggested that the House lacked basic financial information. This was irresponsible, untrue and defamatory of capable executives. It may have reflected the difficulty in predicting costs and income during the uncertainties of closure. It certainly did not apply in my time. Audited accounts testify the opposite.

I was sorry to lose Philip Jones, and sorry, too, to lose Richard Wright. Richard bore the brunt of ROH industrial relations for a decade; he was respected by all because he was straight and fair. Philip Jones put his head round the door of my office daily; we were not out of the wood, was the invariable message, only in another part of the forest. Ours was a labour of Sisyphus; every year we rolled the rock up the hill; at the start of each new year it had rolled back again. The arts in Britain owe much to Philip Jones and Richard Wright, and their like.

Clive Timms, ex-BBC, ex-ITN, succeeded Philip Jones; he would find the going even tougher than he must have expected. Mike Morris, also ex-ITN, who came in for Richard Wright, brought a new energy both to personnel matters and to the industrial-relations front. Where Richard strove, Mike succeeded.

For each of the three years after the Warnock Report, without too blatantly lowering standards, we earned an operating surplus on the current account. This had never happened before at Covent Garden. In cold print it seems something to write home about. It provoked little celebration at the time. The press never reported it with any prominence;

the BBC TV series *The House*, which I authorized and which drew such large audiences, managed not to report it at all. The point was not of interest to the programme-makers. I never met anyone who viewed *The House* who had grasped that we achieved a surplus in the year we gave the cameras house-room. Docu-soap has other fish to fry.

I took too little satisfaction from our success because I knew well how it was achieved. We secured high paid attendance, far higher than that of ENO and most of the West End. But, in the lower part of the House, we were charging steep prices; they helped keep us viable at some social cost. And the staff made real sacrifices; in one two-year span their earnings rose by 30 per cent less than the inflation rate. Fifty staff members, some of whom we could ill spare, lost their jobs. There would have been more to spend on wages if we had spent even less on production. But the point of our being there was to do work of excellence; everything else I saw as a means to that end. Coping with the endemic deficit was like a game of pass the parcel: you could hand it to the public in ticket prices, or to the staff in wage cuts and job losses, but it would not go away.

Itself starved of funds, the Arts Council was concerned neither with the prices we charged nor with the wages we paid – nor even, at the top level, with the quality of our work. Interested, it seemed to us, only in the financial outcome, the Arts Council reduced itself to the role of 'accounting officer', required to ensure that clients tread the line government set. A partner in the making and dissemination of the arts in Britain ceased to exist. Their grant to us eroded each year. Because our work appealed, box-office remained high, nudging upwards to the £19 million mark. The third leg of the tripod on which we balanced so precariously was private funding. If that collapsed, we would be in real trouble.

8

ON POINTE

Ballet 1991-1995

'Did you see that?' We were standing in the opposite prompt corner watching the curtain calls after the first night of the Royal Ballet's new *Don Quixote* in April 1993. The audience was vigorously applauding Irek Mukhamedov and Viviana Durante as the virtuosic young lovers. Anthony Dowell was letting Monica Mason, his Assistant Director, know that for him the achievement of the evening was a newcomer's. In her first important solo role, the young Sarah Wildor as Amour, in white tutu, her hair crowned with a sort of bathing cap, had bobbed her way through the ranks with such dainty precision and aplomb, effortlessly commanding the stage, that he knew at once the company had another ballerina who could in time dance anything he asked her to. To the roster of Lesley Collier and Fiona Chadwick, Darcey Bussell and Viviana Durante, Deborah Bull, Leanne Benjamin, Nicola Tranah and Principal Guest Artist Sylvie Guillem, he could now, very shortly, add the name of Sarah Wildor. She would not disappoint; indeed no one in the company better combined technical facility and feeling than Wildor: panache and pathos were equally hers. Anthony Dowell has an unerring eye for a dancer's abilities, and showed skill and judgement in bringing them on at the right pace. In his time – and he has been Director of the Royal Ballet for over a decade – the standard of dance in the company consistently improved. For that alone, Anthony Dowell well deserved his knighthood.

He found, though, that the recession made repertory planning difficult. The pressure was for longer runs of fewer pieces; that meant familiar three-acters, rather than the uncertain chemistry of the triple bill. The company gave plenty of performances, if you counted those given abroad, but the number of different programmes gave cause for concern. Dowell wanted twelve to fourteen programmes a season, including more new work. But with a company of limited size and studios split between Barons Court and Covent Garden his options, as Warnock acknowledged, were always limited. The opera company could mount a new production by hiring in *ad hoc* a new creative team; the ballet company worked always from within its own resources. One group of dancers created everything new we performed.

We put on fine things. In autumn 1991, David Bintley, fertile as ever, gave us a new three-act ballet, *Cyrano de Bergerac*, with a demanding lead role for Stephen Jefferies. There was plenty to look at in Rostand's Paris, and in the wars. Hayden Griffin's sets caught the eye, held the stage. Did the dancing? At the end, Cyrano reveals that the love he professed to Roxane on another's behalf was his love for her. But by then Cyrano is too old and frail to dance his feelings out. Could a young Cyrano have returned for the denouement? In ballet it happens often enough. Bintley was content to leave the final scene as he had made it. His next piece, *Tombeaux*, designed by Jasper Conran, was measured, classical, more abstract; dance came first.

Urged on to the new, and looking for choreographic energy abroad, Anthony Dowell invited William Forsythe, an American directing the Frankfurt Ballet, to work with us, and make a new work for Covent Garden. Forsythe's personal circumstances – his wife was dying – made that impossible, but he let us use a strong piece of his, *In the Middle Somewhat Elevated*. This explosion of physical virtuosity was seized on with alacrity by the company's strongest dancers, much admired by Forsythe: Guillem, Bull and Bussell, Cope, Trevitt and Kumakawa hurled themselves about the stage in jagged bursts of electrifying energy. I never knew what the title meant. I always knew it signalled a breakthrough for the company. A new audience, sometimes skipping earlier works in the programme, came and, revelling in it, came again. I marvelled that the dancers who did it such justice could return so easily to the classical restraint of Petipa and Ashton, *The Sleeping Beauty* and *The Dream*.

Kenneth MacMillan was not going to be upstaged by William Forsythe, or by anyone else. In *Romeo and Juliet*, in *Manon* and *Mayerling*, songs of love and death, he had shown how physical passion could express itself in great romantic *pas de deux*, expanding, without bursting, the bounds of classical form. Guillem's frenzied sexual ecstasy as Manon, Wildor's physical awakening as Juliet are indelible memories. Since his serious heart attack in Australia Kenneth had given us *The Prince of the Pagodas*, and *Winter Dreams*; now, in 1992, he created *The Judas Tree*. His wife Deborah heard a work by the Bombay-born British composer Brian Elias, and brought him to meet Kenneth. He told Elias roughly what his ballet would be about, and what length, and commissioned him to write the music. Elias's music for *The Judas Tree* is harsh, dissonant, pulsing. We paid for a recording, and MacMillan choreographed to a tape. *The Judas Tree* is set in a derelict Docklands, a marvellous evocation by Jock McFadyen; Canary Wharf, visible from the windows of my home in Bermondsey, is in the distance. The ballet is a brutal tale of sex, gang rape, betrayal, suicide. Racing across the evening, the company gave it everything; Irek Mukhamedov, Viviana Durante, Michael Nunn and others, were superb. *The Judas Tree*, though not for the faint-hearted, was a formidable piece of work, vibrant, uncompromising. It was televised with great success, directed by Ross McGibbon, himself a former Royal Ballet dancer, and won an Emmy. But it was to be MacMillan's last ballet.

In the late autumn of 1992, the Royal Ballet mounted a major revival of *Mayerling*, the story of Crown Prince Rudolf's forbidden love for Mary Vetsera and their eventual joint suicide. Irek Mukhamedov, given a new lease of dancing life by MacMillan's choreography, would dance Rudolf. Kenneth had made minor changes, tightening the piece. In the Opera House his seat was across the aisle from mine. On the first night, I moved across before the work started to touch his arm, and wish him luck. He thanked me, smiled back. In the first interval, I saw him talking to someone. In the third act, he was not in his seat. Someone plucked me by the sleeve, 'Come quickly.' In a corridor to the dressing rooms, Kenneth was lying, face down, arms and legs sprawled as in a twisted cross. He did not move. He had lain there for some time – a security man had found him. First aid had been attempted and an ambulance sent for. He was dead. Deborah was holding him in her arms, not wanting to let go. Monica Mason, a colleague and dear friend, was there beside her. Upstairs, on stage, *Mayerling* was nearing its end. We suggested to Deborah that she go back to Wandsworth to break the news to their daughter, Charlotte. I now see that someone else could have gone.

Deborah deeply regretted leaving Kenneth; she would have preferred to go with his body in the ambulance to the hospital, but she went home to tell Charlotte and fetch her to see her father.

Without much hesitation, I decided the audience should be told at curtain down. The word was out backstage that something terrible had happened. Even if it were still only rumour, the cast were shaken, and could not take their bows smiling. Besides, it would be obscene, it seemed to me, to rejoice with Kenneth dead. And the audience, in the presence of greatness, was entitled to know that that evening, while they were there, an era in the story of dance had ended. The curtain came down at the end of *Mayerling*. It rose again to show the cast on stage, Irek Mukhamedov fighting back tears. I said: 'It is with deep sadness, and in shock, that I have to tell you that the great master whose work we have seen performed here tonight, Kenneth MacMillan, has, during the performance, suffered a heart attack, and died. I ask you to stand, and to leave the theatre quietly.' Solemnly, without a word spoken, the auditorium emptied.

What I had done was wrong, even illegal. You may not say that someone is dead until a doctor has pronounced him so. The proper form is to say, 'He has been taken to hospital.' Indeed, ambulances are not supposed to carry the dead: if one is sent for, it is on the presumption that the person to be conveyed in it still lives. And Deborah, I think, would rather I had not given the news. But I believe that everyone there was entitled to know then that in their presence a great spirit had departed, rather than reading the news of his death the next day.

Kenneth MacMillan was irreplaceable. Anthony Dowell and I quickly agreed not to replace him, not even with David Bintley. He had very strong claims on the post of Principal Choreographer, but we decided against. Anthony had not been over the moon about two of Bintley's recent works for the Royal Ballet, *Planets* and now *Cyrano*. Nor, really, had others. If he had taken on the role, there would still have been, given the company's other repertory and the shortage of slots, too few new opportunities for him. Bintley resented the slight, and soon moved on, finding employment very easily elsewhere. If Anthony had urged appointing him, I would not have resisted, but I had my own agenda for David Bintley. Peter Wright was now well past the Royal Opera House's agreed retiring age. I wanted to see David Bintley, choreographer and showman, succeed him and take charge of the Birmingham Royal Ballet. There would not be too long to wait.

The show went on. For Christmas we had a special treat for children of all ages: *Tales of Beatrix Potter*. In 1971, Frederick Ashton had contrived a film ballet using Mrs Tiggy-Winkle, Jemima Puddleduck and other Beatrix Potter characters. The film was much enjoyed. Some felt we should leave it at that, others that it could be revised and made into a staged ballet. This would mean dancers wearing the heaviest of costumes as pigs, mice, ducks and other, cuddly and uncuddly, feathered and furry beasties, and dancing, twice daily, the testing roles which Ashton had devised for the one off film. (While filming, of course, the dancers could rest between takes and re-takes.) Other companies might have turned up their noses at *Tales of Beatrix Potter*. Some critics did. But I told Anthony Dowell to bar nothing that family audiences would enjoy. If he wanted to do it, I would back him. As my old friend Seamus Kelly, drama critic and diarist of the *Irish Times*, used to remark, there was not a dry seat in the house.

The Director's key function is the choice of dancers and of repertory; the arrangement of a season's, and of an evening's, programme. We know him by the pieces he decides to put on; the choreographers he chooses to work with; the designers he assigns to new productions of works already made. Now, looking for a new crowd-pleaser which would provide multiple opportunities for the company, as any Director must, Dowell brought in Baryshnikov's version of Petipa's *Don Quixote*, as given by ABT. He would follow that with a remake of the Royal Ballet's calling-card piece, for which it was known and loved in London and New York, *The Sleeping Beauty*. He had entrusted *Beauty* to Maria Bjornson to design. For *Don Quixote*, he turned to a new designer for ballet, Mark Thompson, who had just done, fresh as paint, a bright and sunny *Il viaggio a Rheims* for the opera. Thompson responded to the good humour in *Don Quixote*, and to its Spanishness, with reds and blacks for the peasants – you could smell oranges, onions and garlic – and, in a central dream sequence, white, with headdresses of tiny toy windmills for the corps. The critics, who never seemed to me to possess much sense of humour, were not amused. Earlier, showing him the model in the hope that the Linbury Trust might sponsor the production, I found John Sainsbury objecting to the scale of the single wine-barrel which, standing for ever so many little barrels, Thompson had hung huge and high on the tavern's wall. John could not see why it needed to be so big. I thought this view a shade literal, and said so; he would not budge. Then, on the night, the critics complained that, against the dark colouring of costume and scenery, the dancers' limbs could not easily be seen. Was this a point of substance? I could see well enough, looking down from my seat in the Grand Tier. Was it harder from theirs? The displays in the bodega were set, admittedly, against a crowded rear wall. Story ballets are not often set in uncluttered abstraction. Perhaps they should be. At least one critic had decided in advance that what he was going to see would be the wrong version of *Don Quixote*; it ought not to be Baryshnikov's for ABT, but Nureyev's for Paris Opera Ballet, more elaborate, and, I guess, much more expensive. In any case, this *Don Quixote* was stylish and touching. It was danced dazzlingly. The public loved it.

Behind some antagonism to what Dowell did was a concern to keep the past, and not to change it. The argument was similar to that rumbling on, occasionally violently, over styles of opera production. Opera-lovers wanted everything to stay as Visconti and Zeffirelli had left it; balletomanes fervently wished that Oliver Messel were with us still. They had an almost Platonic, idealized view of how ballet's classics should look. No one complained at seeing William Forsythe's work on a bare stage, though they may have loathed the work itself. But they did not want to see a new look for Petipa; the old familiar one – wispy, filmy, feather-light tracery – against which the dancer, well lit, easily stood out, would always do. Some designers still practise that successfully. Anthony Dowell's preferences were bolder. I approved.

The Sleeping Beauty is the grandest ballet in the repertory. With *Phantom of the Opera* behind her, Maria Bjornson seized her chance. Her sets were huge. They showed the Royal Palace, smitten by the wicked Fairy's curse, curved over at a dramatic angle to the universe. The magic of the transformation scene awoke a grander and more elaborate court than normal to new life. This brought gasps of pleasure and admiration. Doubters questioned the scenery's grand scale, claiming it dwarfed the dancers. It did not for me, or for audiences in their tens of thousands.

This was the most expensive production of my time at the ROH; not just because of the sets, but the costumes also. In opera one ample cloak covers very different singers, from a Luciano Pavarotti to a Dennis O'Neill. Wardrobe simply takes it in, or lets it out. In ballet, every millimetre counts. Aurora's costume, and that of every other dancer, must fit like another skin; one wrinkle spoils the effect. No help for it, therefore: each Aurora has to have a costume made for her, and for her alone. And there will be six Auroras, and six Florimunds, and six Lilac Fairies. To sustain long runs of a piece like *Beauty*, as the public insist we do, and to give opportunity to dancers claiming a role, we needed several casts. So the initial cost of a new production of *Swan Lake* or *Sleeping Beauty* strains the budget. Yet Bjornson's *Sleeping Beauty* has recouped its cost in the theatre over and over. We had prepared it in good time, but could not afford to perform it in the 1992/93 fiscal year. Each twelve months was separate. Taking in the cost under the accounting convention we followed would have forced us into deficit. We postponed *The Sleeping Beauty* just over the border-line into the next financial year, but in April the company would tour the United States. The world première of the Royal Ballet's most important new production for years was to be given at the Kennedy Center in Washington DC.

We performed *The Sleeping Beauty* in the presence of the President of the United States, Bill Clinton, the First Lady, Hillary Rodham Clinton and, a genuine ballet fan, their daughter Chelsea. Princess Margaret was there too. The show was admired; the company did well, though Darcey Bussell was a little below her radiant best as Aurora. (Viviana Durante, in performances in New York in the same role, held the solo unsupported balances in the Rose Adagio longer and more steadily than anyone I have ever seen.) Fiona Chadwick danced the Lilac Fairy, who protects Aurora from ill-wishers and fatal hurt. Backstage afterwards, going down the line with the Chair of the Ballet Board, Tessa Blackstone, I introduced Fiona to Clinton: 'Mr President, this is Fiona Chadwick, who danced the Lilac Fairy. She made sure Aurora came to no harm.' He turned to the press: 'There you are boys, just what I need – a Lilac Fairy.' He never found one.

Sylvie Guillem would make a formidable presidential bodyguard. She has muscle. She reminded me of the remark Philip Hope-Wallace over-heard in the Covent Garden stalls: 'Remember, she could kill a man with a blow of that leg.' In Forsythe's *Herman Schmerman*, Guillem was paired with Adam Cooper. They gave an exhilarating display: two wilfully free spirits, coming together and parting, partners and individuals at once. Guillem left the stage briefly, and returned wearing a skimpy yellow skirt over her leotard. A minute or two later, Cooper exited also, and re-entered in an identical skirt – no one quite knew why. *Herman Schmerman* pulled in its own ecstatic following. Adam Cooper emanated the sweet scent of dangerous sexuality that he carried as the lead swan in Matthew Bourne's all-male *Swan Lake*, bowling over men and women alike.

Rehearsing 'Sleeping Beauty' ...
Waiting to go on ..
Back with 11, Steve!
My left shoe's too small ..
Come in on the TABS, John ..
Arthur - TRIM THE GAUZES!
DAILY

Admiring Glen Tetley's work, Dowell invited him to stage *La Ronde* at Covent Garden. This schnitzel should have sizzled, but did not. Korngold's precocious score – he wrote it when he was only fifteen – seemed over-inflated. Perhaps the piece is too. Next season, 1994/95, we had another Forsythe for macho dancers, male and female, *First Text* and *Step Text*. Ashton's *Daphnis and Chloë* was given with deft new sets by Martyn Bainbridge, and with the Royal Opera chorus as well as the orchestra under Haitink. Injury spoiled the effect Dowell sought; Sarah Wildor could not get on in the lead role. We also saw two new pieces by Ashley Page: *Fearful Symmetries* had a John Adams score and a demanding role for Mukhamedov. *Ebony Concerto* had music by Duke Ellington. Both had vivid and effective sets by Anthony MacDonald. With these two ballets, Ashley Page staked a claim to be, one day, the company's resident choreographer.

The Sleeping Beauty was very successfully staged, in the autumn of 1994, at Covent Garden. Ballet paid attendances were up to 88 per cent in 1993/94 and in 1994/95 86 per cent across 107 performances – touring took the total to 170. Anthony Dowell could rest on laurels. In his statement in the 1994/95 Annual Report, cheekily he pointed out that the Royal Ballet was the only ROH company to have exceeded its target income. No one gave him a large cigar, or offered to increase the company's grant.

It is the companies' Directors who should take the credit for their achievements in my time: Anthony Dowell; Peter Wright; David Bintley; Paul Findlay and Nicholas Payne. I was consulted on major repertory, I asked that they accommodate an occasional whim of my own, but I delegated to them virtually every other question of what to do and who should do it. Except as a backstop, in dire emergency, I did not spend my time soothing dancers' or singers' anxious brows, or calming artistic temperaments. When Maria Almeida and her husband Jonathan Cope both decided to leave the Royal Ballet at the same time – she unhappy and perhaps anorexic, he, we were told, suffering agony at the endless battering his shins were taking – I did, over a cup of tea, urge him to come back one day. So repeatedly did Anthony Dowell. After a year, good sense and our plea prevailed. Jonathan Cope is our great *danseur noble*, Maria Almeida a lost star.

Each Director operated within budgetary parameters laid down by me, and agreed by the Main Board. Over a year, these were never – I mean never – exceeded. Each Director, with his colleagues, ran each company himself. This was the devolution Priestley had proposed in 1983. No one took more effective charge than Peter Wright in Birmingham. In budgeting, with Christopher Nourse or Derek Purnell beside him, he was scrupulously responsible. Subject to that, in repertory he was entirely his own master, deciding what his company was suited to, knowing what bold *mélange* would keep the ballet world's eye on Birmingham. Peter Wright unerringly mixed old and new. He commissioned new work from promising beginners, Oliver Hindle and Matthew Hart. He prised jewels from the Balanchine estate, which spunky ladies who had worshipped 'Mr B' drove into BRB's consciousness, and on to the stage. He revived, flatly, Massine's *Le Tricorne*, costumes by Picasso – no garlic – and, very feelingly and truly, Ashton's *Enigma Variations*. To achieve this last, he enlisted Michael Somes to stage it, and Antoinette Sibley, Anthony Dowell and Deanne Bergsma, among others, to assist; they dug into their memories and passed on what they knew. Peter chose to do Agnes de Mille's *Fall River Legend* – 'Lizzie Borden took an axe and gave her mother forty whacks'. This had a great role for Marion Tait. It worked. He brought back from the dead, and from his own 1930s past, Kurt Joos's *The Green Table*, a satire on peace processes and cynical diplomacy, war looming. I remembered a picture of *The Green Table* among the League of Nations literature and Left Book Club volumes on a coffee table in my parents' home. A pre-war period piece came back to life. From David Bintley, Peter Wright obtained a new production of *Sylvia*, something of a romp, but with much virtuosic choreography; and in classical vein, a fine new piece, *Brahms/Handel Variations*.

Ballet, as Peter Wright understands better than any, should reflect a living past, as well as an urgent present. In that spirit, on 11 November 1993, Peter presented in Coventry Cathedral Ninette de Valois's *Job*, to the music of Ralph Vaughan Williams. Madam had always wanted to see *Job* given in a cathedral; it never had been before. Now Peter, in homage to her, managed to stage it. Michael O'Hare, high against Coventry's West Window, leaped Satan's part. *Job* shone like a candle in the dark, vindicating art and Old Testament religion.

I urged Peter, well past the Opera House's fixed retirement age, to step down and hand over to someone younger. A workaholic, constantly crisscrossing the globe to rehearse his own productions in Tokyo or Rio de Janeiro, he was finding BRB's touring pattern taxing. He could no longer, with undimmed enthusiasm, look forward to being with them in Sunderland or Southampton. A write-in campaign to keep him on tried to tell me otherwise, but I knew it was time for him to go.

When Peter Wright's retirement was announced, the post of Director of Birmingham Royal Ballet was advertised. The City of Birmingham and the Royal Ballet Governors were consulted, Pru Skene from the Arts Council and Antony Sargeant from Birmingham City Council were in attendance on the selection panel, chaired by the Chairman of the Ballet Board, Tessa Blackstone. The main competition came from Maina Gielgud, then Director of the Australian Ballet, who has since taken and given up charge of the Kongelige Ballet in Copenhagen, but the panel's unanimous choice was David Bintley. This was the outcome I wanted. David undertook to sustain the company's classical core repertory, to honour the heritage of Ashton and MacMillan, to supply new choreography of his own, but to leave space for others. He knew each company member's strength or weakness. And he knew what he wanted to do. In interview he was assured and decisive. I was as sure as I have ever been of anything that his was the right appointment, and was happy to know that the company would be in his keeping.

Ballet, more than any other art form, depends on memory, on the physical re-creation of poses, gestures, step sequences once struck. Until the invention of Benesh notation in the 1950s, and later of video, ballet steps went unrecorded; choreography was almost as ephemeral as if written on the wind. Only memory saved it. Michael Somes, on whom Frederick Ashton created leading roles, knew just how *Enigma* or *Symphonic Variations* should be done. So did Dowell and Sibley of *The Dream*, or, from New York, Pat Neary of Balanchine's *Serenade*. All companies should be shaken up from time to time, but the physical transmission of a living tradition through the directorship counts for more. At a farewell ceremony in the Crush Bar at the Royal Opera House, Peter Wright paid heartfelt tribute to Madam, Dame Ninette de Valois, sitting in front of him. Standing to one side, I told David Bintley my thought about the handing on of the grail, from one generation to another, the laying on of hands. He nodded. Regularly, he told me, he took tea with Madam, consulted her, kept in touch. De Valois, supported on leaving, came slowly towards us. I stepped forward. 'Madam,' I shouted in her ear, 'here's David Bintley.' 'Ah yes,' she said, 'my old chum.' She reached up her hand and placed it on him.

9

ON SONG

Opera 1991-1995

The German mezzo Waltraud Meier complained to the *New York Times* before her opening at the Met as Carmen in 1996 that no one paid attention to her interpretation of the role. She threatened to go home. The producer, Franco Zeffirelli, erupted: 'No one is interested in her performance. I cater for the Metropolitan's audience. They want spectacle; I provide it. They are not interested in Miss Meier's ideas about her character. She is in any case a German *Hausfrau*.' Nothing like this instructive tiff occurred at Covent Garden in my time.

The Zeffirelli *Carmen* was paid for by Walter Annenberg when he gave the Met $5 million for two new productions. They do things differently in New York. Over the years the late Mrs Donald D. Harrington, Sybil, gave the Met $26 million, and several productions. She would insist only that the opera she paid for be *Bohème*, or *Turandot*, or *Butterfly*, that Zeffirelli direct, and that every cent of her gift be visible on stage. The *Carmen* that Annenberg paid for had 350 in the cast, three horses and two donkeys. This made it more crowded than Nuria Espert's for us, and almost as busy as a famous show at the Paris Garnier when Grace Bumbry, making her début as Carmen, without rehearsal, looked vainly for the tenor through hordes of gypsies, soldiers and vendors offering oranges, postcards and cigars. In despair, she clutched at an extra's arm: '*Où, donc, est Don José?*' '*Suivez-moi, madame,*' he said, and led her through the maze. Alberto Vilar, the Met's new Maecenas, is determined to be their biggest patron ever, and is well on the way. He gave $2 million for

Zeffirelli's *La traviata* and told the *New Yorker*, 'I believe that this is the Met, the Met does lavish things, and the best person for lavish is Franco Zeffirelli.' Mr Vilar likes to see it all up on the stage. 'When the curtain opens, and the audience applauds like mad, that's what I like to see.'

Some of our new productions had adequate budgets, shared with other companies. A very few were expensive, £300,000–£400,000 say. None cost half as much as the *Ballo in maschera* that John Schlesinger did for Karajan at Salzburg, or Faggioni's production of the same opera for the Met.

We mounted a co-production with the Met. Britten's *Death in Venice* went from our stage to New York rather as it had done after its première in 1973. Colin Graham produced. A clever set projected Mariano Fortuny's photographs and John Piper's paintings. There was apt, admired, choreography by Kim Brandstrup; Giacomo Ciriaci, from the Royal Ballet School, danced Tadzio; Philip Langridge gave a moving Aschenbach; Steuart Bedford conducted. This was a marvellously realized show, which forced a re-evaluation of an underrated opera. It won golden opinions in London but, by the Met's rigorous standards, failed at the box-office in New York. *Death in Venice* is something of a rarity in a major house.

No opera of Prokofiev's had ever been given at Covent Garden before. Ted Downes, who reads Russian, is the composer's passionate advocate. He kept telling us this was a lack we should remedy, and he won the day. For Ted's fortieth anniversary at the Royal Opera House, we put on Prokofiev's *Fiery Angel*. This gave us a chance to employ as director David Freeman of Opera Factory. He went to St Petersburg (the city had by then reclaimed that name), spent time in the back streets, and came back enthused. He had found the Mariinsky Acrobatic Troupe. When the curtain rose, the acrobats, embodying the devils plaguing the protagonists, hung upside down, high up stage right, hooded like bats in a cave. Galina Gorchakova as Renata, Sergei Leiferkus as Ruprecht, Paata Burchuladze as The Inquisitor, gave powerful performances. Chorus and orchestra excelled. Ted Downes, and Prokofiev, had a deserved triumph. We put the acrobats up in the Strand Palace Hotel, at a special rate, full buffet breakfast included. They were unhappy. So was Burchuladze, who reported to me that they did not have enough to eat. 'But they have a daily subsistence allowance.' 'Yes, but they want to keep that and take it home.' We gave them vouchers for the staff canteen.

Luciano Pavarotti was supposed to appear for us that season in *La bohème*. We were keen to have him in almost anything. Luciano changed his mind about singing Rodolfo; he had some inhibitions about portraying Puccini's ardent young lover, though later he sang the role in Turin on the 100th anniversary of the première, with Mirella Freni as Mimì and his 86-year-old father as Parpignol the toy vendor. For us he proposed to sing Nemorino in *L'elisir d'amore*. Not keen, because he had recently sung it here, we conceded. We could use the revenue he would bring in. Late, he cancelled *L'elisir*. By good fortune we were able to engage not just Sumi Jo as Adina, but Alfredo Kraus as Nemorino. Alfredo was then well into his sixties, but sang with line and style and delicacy as if he were half the age. Alfredo Kraus resented his exclusion from the magic triangle of the three tenors. He had looked after his voice better than any of them. For the *Bohème*s we had lined up another cast to follow Pavarotti: Roberto Alagna and Angela Gheorghiu. This was the début pairing of two artists who hardly knew each other, and whom the public scarcely knew. There were no tantrums, no cancellations, just the voices and pleasant personalities of two ambitious young people in search of stardom. Those who heard them sing 'O soave fanciulla' at Covent Garden will not forget it.

Bel canto has been in short supply in Britain and worldwide in the last two decades; the right voices are scarce. We rented Bellini's *I Puritani* from Welsh National Opera. Daniele Gatti, a young Italian conductor we admired, agreed to show us what he could do in it. Gatti was recommended to us by his agent, Luciano Pavarotti's then wife Adua. Adua

No! We are not waiting for Domingo – This is the queue for the Canteen.

knows her job. We had four fine voices for *I Puritani*, the American soprano June Anderson, Giuseppe Sabbatini the tenor, and Dmitri Hvorostovsky and Robert Lloyd. They sang wonderfully; Sabbatini spun out the long line of 'A te o cara' so that I wished it would never end.

By May in New York and at many other houses, the season would have been over. But Covent Garden could not afford to be dark for more than four weeks in August. We brought back Peter Hall's *Salome*, with Maria Ewing, giving Ted Downes his eyeful. And we revived Saint-Saëns' *Samson et Dalila* with Plácido Domingo, tired from too much travel, as Samson. Olga Borodina sang lushly as Dalila. Determined to assert her prospective status as diva, she managed, by delaying an hour or so, not to arrive at the Crush Bar reception till after Plácido, who had been signing autographs. I knew then she would make it to the top; in 1998, with Domingo, she opened the Metropolitan's season in the same piece.

And there was more to come. Christoph von Dohnányi would conduct a new production of *Der fliegende Holländer*, produced by Ian Judge and designed by John Gunter. This replaced the previous *Dutchman* which Haitink had hated so. Gunter came up with the most physically exciting staging of my time. His grand design took us from the Dutchman's ship, to Daland's house, to the cliffside harbour of the final act, without pause or interruption. To the dismay of our bar staff, the opera would be given without an interval, as Wagner originally intended. I was reluctant to give up the bar takings, but Dohnányi was keen to do it in one sweep of just over two hours.

The set was huge; getting from one act's structure to another was always going to involve a determined assault by the stage crew. To manage it without pause, as the music continued, would be something of a miracle. When we reached the general rehearsal, the last before the first night, we had not yet managed a complete run-through. At the general we had to. At the end of Act Two, as he came to the music introducing Act Three, Dohnányi at the podium looked up, saw the set was not yet in place, and stopped. He did not realize that as the music went on, so would the set; the chorus, all of them, sailors and fishwives, would mount from either side and be ready, on his upflung cue, to hurl their voices out at us. We told him it would be all right on the night, and crossed our fingers. Dohnányi warned the orchestra that he might have to stop and wait. In the event, on the night, determination prevailed. I gave a party for orchestra, chorus and for the stage crew; they had worked the miracle.

Kenneth MacMillan seized the chance to create roles on Irek Mukhamedov, here with Darcey Bussell in *Winter Dreams*.

Sylvie Guillem in Forsyth's *Herman Schmerman*; most physically thrilling of ballerinas.

Jonathan Cope as Balanchine's Apollo. Pleading sore shins, Jonathan left the company; the muse brought him back.

Manon. MacMillan's pas de deux moves dance on from romance to erotic ecstasy. Viviana Durante and Bruce Sansom.

Bussell and Dowell, Rose Princess and Emperor, in MacMillan's homage to De Valois, *The Prince of the Pagodas*.

Durante, sex-pot and victim, with Mukhamedov, in *The Judas Tree*.

Maria Bjornson's designs for *The Sleeping Beauty* were too strong for some; Aurora's world, cursed by the bad fairy, is at an angle to the universe.

Bjornson frames the happy ending in traditional glory. Zoltan Solymosi partners Viviana Durante.

'Saturn' from David Bintley's *The Planets*. On the first night designer Ralph Koltai's globe retreated on cue; the ring refused to come down.

Twyla Tharp's *Mr Worldly Wise*; Mukhamedov and Teddy Kumakawa at full stretch.

'Put me among the girls.' Peter Wright, Director of Birmingham Royal Ballet, and company.

If a shoemaker's apprentice can't clog dance, who can? Michael O'Hare as Will Mossop in Bintley's popular masterpiece, *Hobson's Choice*.

David Bintley creates new work on the Birmingham Royal Ballet.

Birmingham Royal Ballet rising to the challenge of Balanchine's *Serenade*.

Madam, Ninette de Valois, en route to BRB's new premises.
She would have liked to drive the train.

Kenneth MacMillan works with Durante on *The Judas Tree*, his last ballet.

Julia Varady as Senta gave performances of pure intensity, so that we all wished we could tempt her to London more often. The production was disliked by the critics as uninvolving, but the public were thrilled. This *Flying Dutchman* will grace the new House. It may not again, however, be given without an interval. My successor will want to give the paying public the run of the Floral Hall, and of the new amphitheatre bar with its views across London. This will please the Wagnerite who wrote to me to complain that I had no thought for the infirmities of age. Could I not envisage the discomfort he suffered in sitting through the opera without a break? He had especial difficulty because, as was his wont, he had refreshed himself beforehand with a pint or two of Young's excellent bitter at the Marquess of Anglesey. I wrote back that I sympathized – a full bladder and a tickly throat are the worst hazards of opera-going – but suggested that in future he confine himself to a half of lager, or a small brandy.

The season proper ended. The Royal Opera, promoted by the Japan Arts Foundation, administered by the admirable Mr Sasaki, set out for Tokyo to tour Japan with Mozart's three Da Ponte operas, *Figaro*, *Così* and *Don Giovanni*, with starry casts, and Bernard Haitink and Jeffrey Tate conducting. I went out too, briefly, and was staggered at how the Japanese admired our work and how much they had paid for their tickets. Two students I met on a train had booked for all three operas and spent thousands of pounds each. Back at Covent Garden, we added a coda to the season. July 1992 saw the United Kingdom assume the Presidency of the European Commission, an agonizing crux for John Major's government, split down the middle on Europe. Paul Findlay suggested that we should mark the event with performances of Rossini's *Il viaggio a Rheims*, a European *pièce d'occasion*. Before a *Dutchman* performance I saw Peter Lilley, then Secretary of State for Social Services, in the Crush Bar, and told him we were putting on a Rossini opera in July, with parts for nearly all the countries of the European Union. Lilley, a Euro-sceptic, said, 'Make sure you have a Dane.' The Danes, in a referendum, had just voted No to the Maastricht Treaty. I asked the producer, John Cox, to include a Dane.

Rossini wrote *Il viaggio a Rheims* for the coronation of Charles X at Rheims in 1825. It needs ten star singers. Travellers, on their way to the coronation, put up at the Golden Lily Inn. When their luggage is delayed, they stay on and entertain themselves in a concert. The result is that

Viaggio contains more marvellous solo numbers than almost any other opera. With the resources of a gramophone company and the city of Pesaro, Rossini's birthplace, behind him, Claudio Abbado put this on there in 1984. We planned to give *Viaggio* with good young singers. The cast we lined up included Sylvia McNair and Renée Fleming. At almost the last moment, to lift the box-office, Paul engaged Montserrat Caballé, who had not, perhaps for good reason, been heard at Covent Garden for many years, to sing Madam Cortese, the lively Tyrolean lady who keeps the inn. The box-office duly lifted. John Cox produced – his contract with us guaranteed him one new production a year; this was it. For a brief ballet in *Viaggio*, John Cox, thinking perhaps of The Mall on a State visit, gave everyone a flag. Thus, in a non-singing role, a Dane squeezed in: voting 'No' with her feet, she made off fast. Good fun, entertaining, well conducted by Carlo Rizzi, and beautifully sung, by everyone except Montserrat Caballé. Madame Cortese opens the opera with an aria of welcome to her guests. We should have been prosecuted under the Trades Description Act. This Madame Cortese turned her back on the audience and, shamelessly, managed to avoid singing out on many of the notes written. John Cox connived in this by giving her attendants who cavorted round her; turning to them, she had an excuse for turning away from us. And Caballé created havoc with green apples which, as hostess in the spa, she distributed to her guests, to keep the doctor away. She threw one to the conductor. On the first night an apple rolled across the protective netting into the orchestra pit; the orchestra was not amused. Orchestra players with vulnerable instruments are sensitive about objects propelled into the pit. Pompously the Orchestra Committee wrote to Madame Caballé asking her not to do it again. Montserrat, at the next performance, read out the Committee's letter to her, and went on throwing apples. Rossini's music survived these diversions. We gave it as a *pièce d'occasion*. The occasion over, after a year or two in storage, storage space being expensive, we had to burn it. It would be helpful to be able to keep all new productions for eventual re-use. The Opera House could not afford to do so.

As international opera houses contract artists up to three years ahead, retrenchment, which I had promised the Board, is never easy. Cancellation is costly, and tempers the axe. We could only afford to cut so much. Subsequent seasons therefore, in spite of the change of course promised in autumn 1992, remained a mix of high ambition and now, in heftier dollops, more routine fare. A well-cast, well-conducted, well-produced revival gives pleasure. A long run of a too familiar piece, necessarily entailing successive changes of cast, disappoints the keen subscriber. And overlong runs will fail, in the end, at the box-office. The 1992/93 season would not see *La Juive*, cancelled long before; the starry cast planned for it, including Karita Mattila, Deborah Riedel, Jerry Hadley and Thomas Hampson, gave us *La bohème* instead. But this season, which would be Paul Findlay's last as Opera Director, had goodies enough. From Glyndebourne, we rented Gershwin's *Porgy and Bess*, in Trevor Nunn's fine production, conducted for us by Andrew Litton. Willard White was a memorable Porgy, Cynthia Haymon a touching Bess. There were more black faces than usual in the auditorium. We managed to shoehorn in an extra performance. *Porgy* was followed by *Otello*, with Plácido Domingo blacked up, and Kiri Te Kanawa and Sergei Leiferkus as Desdemona and Iago. Georg Solti, marking his eightieth birthday, conducted. The Prince and Princess of Wales, rarely seen together, were there for him.

Riding a crest, we went straight on to a new *Die Frau ohne Schatten* – Bernard Haitink conducting, John Cox producing, designs by David Hockney. David is very deaf, but fills his head with music; opera is a vital part of his life. The stage, he passionately believes, needs light and colour. For *Frau* he gave us both in abundance, but the great upward path to the light he had designed, displayed by a reveal, did not always work in performance. On the night I gave him supper afterwards, there was a notable miscue. He was not pleased, and muttered throughout the meal. But at least, with a fine cast, we put the work on, sharing the cost with Los Angeles, who took it after us. In LA, in the dining room of the Dorothy Chandler Pavilion, I saw David – who had left England for California to be free to be gay – faced down and menaced by fellow-diners because he had threatened to light a cigarette.

We had a lovely cast for Handel's *Alcina*, but a less than lovely production and leaden conducting, by the standards of today's Handelians. John Copley was due to direct; Jon Conklin would do the sets. They were attractive, but too expensive. We jibbed. Rather than be party to a botch, Copley and Conklin, honourably, withdrew. To save the piece, we borrowed a production, recommended to us, from St Louis, Missouri. *Meet Me in St Louis* it was not; one single plain hedge of stunted leylandii served for scenery virtually throughout. But some so enjoyed the music as to forgive the production. *Alcina* is a cross-dresser's dream. Bradamante is disguised as her brother, Ricciardo. Morgana, Alcina's sister, is immediately attracted to the handsome 'Ricciardo', etc. Besotted, Jeanette Winterson came to every performance.

Next we offered a *Damnation de Faust* under Colin Davis, greatest of Berlioz conductors, and *Pelléas et Mélisande* under Claudio Abbado. The event of the season was neither of these, but a production of a comparatively early Verdi piece, *Stiffelio*, never given before at Covent Garden. *Stiffelio* was urged on us by Ted Downes and hinted for by José Carreras. He had recorded the role, and could still creditably, nobly even, sing it. Lured, he came. *Stiffelio* crowned the season and helped make the case for an annual Verdi Festival. As in *Attila*, the audience revelled in Verdi's confident melodies for the voice, and with the help of surtitles hung on every syllable. They had no idea how the story would end; not till the final bars did they discover whether the Protestant pastor Stiffelio would forgive his wife's adultery. Alan Yentob, Controller of BBC2, with something to prove at the time, was so bowled over that he cleared the schedule one evening to broadcast *Stiffelio* live. The production, one of Elijah Moshinsky's finest, went to La Scala, Vienna and Los Angeles, and, flatteringly, prompted another at the Met. There Domingo sang Stiffelio; the soprano was on the ample side. When Gillian doubted her dramatic credibility as an adulteress, Beverly Sills, in the box with us, sighed, 'Well, there's sure enough for two there.' The first ever *Stiffelio* at Covent Garden was followed by the 319th performance of *The Barber of Seville*. In a starry cast, Ruggero Raimondi was Basilio; one night when he was unwell, Sam Ramey, in London for *Damnation*, came on instead.

To mark Mozart's bicentenary year, Jeffrey Tate, a convincing Mozartian, suggested doing *Mitridate, rè di Ponto*, written when Mozart was fourteen years old and never previously given at Covent Garden. Paul Findlay invited Graham Vick to direct and he engaged Paul Brown as designer. Together they made the most perfect production up to then of my time as General Director. *Mitridate* is *opera seria*, slow and stately, with long, florid, repetitious arias. Graham Vick gave us an object lesson in how, working from inside it, he could bring this piece to life. Everyone, in Ron Howell's choreography, moved with schooled control and precision. Paul Brown's sets were very simple, the stage was mostly bare. But he used bright saturated colours and the period feel was captured by modern art. What he saved on the sets, he spent on costumes. Consulting theatrical records, Paul Brown created dazzlingly elaborate clothing which seemed to demand, through its weight, the grave postures the singers adopted. In this setting the music acquired a steely strength; the singing did justice to every florid twirl. Bruce Ford as Mitridate, in steel breastplate and a stiff, brocaded carapace, looked every extra inch a king; Jochen Kowalski, in dark green as Farnace, Mitridate's eldest son, got to wear the frock of a lifetime, and let us know he knew it. *Mitridate, rè di Ponto* was a treat for eye and ear.

When in 1994 we revived *Mitridate*, the first night audience cried 'Scandal'. The cause was a bird. In Act One, a falcon was shackled to the edge of a grave downstage, at the front. Instead of perching high above us, it was to remain still on the floor as Mitridate's Queen poured out her grief at her consort's supposed death. Birds of prey are not happy on the ground. The falcon, wretchedly, fidgeted, fell down into the hole and could not get up again. Shackled by the leg, it hung upside down like a pheasant in the butcher's, while the soprano sang on and on. Angry audience members called out: 'Do something. Stop the show. This is a disgrace.' A handler came on and hoiked the bird off. It turned out that this was not the falcon rehearsed for the part, but a more attractive-looking bird supplied as a substitute. The Russian soprano Luba Organosova, understanding no English, scarcely aware of what was happening beside her, left the stage, perturbed. She had not expected cat-calls. In the interval, we announced that the feathered member of the cast was perfectly all right, but would take no further part in the proceedings. Neither that night, we meant to say, nor any other night.

Over Christmas and New Year, with ballet filling the Opera House, we broke completely new ground. Following intriguing examples of arena opera at Earl's Court, the opera company staged our *Turandot* production at the Wembley Arena. This was a collaboration with the popular impresario Raymond Gubbay, who persuaded the *Daily Telegraph* and Emap to invest. We would, using amplification, give ten performances in an auditorium seating nearly 7000. The *Telegraph* promoted the event like billy-ho. Gubbay greeted us on the first night. Bypassing the hotdog and hamburger stall, he suggested champagne. 'Things are going pretty well,' he said. 'The bad news is that we are going to lose money. The good news is that it will be less than £1 million.' The *Telegraph* and Emap lost £800,000. The Opera House was not at risk. We had hoped to sell 60,000 tickets; in fact we sold only just over 40,000. That meant that 40,000, many new to opera, who had never been to Covent Garden, saw and enjoyed *Turandot* – the equivalent of twenty full houses. No one could say we were not reaching out to new audiences. Prime Minister John Major was impressed: 'Just what you should be doing, Jeremy.' Not quite, I thought. But it kept us on our toes.

In the New Year, we gave a new production of *Don Giovanni*, directed by Johannes Schaaf, with dark designs by Peter Pabst. Giovanni, rapist, murderer, compulsive seducer, has something of the night about him. Schaaf's production had mildly prurient moments. At the end of Act One we glimpsed Zerlina, way upstage, half-clothed, awaiting the sadist's lash, before Masetto rescued her. In the last scene Don Giovanni, dining alone before the Commendatore arrives to drag him down to hell, ate dinner off a naked lady, her charms hidden by lavish helpings of fruit salad. As she hurried off, her figure was much admired.

On 10 February 1992, to mark the fortieth anniversary of her accession to the throne, the Queen had agreed to attend a performance of *Don Giovanni*. Angus Stirling, ROH's new Chairman, was particularly proud to receive the Palace's acceptance of our invitation. We still imagined that royal patronage – the fact that we were the *Royal* Opera House – constituted part of our claim on public funds. Famously, when invited to Glyndebourne on their fiftieth anniversary to see *The Marriage of Figaro*, the Queen had commented, 'That's the one with the pin, isn't it? I have seen that.' On a later occasion, at lunch at Buckingham Palace, I suggested that she consider coming to the House in February 1996 to see *The Sleeping Beauty*, fifty years to the day after she had attended with her parents and her sister the performance which opened the House. Prince Philip interrupted: 'No, not that. It is far too long. We can't sit through that.' Although the Queen did come to that *Sleeping Beauty*, the *Don Giovanni*, broadcast live on BBC television, was almost the last occasion – the principal public event celebrating her fortieth anniversary – when it seemed to her advisers that her visiting us might benefit her.

That night trumpeters of the Royal Horseguards, stationed on the Crush Bar balcony, sounded two fanfares, one outside as the royal car arrived at Bow Street, the second inside as, after being escorted up the grand staircase, she took her place in the centre of the Grand Tier. Bernard Haitink was waiting to conduct the National Anthem. He had been told that the second fanfare was his cue, and to begin when he heard it. We did not think he'd hear the first fanfare. Alas he did, and began on that. Meanwhile, in the foyer, the Queen had been greeted by Angus and Morar Stirling, by me, and had just reached Gillian when she heard the National Anthem. Gillian, wearing a very posh frock given her cheap by a couturier friend closing his business, was in deep curtsey when the Queen said sharply, 'They've started without us.' In the auditorium the audience rose, turned, and saw so many other members of the Royal Family in the Grand Tier that they did not realize the Queen was not yet there. After a frantic message to the pit, the Anthem was played again. Three hours after that, I escorted the Queen around the back of the Grand Tier, down the stairs and on to the stage to meet the cast. She uttered not one word. I did not ask if she had enjoyed herself; her face said all. Prince Philip did enquire what the flats he found at the side of the stage were for, and seemed astonished to be told they were the scenery, the walls and doors of the Don's palazzo he had just seen. Gracious letters arrived from the Palace, congratulating us on the success of the evening.

The House was honoured to have the Queen present, even if we knew she scarcely looked forward to the occasion. But being called the Royal Opera House no longer brings tangible advantage. The Queen and Prince Philip are neither enthusiasts nor active supporters. Queen Elizabeth the Queen Mother is both; with a small party of friends, well into her nineties, she would celebrate her birthday in the Royal Box at Covent Garden. She enjoyed the ballet, whether her dear friend Fred Ashton's *La fille mal gardée*, or Kenneth MacMillan's *Romeo and Juliet*. She enjoyed the audience and the crowd which gathered outside. Enjoyment is infectious; all rejoiced to see her there. Prince Philip did come one day to see how our stage machinery worked, and took a lively interest. The Queen spent a happy morning visiting wardrobe, millinery, wigs and jewellery, in the rabbit warrens of 45 Floral Street. She asked questions, palpably had a good time. But as far as one could tell, neither she nor Prince Philip ever looked forward to an evening performance.

Princess Margaret loves ballet – its physical appeal, the dancers' virtuosity, grace and charm. She enjoys the colour of sets and costume, and the courtly procedures of those nineteenth-century masterpieces. That is what it really means to be a princess, you imagine her saying to herself. Conscientiously she serves as President of the Royal Ballet, meaning both the Royal Ballet companies. Several times each season she receives a detailed written report on their activities. She comes to rehearsals, when something particularly appeals, and to performances.

She has come also to appreciate the athleticism of modern dance, as Guillem, Bull, Mukhamedov or Kumakawa hurtle about the stage. What she has never liked is the music that accompanies new work. Not only is anything after Stravinsky distasteful to her, so is Stravinsky! Which strikes *Les Noces* or *Rite of Spring* or even *Petrushka* off her list. Actually, I suspect she does enjoy what she sees, but still cannot resist telling anyone in earshot that she hates the music. But the President of the Royal Ballet is a real trouper. Rain or shine, London or Birmingham, and, if someone else paid her fare, in Washington, San Francisco or even Tokyo, she would turn up to attend a performance and fly the flag for Britain. The dancers appreciate that. Her support counts.

Prince Charles used to play the cello, loves music, cares about opera. He is Patron of the Royal Opera. He has conservative tastes. In August 1990 he put on a concert at Buckingham Palace for his grandmother's ninetieth birthday. The programme included a piece specially commissioned by him for the occasion, a cantata for soprano, chorus and orchestra by Patrick Doyle who wrote the music for Kenneth Branagh's film of *Henry V*. In this work, the soprano's vocal line, instead of standing out from the female chorus, merged, replicated, into it, and was lost to the ear. Marie McLaughlin, the soprano, took a dim view. Later in the evening, Prince Charles suggested to me that we commission a new opera from Doyle, just the sort of composer you should be getting work from, he thought.

Charles brought his interest in architecture to the scheme for a re-developed Opera House. Although Jeremy Dixon is not a modernist, and had matched aspects of Inigo Jones's seventeenth-century plan for the Covent Garden Piazza, the Prince of Wales at first was grudging in his approval. He picked fault with Dixon's early and, to be truthful, not very satisfactory proposals for the Bow Street/Russell Street corner; Charles wanted a pepperpot effect, like the corner opposite. Looking at the model, he displayed little interest in the functions the building served, only in the façade. Happily, he did not suggest a thatched roof.

Prince Charles has a real concern for the Opera House – I hope his interest in it will grow. When he and Diana married, we hoped they might come often to Covent Garden together. In my time, they rarely did. Soon, to our mild surprise and pleasure, the Princess of Wales began to come on her own. She visited the craft workshops in Floral Street, and wrote me a note of thanks; she had very much enjoyed it. With a friend, or a lady-in-waiting, and a security man, she would come sometimes to the opera. She asked for no fuss. She would be met by our House Manager, Trevor Jones, at the side entrance to the Royal Box in Floral Street. She declined the use of my private retiring room, kindly decorated for me by Tricia Guild; in the interval, she sipped something in a corner of the Crush Bar. She appeared happy. Afterwards, she drove herself off into the night. Years later we surmised that the opera may have been only part of her evening, and that she was on her way to a rendezvous elsewhere. Charles, though I once found him in the Royal Box ante-room with Kenneth Branagh and Ben Elton, came rarely. As Patron of the Friends of Covent Garden he used to attend the annual Christmas party and perform in it. Princess Margaret, too, once appeared there in the fols-de-rols on stage, making her entrance on a swing. And Diana danced with Wayne Sleep. But the Friends' Christmas party venue shifted, as pressure grew on the stage. Informal royal visits grew fewer and farther between.

Audience's behaviour and attitude over my time reflected changing feelings about the Royal Family. When I arrived, the opera and ballet seasons each began and ended with the National Anthem. That custom we kept up as long as we could. We continued to play the anthem before the performance at the season's start. It was harder to do so as the season ended, with half the audience out of their seats on the way home, so we dropped it then. What audiences principally resented, I found, was being asked, at a gala performance, to be in their seats early to suit royalty's convenience, and to be kept waiting there, for twenty minutes or more, before the royal arrival, and then to sit patiently through the greeting and the introductions in the Crush Bar until, finally, the royal entry into the auditorium. In 1987 they did not grudge that; they did a decade later. But the National Anthem rang out loud and clear as the House closed on 17 July 1997.

Peter Jonas announced in 1991 that he would leave his post at the English National Opera, where, under George Harewood, he headed the triumvirate that determined artistic policy and ran the theatre. As General Director he had overall charge of ENO's fortunes. Peter Jonas had been sounded out, he told me, about Salzburg, but they took Gerard Mortier from La Monnaie in Brussels instead. Now Jonas had been appointed Staatsintendant at the Bavarian State Opera in Munich, where he would enjoy a subsidy more than four times what he was used to at ENO. My antennae twitched. Paul Findlay had been Director of the Royal Opera since 1987; I wanted to make a change. I knew Nicholas Payne, a success both as an impresario and a ruthless manager at Opera North, would be a prime candidate to succeed Jonas at ENO. I guessed he would be George Harewood's choice. Harewood had started Opera North as an offshoot of ENO, and had seen Nicholas put in charge. I wanted to bring Nicholas Payne to take charge of opera at Covent Garden, and I saw instantly that this would be my only chance to bring that about. I told Paul Findlay that, when his contract expired at the end of the 1992/93 season, it would not be renewed.

Findlay, as these pages make clear, achieved prodigies as Director of the Royal Opera. He was Bernard Haitink's chosen collaborator. I admired his energies, and was grateful for his taking on all the job's fraught and tedious minutiae – what Frederick Gye, who managed Covent Garden in the nineteenth century, called 'the dreadful business of opera management'. Paul knew the world of opera; he knew his stuff. But too much we did, it seemed to me, was arrived at opportunistically, on the wing even. We hired other houses' productions because they were there, rather than engaged in genuinely creative collaborations. Some productions we rented did not fit, and had to be re-made. The Opera Board, too, found his restless activity disquieting. I took exception – my fault, of course, for agreeing to it – to a commitment he gave to Valery Gergiev and the Kirov, by which we made for them Prokofiev's *War and Peace*. Timothy O'Brien designed it, Graham Vick directed. Our share of the cost was £200,000. They staged it in St Petersburg but before we could do so here, BBC TV relayed it from the Mariinsky Theatre to British audiences. We had no control over that, and should have done. When the question arose of putting it in our repertory, it was clear – this was what I had not grasped – that in no foreseeable future would we be able to afford to pay the chorus for the hours it would take to learn their parts in a language they did not know. The sets sat out the Russian winter. In the end, I wrote the production off. (Now, years later, Paul Findlay is General Manager of the Mariinsky, freeing up Valery Gergiev to conduct abroad.)

The real point was that I thought we could do even better than we had been doing: opera seasons should be fashioned within an explicable artistic framework or rationale. Paul had worked for the Royal Opera House, as assistant to John Tooley, and then as deputy in charge of all opera and ballet touring, for twenty-five years. It was he who suggested hiring Terry Edwards as Chorus Director, and bringing back Ted Downes. He had done his damnedest. He had cause for pride in his achievement. Yet I knew I must make the change.

Making it was another matter. Paul's post would be advertised. Nicholas Payne was not easily persuaded either to apply or, when offered the job after a sequence of interviews, to take it. During the selection process, I found another admirable candidate, Elaine Padmore. She had run the Wexford Festival with success, and was now in charge at Copenhagen. I would have been happy to see her in the post. But in the end Payne accepted. Nicholas is a self-assured Etonian who has loved opera all his life, hanging out night after night in his youth in the amphitheatre at Covent Garden. He had attended the same arts management course as Paul Findlay and Brian McMaster. With McMaster he ran WNO, before taking charge in Leeds. Private and ebullient at once, he agreed to come to Covent Garden. The 1993/94 season would be his first, giving him a year to prepare. Some of the work planned, of course, he inherited from Paul Findlay, while one or two productions had his mark on them.

There are evenings in the theatre I shall remember all my life. *Die Meistersinger von Nürnberg*, produced by Graham Vick, conducted by Bernard Haitink, with John Tomlinson as Hans Sachs, gave me several of them. As Music Director, not Artistic Director, of the Royal Opera, Bernard chose what he wanted to conduct. He did not choose the producer and the designer; dolefully, he left that to us. He had not admired the sets and costumes for the *Parsifal* he conducted, nor for *Il trovatore*. He had wanted to put Lyubimov's *Ring* behind him; he respected Götz Friedrich, but not Peter Sykora's sets for those *Ring* cycles. He would not be happy with Nigel Lowery's designs for Richard Jones's *Ring* cycle still to come (though he understood that Richard Jones knew the work inside out). But this *Meistersinger*, designed by Richard Hudson, might have been made for him. Handsome and practical, St Catherine's church, the town square with the lime tree, Sachs's workshop, the meadow crowded for St John's Day – all were good to look at. The sets must have warmed Bernard's heart. Graham Vick gave the comedy a sunny production. Peter Katona had found an excellent cast. The orchestra, and the chorus trained by our new Chorus Director Terry Edwards, responded to his baton. Triumph. For many regulars, this *Meistersinger* was one of the best things we had ever done. A guest at one performance wrote of John

Tomlinson's Hans Sachs: 'It was a noble achievement,' and added, 'so indeed was Covent Garden's in mounting so marvellous a new production of this great work.' That, from George Harewood, kept me chipper all day. The warmest tribute came from Bayreuth. Wolfgang Wagner and his wife Gudrun were my guests. They admired everything about the production and the performance. 'We thought', Gudrun wrote, 'we saw not a *Meistersinger*, but THE *Meistersinger*.' (Later they came to every opera in Richard Jones's *Ring* cycle. This time Gudrun Wagner wrote to my assistant Nini Aldridge to thank her for 'the excellent arrangements, help and kindness you extended to us preparing our stay in London'.)

Bernard Haitink, in this season put on under the lash of economy, also got to conduct Janáček's *Káťa Kabanová*, directed by Trevor Nunn, with Maria Bjornson's extraordinary set, like *The Scream* by Edvard Munch. Trevor Nunn framed *Káťa*'s drama in the life of the village. He had Tikhon leave for the market at Kazan, with goods piled on a wagon drawn by two heavy dray-horses, never, to my knowledge, seen in the piece before. Bjornson's set was expressionistic, the horses all too real. Real horses distract, and these were no exception. Would they be still and calm? Would their bowels? Thick felt was laid at the side of the stage to muffle noise before they came on, but we still heard them clumping about. And we worried about their footing as they moved off. The TV series showed an accident in rehearsal: one stumbled and fell, but was not hurt. I could not rest each evening till they were off and on their way back to the stable. With them on stage, it was hard to look at anything else. When they were gone, it was hard not to look at Elena Prokina as Káťa; she gave a moving performance, fluttering like a wounded bird. Prokina could act as well as sing, and she sang like an angel. Trevor Nunn's production of *Káťa* was a very considerable success.

So was Massenet's *Chérubin*, Nicholas Payne's personal choice for a première on St Valentine's Day, when it had first been performed. Tim Albery made his début as a producer in the house; what he gave us was light, frothy, fun. He also helped engineer the departure of Gennadi Rozhdestvensky as conductor. Rozhdestvensky took a broader, more measured, view of Massenet's score than did Albery. But he had not, according to Albery, deigned to attend many rehearsals. Hoping perhaps to be summoned back on his own terms, Rozhdestvensky went home. Nicholas had chosen the Russian maestro; with immaculate timing, he bade him goodbye. Before you could say Machiavelli, we were able to whistle in another conductor, Mario Bernardi, who actually knew the piece. Bernardi came in such a hurry that he brought only one shoe. Susan Graham, as a radiant Cherubino who cannot stop falling in love, won all hearts. No one but Nicholas would have thought of giving us *Chérubin*. We also gave Giordano's *Fedora*, which Mirella Freni, José Carreras and Ted Downes made count, in a production rented from La Scala. Tosh perhaps, but enjoyable tosh.

The season was let down by performances of a *Magic Flute* rented from Scottish Opera. It had worked well in the Theatre Royal, Glasgow, in a Glasgow accent. In German for us, it failed over too long a run – financial imperatives again. Sixteen *Carmen*s sent the same grim message: another opera has been cancelled here. Patrons may have been surprised to hear Anna Tomowa-Sintow as *Tosca*; she should have been singing Yaroslavna in a revival of *Prince Igor*. We revived *Mitridate* – this was when the chained bird spoiled the first night – and *Elektra*. Here, Christian Thielemann's conducting conclusively demonstrated his greatness. We brought back Birtwistle's *Gawain*, with Anne Howells joining the cast as Lady Hautdesert. Again, *Gawain* filled the house. And a first: *Gawain*, in English, was surtitled throughout its run. A new *Aida* went off at half-cock, mostly because we lacked a commanding Aida; Cheryl Studer did not rise to it. I was glad a performance elsewhere kept me away from the first night of a revival of *Manon*, though Colin Davis was conducting. Anthony Michaels-Moore, singing Lescaut, lost his voice in the last act. David Syrus, Head of Music Staff, sang the role from the pit, with the staff producer Stuart Maunder on stage acting. David Syrus has a voice like a hacksaw.

Next season, Nicholas Payne got into his stride. He launched a new *Ring* cycle and offered a *Così fan tutte* on a shoestring (costumes by Armani): Jonathan Miller's absurdly belated house début. He introduced a Luc Bondy *Salome* from Salzburg, and a *Billy Budd* from Geneva. We also paid tercentenary tribute to England's greatest composer, Purcell, with *King Arthur*, begun at the Châtelet. For three performances only, this was stunning, if very expensive. And we embarked, at the season's end, on an annual Verdi Festival, designed to see all his operas performed by 2001.

The 1994/95 season had already brought us a new *La traviata*, conducted by Georg Solti and directed, to my delight, by Richard Eyre, consistently one of Britain's finest directors. For both it was their début in the piece; for Richard, his début in opera. He had promised me he would direct opera at Covent Garden when his commitments at the National Theatre allowed. Now he came and struck up a partnership with Solti, not quite concealing the disdain he felt for it all: he wrote later that opera was 'an elaborate conceit as remote to me as the courtship rituals of the Inuit Indians'. It did not show on stage. Bob Crowley did the fine sets; a gilded cage for Scene 1, and a wonderful transition from the country estate to the gambling party in Act Two. The production, although to some it seemed not to catch fire, pleased very many. Angela Gheorghiu, making a début as Violetta, rocketed to stardom. Slim, beautiful, elegant in white, she delivered every last note of 'Ah, fors' è lui' and 'Sempre libera' with faultless 'ping' and musicality. She was, deservedly, the toast of the town. Richard Eyre had stipulated to Solti for credible lovers to work with, and especially a young Violetta. Carol Vaness had been Solti's choice. She was due to make the recording in the following summer. When she was unavailable for the autumn première, we put forward Angela Gheorghiu, whom Peter Katona had been nursing along for just this moment since he heard her years before in a Belvedere Competition in Vienna. Richard Eyre was immediately convinced by what he called her defiant energy and 'a waist the size of a teapot'. Solti, at first reluctant, was won over. Now he shared Gheorghiu's triumph.

Immediately before *La traviata*, but with similar excitement and réclame, we had given Gounod's *Roméo et Juliette*, co-produced with Toulouse, Lyon, and the Opéra-Comique in Paris. As Romeo, Roberto Alagna was magnificent. Alagna came late to opera. He made his reputation at La Scala in *La traviata*, and was asked to sing Alfredo all over the world. But his wife was then dying of a brain tumour and he could not bear to sing Alfredo to a dying Violetta. Now, after her death, and with his young daughter and his parents in the dressing room, he sang Romeo instead. When he came to the aria '*Ah! lève-toi soleil*', he sang with bravura and poignancy, better perhaps than he ever would again in his life.

By the end of the 1994/95 season, Nicholas Payne had shown what he could do. Opera at Covent Garden was where it should be, on top of the world.

I had originally thought I would leave the Royal Opera House in 1995. Seven years is a longish stint for me in any job. If closure had come, as envisaged, in 1993, and been completed in the tight two years scheduled,

I could have rc-opened the House in late 1995 and moved on. It had not worked out like that. Closure would now come, we hoped and believed, in 1997. I would reach sixty-five, retirement age, that September. The Board extended my contract to that date.

The next two years would be among the most difficult of my life.

10

DEVELOPMENT

'Vollendet das ewige Werk!' By the time this book appears, the work will be completed; the new, redeveloped Royal Opera House will be in action again, the public enjoying it; Wotan and the other gods in Valhalla. (Loge, lurking somewhere, will warn us they are going to their doom.) I take pride in what has been achieved, as I have taken pleasure in watching construction rising to completion, on time and on budget, since the House closed its doors in July 1997. A week was allowed to clear up after the closing gala; then the builders' men, poised to begin, as they had been for months, were in and at it. Demolition of the old was under way. Not of the auditorium itself; that Victorian Grade I listed structure would remain. But the stage area and the fly-tower would need to be transformed if a theatre equipped for the nineteenth century was to continue to serve audiences in the twenty-first. The twentieth century had passed without serious alteration or improvement.

When I joined the Board of the Royal Opera House in late 1985, work on a scheme for redevelopment was well advanced. In 1974 government bought the land on which the theatre sits, extending from Floral Street in the north to Russell Street on its southern boundary, and from Bow Street in the east to James Street in the west and the eastern edge of the Covent Garden piazza. They gave it to the Royal Opera House to enable the theatre to be redeveloped. Drastic improvement of the cramped, poky, squalid conditions in which staff worked, and had their daily existence, now became possible. An appeal was launched. Prince Charles and

Princess Margaret were active in support, and £10 million was raised to build what was described as Phase 1. Artists' dressing rooms, some offices, opera and chorus rehearsal rooms, and two ballet studios were added behind the stage, creating a new building on James Street. Money ran out before the windows could be double-glazed, so that the loudest noise heard in the opera rehearsal room was made by buskers and ghettoblasters in the street outside. The doors to the rehearsal room through which scenery passed did not line up directly with the stage. When work on Phase 1 was under way, the Treasury, in spite of its proclaimed curmudgeonly refusal to contribute, actually agreed to match private funds by making two separate donations of £1 million. The Greater London Council (GLC), at that time still London's government, gave another £1 million. Phase 1 was formally opened in 1992, and very much improved working conditions and the House's functioning. But it was not enough. These changes scarcely began to fulfil the Board's modest aspirations for a living lyric theatre: an efficient stage, a base for the ballet, pleasant spaces for the public. Much remained to be achieved.

The Royal Opera House, Covent Garden, was only ever royal in name. There had been a theatre on the same site since the early eighteenth century, but differently aligned. The present auditorium was built, to a design by E. M. Barry, in 1858, replacing one by the same architect burned down the previous year. (During that year of closure, the manager Frederick Gye took his business down the road to the Lyceum, plumping up the season there with occasional performances in other venues.) Other large lyric theatres put on opera in eighteenth- and nineteenth-century London, including the Theatre Royal in Drury Lane and His Majesty's in the Haymarket. All were under commercial management, there to please and to make or lose money. None aspired to serve the state.

The Royal Opera House that lasted from 1858 to 1997 was essentially a modest structure. The auditorium, seating just over 2000, dressed in red and gold, with a fine decorated dome and Queen Victoria's profile above the proscenium, made a striking impression, particularly as you entered the stalls. But compared to the vestibules, salons and staircases of Munich or Vienna, or of the new Metropolitan Opera House at Lincoln Center, New York, space was limited. At the Palais Garnier in Paris, flights of stone steps rise from the street to the entrance porticos. You pass across the entrance hall, up the imposing double staircase through vast salons and balconied walks, for yards and yards and yards before, at last, you reach the back wall of the auditorium. Heads of state – saluted by a presidential guard of honour, shakos shining, sabres drawn, fanfares ringing out – have done so before you. Garnier designed for the glory of France. At Covent Garden, it was ten paces from the front door till your ticket was demanded at the rear stalls, or at the foot of the grand staircase. Compared with any of its peer houses, Covent Garden's floor plan showed a minimal stage area and severely restricted public space. The Crush Bar was not called that for nothing. Amphitheatre audiences were kept segregated from it, and from the Pit Lobby; allowing their numbers in the lower house constituted a safety hazard.

Barry's theatre was lit by gas, offering performances staged in front of painted cloths. For that, it was more than adequate. Singers, lit from below by naked flares along the front of the stage, came down to the footlights to sing. Behind them, cloths rose and fell from the flies as the scene changed from castle to dungeon to witches' den. These were stored deep beneath the stage. (One perk no one grudged our stage crew was the extra payment received for working in that dark and dangerous hole.) Covent Garden's stage elevators, raising and lowering portions of the stage floor on sections known as bridges, rebuilt in the early years of the century, were powered by the engines of First World War submarines. They worked well.

But today, neither *Carmen* nor *The Sleeping Beauty* is given in front of cloth. The stage was wholly inadequate to cope with the weight of scenery customary in the century's second half. And, as we have seen, an opera house faces a difficulty that never arises for a theatre housing a long-running musical: the need to change over from one show to another. However massive the set for *Miss Saigon*, *Les Misérables* or *Starlight Express*, once the scenery is in the theatre, it stays there for the duration of the run; it shares the stage with nothing else. But to change over from one opera to another, or from opera to ballet, or from rehearsal to performance, requires both space and modern stage machinery. Covent Garden possessed neither.

In the 1920s and 1930s, the difficulties could readily be overcome. Opera scenery was still on the light side; the emphasis still very much on the singers and the conductor. And performances were well spaced out. Opera-going in those days was something to dress up for, part of the social season. One evening in my time, Lord Deedes – the Dear Bill of *Private Eye* – delightful fellow, turned up during an interval and propped up the wall of my retiring room. I was most happy to find him there. He closed his eyes, dreamily summoning up the past, and drawled, 'I seem to remember that last time I was here, we wore white tie.' I thought to ask which post-war royal gala he had attended – that for President de Gaulle perhaps. And then I understood. He did not mean that sort of dress occasion. He remembered attending a pre-war performance in white tie and tails; had dined before, and danced after. Another world.

During the Second World War, the Royal Opera House served as a dance hall. Thousands of soldiers, sailors and airmen, men and women, enjoying the freedoms war brings, danced the nights away. The band was on the stage, the pit was floored over and reached out over the stalls. The theatrical old lady showed her medals. A riotously good time was had by all.

In 1946, the theatre re-opened with a performance of *The Sleeping Beauty* by the Sadler's Wells Ballet, the first of seventy-eight consecutive performances! The décor was by Oliver Messel; Margot Fonteyn danced the Princess Aurora. Opera and ballet shared the stage, with the ballet at first in prime position. The demands put on the Covent Garden stage grew weightier. Performances followed each other, night after night. Each day there were rehearsals, with technical rehearsals, expensively, on Sundays. The theatre took a break for some weeks in the summer, but this had reduced by the late 1980s to as little as five weeks or even four. Every day of that was needed for annual repairs to the stage, laden with scenery, carrying the weight of singers and chorus, pounded by dancers' feet. The House was in use the whole of the rest of the year, six evenings a week, with matinées in addition. Pressure on the stage was intolerable. Either a major redevelopment or a completely new theatre on a different site was needed.

The theatre sat on top of the Covent Garden fruit and vegetable market, where, every day except Christmas, lorries trucked in and porters humped by basket and barrowload tons of prime perishable produce. Covent Garden's streets could no longer cope with the heavy lorry traffic. When the market closed, something earthy and lively in London's life died with it. Coffee-stalls had kept open all night for revellers; pubs had opened before breakfast to serve market porters whose work began at 4am. But that Covent Garden could not be preserved. In an age of ambitious, not to say megalomaniac, town-planning there were those who proposed to alter the area's nature by razing much of it to the ground, changing the street pattern and rebuilding on a vast scale. One constraint on the Royal Opera House's possible expansion was Floral Street to the north. This pre-empted the chance of a cruciform stage pattern, main stage and side-stages, common elsewhere in theatres built or rebuilt since the Second World War. One plan for the Covent Garden area shows Floral Street abolished, so that a new opera house on a new alignment becomes possible. Another plan, favoured once by the GLC, was for an area of vast office development. This was bad news to the local community whose families lived and worked in the market, and the small-scale retail businesses and artisans' workshops that surrounded it. They wanted to preserve the area's character if they could. When a plan for massive redevelopment was put forward, the Covent Garden Community Association (CGCA) fought it unrelentingly, saw it off at an inquiry, and won a famous victory. Unfortunately for the Opera House, that war was not over. The leaders, if not all the members, believed in continuous struggle – *la lotta continua* – which became for some of them almost a reason for living. Any coming developer, however well intentioned, was likely to meet serious resistance. The Royal Opera House was next in line.

When government – a Labour government, in fact – gave the Opera House land on which to develop in 1974, the House knew it must seize this chance, or crumble into decrepitude. 'Not one further penny would be provided from public funds,' the Treasury insisted, and has continued to insist. The Opera House was now on its own. The land made over, held in trust to realize its purpose jointly by the Royal Opera House and the Arts Council, had a value in 1975 of about £3 million. Without the land given, redevelopment would not have been possible. Now it became conceivable, even likely, on that site. But the entire capital cost of redevelopment was still to be found.

'In Xanadu did Kubla Khan a stately pleasure dome decree . . .' In Austria after the Second World War, national pride and a commitment to an operatic heritage that lives rebuilt the Wiener Staatsoper. Bavaria's self-respect did the same for the Staatsoper in Munich. Civic pride paid for both, from public funds. In Berlin, when the Cold War divided the city, cutting off West Berliners from the Staatsoper on Unter den Linden, the Senate and Federal Government gave funds to build the Deutsche Oper. Opera-lovers in New York, tapping private wealth beyond Europe's dreams, collaborated to move the Met from its old, loved haunt on Broadway and 38th. They were aided on a generous scale by the state and city of New York, determined to revive a run-down area of Manhattan above Columbus Circle. Lincoln Center, with its two opera houses, its theatres and concert halls, its vast new promenade, stands gloriously where only twenty years before urban decay offended all eyes and the city's *amour propre*. New South Wales used a state lottery to bring Jørn Utzon's design for the Sydney Opera House to completion. This building caused endless controversy, took fourteen years to build, ten more than expected, and cost 102 million Australian dollars, ten times the original estimate. When they looked inside, they had to turn the concert hall it contained into an opera house, and vice versa, before performances could proceed. But Sydney now boasts one of the most beautiful contemporary buildings in the world. Bilbao has recently responded with Frank Gehry's Guggenheim Museum. He was commissioned to create 'the most important building of this century'. Kubla Khan would have applauded.

In 1982 François Mitterrand decreed that, for 1989, the 200th anniversary of the French Revolution, Paris should have a new, popular opera house on the Place de la Bastille, one of a series of grand projects on an east–west axis across the city. Paris got one. The design, by the Canadian architect Carlos Ott, was chosen in open, anonymous, competition. Scurrilous rumour has it that jury members, under patriotic pressure to choose a Frenchman after seeing the Beaubourg Centre Pompidou designed by Renzo Piano and Richard Rogers, were wrongly tipped off about whose design was which, and came up with it by mistake. Now they had to cost it and build it. I toured the site with a key member of the team, Michael Dittman. He had taken a telephone call from the Finance Ministry: 'The Minister likes the scheme; he wants to know what it will cost.' 'We'll do some work and let you know.' 'You don't understand. The Minister needs to know by tomorrow.' Dittman had been involved in building two opera houses in Germany. He looked up their cost, did a calculation based on volume, added 20 per cent for safety, and arrived at a total whose sterling equivalent was £350 million. He reported this figure. A few weeks later the expenditure was authorized. The Bastille was built, in time to open for the anniversary, at that cost. Not a moment had been lost. Not everyone liked it. Hugues Gall was asked what he thought of it and replied: *'Mauvaise réponse à une question qui ne se posait pas!'* – 'The wrong answer to a question which did not need asking.' He is now running the Bastille and the Garnier.

British government, by contrast, invited the Board of the Royal Opera House, a penurious charitable institution, to find on its own the funds to redevelop a theatre a century and a half old, without directly providing a penny of the cost. The registered charity had to turn property-developer, or discover a crock of gold, to have any hope of succeeding. The process, though not as drawn out as the building of the British Library, or the long labour and induced birth of the National Theatre, took nearly twenty-five years. The high-speed rail-link to the Channel Tunnel will take as long. We order things differently here.

The first determination of the Board of the Royal Opera House was to see the job done, the task completed. I honour them for it. They could have said, 'Running this place is quite hard enough, thank you very much. Let someone else rebuild it.' But, acting out of love, they saw their duty plain. Accepting there would be no further help from government, they set about trying to raise what was needed themselves. In deciding to use the land government had given, they had taken a major strategic decision. They would rebuild on this site, not on another; they would preserve and add on to the existing Victorian auditorium, rather than obtain permission, which would never have been granted, to knock it down and build a completely new theatre. But by deciding to continue to use the Victorian theatre, with its horseshoe-shaped auditorium, they were committing to compromise; they would add modern facilities to an old-fashioned theatre, creating a complex of buildings which would sit well with its neighbours in Covent Garden. They would not, as Vienna or Munich had done, simply replicate the past; they would not, as had the Met, remove to a new, vast, dedicated site; they would not strike out, as had Sydney, for the architectural stratosphere. Covent Garden would do none of these things; it would both preserve and create; it would marry its surroundings. A complete new theatre on another site would have been far more expensive; the decision to build at Covent Garden was the right one.

After an open competition in 1984, Jeremy Dixon was selected as architect. Since his practice was a small one, and his company's strengths lay in design rather than engineering, the ROH Board decided to appoint him jointly with an ally in a larger firm with expertise in construction, in engineering services, in project management, in commercial matters: Bill Jack of Building Design Partnership (BDP). Later, Jeremy Dixon persuaded his partner and friend Edward Jones to return from Canada to help finalize the overall appearance and its infinite detail. Jones turned down a full professorship at Princeton to do so. The main thing Dixon and Jones needed was patience.

At a Board meeting I attended in 1986, Jeremy Dixon described his plans to Board members and to those who would have a crucial role in helping bring them to fulfilment. A key figure here was John Sainsbury. He and Vivien Duffield would, at vital moments to come, personally act to clear the path forward. Dixon's scheme would achieve the objectives set for it in the brief. It undertook to preserve and refurbish the auditorium, improve amenity and space for the public, modernize the stage facilities; rehouse the Royal Ballet, moving its studios and offices from Barons Court to Covent Garden; provide a second auditorium for smaller-scale work, opera and ballet; and, importantly, add to the cityscape by completing the eastern edge of Inigo Jones's Market Square. The Opera House's staff, facilities and functions straddled Floral Street and were scattered across London from King's Cross to Mile End. The scheme would bring as many of them as possible on to the island site, bounded by Floral Street to the north and Russell Street to the south. Offices, workshops making scenery, props, hats, costumes, scenery storage, opera and ballet rehearsal studios, would be crammed on to a limited space – less in volume than is occupied by the Met or the Bastille. The building would have to be dug deep, as well as rising high. Westminster City Council, the planning authority, had demanded we build a multi-storey car park under the Russell Street/Bow Street corner – accessed by a steep ramp in Bow Street. And, towering over Russell Street, where stood some modestly attractive part-Georgian buildings, then occupied on short leases by restaurants and shops, there would be a sizeable office block, providing some 175,000 square feet of accommodation. The value of this, realized in a booming market, would supply funds which, added to the proceeds of an appeal to the private sector, would see the scheme built. That was the theory. But the sums did not add up. And, in the vain attempt to serve both Muses and Mammon, it was doubtful if the House's technical needs were adequately met.

Jeremy Dixon's design imaginatively integrated the Opera House building into the area. Inigo Jones, in the seventeenth century, had designed Covent Garden as a whole: St Paul's Church to the west, and to the north, south and east colonnaded facades, of equal mass and scale, gave a unity to the space they enclosed. In the centre of that space, there

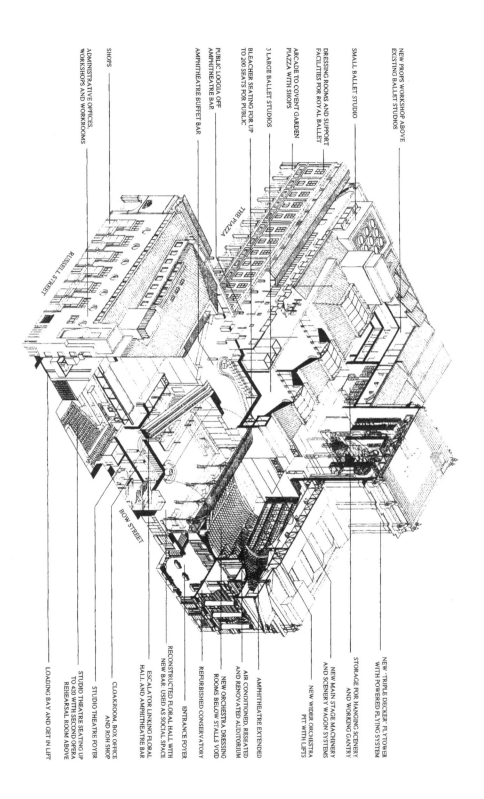

now stood the market buildings. A pale Victorian imitation of Inigo's plan could still be seen in colonnades on the northern edge, west of James Street. To the east was an ugly, derelict vacant site – the market's lorry park – extending through to Bow Street, crying out to be built on. Dixon proposed to follow Inigo Jones by completing his piazza with porticos and colonnades. The Opera House would present a friendly, useful face to the crowds promenading in the square, rather than the high, bare curtain walls other theatres forbiddingly show. Covent Garden was to be, in Inigo's intention, an open rectangle. It did not aspire to the closed perfection of the Place des Vosges in Paris, or the Plaza Real in Salamanca. The Piazza degli Armi in Livorno was a likelier model. To restore the square, even in part, would be a change worth making.

The same could not be said of the proposed office block. Who needs offices? In the 1980s, developers were queuing up to answer: 'We do!' As Britain's service economy boomed, the City of London prospered. Demand for office space was strong, and growing stronger. Offices in Covent Garden next to the Inns of Court, not far from the City itself, could not fail to realize value or to earn income. Or so it was believed. But there was a snag; any office block on the Russell Street/Bow Street corner of the Opera House site would be small by comparison with the NatWest Tower, but to those opposed to the Royal Opera House development, for whom the auditorium itself threw too big a shadow, even a modest office block seemed wholly undesirable. What was more, large-scale development in Covent Garden was contrary to planning guidelines laid down by the GLC and promulgated by the planning authority now responsible, Westminster City Council. If Westminster granted planning permission to the Royal Opera House scheme, in its then form, the Council, it was argued, would be in direct breach of its own planning regulations. It could be held to be acting *ultra vires*. Its action would certainly be liable to judicial review.

We debated the way forward at meetings of the Development Board, a subsidiary of the Main Board. Its members, experienced in property matters, included Philip Beck of Mowlem, and a successful developer, Trevor Osborne of Speyhawk. The professional advisers were of the highest quality. At these meetings, the House claimed space that clashed with the revenue-raising needs of the development. Looking hard, and acquisitively, at model or plan, I would insist that room must be found for the House's operations: paint-frame, props, wardrobe, must be accommodated on site; education needed to expand, and so on. Trevor Osborne, a cheeky chappy with a keen mind and a prodigious appetite for hard work, used always to reply, 'Don't cut into the commercial block. We shall need the revenue if we are to build the scheme.' As things were then, this was unchallengeable. If we were to persuade the Arts Council, the Office of Arts and Libraries, and behind them the Treasury, that it was safe to go ahead, it would be necessary to raise more than half of the total sum required through property development. The offices were a vital part of the scheme. The architects never liked them: they saw the scheme as an aggregate of individual buildings – Barry's auditorium sitting next to Barry's reconstituted Floral Hall; distinctive façades on the piazza; ballet studios and fly-tower as roofscape. They wanted as much variety on the site as the differing functions there. A monolithic office block, whose regularity enhanced its commercial value, was quite contrary in spirit. They would have wished it away if they could, but needs must when financial devils drive. No other source of funding was then in evidence.

Central government would not provide it. Could London? The obvious source of funding for great civic arts projects which enhance a nation's cultural life but benefit principally those who live in, work in and visit a city, is local pride. The city of Munich joins with the *Land* of Bavaria to support the opera in Munich. In Paris, city and state, mayor and president, contend with each other to excel, and to be seen to excel, in support for the arts. The French State – the President, that is – and his ministers fund the Bastille, the Garnier and the Opéra-Comique. The City, the Mayor and Lady Mayoress, support the Châtelet and the Champs-Elysées. The Théâtre des Amandiers at La Défence, where Patrice Chéreau did some of his finest work, and the Théâtre at Bobigny, where, during closure, the Royal Opera toured Deborah Warner's *The Turn of the Screw*, receive funds from lesser municipalities, the equivalent of London boroughs in size, each determined to make the arts a vital part of their citizens' lives.

But by now London was without a government. In a determined fit of political pique, Margaret Thatcher exercised her whim of iron to abolish the GLC, taking back into Whitehall (and distributing to thirty-two disparate London boroughs) powers that had been wielded at County Hall. Whatever the rights and wrongs of this seizure – no doubt the GLC was bureaucratic and top heavy – the intention and the effect were clear: London was left leaderless. There was no London to which the Opera

House could turn. From its financial treasure, the archaic City of London funds the Barbican Centre and the good things that go on there. All credit to it. The City matches the grant that the London Symphony Orchestra (LSO) receives from the Arts Council, making it the only half-adequately funded orchestra in Britain; the LSO now gets a quarter of Berlin's grant to the Berlin Philharmonic. But the City, understandably, has up to now virtually confined its funding within its own walls. Approaches to officers, and the sounding out of successive Lord Mayors, failed to alter this natural order of priorities. That left the City of Westminster. But the borough was not prepared to help with major capital schemes. Westminster was proud to have the ROH within its city limits. Its leaders welcomed a thriving opera house in Covent Garden, rather than a derelict shell. They looked with favour on the House's aim to redevelop. They supported our outreach work. But they were not a major source of funds.

The National Lottery did not exist in 1988, and was not a serious prospect, only a bright gleam in a fanatic's eye. Denis Vaughan, a multi-parted eccentric, resident in Covent Garden, had been a musical colleague and disciple of Thomas Beecham; he was a conductor, and an authority on acoustics. He was an eager proponent not of an expanded Royal Opera House, but of a loosely defined and grandly conceived international centre of the arts on the same site, our site. He was also, ahead of his time but vindicated during it, an enthusiastic advocate of a national lottery to benefit the arts. The trouble was that, while Thatcher was in power, no one listened to him. Scarcely a week went by without a lengthy letter from him reporting his views and their progress to acceptance. Each one I received was individually addressed to me but copied, if I looked carefully, to a list of dignitaries which always included the Prime Minister, the Chancellor of the Exchequer, the Minister for the Arts, the Chairman of the Arts Council, and sometimes, though I may have imagined it, the Archbishop of Canterbury. To acknowledge one of these round-robins was fatal. Promptly, another would be delivered, this time informing everyone that a most encouraging reply had been received from Jeremy Isaacs, General Director of the Royal Opera House, welcoming and endorsing the recommendations made in the previous letter. Politeness cultivated over the years led me at first to read and respond to Denis Vaughan. Soon, like others with whom I checked, I consigned his missives, unread, to the wastepaper basket.

Margaret Thatcher was opposed to the idea of a national lottery. Not averse to pleasure, she nevertheless disliked the idea that it could be come by too easily. People should pay for their pleasures, she thought. Her government could not dispense with the state's dependence on gambling, through taxes on betting, on horses and dogs and football pools. But she would not be party to extending it. Britain must be frugal in its habits, she urged. A vastly increased dependence on gambling, let alone glorying in it, did not sit easily with her belief in self-help. And in 1988, Mrs Thatcher was still securely in power.

At this time, I had a cheerful encounter with her at a cocktail party in Pimlico given by Kenneth Baker, then Secretary of State for Education and Science. The police presence in the street beforehand had suggested to me that she was expected, but I did not see her in the crowded rooms. As I was leaving, Kenneth Baker seized me and presented me to her. She gestured to those nearest. 'This man', she announced, forefinger prodding me in the chest, 'is the devil. Nine and a half years of doing absolutely everything right, and he doesn't believe a word of it.' It took me a moment or two to realize she meant *she* had done absolutely everything right. 'I believe some of it, Prime Minister,' I muttered, 'not all of it.' What was striking was the strength of her self-belief. If she was opposed to it, a national lottery would not happen in her time. Denis Vaughan was promising 'pie-in-the-sky'. No viable plan could take notice of it. We must soldier on without.

And the need to build was urgent. There was a real question as to how long the House could operate effectively in the condition it then was in, groaning and creaking under the load of work, the flow of performances and rehearsals, the demands of the new productions we came up with each season. The structure was sound, but the fabric was showing the strain. Rain regularly came through the roof, dripping through on to certain seats in the stalls and the amphitheatre, and soaking areas of the stage. The wiring was ancient, and growing older by the year; in 1988 the House had not been rewired for nearly thirty years. Westminster's health and safety inspectors, on their regular visits, might not tolerate that much longer. Running repairs or slight structural modifications often came across pockets of asbestos in corners of the fabric which, with due precaution, must be removed. The sooner these faults could be attended to, this neglect repaired, the better. But rewiring alone was a six- or nine-month job at least. The House would have to close anyway to see that done. Better to crack on to closure for development, and carry out all necessary repairs then. With urgent need our watchword, we pressed on with the planning application to Westminster, the office block still part of the scheme. We faced formidable opponents.

The Covent Garden Community Association had maybe 1000 members. They had premises nearby in Earlham Street, where local residents could drop in for a cup of tea and a chat. They stood for the well-being of the community, and the environmental interests of those who lived and worked in the area. In other circumstances, they might well have supported the Royal Opera House's development plans. It could not be in their interest if the theatre crumbled and closed: too many local people worked there; a great many local restaurants depended on custom attracted by opera and ballet performances. The Royal Opera House ought to have had their support. Instead, at every turn, we met violent antagonism. Was this our own fault? Were we arrogant and aloof? Perhaps. But there is more to the story. The CGCA was heavily politicized around a single issue. Most of its members, who used it for social purposes, had little objection to what the Royal Opera House sought to achieve. But most of its members, even if they were properly concerned about the noise, dust and disruption that would be caused by a major building going up in their midst, never went to meetings. The CGCA, still cherishing memories of victory over the GLC, was led by a polemicist whose frenzied and untiring energy in single-minded opposition to the Opera House and all its works proved a constant thorn in our flesh – James, Jim, Monahan.

Jim Monahan is the son of another James Monahan, from the Opera House's world. The father had been principal of the Royal Ballet School and, under the *nom de plume* James Kennedy, ballet critic of the *Guardian*. He married more than once. By one wife he had a son, Jim, and a daughter, Judy. The marriage ended and he married Merle Park, the dazzling ballerina of the Royal Ballet of the 1960s and 1970s, and from 1983 to 1998 herself principal of the Royal Ballet School. That marriage too ended in divorce. Did this family history rub off on Jim Monahan, fuelling part of his hostility to the Opera House? I sometimes thought so.

And then, Jim Monahan is himself an architect. After the successful campaign to prevent large-scale redevelopment of the Covent Garden area, he was commissioned to design the Jubilee Hall, an undistinguished market building on the south side of the piazza. What he did not win was the commission to design the redeveloped Royal Opera House. He entered the competition, and did not make the shortlist. I once agreed to meet Monahan in my office and hear him out. On the particular matter he was pressing – objections to the Bow Street façade – it seemed to me that his critique boiled down to one simple fact he could not live with: Jeremy Dixon was architect of the scheme, he was not. I saw no point in continuing the dialogue. Happily for us, Monahan was formidable only until he made his case. Then fury gripped him and his audience was lost.

Planning permission for a major scheme, I learned to my cost, is not achieved by one all-embracing set of documents, but by an endless succession of detailed applications adding up to a complex whole. To any written submission to Westminster by the Royal Opera House, Monahan was ready with his objections. Every submission was published precisely to allow time for objection. Monahan invariably objected. Westminster encouraged consultation; when consulted, he objected the more. In the naïve belief that Westminster's councillors would act on the well-reasoned papers which their officers, with whom we were in weekly contact, put in front of them, I paid less attention to appeasing the CGCA than I might have done. I did not appreciate that for the councillors it was the very fact of an objection, not its substance, that counted. Every objection must be countered in kind, or it told against us. The officers, expert and thorough as they were, were mere advisers. Councillors on the Planning Committee or sub-committee would take the decision. The Chairman of the Planning Committee was a key figure. We made contact and kept in touch, particularly when a new Chair took office. Tremendous respect was accorded by the committee to the views of two local councillors, representing the ward in which Covent Garden itself was sited. For these two, the CGCA appeared to have quasi-representative status. It claimed to speak for opinion in Covent Garden, and was assumed by them to do so. It certainly did not, but unfortunately no one else did. It took us far too long to set up a Community Liaison Group in which we made the running, and the CGCA representative – Monahan – was only one of several present. Monahan's language could easily be detected in any CGCA written submission to Westminster, whoever had signed it. But, as the dramatic events involving Dame Shirley Porter and council housing policy made clear, few things mattered more at Westminster than winning elections. Every ward and every vote counted.

Heaven forfend that a single ward should fall to Labour because of voters' disaffection over the Royal Opera House's plans. At all costs, the local councillors believed, note had to be taken of the CGCA's views. At one point, the local councillor, before a crucial Planning Committee meeting, reported to us her concern that a petition against a particular application had been received, and gone unanswered. 'How many signed?' I asked. The answer: fifty-four. There were two days to go. I sent for volunteers. In half that time, more than 200 local businesses willingly countersigned in our favour. From then on we played tit for tat. Yet I still find it extraordinary that over a scheme of national consequence so much attention needed to be paid to tiny, vociferous, unrepresentative minorities. I used to point a contrast by telling an apocryphal story of a British and a French civil aviation minister of two decades ago. 'Monsieur,' says the Brit, 'tell me something. In Britain we have been arguing for twenty years now over whether London needs a third airport, and where to put it. In France, you decided only seven years ago that Paris needed a third airport, and today the planes are taking off from Charles de Gaulle, at Roissy. How do you do it?' The Frenchman replies: 'It is very simple. In my country, when we propose to drain a swamp, we do not consult the frogs.'

In June 1987 Westminster City Council granted the Royal Opera House full planning permission for its controversial scheme. In August 1987 the CGCA applied to the High Court for a judicial review of Westminster's decision, citing guidelines against offices in the area as their principal ground. This was a major setback, the press said, to the House's plans. That it certainly was, if only because the hearing was likely to be a year away; and, even if a ruling went in our favour, there was always the possibility of an appeal, and further delay. The news in October that the High Court had set a date for the hearing meant an immediate change in our plans. The House could not now close in 1993, but only in mid-1995, at the end of the season, at the earliest. David had challenged Goliath, with a vengeance.

But David was not alone. Judicial reviews are an expensive business. The CGCA could not afford to do this itself; someone else was paying the bills. Threatened by the development in Russell Street were busy cafés and restaurants, one of them called Brahms and Lizst – less a tribute to nineteenth-century Romantic composers than highbrow Cockney rhyming slang for 'Pissed'. The proprietor, a Mr Stein, traded there on a short lease. We were the landlords. We gave all our tenants statutory notice of our intentions to redevelop. They knew they would have to close when we determined. All naturally wanted that day postponed as long as possible, and then, ideally, either to be handsomely compensated for going, or to be rehoused on the site. The proprietor of Brahms and Liszt was particularly tenacious; the solicitor who represented him was famously belligerent in a tenant's cause. We always believed that Brahms and Liszt's proprietor bankrolled CGCA's continuing campaign, as he was legally fully entitled to do. (Later, we rehoused him in James Street.)

Both Westminster and we ourselves briefed counsel, and prepared for the High Court's judicial review hearings. A serious point of planning law was at issue. As we waited, using the time to revise and re-revise the scheme, the bills mounted. In February 1988 Mr Justice Scott pronounced, and vindicated Westminster completely. The Council should observe guidelines set for it, he noted, but not as absolutes; they were rules to be taken account of, not diktats to be obeyed. The financial circumstance of the planning applicant was a material consideration, which the planning authority could properly take into account. If convinced this was the case, the Council was entitled to choose the planning gain of a handsome new opera house in the vicinity over the awkwardness of an office block, as its price. Property was built not in an abstract juridical landscape, but in the real world. Planning authorities must weigh conflicting considerations, and decide. He dismissed the application. The CGCA appealed. In September the Court of Appeal upheld Mr Justice Scott's decision. The CGCA's request to appeal to the House of Lords was denied. The CGCA was left with its costs. Their initiative cost us a delay of two years. It was back to the drawing-board, but the scheme would be better for the setback. Westminster, without a whisper of complaint, had staunchly withstood the legal challenge. They were brusquely rewarded. The Royal Opera House abandoned the scheme which the courts had approved, and submitted another application instead.

For years before I arrived, the Development Office juggled with the scheme's conflicting elements, shifting the boundary between space for the House's own needs and the offices which would pay for them. Wherever the divide, there was always a financial gap that could not be closed. If the sum seemed feasible, that would be met by public appeal. When I came in, I examined the scheme we were then putting forward, to satisfy myself that the House's gains were adequate. The theatre could not cope much longer with the technical demands placed on the stage. Could I be certain the new House would? This review intensified when

John Harrison, the new Technical Director, joined us in November 1988. Harrison was taken aback at what he found. He urged that more space for scenery storage and assembly was certainly needed, and that, if we really sought revenue savings, more of the House's service facilities, scattered across London, should be concentrated on the site. But the stage, the hub of our operations, was the key. There we should aim, in stage lifts, in the flying system and above all in the delivery and movement of scenery, for the best modern technology could deliver. If the House was to be re-developed, then, I was easily persuaded, we had to ensure that lasting benefit resulted. A new Chief Executive of Development, Dick Ensor, had joined that summer. He too was willing to rethink what we were proposing, to redefine our aim. The staff canteen, for example, remained below ground, airless and windowless. We could do better for the staff than that. We agreed that the 1986 scheme was inadequate and that the Opera House's space within it would have to be drastically enlarged. So revision was called for, and put in hand.

The House had been engaged in furthering redevelopment now for nearly fifteen years and had very little to show for it, except a plan that needed changing, and a very substantial overdraft run up by architects' fees, the costs of running a development office, of preparing the planning application, the expense of time, and the interest on borrowing. With no funds yet available, all was financed by a bank loan. We owed Coutts, our understanding bankers, £15 million, secured by a charge on Royal Opera House properties, against the expectation of the success of an appeal and the realization of property values. They would be repaid in the end. We had pledges of private help, but these were dependent on the state's pro-viding funds also. Of that, there was no sign.

When Dick Ensor took over the development, several people were dis-satisfied, including Ensor's predecessor Robin Dartington. Perhaps not surprisingly, a series of hostile stories found its way to the press; some were based on the leak of Development Board minutes. On 7 February 1989, at a critical moment in our relations with Westminster, the *Guardian* gleefully claimed a scoop: 'Opera in Disneyland: Secret talks to ring Covent Garden with theme cafés'. The paper's noted investigative correspondent David Hencke attached excerpts from papers stating that it had been agreed to consider such a proposal. Apart from the sheer impracticality of accommodating a Disneyland theme park of any sort on a corner of the Bow Street site, Hencke could have discovered, by a single telephone call, the unlikelihood of such a partnership. He did not check with us, but ran the story. There was this grain of truth in it: the Development Board felt, responsibly, that it ought at least to look at any proposal for commercial partnership that was made to it, perhaps avoiding the need to build offices thereby. When I saw the theme-park proposal, I put it immediately in the wastepaper basket. Solemnly, feeling that Westminster were entitled to a public denial from us, I gave a press conference – very tedious it was too – to put the record straight: no Disney.

Sir Michael Tippett OM, in his eighty-fifth year, sent me a postcard:

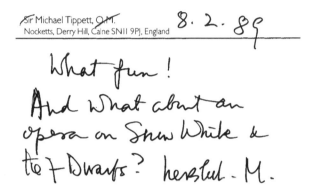

Later Tippett's agent wrote to say that Sir Michael's commission fee for the work would be £10,000 per dwarf and £20,000 for Miss S. White, but that he was too busy to get down to it before 1995.

Westminster's concerns about the various versions of the scheme were aesthetic, conservationist, social: the height of the fly-tower; the proposed demolition of Georgian buildings in Russell Street; a request for some modest residential content – flats in Floral Street, Long Acre – to compensate for the volume of new offices. English Heritage fought the conservationist case. On the auditorium itself we had no quarrel; Barry's theatre would be preserved, enhanced, improved, with air-conditioning as a top priority. But it would not be altered. The Floral Hall, beside it, was another matter. We could not keep all of that. Decrepit as it was, it was still a superb example of Victorian ironwork. The barrel-vaulted roof had been destroyed by fire in 1956. English Heritage would have wished the whole restored and preserved on site. That could not be. If there was to be efficient movement of scenery we had to add, as well as a rear-stage, a side-stage. Floral Street cut off expansion to the north; a side-stage must lie to the south, where the rear of the Floral Hall now stood. We would preserve as much of it as we could, and would restore the barrel-vaulted roof, turning it into one of London's finest public rooms. But part would be deconstructed, stored and perhaps re-assembled elsewhere. English Heritage would, reluctantly, have to wear that. In the end, they did.

As time dragged on, the Development Office was not idle. Ensor grappled manfully and inventively with the problems he faced. He was content, as we all had to be, with the planning envelope – the scale of the scheme above ground – for which permission had been granted. But he sought two further objectives: to accommodate on the island site virtually all the House's departments. When Westminster abandoned its insistence on a deep basement car park, this freed space for the Opera House workshops underground. And he plotted a flow-path for the build that would ensure the Treasury's assent. What they wanted was to know that we could afford to complete each phase of the scheme as we undertook it. Ensor decided to match this by breaking the build down into several separate phases, none to be embarked on till the previous was completed. Since few funds were available upfront, we would start by building and letting the commercial element of the scheme, creating value that would help fund the rest. He formally submitted a lengthy document setting all this out in sequence. The Treasury agreed to it. One step at a time, they said, seems the prudent way to us. The fact that it was precisely this super-cautious, crab-like progress that had led to a protracted build and vast overspend on the British Library completely escaped them. In 1990 a newly revised scheme won Westminster's approval. The build Ensor envisaged would extend over nearly a decade, commencing before the House closed, continuing after it re-opened to 2002. When the Board was presented with Ensor's proposed timetable, Vivien Duffield, now principally responsible for our fundraising effort, blew it away with one sentence: 'I cannot raise funds for anything that takes so long.' The donors she was preparing to tap for six- and seven-figure contributions, philanthropic individuals, charitable trusts or corporations, would want to see far quicker results. Ensor's proposals were too complicated, and probably unworkable.

The Board and Development Board thought it sensible, before finally proceeding, to invite an independent review of our plans. We should test their viability, their likely cost, the probable duration of the build, and its effect on the closure period. Our Development Board bristled with expertise in property. Trevor Osborne, the principal link with Westminster's officers, could properly take pride in the planning permission he had helped win. But now, in 1993, another property company, Stuart Lipton's Stanhope plc, was invited to run a ruler over our intention. And they came at a critical juncture: the property market was changing and a bill bringing into being a new source of funding, a national lottery, was making its way through Parliament.

Stuart Lipton was the successful developer of Broadgate – though later he lost control of the project. He had won praise for advisory services provided, *pro bono*, to the new opera house at Glyndebourne, and to the Sainsbury Wing of the National Gallery. He brought with him, as eyes and ears, Peter Rogers, an eager beaver with an analytical mind and bold taste in neckwear, the half-brother of architect Richard Rogers. They did not like what they saw. Their view, simply put, was that there was too much on the site. We were overdeveloping it. It could not carry what we were loading on to it. The office block, rising on part of the site to roof level, forced Opera House functions underground. Digging deep would be costly. We would encounter more problems below than above ground. Some were concerned for the health and morale of workers below ground. I was not. I had seen airy rehearsal spaces several levels below the stage at the Met in New York, and vast pits for scenery storage, assembly and movement at the Bastille; confining scenery storage and assembly to lower levels would free up space for other activities above ground. But all added to the complexity of the build. Our advisers had not formally advised that what was being attempted was impossible, only that it was difficult. Ensor had no qualms about the difficulties. Stanhope did. They urged we go for something far more simple, accommodating everything we needed on a horizontal plan; one deep basement only, everything else at ground level or above. But there was no way even the Opera House's minimal needs could be met on the site if 130,000 square feet of space was given over to commercial development. 'Get rid of the office block,' said Stuart Lipton. 'Do without it. Offices won't pay anyway. They were the 1980s; this is the 1990s. Let's see what the scheme will look like without them. Let's reconfigure, emphasizing simplicity in the build, and in the structures we erect.'

This liberating view helped transform the situation. It was able to do so, however, only because of an equally dramatic change at 10 Downing Street. Margaret Thatcher had gone. John Major was Prime Minister. A national lottery would soon be a reality. Help, from this unexpected quarter, was on the way.

11

LOTTERY

New Year's Eve 1990: a gala performance of *Die Fledermaus* to mark the farewell to the stage of one of the very brightest stars in opera's firmament, Dame Joan Sutherland. This was the moment I first realized that a national lottery might become a reality.

Joan Sutherland had been a member of Covent Garden's resident company of singers for eight seasons before rocketing to stardom in 1959 in *Lucia di Lammermoor*; since then her immaculate and dazzling high soprano had delighted the world. Now her career was ending. Joan's last proper performances at Covent Garden had been for John Tooley, in the 1986/87 season, as Donizetti's Anna Bolena. She was in pretty good voice, at least some of the time. (For management, the principal preoccupation during the run had been the mezzo-soprano, the excellent Susanne Mentzner, who sang Jane Seymour; she was pregnant – eight and a half months pregnant by the final performance. She made it to the curtain, giving birth safely a few days later.) After that last *Anna Bolena*, John Tooley gave a supper party. Courteously, he seated Joan beside me. As we chatted, she told me her great joy now was that she was a grandmother; her great pleasure from now on would be to knit for her grandchildren. One more farewell performance?

Paul Findlay put *Die Fledermaus* in the schedule for Christmas 1990, and hoped to persuade her to sing Rosalinde for a last time. The final per-formance would be on New Year's Eve. From then on he and I were to remind Luciano Pavarotti, whenever we saw him, of that date. *Die*

Fledermaus is a famously versatile piece; the ball in the middle act presents an opportunity for all sorts of guest artists to do a turn, a party-piece. Luciano had first sung with Joan when she was a star and he a newcomer. They sang *La fille du régiment* together at Covent Garden in 1966, a big step forward for him. Throwing off high Cs by the half-dozen, he scored a huge hit. Triumph at the Met followed. Pavarotti learned much from Joan, and always owned to the debt. Yes, he would sing at her farewell. He put the date in his diary. Paul Findlay had a fallback plan. If Joan would not sing Rosalinde, then perhaps she would come anyway, and do a cabaret turn at the ball. The half-expected call came. She would not sing Rosalinde – 'It's my knees, dear, not the voice,' she confided – but she would appear.

In November 1990, Michael Heseltine stood against the Prime Minister, Margaret Thatcher, for the leadership of the Tory party and toppled her from office. The spoils went to John Major, who won the ensuing election against Heseltine and became Prime Minister. His wife, Norma, had written a biography of Joan Sutherland. Invited by the Chairman, John Sainsbury, to join him in the Royal Box on New Year's Eve, the Majors accepted. Days before, I had read that Major was looking at a lottery as a way of funding sport and the arts. In the Crush Bar at the interval, snatching a moment's meeting, I told him I thought it an excellent idea. If the recipients were spread across the community, a lottery could command general assent.

On stage, the tenor Bonaventura Bottone, singing Alfred, flapped a white handkerchief to send up Pavarotti. '*Bella voce*,' said Luciano. In the cabaret on stage, Joan Sutherland sang 'Home Sweet Home'. At the end I welcomed the Prime Minister on one of his first public engagements, and offered a brief tribute to Joan. The audience cheered themselves hoarse. The television recording was seen round the world; Covent Garden on top form. It was a good night, all round.

Next year, 1991, the government looked at a national lottery in earnest. Tim Renton, Minister for the Arts, went twice to see how it worked in Ireland. His counterpart in Greece, Madame Benaki, told him: 'I am saved by the lottery.' This struck home. Renton, against the Treasury's opposition, including that of the then Chief Secretary David Mellor, became the lottery's principal advocate in Whitehall. He won over the Home Secretary; the Prime Minister was also on side. A proposal to create a national lottery was included in the Conservative Manifesto for the 1992 General Election. Major won. On 21 October 1993 the National Lottery Act received Royal Assent.

In other societies, revitalizing the Royal Opera House, the prime national lyric theatre, might have been seen as a proper modest charge on the public purse, costing much less than a submarine, say, or a clutch of tanks. But the British government, maintaining expenditure on the arts at the lowest level in Europe, except for Ireland, would not countenance meeting that need by a direct call on Treasury funds. Successive ROH Chairmen, granted audience, briefed successive Prime Ministers that a structure erected in 1858 would need to be redeveloped if it were to serve another century. Government, in effect, had acknowledged the need in 1974, when it gave the site. John Sainsbury, going to Downing Street to plead our cause with the aura of the Sainsburys' munificent gift of a new wing to the National Gallery around him, did not ask for the total bill to be met, only for a state contribution. The Treasury might be deaf to such a public benefactor; the Prime Minister could not be. John Major knew well that the case for the Opera House's redevelopment was irrefutable. But he had to find another way of funding it. That way was the National Lottery. So far from the Royal Opera House being an inappropriate recipient of the Lottery's first sizeable grant, it was actually the most suitable. Without the evident need to redevelop the Royal Opera House there might never have been a British national lottery at all.

Britain likes a gamble. Early forecasts predicted a rich flow of funds. Fifty per cent of the money wagered each week by punters would be redistributed in prizes. Of the remaining 50 per cent, half would be divided between the Lottery operators and, a new betting tax, the Treasury. Not only would the Treasury escape the need itself to fund Lottery projects, it would even benefit. These two depredations reduced the amount available for distribution to nominated 'good causes' to 25 per cent of the whole. This 25 per cent would be split five ways, 5 per cent each going to the arts, sport, heritage, charities and to celebrating the Millennium. Government had found a way to pay for rehousing the arts. Lottery funds would be made available for arts capital projects.

Government had no strategy on how the lottery should be introduced to the public. It was meant to spread benefit throughout the community; by offering something to everyone, and by simultaneous doling out of grants across the spectrum, it would win consensual support. But some of the five distributive agencies would be ready to deal well before the others.

Those whose statutory bodies already existed – the Arts Council, Sports Council and National Heritage Memorial Fund – would be first. A Charities Board, which might most easily touch public heartstrings, would come on stream last.

The Secretary of State chaired the Millennium Commission, and the Deputy Prime Minister was a member. They had licence to invent what to do with our money, their most extravagant invention being the Millennium Dome – at a cost of £750 million. The other four conduits would be reactive, not proactive; except in the loosest sense – spread it about a bit – they were given no guidelines on which to operate. They set these themselves. They would choose from those who applied to them; first come, first served.

Government, perhaps abashed at its new dependence on gambling, always seemed hesitant at claiming credit for the Lottery's benefits. Cautious estimates suggested that total Lottery income might run as high as £2 billion a year, bringing to the five beneficiaries as much as £100 million each annually. The actual sums far exceeded these hopes. On Saturday night, 19 November 1994, with Noel Edmonds presiding live on BBC1, the numbered balls whirled round and plopped, one by one, into the winner's groove: 3, 5, 14, 22, 30, 44. The jackpot of £5.9 million was shared by seven winners. The British punter, voting with the purse, contributed £48.9 million in the first week; this grew to £55.2 million on Christmas Eve. When the Royal Opera House submitted its application on 4 January 1995, Lottery income was higher than anyone had expected; each of the five good causes could well benefit by £250 million in 1995, and again in 1996. The Royal Opera House had been nursing a development project for twenty years. This was our chance.

I had fondly imagined that I, or the Chairman, would write a simple, eloquent letter stating our need. When I saw the application form, I put my colleague Keith Cooper, Director of Corporate Affairs, in charge. The information sought was extensive and detailed: precisely what we intended to build, what purposes it would serve, what it would cost, what the redeveloped House would achieve, what it would cost to run. There were hundreds of questions; they would take months to answer. And nothing we stated in our application was to be taken for granted; every assertion would have to be backed by consultants we might be asked to appoint, and reassessed by assessors the Arts Council appointed. Next to the jackpot winners and the directors of Camelot, the franchised operators, the largest fortunes earned through the Lottery have gone to accountants and consultants. At one point, late in the process, the Arts Council, distrusting both our figures and their own ability to appraise them, asked us to appoint consultants to process the figures before we resubmitted, and themselves appointed consultants to check them. However many runs of the computer resulted, the figures remained essentially the same. But we, though impoverished, would spend another £30,000 in fees, and so would they. In one year, 1998, administering the Lottery, the Arts Council spent £8.4 million on 'external assessment costs' – consultancy fees. Nice, if you can afford it.

The Arts Council's liaison officers dealing with our application could not have been more helpful; Jeremy Newton and Joan Cunningham were prompt and generous in their advice and guidance at every stage, repeatedly stressing the absolute importance of getting every item down on paper, and every detail right. Nothing escaped them. What work would be performed in our modest second auditorium, what other companies would we invite to perform there? What arrangements would we make for the disabled? There would, we said, be seats reserved at every level of the auditorium, and yes, there would be access by lift to every level. But would minders be able to sit next to wheelchairs, and not behind them? We tried to show that whatever could be done, would be.

We needed a decision at the earliest possible moment. Obtaining the Lottery grant would enable Vivien Duffield to launch her appeal, completing the funding circle. We were planning now on closure in July 1997. We would book artists for the 1996/97 season, but for the moment not beyond. Closure in summer 1997 meant that procurement contracts had to be entered into and orders placed, on a strict timetable, from summer 1995. There was not a day to lose. All through 1994 Keith Cooper and his aide, the peerless Siri Fischer-Hansen, slaved away day, night and weekends on the text and the swathes of factual information it contained. Applications could be submitted from January 1995. In November 1994, we were ready.

We would apply for £58.5 million as a contribution to the total cost of the development, £193 million. The rest we would raise ourselves. Most Lottery applicants for large grants have been asked to find 25 per cent of the cost of the schemes they proposed. We undertook to find 66 per cent. The Lottery's £58.5 million would help provide a gloriously reconstituted Floral Hall, a modest second auditorium, three new studios for the ballet (making five in all), a modernized stage, vastly improved sight-lines and air-conditioned comfort in the auditorium. It would make possible 300 performances a year, plus those in the studio theatre. All this was capital cost, meeting it our prime object.

We had another crying need. There was, as yet, no agreed external contribution to the revenue costs of the closure period; the guidelines specifically excluded revenue purposes. But during closure the House would incur new costs, such as theatre rental, and suffer drastic falls, though we did not realize quite how drastic, in box-office revenue and in private funding. This ticklish issue had been evident for years, but had lain unresolved. The Treasury line was, don't look to us; the Arts Ministry line, we see the problem but cannot help you. The Arts Council also saw the point, but would do nothing about it. But the problem would not go away. The Opera House argument was that to turn this difficult corner, a special provision – a one-off grant – would be necessary. One Minister for the Arts, Richard Luce, his civil servants shifting uneasily beside him, did once concede to me in his office that we had a clear case for additional funds. There might have to be a direct approach to the Prime Minister. That was our intention of last resort. We hoped the Arts Council, co-trustees of the development, would join us. Ministers came, and went; the Treasury remained as adamant as ever. In 1994, no one was putting their hand up and saying, 'We will go with you to Downing Street.'

As we prepared to submit our bid, I pondered what to say about closure costs. We could take the position that they were separate, and that we would make a separate application to government; or, on the argument that they were the direct consequence of the development and could not be divorced from the total cost of the build, we could include them. I did not want to jeopardize the grant to the building by adding an inappropriate supplementary request. On this there was no early guidance from the Arts Council. Mere days before our application, an inch thick and weighing over 2lb, had to go to the printer, word finally came. The liaison officers advised that the Chairman of the Lottery Advisory Panel, Arts Council member Peter Gummer, thought it best that we include a reference to closure costs, not as the essence of the application, but not separate from it either. We should avoid a separate plea to the Prime Minister; we must put our request in the document instead. Fatefully, we reviewed our figures. Based on estimates of box-office income in our preferred venue and on then current projections for private funding, we added a paragraph to the text requesting an additional £20 million towards closure costs directly due to the development. This sum was the largest I dared imagine we could hope to receive. In the event it was to prove inadequate. Had I requested £30 million, and had we been granted it, the story of the House's affairs over the two and a half years of closure would have been very different. In December 1994, though, we were relieved to be submitting a comprehensive, well-set-out, well-argued Lottery bid, on time. If Keith Cooper had done nothing else at Covent Garden, he would have earned his salary by the skill and determination he put into this.

On 4 January 1995, at 8.30am, I was outside the Arts Council building in Great Peter Street. Darcey Bussell and Bruce Sansom for the Royal Ballet, Tom Allen and Simon Keenlyside for the Royal Opera, came too. So did two students of the Royal Ballet School, the real future bene-ficiaries of the development. We handed the application in, posed for photographs, had coffee and a bun in the canteen, caught a taxi and came back to Bow Street. The waiting began.

Our case was a persuasive one, and in that lay our strength; the need was clear, the plans were detailed, the proposed building attractive. Redeveloped, the Royal Opera House would serve in the next century as a more efficient lyric theatre, with vastly improved public amenity; the ballet would be under one roof for the first time; the development would add to the cityscape, elegantly completing the Covent Garden market square, as Inigo Jones had intended. The sums made sense, and offered generous value for public money. From a weekly spasm of gamblers' optimism which would raise £4 billion a year, the public was being asked to stump up £58.5 million towards the cost of a national lyric theatre, attended by 600,000 souls a year, its music enjoyed by millions on radio and its spectacle by millions on television. The total sum applied for, including £20 million for the closure period, was under £80 million. This represented less than a third of Lottery income to the arts in one year, less than a thirtieth in ten years. The law was on our side; the Arts Council Lottery Panel was required to receive submissions and, if they answered published criteria, to meet them. That was its statutory duty, and was the view its Chairman, Peter Gummer, took of his role. But government, now that it had begun to contemplate the public-relations consequences of the train of events it had set in motion, was not so sure, at least about timing.

Most people give to good causes they believe in, but I had always supposed that they buy Lottery tickets not principally to repair the village hall, or erect a new national football stadium, but because they fancy a flutter, and dream, against odds of 14 million to one, of becoming millionaires. Government chose to believe otherwise. Late in the day they were anxious to ensure, if they could, that early grants would go to genuinely popular causes. But they could not ensure it; the matter was out of their hands. They may have wanted to help children with leukaemia, or provide kidney dialysis machines, but government would have to live with what the distributive bodies chose to do, and with the order they chose to do it in.

The National Heritage Lottery Fund (NHLF), chaired by Jacob Rothschild, was first to deliver. Its first major award provided a rude shock. The award went not to repairs to York Minster, nor to a village church near you, nor to preserve a parcel of glorious landscape for the public use. Instead, NHLF set aside £13.2 million to purchase for the nation the Churchill family papers from the Churchill family. Winston Churchill's services to this country are beyond measure, and beyond praise. It is proper that his private papers should belong to us. What people failed to understand, when the announcement came, was why they needed to be purchased; could they not simply have been given? Whatever the intrinsic worth of this acquisition, it did not go down well with the press or with public opinion. Government, embarrassed, stood its ground, and waited for relief; perhaps a new national football stadium could come to the rescue? There were vocal contenders for such a grant – Manchester, Birmingham, a revived Wembley. But none was ready to make an application. The Arts Council would, in spite of all ministerial hints and pressures for delay, be next in line. Top of its in-tray was its own Lottery Advisory Panel's recommendation that the Royal Opera House's application be acceded to. 'It meets the criteria,' the word was. 'It has survived our scrutiny. It may be a metropolitan project; opera and ballet are not, it is true, everybody's cup of tea. But this sort of redevelopment, which cannot be undertaken without us, is exactly what we were set up for. Let us get it over with.' On 21 July 1995, the Arts Council's Chairman, Lord Gowrie, stood up to make his announcement.

Grey Gowrie had been Minister for the Arts under Margaret Thatcher, and Minister for the Civil Service. Lunching with him one day at the Savoy Grill, I was dismayed then to discover that he was keener to be seen to be saving money in the latter capacity than to be increasing the public spend on the arts. However, he was a poet, a lover of painting and film, and he liked the same detective stories as I did. Now he pointed out that, since making their first allocation of grants in March, the Arts Council had given around £100 million to 159 organizations; this month they would make awards to London's two great opera houses. English National Opera would have £1,384,000 to commission a comparative study on the best location and design for the future housing of the company; ROH would receive, in two separate tranches, £78.5 million – £55 million to enable the development project to proceed; the balance of £23.5 million subject to the receipt of satisfactory proposals on the use of the second auditorium and the closure period. 'We are confident', Gowrie stated, 'that these will be forthcoming and a further grant will be awarded.' In his presentation, and in guidance notes provided to editors, Grey Gowrie was careful to explain that these sums were not disproportionate, that others of equivalent size would probably go to the Tate, to Cardiff, to Salford, and that overall the Arts Council intended to distribute its largesse very widely across the UK. But his tone was unapologetic: this was London's turn. 'We are proud at being able to assist in securing the future of two of this country's most celebrated artistic institutions.'

Conditions would be attached to both tranches of grant made available to us. There were eighteen in all. At his press conference, Gowrie called particular attention to changes he said he wanted to see made to the Board, ensuring that property-development expertise be available full time.

> While the Council has every confidence in the Royal Opera House as presently constituted, it does believe that the scale and complexity of the project, involving closure and temporary accommodation as well as on-site activity, requires supervision by a Board not only consisting of people who in the nature of things can only devote but a small proportion of their time to Royal Opera House affairs, however able or distinguished they may be.

This came rather out of the blue; it was not clear whether it was a dig at the Chairman, Angus Stirling, full-time Director General of the National Trust, or whether it was a plea to take on more property expertise. In either case it was a huge and belated admission that those volunteering to supervise arts management in Britain faced gigantic responsibilities. We were invited to submit proposals. Still stressing that this was no irresponsible give-away, Gowrie added, 'Payment will be released in stages as the development progresses.' This concealed a little-known fact of huge consequence: the Arts Council handed over no money upfront. It paid on sight of receipted bills of expenditure, to which it then contributed 75 per cent. This was prudent and a properly accountable use of public funds, no doubt. But we, and all their other clients, could have made much better use of interest earned on the sums awarded than they ever could. '*Bis dat qui cito dat*' – 'He gives twice who gives quickly.' The Arts Council gave as slowly as possible. Too slowly for some recipients, whose schemes foundered in consequence. The devil, as ever, is in the detail. But the big picture was bright. I put on the noticeboards:

GREAT NEWS

The Arts Council has today announced it will award us, in two instalments, and on certain conditions, the sum we asked for for the development and for the closure period, £55m on immediate offer, £23.5m provided that, in further discussion, we satisfy them on some of those conditions. We can do that.

This means that the development will proceed.

Our news is good for us, for our neighbours in Covent Garden, for our audiences, for the lyric arts, for London and for Britain.

Hold your heads high! Have a good summer.

Jeremy Isaacs

Now for the press. It had been arranged that as soon as they had finished in Great Peter Street, they would come to us. We gave the matter some thought; instead of receiving journalists in the Crush Bar, we decided a more suitable space would be the Floral Hall, then in use as a makeshift scenery store, because its restoration would be a stunning feature of the redeveloped House, and because the muddle and mess inside it then encapsulated the need to redevelop. When I got there, I found that, without consultation or undue thought, our catering manager, Aydin Hasirci, had laid on celebratory champagne. Feebly, we sent it away in case it gave the wrong impression: the people's Lottery fuelling a toffs' do. Orange juice and white wine were offered instead. Angus Stirling and I said a few words and posed together for the photographers. In spite of

Gawain. The Green Knight – John Tomlinson – loses his head to Gawain's axe-blow, and goes on singing in Harrison Birtwistle's masterwork for Covent Garden.

Les Huguenots; the Royal Opera chorus in bathing costume. Voices in the auditorium: 'Isaacs, this is rubbish. Go back to television.'

Paul Brown designed sets and costumes for Graham Vick's production of *Mitridate, ré di Ponto*. Bruce Ford as the King.

In Bill Dudley's set for *The Cunning Little Vixen*, the acrobat, Deborah Pope, soared high.

Josephine Barstow's Odabella sets Verdi's *Attila* alight.

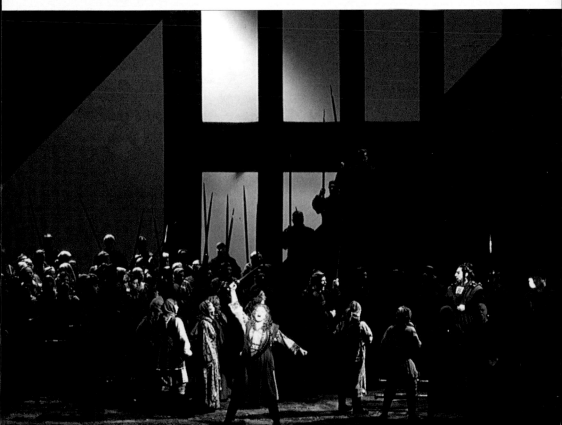

For David Hockney, opera is colour. *Die Frau ohne Schatten*, for producer John Cox.

Bjornson's set for Trevor Nunn's production of *Káťa Kabanová* echoes Munch's *The Scream*.

Fiery Angel, the first opera by Prokofiev to be given at Covent Garden, directed by David Freeman. Ted Downes talked us into doing it.

Susan Graham, knockout as Massenet's Chérubin.

Mattila in Luc Bondy's production of *Don Carlos*. We closed for a week to rehearse.

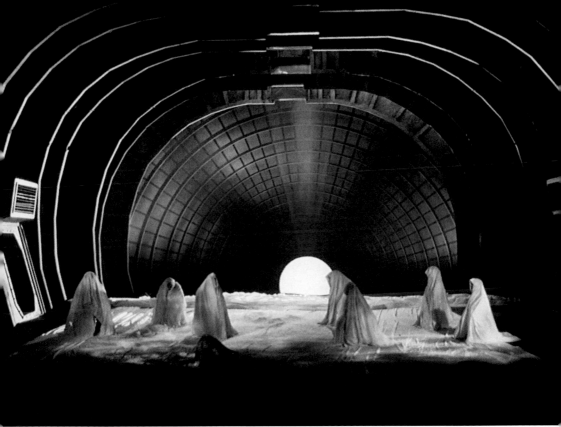

The time-tunnel in the Friedrich *Ring*; the Norns set against infinity.

Rheingold, Scene One. Richard Jones's and Nigel Lowery's *Der Ring des Nibelungen* took the Royal Opera securely into a post-modern age.

Incestuous lovers, Siegmund and Sieglinde – Poul Elming and Ulla Gustafsson – in *Die Walküre*. A mime plays the tree.

Nigel Lowery's front cloth for *Götterdämmerung*. By this point of the cycle, audiences were ready for anything.

John Gunter's set for *Der Fliegende Holländer*; new stage machinery will cope more easily than we could.

Graham Vick's production of *Die Meistersinger von Nürnberg*; the unqualified triumph of my time. Gwynne Howell as Pogner, Nancy Gustafson as Eva. Richard Hudson's set.

the delight we both felt that at last, after years of frustration, we could see a way forward, at first we both looked solemn enough. But the photographers wanted a smile; I grasped Angus's hand and raised it in triumph. That was the picture that hit the front pages next day.

To journalists, on radio and television, we could explain that this award was the answer to all our hopes. But the interrogation was mean, carping, hostile. Not a single interviewer seemed to believe we deserved it, or that good would come of it. 'Why not spend the money on hospitals instead?' we were asked. Keith Cooper drew the short straw. On the next morning's television he was asked how he could justify an award to an opera house instead of towards providing more kidney dialysis machines; the questioner depended for her life on one. It was not easy, with a studio audience baying for blood, to point out the false dichotomy. Society can have both, if it chooses.

The press was at its sourest and stupidest. Headlines and moralizing features had a field day. A decision to help sustain the arts, with funds especially hypothecated for that purpose, would in any other society have been quietly noted with approval. Here it was greeted with antagonism and hysteria. The *Sun* excelled itself, dressing up half a dozen of its readers in top hats and Moss Bros finery to take seats in the amphitheatre. They must have felt as out of place as an ermined peer on the Northern Line. Gowrie had pointed out that the first tranche to us of £55 million represented 3.4 per cent of the £1.6 billion available for the arts over the

seven years of Camelot's franchise. No newspaper noted this prominently, nor how much smaller a portion it constituted of the total disbursed by all five Lottery distribution arms. No minister of the Crown cheered us on; a very new Secretary of State, Virginia Bottomley, two weeks only in the job, remained inscrutably, unhelpfully silent.

One good friend, Rodney Milnes, editor of *Opera* magazine, always refers in his fulminations against the underfunding of the arts in Britain to the 'public-relations disaster' of the handling of our Lottery announcement. If it was a disaster, it was government's, not ours. A dream for which we had long laboured had come true. I do not regret the happiness I felt and showed that day.

I told the staff and the Board that we could fulfil all the conditions the Arts Council had set us, and in good time. Two of the eighteen would prove demanding. As ever we had to satisfy the Arts Council that we had a viable business plan, that we were solvent. But we knew, and they knew, that our viability was precarious. And we had to present satisfactory plans for the closure period; these were far from presentable. There were two years to go.

A curious feature of the Arts Council announcement, unnoticed by the press, was the division of the total amount awarded into the two tranches proposed. We had applied for £58.5 million towards the development and, as an afterthought associated with that, for £20 million towards the cost of closure. Varying the figures without explanation, the Arts Council split their grant £55 million and £23.5 million. Our application made explicit the distinction between capital cost and a grant to revenue, specifically excluded by their own guidelines. The Arts Council deliberately fudged it. It later turned out that they were much agonized as to which revenue purposes, if any, could be funded, and which could not. Who were we to complain?

The great fact, however, was that since our application met each of eight criteria, they awarded us a grant. This was the decisive contribution. We could now assure Westminster that we would have ready, when we needed them, all the funds we must find to complete our scheme. The development would proceed. The Royal Opera House would close for two years in July 1997.

12

THREE TENORS

'$\mathbf{M}$r Isaacs, do you know the effect the antlers of a rutting stag have on the female deer?' an attractive woman once asked me at lunch at Merton, my Oxford college. 'No,' I muttered, 'but I can imagine.' 'Well,' she told me, 'that is the effect the male tenor voice has on me.'

When I came to the Royal Opera House in 1988, there was no such phenomenon as 'The Three Tenors'. There were plenty of really good singers, male and female, combining beauty of voice with musicality, some of them also gifted interpreters. There were singers of fame and reputation, whose presence on a cast list was guaranteed to sell out the house. And there were some – Joan Sutherland, though fading fast, was still among them – who carried with them an aura of superstardom that lifted them into a class of their own.

But three tenors were thought to be somehow special: Plácido Domingo, Luciano Pavarotti, José Carreras. Of these three, Domingo – his voice dark, baritonal, like a cello – was a consummate musician and still appeared at the height of his powers. Pavarotti, a pure Italian tenor rather than a pushed-up baritone, no longer sang with the angelic simplicity of his early recordings; yet, in several great roles, none surpassed him. José Carreras, not quite the calibre of the other two, always aspired to be. At the beginning of his career he had sung with light and effortless sweetness.

In 1988 Carreras was out of action, fighting for his life against leukaemia. In heroic isolation, he had undergone bone-marrow transplants in Seattle. His courage earned admiration; if he recovered, would his voice recover too? Would he have the stamina to tackle opera's most demanding roles? At Covent Garden, we impatiently awaited news of his recovery.

Luciano Pavarotti had not sung at Covent Garden since an ill-fated *Aida* in June 1984. In this production, directed and designed by Jean-Pierre Ponnelle, Pavarotti was not in a co-operative mood. Richard Jones, later to produce a *Ring* cycle on this stage, worked as a young assistant to the director. He remembers approaching Pavarotti during rehearsals: 'Monsieur Ponnelle asks that, at this moment, you move ten paces to your left.' Pavarotti answered: 'No.' Jones, wondering if he ever wanted to work at Covent Garden again, admired the tact and patience of the conductor, Zubin Mehta, in keeping the show together. Pavarotti had had a great falling out with Covent Garden when contracted to sing in *Tosca* in February 1983. He failed to appear for rehearsals and all five performances, telexing from Australia to say he was indisposed. This cancellation appeared to be a breach of trust when the press reported that Luciano had turned up on a South Sea island with a girlfriend. Bad blood was shed. Pavarotti would need to be wooed back by me.

Plácido Domingo bid fair to be considered, if not the greatest voice among this trio, certainly the greatest artist; his stature, his handsome features, his dramatic involvement in a role, his fine musicality in the shaping of a phrase, all commended him. Some doted on Pavarotti, others yearned to care for Carreras, but Plácido, on stage and off, carried a charge of electricity, an aura of danger, that bowled women over and roused admiration in men. He had been a Covent Garden regular since his début in *Tosca* in 1971. Recently he had scored in *La fanciulla del West* and had scaled that pinnacle of tenor roles, Verdi's *Otello*. From the opening 'Esultate!' to the starlit love duet, 'Già nella notte densa', to the final act's agony, 'Niun mi tema', he sang and acted with supreme authority. Due, at his own wish, to sing Lohengrin, perhaps the most Italianate of Wagner's tenor roles, at the end of John Tooley's last season 1987/88, to everyone's disappointment he had cancelled. He had not found time to learn the role. He would sing Manrico in *Il trovatore* in my first season.

When the agent Herbert Breslin first heard Luciano Pavarotti sing at the Met, and recognized the power and lyricism of his voice, and the warmth and openness of his personality, he offered to put him on stage, solo, at Carnegie Hall. The evening was a sell-out. Pavarotti's fortune was assured. But great singers had always given solo recitals in concert halls to audiences of two or three thousand. Apart from the hire of the hall, and a poster or two, the only other costs were the singer's and accompanist's fees. The rest was profit. This meant a living; it did not make millionaires. But we live in the age of sophisticated sound systems and acoustic techniques, of media hype, of the pop-music megastar. When Mick Jagger strutted his stuff, he did so for tens of thousands. The Beatles had filled not Carnegie Hall, but New York's Shea Stadium. Why could not Pavarotti do the same?

This was the idea of a successful Hungarian entrepreneur, Tibor Rudas, who conspired with Herbert Breslin to make Luciano Pavarotti a multimillionaire and themselves, I guess, very rich into the bargain. They would do so by bringing a megastar opera singer to hundreds of thousands who, unable to cram themselves into La Scala, the Met or Covent Garden, would flock to fill ice-rinks, exhibition spaces, football stadia, to savour something rare and new. Not any old space would do: the trick, Rudas saw, was to get the acoustic right. Luciano's voice would be miked. Decca's engineers, used to the recording studio and to handling rock stars, could be trusted to do him justice in a vast arena, holding 20,000 paying customers. And if those 20,000 each paid £50 for a ticket, and perhaps 500 paid £150 for the privilege of dining with him afterwards, and if there were 5000 more, as I saw once in Glasgow, in an overflow hall, paying £10 to watch Luciano's tonsils and his broad grin on a big TV screen, why, before you knew it, you were looking at a take of maybe £1 million a night. In Glasgow, banners said: '£75 Pavarotti! Whit aboot the poverati?'

When, in New York or London, I peeped at the pages of Luciano's five-year diary to see what periods he could offer Covent Garden, the months ruled out were occupied no longer, as they might once have been, by engagements at the opera houses of the world, with adequate rests in between, but by jet voyages to the far corners of the globe, Sydney and Rio, Moscow and Madrid, in whose biggest venues a single performance would yield revenues worth a season's work at La Scala, Covent Garden or the Met. In the years I knew them, Pavarotti and Domingo still sang the circuit of the great opera houses. They needed to remind the opera public of what they could do. In Luciano's case, however, the great bulk of his income already came from solo arena performance, rather than from singing complete operas.

At a solo recital by a famous tenor in a spacious auditorium, seating thousands, the occasion itself is the thing. It is being there that matters. The megastar sings to produce the maximum effect with appearance of effort, but minimum real strain on the voice. The recital becomes a series of short, sharp bursts, arias, familiar melodies, songs of love and death, none lasting more than a minute or two, each climaxing, in effect sexually, in a high, long jet of sound demanding recognition and applause, a mating call. 'How was that for you?' the singer asks after each number. Men and women, like my easily aroused Oxford friend, seem satisfied enough.

In the last two decades, Pavarotti has given audiences vast pleasure and made millions from these recitals. But there were peaks of box-office income still to scale. The promoter Tibor Rudas had another bright idea: to bring together on one platform, not one tenor, nor two, but three. Suppose those well-known rivals Pavarotti and Domingo, friends but competitors, performed together. Suppose one added Carreras, of whom the others had been so supportive when he was ill, and whom illness and recovery had pushed into audiences' hearts. Then you would have something remarkable: less song from each, but more jolts of pleasure for the audience; a concert that would be the event of the decade; a ticket to kill for; a telecast worldwide; a CD that would sell in millions. Three tenors' individual identities altered at that moment. A monster, 'The Three Tenors', was born.

Their first concert was given in Rome during the 1990 World Cup, in the Baths of Caracalla. (Here, in 1954, I first heard *Aida*. The crowd hummed 'Celeste Aida' a beat before the tenor. Vendors shouted '*Caffè caldo*'. A camel from Rome's zoo crossed city and stage to saunter along the Banks of the Nile and, without pausing, returned to the zoo.) All three, after much haggling over who would sing what, excelled. It was a case of 'Anything you can do, I can do better.' Each delivered the orgasmic scream, but in his own way. At the end, in 'Nessun Dorma', they sang together. Zubin Mehta conducted. The world tuned in; millions watched. Millions more bought the CD. Decca, jolted into action by Bert Chappell, paid a fortune for the recording rights, and never regretted it. The three musketeers were said to have obtained a fixed fee of $1 million each – an unheard-of amount. In this insistence they lost out. The revenues worldwide were gigantic. The artists suggested an injustice had been done them, and demanded reparation. They probably got something more in the end.

Great singers still came to Covent Garden because, with New York, Paris, Vienna, Milan, it counted as one of the great houses of the world. For the débutant, it was important to be invited to sing in London; for the master, it is useful to go the rounds of Europe's operatic capitals, keeping in touch with the public. Record companies are happy that their star should be heard, and London, with its fine musicians and technicians, is still a city where recordings are made. Covent Garden expected, therefore, that three or four years ahead in the five-year diaries that busy singers carry, there would be pencilled in periods each year for us. Covent Garden practised the *stagione* system: every production, new or revival, was rehearsed. For a new production we would need three or four weeks of rehearsal, and then performances spread over two or three weeks. With a superstar this was always hard to achieve. A favourite role in a revival took less time: a week's rehearsal, say, and a fortnight's performances. No great singer performed without any rehearsal. But none of these three rehearsed an hour or a day more than seemed, to them, necessary. In the far-off days when singers arrived by ocean liner, they would take up residence in the new city for a short season. Today, in the age of the private jet, they commute frantically between engagements. Domingo would arrive, rehearse, rest to prepare for the first night, sing, sign autographs, stay up late, recover and, sometimes, record before the next Covent Garden performance. He might sneak off for a concert elsewhere. No one who protects his voice at all times can safely undertake strenuous engagements during a demanding run of opera. But some roles are more demanding than others. It is surprising how space that was free in the diary three years before can become stuffed full of engagements when the day for the great man's visit arrives.

Counting galas and concerts, Plácido Domingo sang thirty-six performances (and conducted two) in my nine seasons at Covent Garden; Luciano Pavarotti sang fifteen; José Carreras eighteen. Virtually all of these performances were sold out; all were enthusiastically received. In each case, a high level of expectancy prevailed, so that the appearance of the General Director in front of the curtain brought an automatic groan of anxiety. Would the megastar appear, or had sudden laryngitis struck him down? Some were evenings of memorable music-making – *Otello*, *L'elisir*, *Stiffelio*. Many in the audience heard what they came to hear, and would long remember enjoying every note. On some nights, though, there was, tangibly, an air of faint disappointment, perhaps because expectation was too high, or because the performance itself failed to catch fire; but sometimes, I thought, it was because the artist the audience heard was no longer the talent of memory, first encountered on the stage, or in early recordings, his voice in the full, rich bloom of youth. Several performances these three tenors gave are among my happy memories. Only one or two, with Kleiber, Solti or Downes in the pit, carried that extra charge of excitement that transcends the evening and memory alike.

Plácido Domingo sang Manrico, at the end of the 1988/89 season, in a baleful, dark production of *Il trovatore* designed, lit and directed by Piero Faggioni; half-designed and half-lit would be nearer the mark. The vast single mountainous set, cast in fibreglass from volcanic cavernous shapes, and closed in by a heavy, sombre canopy, was supposed to be at least partly transformed by props, costumes and lighting as the scene changed from palace gardens, to a convent's cloister, to a gypsy encampment, to a military camp. Occupying different levels of the stage in one undifferentiated mass, Faggioni's set remained resolutely dour. The soprano was uncertain, so her great aria at the start, 'Di tale amor . . .' failed to get the house going; the baritone was striking but, being Russian, deemed lacking in *italianità*; Azucena, the gypsy, the producer's preference, not our first choice, was goodish. Faggioni didn't believe he could get a strong performance from the big growly-voiced mezzo we had wanted to cast (he was wrong). Bernard Haitink was plainly not at ease with one of Verdi's most tuneful blood-and-thunder scores. Plácido looked wonderful in doublet and high boots, but could not impose himself against a set which, instead of showing the singers off to full effect, dominated everyone. This new production scaled no heights. The tenor's high point is generally reckoned to be 'Di quella pira' in Act Three when he abandons the bridal altar to try to save his mother from the pyre. Visconti, in his film *Senso*, used 'Di quella pira' in a performance at La Fenice as a call to arms, inspiring Italians in the audience to rise against the Austrian yoke. First time round it is stirring stuff; repeated, in the cabaletta, it should bring the house down. Before we opened, Plácido insisted on giving a press conference to explain that he would not sing the ringing high C in 'Di quella pira'. Verdi had not written it; it was a later interpolation by singers showing off. This was true, but unlikely to set the blood tingling. The press conference went off reasonably well, though Faggioni, joining late, was indignant that so much attention was being paid to a few notes of the score, rather than to his production. On the first night there were less

Il trovatore

than ecstatic curtain calls. Next morning I received, sent round by messenger, a letter of congratulation from the sponsor Peter Davis of Reed plc, now 'The Man from the Pru'. Peter, a gentleman, did not wait to read the reviews but wrote at once. I have always been grateful to him for this courtesy.

Domingo's visits were always events. Between them we kept in touch. Paul Findlay, Nicholas Payne, occasionally I myself, would attend his performances in New York or Paris or Milan and seek a few minutes of his time. He was always glad to see us, not always able, in a crowded dressing room or at supper, to attend fully to next season's London engagements, or to the season after that. Sometimes, with the brochure ready for the printer, we had to get on a plane to get a firm yes from his lips. The actual contract might not be signed until mere weeks before he arrived.

For Plácido money was never the issue, only time. He would want to know our choice of conductor, and the rest of the cast, particularly the female lead. He might express a preference; he did not impose or dictate. It was for him to agree the role. No use any longer suggesting Alfredo in *La traviata* or Rodolfo in *La bohème* – 'I am a little old to play the young lover, Jeremy, don't you think?' he might say, while agreeing to Don José, or Cavaradossi or Otello. He might request some help with expenses; and it was of interest to know that a performance would be televised, though that took careful negotiation. But he never asked for an uplift in fees. Domingo and Pavarotti, whom solo concerts, themselves boosting the sale of recordings, have made multimillionaires, each wanted only the assurance that their fee was the House's highest. This was understood; they were our biggest draws. Nor were those fees exorbitant. Plácido's fee, expressed in Swiss francs, edged upwards over a decade from SF20,000 towards the SF30,000 mark. A single performance elsewhere, off the loop of the great houses, might bring him twice that, as much as DM100,000 to sing in Hamburg, say, or several million lire for Pavarotti at a smaller Italian theatre, keen to make an occasion. Plácido earned far less from circus appearances than Luciano, but a Covent Garden fee was hardly worth arguing over.

To the theatre, on the other hand, their appearances were worth a lot of money, way over the cost of fees. Well before the Three Tenors phenomenon, their names announced for the season enabled the Met or Covent Garden to sell tickets, not only for their own performances, but for subscriptions. At the Met a package of four or six performances will get you one with Domingo among them. We would have liked to make the same offer, but I could never obtain enough megastar appearances to assure each would-be subscriber of the prize. Any Domingo or Pavarotti performance in a popular piece would sell out our 2000 seats. Offering only four or five starry performances would leave tens of thousands disappointed.

For these tickets it was always a seller's market: first come, first served. Sometimes we ran a ballot. Touts who had packed the queue for personal sales sold good seats in Floral Street for many times their face value. I decided to boost our revenue by raising prices for Domingo and Pavarotti performances. *We* sold the tickets. The touts disappeared. The House benefited tangibly. Domingo always dissociated himself from high ticket prices; but he never asked us to bring prices down – that was our business. He knew how desperately we needed the box-office revenue. He was happy if a performance was to be broadcast, or would be relayed free on a big screen to the piazza. He likes to think of himself as a popular figure; he enjoys contact with the crowd.

Repertory is planned, and quality of performance evaluated, by the season. But Covent Garden's financial management is measured by the fiscal year, April to March. I had one fiscal year that contained per-formances by Carreras and Pavarotti and Domingo. That year we balanced the books.

When Plácido arrived in London, I would make a point of greeting him, at his hotel, his apartment or at the stage door. Sometimes I only caught up with him on stage, or in his dressing room. Everyone was glad to see him; his regular dresser, Julio, had his costume ready. Chorus and orchestra found extra zest in working with one of the great talents, an artist of in-disputable world class. At his rehearsals we restricted entry to the auditorium. Habituées of the House, without a ticket for the performances, hoped to hear him at rehearsals instead; 'friends' would write begging admittance, assuring me that Plácido himself had expressed the wish to meet them there. But you cannot rehearse properly with an audience – there must be freedom to stop and start, criticize, do it again. So we had to deny entry. Sometimes I would attend each of his performances, sometimes not. Gwyneth Jones had given me sound advice: 'Singers like to see you, to know you are there. They welcome a visit to the dressing room, and to be asked to supper. But they don't expect you at every performance. Just make it clear when you will be in, and when you will be away.'

When it was known that Plácido was to come, Floral Street filled with
well-wishers; fans and passers-by crowded the stage door, hoping for a
glimpse. After the performance people queued for his autograph. Paul
Garner, his secretary and amanuensis, would arrive some days before he
did. Weeks before that I would enquire: 'Which night will Plácido be free
for supper?' The least we could do for him, we thought, was take him out
after a performance. Yes, he would like to come, but he would have guests,
friends from Madrid, or from Mexico. Many of these were regulars; some
were addicts. I have had supper with Plácido after a performance at La
Scala, not just with his wife Marta and other cast members, but with half
a dozen blue-rinsed ladies from Florida or California – each seventy or
eighty years old – following in his caravan from performance to performance. I presumed they were generous contributors to a company that
Plácido served, Los Angeles perhaps. But is this fun? Other of Plácido's
friends are wealthy jet-setters. At a supper party I hosted I found myself
sitting between beady Marta Domingo and glamorous Ivana Trump, after
her divorce. Ms Trump told me she was writing a novel, marketing a
perfume – Ivana – and launching a line of lingerie. We did not discuss
opera.

Martin Feinstein, lately director of the Washington Opera – Plácido
succeeded him there – used to tell a story of six Domingo performances
of *Tosca*. On the morning of each, Plácido telephoned to say he was not
well, and must be doubtful for the evening's performance. Martin rang
the Met to find out if the Russian tenor Vladimir Popov was there; if so,
would they put him on the shuttle. His colleagues remonstrated: 'Don't
do that, Martin. If Plácido knows he's here, he won't sing. If he doesn't
know, Plácido will sing.' They took Popov off the shuttle, but Martin had
to make several announcements from the stage. One evening it went like
this: 'Ladies and Gentlemen, good evening. I am Martin Feinstein,
Director of the Washington Opera. I have to tell you that Mr Domingo is
unwell.' Cries of anguish from the audience. 'He is at this moment on his
way to hospital.' More anguish. 'He is in costume. There is something
wrong with his ear. If that can be fixed, he hopes to sing for you. So please
go to the bar and have a drink, or two drinks. We hope to start the performance in about forty-five minutes.' On the last morning of the run,
Plácido said: 'Martin, you have been very good to me this last fortnight.
Tonight, I will do something for you. I will go out before the curtain
and say: "Good evening. My name is Plácido Domingo, and I have to

tell you that Mr Feinstein will not be appearing this evening".'

I had to make only one appearance before the curtain to explain a non-appearance by Plácido. It was in a short run of *Otello*, conducted by Carlos Kleiber. Plácido had a temperature of well over 100°, and could not possibly sing. The danger was that the autocratic Kleiber would refuse to conduct. But, choosing to work with the Welsh tenor Jeff Lawton, star of Peter Stein's WNO *Otello*, who did well, he got on with it. Katia Ricciarelli, however, feeling neglected as Desdemona, insisted that, in the same breath as my apology for Plácido, I tell the audience that she was not feeling well but would nevertheless sing. Later I decided, as my job at Covent Garden got more difficult, that I should have someone stand outside my office in the morning to proclaim: 'Mr Isaacs did not feel at all like coming to work today. He will go through with it, but asks for your understanding.'

Plácido Domingo gave memorable performances in *Tosca*, in *Otello*, with Solti as well as with Kleiber, in *Samson et Dalila*, in *Stiffelio*. No one in my time, with the exception of John Tomlinson as Sachs and Wotan, bestrode the stage as he did. He guarded his voice, and his career, with exemplary care. He was always growing as an artist, even if the power of his vocal cords detectably diminished. He chose carefully what to sing and what not to sing, putting behind him not just the inappropriate tenderness of teenage love, but also some of the most demanding tenor roles – Calaf in *Turandot*, Radames in *Aida*. With Carreras, he began to hint that certain operas in which he had not previously sung, and not yet recorded, might tempt him now – the temptation being partly that the tenor role was less taxing than Calaf or Otello. There was talk of Massenet's *Le Cid*, and of *Hérodiade* (Carreras sang in this in Zurich). We considered it, lavish production though it required, but thought better of it. Rarer Verdi opened up several possibilities, particularly when we decided to put on every Verdi opera at Covent Garden by 2001. We were happy indeed to mount *Stiffelio*, for both Carreras and Domingo. The tenors welcomed this role because they could sing it without strain, though Carreras, to Ted Downes's fury, refused to sing the repeat to his early cabaletta. Plácido, who appeared in the revival, could only give us three performances, not the six we had promised. He had got tangled up in the 1994 Football World Cup. José Cura sang the other three instead, and made an impression.

The piece the tenors were always keen we do was *Fedora* by Giordano, the composer of *Andrea Chénier*. We rented La Scala's production. The tenor part, Loris, though there is a fair bit to do on stage, is not a demanding one. The aria 'Amor ti vieta' lingers in the mind, but lasts just over a minute. Plácido put a great deal of energy into acting the role; but this is still not the hardest way to earn a living. One London critic thought it not worth doing at all. Audiences, as I pointed out from the stage one night, disagreed.

In my final season, as part of the Verdi Festival, Plácido had agreed to sing in *I masnadieri*, the only piece Verdi wrote for London (not for Covent Garden, but for Her Majesty's, where it was first given in 1847). Then he changed his mind, declining to learn the role. This was a pity, but instead he agreed to sing Adorno in *Simon Boccanegra*, the original 1857 version. With Mark Elder conducting, these were happy evenings.

When we wanted to lure Plácido back, the easiest ploy was to stage *Tosca* in the famous old Zeffirelli/Mongiardino production in which he had made his Royal Opera début in 1971. He sang in that in December 1991 on his twentieth anniversary. In 1996 we were ready to wheel out *Tosca* again for his twenty-fifth. He agreed; it was included in the schedule. It was crucial he come, not just to sing, but because Vivien Duffield, launching her appeal for the development, needed his presence to make an occasion of it. Plácido honoured his commitment but, awkwardly late in the day, he changed his mind about what he would perform. 'I don't wish to mark my twenty-fifth anniversary singing Cavaradossi,' he explained candidly. 'I cannot sing it now as I could then.' Instead he offered to conduct *Tosca*. He is no great shakes as a conductor, but could not have done it at all twenty-five years before. All right, we said, reluctantly, conduct *Tosca*. (There was never more than the most fleeting hint to us of another suggestion, that his wife Marta should direct, as she did in Bonn, in Los Angeles, for whom he acted as Consultant, and in Washington DC, after he became Director there.) For Vivien, and for the House to which he knows his early career owed much, Plácido agreed to the fundraising gala and to a speech at supper afterwards. 'Hurry up,' he told us, 'I want to sing in the new House.' The gala raised £600,000.

We got the best of both worlds, for Plácido also wanted to show he had grown in voice, in musicianship, in range of repertory, and offered to sing Siegmund in *Die Walküre* which no one could have imagined twenty-five years before. He could only offer us a single performance, which is a nuisance, even an extravagance, in a *stagione* house. But we agreed with alacrity. With John Tomlinson as Wotan and Deborah Polaski as Brünnhilde, we were assured of an electric evening. I had hoped Anne Evans would sing Sieglinde, but she was ill. Plácido asked for Karen Huffstodt with whom he had sung Siegmund at La Scala. Only Plácido, so late in his career, would make this transition to Wagner, or at least to the less stressful Wagnerian tenor roles. Critics in Vienna and Bayreuth cribbed at his German in Siegmund and Parsifal. But he dared, and persevered, and carried both off. The lyricism of his 'Winterstürme' in that single performance gave us a truly great night.

'Why have you given the House to that other singer?' Luciano Pavarotti demanded, slamming his hand down on the desk in his New York apartment when I went to ask him to come back to Covent Garden after years of absence. But he wasn't wholly serious, and had already agreed to return. 'I would not come for your predecessor,' he told me, 'but for you I will come.' Luciano had been angry about the hoo-hah that followed his withdrawal from *Tosca* in 1983. But perhaps he knew he could not leave London off his circuit of performances. Judging from the high-powered enthusiasm with which Decca supported his every London visit, I guess his recording company warmly seconded that.

'When I come back,' he said, 'you will treat me as an ordinary person. No fuss.' The endearing thing about Luciano – apart from the fact that he possesses one of the voices of the century – is that he really seems to be a simple soul. It is hard to think so of someone so successful; beneath the surface geniality must lie a steel will and sharp business sense. But on most occasions I have been with Luciano, he has indulged simple tastes – chatting, eating too much, watching or talking football. One evening in London, when Sting was in the party after the performance, an aide of the rock-star's, zonked out of his mind on something or other, got up and insisted on telling us all what a wonderful experience it had been for him to go to an opera – he had never been before. That was exceptional. The folk Luciano likes to be surrounded by are not usually famous, but family and genuine friends. At table with him I have met cousins, uncles, the local butcher and baker. Pavarotti has fans who are very fond of him, but he doesn't have a hero-worshipping band of retainers. At the San Domenico restaurant on Manhattan's Central Park South, dangerously close to Luciano's New York base for his faltering attempts at diet control, his staunch ex-wife Adua left his staff in little doubt that, in failing to insist on fewer helpings, they were neglecting their duty.

Pavarotti sang only three sets of performances in my years at Covent Garden: *L'elisir d'amore* in 1990 was a happy, easeful time, and a considerable success; *Tosca* at the start of the 1992/93 season was also something he took in his vocal stride; *Un ballo in maschera* in April 1995 was agony, one performance out of five cancelled and only one of the others achieving the standard he set himself, or the quality he knew his public were entitled to expect.

When I first met him, Luciano weighed way over 20 stone, though his assistant at the time was reputed to have put a lock on the refrigerator door. He had considerable difficulty moving quickly or lightly. He had a particular abhorrence of steps, either up or down; if he went up he would have to come down, and, worse, if he went down, he might have to go up again. Sets had to be simplified for him, movements eased. In our *L'elisir* he cheerfully attempted an amiable young village lad, ambling about the stage and skittishly essaying a hop, step and dance. In *Tosca*, he did not climb the scaffolding steps up to the portrait of the Madonna that Cavaradossi is painting, but did risk falling down to die when shot in Act Three; fortunately the curtain had closed on Tosca's suicide before he had to get up again. In *Ballo*, his performance as Amelia's lover left a lot to the imagination: he kept leaving the stage to sip liquid during the love duet. Looking for a dramatic explanation, we surmised he was keeping look-out for the conspirators who do, eventually, turn up. (It was of this *Ballo* that a stern colleague, George New, scenic artist, remarked all too audibly in the Grand Tier: 'Bromley Rep!') But Pavarotti as an actor was never in Domingo's league. It was for his voice that people loved him. Alas, in those years he could not always rely on it.

In 1991, 'Una furtiva lagrima' in *L'elisir*, and all the music Nemorino sings, he carried off with *élan* and enjoyment. 'Recondita armonia' from *Tosca* sounded fine on stage, and sensational when uttered complete, warming up in the dressing room. So did 'E lucevan le stelle'. But watching him nursing nose and throat, crouched among the mighty ranks of the Chicago Symphony Orchestra during a concert performance of *Otello* conducted in New York by Georg Solti, was to watch a great singer, who had nothing to prove to anybody, trying to climb a vocal Everest because it was there. He managed it, but only just. The effort was exhausting. If we could find the right conductor, he said, he would sing *Otello* on stage at Covent Garden in my last season. When, in a radio interview, I asked him why, he said: 'Because crazy people like you keep telling me I should.' But of course the suggestion came from him. We never really thought he would and he never did. But, as his powers declined, he wanted to believe it.

It was *Un ballo in maschera* at Covent Garden in 1995 that revealed to me the agony he went through. Drugged on memories of what he had once been like, hyped by the media into believing he could still do it, won over to enjoyment by the price they had paid for their tickets, the public was more easily satisfied than he could be himself. He always sang in tune, on the note. He still sang an elegant line. His voice rang out, if he was in form, loud and clear, though when he wanted to add that extra something, to swell and lift, and called on the voice for more, that more sometimes was not forthcoming. When he was not well, bothered perhaps by a throat complaint, as in London in 1995, the whole thing became too much for him. He cancelled the second performance of *Ballo*, explaining, bizarrely but convincingly, that if he could get back home to Italy for Easter he would recover. One performance, at the end, he was happy about. After another, the look I saw on his face was of such agony, discontent and self-reproach that I was shaken. Stupidly, behind the curtain, before he took his call, I went to him and said, 'Bravo maestro.' I meant 'Thank you for going through with it, and not disappointing the audience.' But at 'Bravo', wearily and scornfully, he raised an eyebrow and looked piercingly through me. He did not at that moment want praise, or applause. Later that evening, when Gillian greeted him, he said bluntly: 'I should stop.' My time at Covent Garden was punctuated by performances by three tenors. The truth is, though, that I coincided not with their promise or their peak, but their decline. This moment was the apogee of that.

Perhaps it was his searing vulnerability that endeared Luciano to me. I liked him; he was always himself. Although the dominant figure in our relationship, he liked politely to imply that I was boss. 'Time to leave, Luciano.' 'Yes, sir. Very good.' When he came to supper after a performance, he came in make-up, in rudimentary costume sometimes, a vast floppy scarf loosely drooped over his shoulders, protecting his throat. I went to see him once in his summer villa above the beach at Pesaro. It was mid-afternoon, but Luciano sent to the kitchen, determined to be hospitable, for hard cheese and a local brawn he liked which he pared and sliced for us himself, insisting we ate. In Florence once I went to hear him in *Il trovatore*. I called on him earlier that day in his hotel close to the theatre. 'You realize I cannot talk, and why,' he said on the telephone.

'You mean because you have a performance.' 'No, because we shall be watching football.' Luciano was hugely pleased that the BBC had used his recording of 'Nessun Dorma' from *Turandot* as the theme tune for its World Cup coverage; and that, when it sold its first 250,000, the great England forward of the 1966 winning team, Bobby Charlton, came to present him with a platinum memento. Luciano himself had once played centre-half. In Florence that afternoon, as well as watching the football, Luciano was also contemplating two ample round cream cakes, presented by admirers. He had already demolished half of one. The cakes were delicious. *Il trovatore* was OK.

When he gives a concert, Luciano holds the note at the end of each number as long as musicianship allows, and then, with hardly a pause, forces his lips open, and his front teeth forward in a broad, fixed grin of triumph. He smiles as we applaud, happy that he has done it again. The public warms to a smile, to an artist who enjoys his work. (Part of Darcey Bussell's star quality, as prima ballerina of the Royal Ballet, is the air of happiness she conveys to us.) I shall never forget the smile that broke across Luciano's face at the start of the open-air concert, 'Pavarotti in Hyde Park', when he realized that his audience, stretching across the park, with royalty and Cabinet ministers in the front row, were being drenched by a rainstorm while he, Luciano Pavarotti from Modena, secure under a canopy, was in the dry. It was a bizarre evening. Prince Charles sat next to Princess Diana, without a word. Sitting behind, I passed Diana a waterproof head-covering. She smiled, but waved it away. Her stiffly lacquered hair survived the downpour like a duck, and looked appealing in the photographs.

Urged on by his ineffable manager, Herbert Breslin, we tried to make every one of Luciano's visits to Covent Garden special. Breslin constantly demanded that we mount a new production for Luciano. You never have, he would point out, though we had for 'that other singer'. The problem was that Luciano would not stay in London long enough for rehearsal to justify it, or he might not turn up at all. In any case, we could not afford it. Perhaps then we could give an assurance that a performance would be televised, with an extra fee added? But broadcasting decisions were not in our gift. It is hard for foreigners to realize it, but neither Her Majesty's Government nor the Royal Opera House controls the BBC. With other pieces of ours to choose from, the BBC's Head of Music and Arts was not likely to make a prior commitment to a creaking revival, even if the production was a vehicle for a star. Breslin was only doing his job in asking; the answer was still no.

But for the *Ballo* visit in 1995, another expedient offered. With a great flourish, a wealthy admirer, Mrs Joseph Haim, had commissioned a portrait of Luciano by an Italian painter, Ulisse Sartini, the Annigoni of Italy. It showed a tall, handsome, idealized Luciano, wearing a big colourful silk scarf. Wanting to make a fuss of him somehow, I accepted it for the House in his presence in the Crush Bar on a Saturday afternoon. Speeches were made, toasts were drunk. After the ceremony I walked Luciano to the grand staircase and the door. He knew I was due to leave when the House closed, put an arm on my shoulder, and said, 'You know, my friend, I shall miss you.' Larger than life, I miss him.

José Carreras was a great artist in his day, and a small, proud man. As a young singer, as recordings demonstrate, he had a light tenor voice of exceptional sweetness and purity. He excelled in young men's roles; his Nemorino was unsurpassed. As he went on and time wore on, he had to press the voice just a little. He was handsome, attractive to women, a glamorous figure.

When he recovered from leukaemia, he came to us in 1989 to sing a short recital. By now he was not just a famed singer, but a phenomenon. His bravery, his will to survive and recover, his determination to sing again, won the admiration of the world. I cannot remember anything he sang that night. I do remember the welcome that greeted him and the almost endless applause after the last encore. To watch his reception was to watch an artist literally buoyed up by his public. He really needed them; they could not do enough for him. The applause went on and on and on. Finally, I seized an armful of gladioli, went out on to the stage and dragged him off it; time to go home.

In March 1991, ready to sing a demanding operatic role rather than a carefully planned recital, he came to Covent Garden to sing Saint-Saëns's *Samson et Dalila*. I met him at the stage door and took him up to the opera rehearsal room. The chorus stood and applauded him, crowding round in welcome to shake his hand, congratulate him, wish him luck. On stage, in Sidney Nolan's fine, red desert settings, Carreras sang Samson well. In the Old Testament story, Samson, seduced and betrayed by Dalila, shorn of his hair, loses his strength. At the end, he regains it to pull down the temple on Israel's Philistine enemies. 'God give me back the strength that once I had,' Carreras sang. God did. The applause, like Samson, nearly brought the house down.

Two years later, Carreras would teach me a lesson in artistic dignity and offended *amour propre*. In January 1993 we mounted Verdi's *Stiffelio* for the first time at Covent Garden, with José in the title role. Usually for an important production the opera company would produce a poster carrying useful information: principal cast, conductor, director, designer, lighting designer, dates of performances. But this time, no poster: hard up against it financially, we had decided to economize. We did not need one, we reasoned – the House would sell out anyway. On a few box sites around the walls of the House in Bow Street and Floral Street, however, there appeared specially posed portrait photographs of Carreras, not as the eponymous hero in costume, but studio shots of the tenor whose name, reputation, and now image, were indeed selling the show to the public. An undertaking to do this had apparently been given in early negotiations. The problem was that the soprano, Catherine Malfitano, objected and the director, Elijah Moshinsky, backed her up.

The first I knew of a difficulty was when word was brought to my office that Malfitano and Moshinsky wanted to see me. Malfitano came, in high indignation. *Stiffelio* was not a solo for tenor, but an ensemble piece; her own role, Lina, was at least as important as Stiffelio's. She certainly had more to sing. The red and gold fish-and-chip board in Bow Street would list the names of those appearing – women first, men next, but each in alphabetical order, with the conductor's name at the end. So would the programme, in order of appearance. But she and her colleagues could not wait for that. They shared her anger that this photograph should appear alone and insult them by their omission. Moshinsky, she said – all this extremely politely – agreed that all their names should appear. If they did not, they would stop work. As for herself, unless her photograph appeared on the wall tomorrow, she would return immediately to New York.

Here I missed my great opportunity. At this point, the operatic game requires the General Director to rise, point sternly to the door of his office leading to the stairs and down those to a door on to the street; in that street can be found a taxi to the airport and New York is just seven and a half hours away. Feebly, I counselled patience. I would see what could be done by tomorrow. My troubles were only just beginning.

I enquired if a cast list could be prepared; of course it could. I went further: could we find room, somewhere, for a picture of Malfitano? We could, and did. Next day, these appeared; rehearsals proceeded. Then came a telephone call from Carreras's agent Carlos Caballé (Montserrat's brother) in Barcelona. Señor Caballé, whom I did not know, came on the line. There was a problem, only a little problem, but a problem none the less. José was not happy about what had happened. He was certain I would understand. José was too much of a Spanish gentleman to mention it himself, but would I go and see him in his dressing room? He was sure that, between two gentlemen, this visit from me would put all to rights. I went to see José. He was quiet, calm, dignified. He was grateful to me for coming. He wished to say nothing to cause offence. He was enjoying working with his fellow cast members, and hated to disagree with them on anything, but an undertaking had been given, an understanding arrived at, that pictures of him alone would appear on the walls of the Opera House, and now other images had joined them. This was quite wrong. He knew I would understand.

I was in a spot, but I had turned once and could not turn again. I much regretted that he should have been in any way upset, but I hoped that he, who was evidently reluctant to make much of this, and was conducting himself in so gentlemanly a fashion, would now agree to let the matter rest. We nodded at each other. I left him. The pictures stayed up.

Another telephone call from Barcelona. José, Señor Caballé put to me with rather more bite than before, was deeply disappointed in me. He had kept his temper. He had not wanted to make a scene. But he had expected me to meet him in this. This was a matter of honour. He could not allow those other pictures, of his colleagues, to remain on the walls with his. If I was not prepared to remove theirs, then he must insist that his photograph come down immediately rather than remain there with them. We took Carreras's pictures down next day.

The first night of *Stiffelio* was a success, musically and dramatically. The audience hung on the music and the libretto's words to the story's cliff-hanging end. The applause was loud and long, the cast all smiles. Carlos Caballé was here to see and hear Carreras triumph. The backstage storm in a *copa* had ended, it seemed, with honours even. Dignity, or the semblance of it, had been preserved.

José Carreras returned once more to Covent Garden to sing in *Fedora*, for the tenor an even less demanding role. He delivered the brief aria 'Amor ti vieta' with style and finish. Mirella Freni, as Princess Fedora, stole the show. Since Freni had sung first at Covent Garden twenty-five years previously, I presented her on stage after the last performance with our silver medal. As I did so, I realized that I had put my foot in it with José again. To make a presentation to her, and not to him, was not clever. Even as he applauded, I could see the Spanish gentleman inwardly wince at the wholly unintended slight. José Carreras, though so courageous and fine an artist, was always, I think, a little prickly that he stood just below others in the pecking order of fame. The Three Tenors concerts promised to remedy that for him, but could not altogether.

The Three Tenors were a media-made phenomenon, and a masterpiece of marketing. Second time round, at Los Angeles in 1994, for another football World Cup, they drove an even harder financial bargain. This time the event, though almost as huge as Rome, lacked the same sheer fun and excitement. But again, cash registers rang. At least it was celebratory in tone. Subsequent repeats in different farflung cities were purely financial occasions. The one in London was anticlimactic. In Paris, in July 1998, for another football extravaganza, we may have heard the last of the Three Tenors jamboree.

The Three Tenors will have a place in the musical annals of our time; their lasting influence is not yet clearly seen. What is certain is that Domingo, Pavarotti and Carreras, three artists equal to opera's full demands, gave infinitely greater performances on their own than they ever gave together.

13

THE CLATTERING TRAIN

I asked the Prime Minister, John Major, and his wife to the opera. They accepted but, at the last minute, he could not come; did we mind if she came on her own? Of course not. Norma Major enjoyed herself, as she always did at Covent Garden. She came, as usual, without fuss. She would ring up sometimes and ask for tickets. She paid for them, and, given our prices, more than once preferred to sit with her friends in the amphitheatre rather than in the stalls. After this particular performance a friend, Kenneth Bradshaw, a former Clerk to the House of Commons, dropped her off at Downing Street. When I got into work next morning, at my usual time of 10am, the message pad was loaded; the Prime Minister had telephoned three times, but found no one to take his call. I winced. He only wanted to thank us for looking after his wife, but he must have thought us a bunch of layabouts.

My day started at 10am and went on to midnight or after. The evening performance was the focal part of the day. In my seat, in a dressing room before the performance, on stage with the cast after it, I could remind myself why I was there. A word of encouragement before and of appreciation after to artists who give their all is the essence of the General Director's role. Everyone I knew outside the House most envied me attendance at rehearsal. Indeed, my happiest memories of Covent Garden are of snatched moments in the rehearsal room, watching Sylvie Guillem and Adam Cooper learn *Herman Schmerman*; catching by serendipitous good fortune Anthony Rolfe Johnson singing 'Where'er you Walk' from

Semele, all the way through, just for me. There were too few such moments. Twenty-five past ten was a good time to greet the cast, or to exchange news or views with conductor or director. Rehearsal proper began prompt at half past the hour; I could rarely stay. I spent most of my time at the Royal Opera House at my desk, or attending meetings, formal and informal.

Every morning I would see my closest colleague, the assistant to the General Director, Christopher Nourse, my principal link to the three performing companies and to the rest of the House. He played a key role in the concentrated effort which kept us giving, come hell or high water, up to 270 performances a season. Not a day went by without a visit from the Finance Director, Philip Jones and his successor Clive Timms; though I valued them both, I wish I'd seen them less often. But since our finances teetered on the knife-edge, there was always some dangerous new tremor to report. The Director of the opera company I saw daily about the House, and regularly each week for a 'routine' report and discussion; so-and-so was confirmed as producer for the Verdi next year; this soprano had cancelled and would likely be replaced by that; the savings sought to compensate for an overspend on that last revival had been found; these repertory changes would be within permitted financial bounds next season. Nicholas Payne had it all at his fingertips. Returning from Vienna or Milan, having heard an artist or chatted up a conductor, he would find time in the air to produce, in a tiny clear hand, a draft programme for two seasons ahead, thoughtful, inventive, exciting even. And practicable. Or just about.

Meetings with him were far more regular than with the Music Director, Bernard Haitink. This was partly because Bernard was away much of the year; partly because, when he was with us, his whole mind and energy were singly bent on the work he was conducting. He never found it easy to switch his attention to anything else. In November 1989, Bernard was in Berlin when the Wall came down. 'How exciting,' we thought. 'The noise was terrible,' said Bernard. 'I could not sleep.'

Bernard took a habitually gloomy view of every prospect. If the matter were problematic, he saw the dark side; if a plain and secure way lay ahead, he suspected a trap. The view from the Polder, I thought of it as, with Bernard pressing a finger to the hole in the dyke lest the North Sea sweep through; Eeyore, someone said, rather than Tigger. Bernard used to complain to anyone who would listen that he did not see enough of me and, sometimes, that he did not like what he saw. The press wrote that we did not get on. I never allowed myself to feel that, and always relished the steep climb up four flights of stairs to the Music Director's room, above the prompt-corner entrance to the pit. Betty Scholar received me there, and would wave me on past the piano, and the tails and white tie hung up beside the wash basin, to the further enclave where Bernard sat with his score. Bernard was seriously committed, as he has proved, to the work and the well-being of the House. He could not understand why we had to close and rebuild in 1997 and no later, but he always wanted the best for the orchestra, for ROH staff, and for all our futures. He was as shocked as the rest of us at the vast amount of francs the Bastille paid Daniel Barenboim – first to come, and later to go. In a profession where ego is all and greed rampant, Bernard remained modest in demeanour and moderate in his demands. ROH benefited. It took me quite a while to break the ice of our early relationship. If I did, perhaps the moment came when I loaned him the video of a film in *The World at War* series on the occupation of The Netherlands by the Nazis. As a schoolboy in Amsterdam, with one-quarter Jewish blood – his maternal grandmother – he had watched with concern and horror as one by one the Jewish boys in his class at school failed to answer their names, and did not return, as they waited at Furst or Westerbork for transports to Auschwitz. This film got to him; it brought his childhood back, he told me. I gave him the complete set of *The World at War*. We understood each other a little better thereafter.

I saw Peter Katona, the Artistic Administrator in the opera company, at planning meetings, or with Paul Findlay and Nicholas Payne. Responsible for opera casting, Peter's was a key contribution to the quality of our work. Although he was always on the telephone, his was a most pleasant office to drop into to find out what was going on, or would be going on two seasons hence. And he baked marvellous small nutty biscuits, crisp and chewy at once. At Christmas I would have forty colleagues to lunch; Peter came carrying a tin. (Since I left the Opera House, he has arrived at my new office each Christmas bearing his tin of cookies.) Assiduous in hearing singers, discriminating in choice, firm in negotiation, diligent in detail, warm in support, Katona was wooed often to leave Covent Garden. We were fortunate he stayed.

The Orchestra Director Bram Gay, rotund and waspish, understanding the orchestra, understood and measured by them, would come to me often for a chat, particularly if Bernard was away, to tell me what the orchestra thought of a new conductor. Usually it was not much, otherwise why would he bother to tell me? 'But Bram,' I would say, 'I am not interested in what the orchestra thinks of the conductor. What does he think of the orchestra?' They hated the martinet Christian Thielemann, for example, when they first played under him for *Jenufa*. Then they realized his talent. In either case, Bram had to mediate. It was to him that the great maestro would address a request for a particular leader or cello or trumpet; to him that the tyro would go for guidance and advice. Bram knew his business inside out, but loved mischief. You had to aim off a bit to get a real sense of any crisis he reported. But in his time orchestral standards improved; thanks to Bernard principally, but Bram too played a role. His deputies Honor Thackrah and Cliff Corbett were each trusted and liked by all. 'I really rate her,' one star player said to me of Honor. 'She telephones me, but when she realizes I am not where I am meant to be, and am off enjoying myself, she stops telephoning.'

Bram was sent to hear Carlo Rizzi and confirm, if he could, Paul Findlay's view that this was a talent we should employ. He could, and did. And there were rare occasions when we agreed, before the critics uttered, that Mr So-and-So would not be re-engaged. But Bram was happiest when one of the great names came to us and he could usher him into the pit to greet the orchestra at their first rehearsal. What the orchestra mainly wants from a conductor, or so Bram thought, is a clear beat. The great are laws unto themselves. I heard Carlos Kleiber in *Otello* tell them, 'You may want me to beat time, but I will not beat time. Please watch my left hand, and follow that.' I watched his left hand myself from the front row of the stalls, as sinuously it curled and weaved, calling forth magic. We never saw enough of Carlos Kleiber; nowadays he too rarely conducts anywhere and when he does, he drives a hard bargain. They say he looks in the freezer and while it is full refuses; he does not need the money. He has a passion for British TV comedy. I sent him *Monty Python* videos, without result. 'You offer me the two things I most value,' he said, when I telephoned once to plead that he should come, 'money and flattery. But I shall say no.'

The ballet companies were further away, and seen less often. Peter Wright and Derek Purnell of Birmingham Royal Ballet came regularly to tell me what they were up to, but I was happy to let Peter get on with it. Derek came to senior management meetings, and I would see him separately at budget time. He was diligent about keeping his finances in line; however difficult, he would always find the savings necessary to balance BRB's account.

At first I found it harder to get hold of Anthony Dowell. The trouble was that one of us had to cross half West London to reach the other. We did eventually set up regular meetings in my office at which he was accompanied by the Administrative Director, Frederick Ashton's nephew, suave, able Anthony Russell-Roberts; by Monica Mason, a great dancer appointed Associate and then Assistant Director; and by a new, outgoing, bright assistant, Jeanetta Laurence. Monica Mason – 'Mon' to all – clear-headed, understanding, practical, expert, was a tower of strength. Together we discussed repertory, striving to find the right balance between familiar works, which would please the public and fill the House, and whatever would add new pleasures, revive old unfamiliar ones, cater to more varied tastes. These meetings, at the end of long days, were positive and co-operative in spirit. We knew what we wanted to do; we did not always, easily, achieve it. A glass of malt whisky helped.

Ballet performances did not markedly decline in number during my time in charge, but the number of programmes the company offered was smaller and, with touring becoming an annual rather than a biennial event, a sizeable number of performances were given abroad. The company seemed to enjoy that; muscles and technique were stretched. Their performance benefited; their relationship with London's dance public wore thin. Russell-Roberts welcomed foreign touring; he liked arranging tours – perhaps because financing each one involved last-minute brinkmanship of a hair-raising sort. Anthony Dowell was happy touring; it gave him chances to bring on talent he could scarcely take at home. When the Warnock Report absolved us from spending our too limited resource on touring the Royal Ballet to Birmingham or Manchester, we came up with *Dance Bites*, a lively mix of new and small-scale work for a group of dancers only, in smaller venues up and down the land – Ashford, Cambridge, Northampton, Bath. With Anthony Russell-Roberts, I discussed dancers' contracts and salaries, retirement and recruitment. The final decisions were Dowell's. The Royal Ballet plays a far larger role in the life of the Opera House than is the case elsewhere. It will play a greater role in the future.

Appointing John Harrison Technical Director was one of the best things I did for the House. John enjoyed only one thing more than bringing me problems: solving them. He would arrive with a tale of woe: a borrowed-in production would not fit the stage, the people who had rented it to us were rogues, the colleagues who had committed to our using it idiots. Yes, John? Well, we'll find a way of cutting it down; it will be all right in the end. It always was. Harrison and his colleagues not only kept productions and performances flowing across the stage, but he and Paul Findlay developed a profitable business for us renting out our productions. *Un re in ascolto*, *Stiffelio*, *Meistersinger* and *The Cunning Little Vixen* were seen in Paris, Vienna, Turin and Washington DC. Older stock also travelled, to Lisbon or to Tel Aviv. Our coffers swelled to the tune of several hundred thousand pounds a year. Labour relations were not Harrison's strongest suit; he left the detail of that to others, notably his very capable deputy, John Seekings. But I know of no one to whom I would rather trust a 'get-in', a fast turnround or a 'get-out' than John Harrison. Every so often, warning that the constant pressure was getting too much, he would announce his resignation. He was always persuaded out of it. It was his vision of what the House required for its efficient operations that determined key elements in the development plan. He saw to it that the stage and its facilities would be adequate to their task, as they never would have been under the scheme I inherited in 1988. He persuaded us to take maximum advantage of regional development grants, and to build a pallet store for scenery in the Cynon Valley, South Wales. There should be a statue to him in the scene-dock, on a moveable plinth.

A crucial regular meeting was with Keith Cooper, Director of Corporate Affairs. What did he forecast at the box-office? Could we improve the figures at all? Drop-dead good-looking and extremely hard-working, Cooper had too much on his plate, combining two quite separate roles in marketing and public relations, and managing staff in each department. Managing staff was not his forte. At English National Opera he had helped sell the company with flair. I hired him principally to market the ROH, and particularly the ballet company. We never had the budget for the sort of campaign we both wanted.

Into each week I would squeeze time to see the in-house development team, led by John Seekings and John Fairclough. As the client commissioning the project, I led an executive group which met weekly to push the work along, reporting monthly to the Board's Development Steering Committee, set up and chaired, firmly and authoritatively, by

Angus Stirling. Seekings and Fairclough had operational charge on a daily basis. The Committee could not determine design detail – that was for the architects – but a design sub-group approved all key questions, particularly as they affected public spaces. This group vetoed a proposal to face part of the scheme in brick, for instance, and insisted on the more expensive option of hard limestone. They had much to say about the granite skirting of the façade in Bow Street, above which the glorious reconstituted Floral Hall proudly rises – 'Not like a bank, please.' And they insisted on calling in an interior designer, David Mlinaric, to work, extremely happily as it turned out, with Jeremy Dixon and Edward Jones on the interiors. The twin giants bestriding the group, like colossi, were two great benefactors of the House, Lord Sainsbury of Preston Candover and Mrs Vivien Duffield. In the last matters of design, from options Dixon and Jones and Mlinaric put in front of them, what these two wanted, they got. When they disagreed, the rest of us ducked for cover. With John Sainsbury, Vivien Duffield was the dominant personality on the Board in my time and, in spite of her lively temper, a great force for good.

As Director of the Royal Opera House Trust, Felicity Clark would brief me on fundraising activity and its success, or lack of it. She and Phyllida Ritter, the Director of the Friends – 20,000 members and something of a law unto themselves – attended senior management meetings once a month. A welcome visitor I saw formally twice a year was Aydin Hasirci, a Turkish charmer in charge of catering. Under Aydin turnover and net catering profit rose substantially each year. He achieved results by increasing volume, as well as price, and not noticeably because the smoked salmon was sliced more thinly. Catering profit became a significant factor in keeping the House in the black. In the new House, an outside caterer of quality will serve meals, snacks and drinks in the spacious Floral Hall and the loggia-level amphitheatre bar, with an open terrace and stunning views west across London. Aydin and his troupe, struggling in cramped corners and with wholly inadequate facilities, worked miracles nightly. They received too little credit for it; our catering staff, with all their moods and idiosyncrasies, had a lifelong commitment to the House and its patrons. Their successors will need to match that.

No two observers could ever agree on how many would constitute the ideal number for the senior management meeting; if it was too many, that at least afforded an opportunity to keep twenty colleagues aware of our plans and progress. If nearer half a dozen, and more capable therefore of executive decision, that necessitated a 'cascade' of briefing down through middle managers who had charge, each in their own 'villages', of specialist departments, each contributing to the finished product – excellent performances achieved within financial parameters.

Much of my time was spent attending Opera House Boards. Boards make policy. What else do they do? Hear monthly reports from the executive, keep an eye on what is going on, mediate with the outside world of politics and public opinion, offer advice on tricky questions of protocol should they arise, occasionally lunch an Arts Council Chairman or address a letter to *The Times*. That is the theory. Perhaps, in an idyllic past, that was all there was to it. But, these days, Boards are in the front line of a never-ending struggle to stay solvent.

In other societies, Boards have another role. In the United States they give money first and help raise money second. To belong, they contribute generously. Belonging is a ticket to New York high society; in the United States giving to the arts confers social prestige. The United States has more than a million millionaires, some of them worth hundreds of millions. There are 400 billionaires. Donations to the arts are tax deductible, so that, in a sense, government subsidy is higher than in the UK. The Metropolitan Opera and the Metropolitan Museum have huge endowments: the Museum's fund stands at $320 million, against a target of $400 million; the opera has over $150 million, and intends to increase that to $400 million. In 1998, a new arrival on the Board of the Lincoln Center handed the Chairman, the smilingly voracious Beverly Sills, a cheque for $25 million, of which $4 million found its way directly to the Met.

The executive still has to manage. Within his artistic lights, Joe Volpe, General Manager of the Met, is as capable an arts administrator as any in the world today. He enjoys a security unknown in Britain: the house he manages has money in the bank. There was a rocky period fifteen years ago, before Volpe, when the Met essayed an element of daring in its repertory, putting on Britten's *Billy Budd* and Poulenc's *Dialogues des Carmélites*. Attendances dropped; financial alarm bells rang. The house trimmed sail and steered for safer water. Managerial adjustments were made. But there was no crisis. The Met had reserves. One Met luminary, Bruce Crawford, who served in that emergency as General Manager, told

me that he once stood up, in his open box, during a performance of Berg's *Wozzeck* and instructed his assistant that the people three boxes along, who were talking loudly during the performance, were making so much noise that they were not to be allowed to take the box again. Then he discovered they had given the Met $1 million. (In Los Angeles, the audience talked so much during the orchestral interludes of *Wozzeck* that Simon Rattle had to explain to them over the tannoy that the music was part of the opera too; would they please keep quiet.) Today, the Met is financially sound and adventurous again: *Moses und Aron*, with our own John Tomlinson and Philip Langridge, has joined *Lady Macbeth of Mtsensk* in the repertory.

As any businessman knows, an excess of expenditure or shortfall in income can be lived with if the business has reserves substantially greater than the blip on the current account. There are no financial concerns for the Board members of a richly endowed house; theirs is a pleasurable social activity, not a demanding task. If the institution is in crisis, that is another matter. Jim Wolfensohn, now Chairman of the World Bank, worked his socks off to raise money to save Carnegie Hall when it was threatened with closure and demolition. American ballet companies – ballet does not have quite the social prestige of opera – have rougher rides. Other major American opera companies live far too much hand to mouth for comfort. But Met Board members sleep soundly and without care, provided they don't pay too much attention to *New York Times* reviews of what they put on stage. London is different.

No one joining the Board of the Royal Opera House was expected to give money. John Sainsbury, my first Chairman, had, with his brothers, endowed the new Sainsbury Wing at the National Gallery. He made known his intention, if matching public funds were also contributed, to make a major donation to the ROH development. His love of the Royal Ballet being what it is, he would have done that anyway, whether Chairman or not. He was emphatic that he would invite no one on to the Board simply because he or she would write a cheque. Nor is anyone invited to join the fundraising arm of the ROH, the Trust, because he or she will pay for a seat at the table. They are there to look for money from others, and will sometimes persuade the companies or corporations on whose boards they sit to fund a production or an educational project. Board members may give, and handsomely, according to their ability, if they choose. But there is no entrance fee. This surprises Americans. What are Board members there for, they ask, if not to give? But private subvention in the UK comes mostly from companies, not from individuals. Social prestige is conferred in Britain through the Honours list; we jib at purchase. Cyril Bennett told me of a conversation he had with Lew Grade, then already Sir Lew, when he received the letter notifying him of his peerage. Lew showed the letter to Cyril: 'The Prime Minister has it in mind to recommend to Her Majesty . . .' 'Congratulations, Lew,' said Cyril. Lew still looked puzzled. 'What does it mean, this "has it in mind"? Does it mean I have to write another cheque to the Theatre Royal, Windsor?' 'No,' Cyril reassured him, 'this is it.'

The Board members of arts institutions in Britain have a testing time. If the arts were adequately funded, their lives would be much easier. Evenings at *Don Giovanni* and *La Bayadère* are an enticing prospect, well worth two hours' monthly attendance at meetings. As it is, they find, when they take their place, that they must bend mind and energy to tackle incipient, ever-threatening crisis. Those who might have expected to be pampered passengers in the first-class saloon soon find themselves on deck in lifejackets, in the teeth of the storm, battening down hatches. They may even have to prepare to abandon ship.

There is no equivalent of our governing bodies at a French or German house, no function for them to perform there. What could it be? The intendant deals directly with government: his budget is precisely tailored to meet the whole of his measured needs; there is no active role for a supervisory board. When Munich, before Peter Jonas's day, overspent by DM8 million on a *Ring* cycle, a member of the Bavarian parliament stood up to speak: what shame it would be on Bavaria, he urged, if such a sum could not be found to do justice to the immortal work of Richard Wagner. When the city fathers of Rome entrusted the extraordinary Gian Paolo Cresci with revitalizing Rome's opera while Italy had the Presidency of the European Commission, within a couple of years he ran up an over-spend, reckoned in sterling, of £23 million. It was said that he spent it on carpets and English lessons for the staff. He had to go. But normally financial management in the great houses of Europe is in essence simple: to keep within a budget adequate for its stated purpose.

All the Board members I knew loved opera or ballet, or both, and brought varied talents to the table; all knew and cared keenly for the Royal Opera House. The Deputy Chairman was Denis Forman, my old Granada mentor, who well understood the creative process. And he knew, from long experience, about the conduct of industrial bargaining. He had a robust and cheerful demeanour in the face of criticism. Martin Jacomb (BZW) and James Spooner (Swire Brothers) were acute students of a balance sheet, and wise in larger matters. So was Bob Gavron. 'Do you think we could get Kit McMahon?' Claus Moser asked me once. He was too busy as Deputy Governor of the Bank of England. Literate and numerate, Kit came in the end and chaired the Development Board. Bamber Gascoigne was knowledgeable and inventive; he chaired the Friends. Tessa Blackstone, Master of Birkbeck College, would sternly remind us that funding in academe was just as scarce as in the arts. John Manduell, a composer and Principal of the Royal Northern College of Music, spoke up for range and adventure in repertory and quality in per-formance, first and last. When Angus Stirling succeeded John Sainsbury as Chairman in 1991, he invited Deborah MacMillan – Kenneth's widow, intelligent and expert – and Christopher Lowe to join. Chris Lowe, Headmaster of Prince William School at Oundle, had long taken a hyper-active and productive interest in education and the arts, and had chaired our Education Advisory Committee. He fought education's corner formidably. Colin Nears chaired the Birmingham Royal Ballet Board. The Board nominated its own membership, and chose well.

When I arrived, our Secretary was Robert Armstrong, now Lord

Armstrong of Ilminster. Robert, son of Sir Thomas Armstrong, Principal of the Royal Academy of Music, rose to head the Civil Service, ending as Cabinet Secretary under Margaret Thatcher. Hurrying from Downing Street with pen and notebook, and dazzling civil servant's virtuosity, he produced full and immaculate accounts of our proceedings. His presence at our table signified a symbolic link within the establishment between the highest level of government and the Royal Opera House. He saw to it, too, that able younger colleagues – who knows, perhaps a future Cabinet Secretary among them – took minutes of the subsidiary boards. They served willingly in return for tickets. The custom ended under John Major, and an era with it.

Main Board members served on at least one subsidiary Board. They might be asked to attend liaison meetings with the Arts Council; two or three formed the Audit Committee; there was the Benevolent Fund to chair, and the Pension Fund; sub-committees were formed to tackle particular issues such as a wage award, or the selection of a senior executive. The development posed a huge constant challenge. One Board member chaired the Trust, another the Friends. Meetings proliferated, agendas lengthened, papers circulated, hours stretched away.

We met in the Boardroom backing on to Long Acre, round an octagonal table with a hole in the middle. It was either too hot or too cold. Meetings were gloomy or cheerful; they were rarely brisk. Serious people, without any reward except pairs of tickets, gave up hours and hours of voluntary time to help manage a private institution with public responsibilities. Supervising projects that depend on multiple sources of funding, keeping all in play, is more taxing than serving a single paymaster. Any body of men and women could take satisfaction in having seen such a task through. But overseeing management in daily detail soon becomes inappropriate and undignified. Managing a revenue account is the task of an executive, not of a Board of part-time directors. They were constantly involved in this, however, because the task of management – attaining standards while remaining solvent – was an almost impossible one. Management should manage, but to manage effectively you need resource. As the Arts Council grant fell from over 60 per cent to under 40 per cent of revenue, we made bricks without straw. Somehow dodging crisis after crisis, the House got by. But the constant threat of insolvency got the Board more and more closely involved in management. In Claus Moser's day, it would debate for hours, and at meeting after meeting, whether the ROH could afford a half or a quarter per cent wage increase for chorus or orchestra. With no reserves, every dash of red in the accounts was a signal of crisis, a matter for recrimination and blame.

At the Main Board, in my time, once a year's budget was approved no one challenged the detail of repertory. By that time, anyway, the pieces we could not afford had already been removed from the schedule – *Iphigénie en Tauride*, *Die Soldaten*, *La Juive*, the revival of *Prince Igor*; the runs of opera revivals were already extended, the long-awaited new ballet already postponed. Here we were, costs under control, box-office up to expectation, but, with private subvention faltering and grant at a standstill, a yawning financial gap was now appearing. The Board stared grimly at the looming deficit. Management repaired to its cubby-holes to trim and tweak to stave off catastrophe. The structural, endemic problem remained. The Board could see no solution that did not involve decimating our work, and that was no solution.

Unlike John Tooley, I was a Board member, not just an employee. I talked and talked, urging always that we keep going, tackle one problem at a time, get the development completed, look forward to a redeveloped House and a brighter future. When we had to impose a wage freeze, we imposed it; when we had to declare redundancies, posts were abolished; when we had to cancel productions, we cancelled some of them, kept others, and tried to hold our heads high. Regularly the Board took advice on its legal position. If bankruptcy threatened, could we go on trading? The auditors, with stern hints of possible qualification narrowly avoided, passed our accounts year on year. The Board more than once asked itself whether it ought not to declare its task impossible and resign. There was never any heart in this – the notion, informally canvassed, never carried. In posing the question, the Board was merely stating a truism: without a vast increase in funds, there was no prospect of an easily viable existence for the Opera House. In the new House, we thought, things would look up; a surplus on the appeal would form the beginning of an endowment; my successors would, in the hour of need, have something to fall back on. That could make the difference. But that was for the future. Now was now. Surrender, or soldier on? There was only one answer to that: Churchill's after Dunkirk.

When the House was in direst trouble in the perilous circumstance of closure, in the extraordinary shenanigans after I left, the Board of the Royal Opera House came in for more than its due share of criticism. They were told they should resign, and they went. They could have chosen to go much earlier. Instead they had shouldered the burden, carrying the House past hazard after hazard, winning planning permission, securing a Lottery grant, launching a successful appeal, seeing the House's books balanced more years than not, setting artistic standards that others applauded and envied. Their service was selfless. It ought not to be thankless. If Britain were a statist society, if all was owned and funded by the state, we would not have independent entities like the Royal Opera House. Life would be the poorer for it.

Unless government funds the totality of an approved arts budget, the British habit of using public-spirited intermediaries to run cherished national institutions will continue. So long as it does, those who volunteer for duty deserve our gratitude and respect.

14

THE HOUSE

'Oh God, not another unflattering story,' my fellow Board members groaned. If they hoped for one thing, it was not to read about the institution they cherished in the newspapers. I was more relaxed. If journalists wanted to write critical stories, there was little we could do to stop them. What mattered was to get things right on the stage; when the world saw we were working wonders – the House full, and ringing with applause – the press would come round. That had been my experience at Channel 4. A unanimous barrage of hostility burst on us as we opened: Storm over IRA Film, Gay Film, Language. I tried not to let this get to me. A *Daily Mail* reporter appeared at my house in Chiswick one break-fast time with a front page calling for my resignation. 'Will you resign?' he asked. I said, 'No.' He asked me to give him a lift into town. The onslaught persisted, peaked, and faded. The media changed tack in part because the Channel was delivering satisfactions that others were not, so that steadily our audience grew; and partly because, having run out of sticks to beat us with, the newspapers lost interest and moved on to the launch of ITV's Breakfast TV – TVAM – a few months later, laden with talent but aimed a mile above its audience's tastebuds. So I thought that at Covent Garden we should simply get on with the job, rather than get into a state over every gossip paragraph or trivial news story or lurid headline.

What I did not at first fully grasp, adjusting to life in a new goldfish bowl, was that two institutions could scarcely have been more different

'I won't quit' says Isaacs

By TARA CONLAN

Royal Opera House general director Jeremy Isaacs has declared he will not resign over the 110 front-line posts managers want to cut to balance the books.

At a packed house meeting attended by all the senior management, Isaacs said management will not be subject to the same cuts as production staff.

Isaacs did not respond to the floor on the issue

demonstration on the steps of the opera house on the first night of a new production of The Midsummer Marriage.

At present there are 28 vacancies and seven fixed term staff, so management is currently aiming for around 70 actual redundancies.

Spokesman Keith Cooper said management is initially looking for voluntary redundancies and that "some staff had already come forward."

He continued: "It's hard to convince people that we have looked at all the other alternatives, but this really is only option."

opera house has to by April

For Union Christian "Follow opera still for

vote of running of has been passed to BECTU is waiting response before deciding whether or not to ballot for industrial action.

Mickey Mouse & Co ride to the rescue of the Royal Opera

M ICKEY MOUSE is coming to the rescue of the Royal Opera House. From

it they may full alloca lottery mil ROH a with offi company,

eager to a plan in y for the be banks uite the London after Mar refur n birth tery ple tey uld use 1997

Disney deal for Jeremy Isaacs?

would not be able to enjoy the lottery's money.

arden's corporate spokes the Opera House volved in ex

re we go phase wark ome d.

Fly on the wall that nearly brought the House down

J eremy Isaacs smelt a rat. Those polite cameramen from the BBC had departed, after a year's unprecedented access to the nation's temple of high culture, the Royal Opera House in Covent Garden, and its boss was feeling uneasy about the ground rules he had agreed. "Trust us," the siren voices had murmured. "If it is to be confidential to screen, we agree to leave it out. That apart, we retain editorial control."

Isaacs decided to ring Roger Graef, a pioneer of fly-on-the-wall documentaries about the Thames Valley police and other institutions. Graef explain his standard devi an agreed ng list of topics and a Jeremy said, 'Ob have done st week. nations. llow in c epi ver

The head of the Royal Opera House letting in the TV cameras first to have

T HE people at the Royal Opera House must feel that whatever they do, they can never get it right. Their grants from the Arts Council have fallen in real terms, until recently sponsorship has boomed, staff numbers have been cut, artistic standards have soared. They have staged special performances with cheap tickets and presented live relays to the Covent Garden Piazza to combat charges of elitism.

None of it has worked. They are still unloved, envied and scorned. The rest of the arts world complains: "What couldn't we do with an extra £20 million, the value of this year's Covent Garden grant? We would give much better value for the money." The guy on the Clapham omnibus wonders crossly why his taxes are spent on rich businessmen, those who can afford a subsidised £70 for a good seat

Both are hardly going to be bankrupted if they pay an unsubsidised £160.

Hardly a day passes without some bad news. Last week the plan to move to a new theatre at Tower Bridge when the ROH closes in 1997 for a few years for redevelopment and refurbishment collapsed. So if an alternative can't be found, they may soon be homeless. A day later, bringing a below-inflation increase in their Council grant of one per cent and a of about £1 million in their business sorship income, the board need a savage staff cutback; proba jobs will be lost. Yesterday, BEC staff union, accused the manage 'losing control of the ship'. Next the launch of a six-part BBC wall' documentary series nt Garden which reveals the rts and all. At Covent Gar come not in single spies. the news is eems to come Then Covent ational tri million, in a triumph s director nd his he tab ti as a had avy e ld ic

Lottery outrage as opera scores £58m

BY PAUL CROSSIN

al Opera House y seat can cost le receive m the

Charity anger over handout

Why we love to hate the Opera House

by ANTHONY EVERITT

out of the impasse, which would transform the V len Duffield, the Clore he ess, is a board member as as well as having prom a hefty personal contri tion to the opera house velopment, is ma minding a public app raise the additional needed on top of the grant. She might able to find enough privately wrink cheques from friends and has in grand

for the live performance of antique melodramas and implausible that sort Those who go to Phantom of than grand than Channel 4 and the Royal Opera House. C4 was a cheeky newcomer, noisy, irreverent, though in news, opinion and the arts much that we did was serious. The ROH was seen as grandiose, stuffy, remote, deserving at all times to be taken down a peg or two. Measured by any objective criteria, far more column inches were devoted to our affairs than they deserved. Health, education, transport, defence, industry, the City, trades unions, matter more than opera or ballet. But newspapers don't select news stories by objective criteria; they want juice. They take aim at recognizable, stereotypical targets – stereotypes of their own making. Because a theatre, employing 1000 people and entertaining 2000 a night, 260 times a year, depends partly on public money, is decorated in red and gold, enjoys – lightly – royal patronage, and occasionally presents Plácido Domingo, it gets far more space, in broadsheet and tabloid, than huge farm subsidies or lurching motor-car manufacture, or GEC, or Unilever or Tesco. The lyric arts are not as overblown in print as pop music or television, but at least those command audiences of tens of millions. Opera and ballet seem rare, exotic blooms by comparison, yet editors salivate as another Covent Garden titbit stimulates a page of moralizing comment. The Royal Opera House, like the BBC, though there is no possible comparison with that body's reach and influence, attracts journalistic interest like pollen does bees. And, because to be instantly recognizable the target has to be a stereotype, it is important, in what was Fleet Street, not to confuse the reader by reporting any good of it. Routine achievement is ignored, random brief interruption given the spotlight. No one will print a feature on the calm preparation that leads to clean performance. Everyone wants the story the night the tenor cracks. No one would report our outreach work in schools and hospitals. Opera singers and ballet dancers performing in primary schools or terminal wards – human interest stories if ever there were any – would not fit the image of the House we love to hate. The *Times Educational Supplement* sometimes reported our educational work. *The Times* did not, nor did its rivals: good news is no news.

Something happened to arts journalism in the 1980s and 1990s because something happened in our society. High culture was devalued, rated at less worth than it had been. Indeed, the very notion of a hierarchy in the arts was scorned and set aside. Absolute values, or our aspiration to them, were rejected in favour of a demotic relativism; roll over Beethoven, here comes Madonna. No one's judgement has preference; all are equal. Blur and Oasis claim space on pages once devoted to Bach and Mozart. Record sleeves, haircuts, body-piercing, ice-creams are seen as icons. Arts pages become culture pages; pop and popcorn push opera to the bottom of the page, making way for the restaurant column. I first sensed what was happening when I was told gleefully, on a green lawn on a sunny Norfolk Sunday, that the *Sunday Times*, for whom Ernest Newman had once reviewed music and Dilys Powell cinema, would shortly, instead of pages devoted to the arts, publish a 'Culture' section edited largely by and for twenty-year-olds. The shock was clinched at a lunch I attended for arts reporters at the Arts Club in Dover Street; baited and biting back, I asked each to say what ballet and opera meant to him or her. I expected one or two might say: 'Not very much.' I had not thought the arts correspondent of a leading broadsheet would reply: 'Nothing at all.' (This was before I encountered the arts editor of another paper who plumed himself on being 'a thorn in your flesh', and later claimed in print never once in twenty years to have found anything good to say about the Royal Opera House.)

These reporters knew that knocking copy was their best chance of getting into the paper; if they had wanted to write pleasant things about us – and there must have been something they could have conjured up from time to time – there was little chance of its appearing. The same was true, in spades, of feature writers, subs looking for headlines, leader writers eager to bang a critical drum. It was impossible to interest them in our outreach work, because it was unassuming. Occasional empty seats in the auditorium were hawkishly commented on, even though paid attendance at the ROH season after season exceeded the West End's average and ENO's by 10 or even, in the aftermath left by their most adventurous work, 20 percentage points. Nobody reported that ENO and WNO and Opera North and Scottish Opera received a higher Arts Council subsidy per seat than the Royal Opera, though we more than once pointed this out. As to ticket prices, nothing would persuade them to print the average price each season; to note the 850 cheaper seats available each night; or to track the price of a – precariously lofty – place in the upper slips from £1.50 to £7 over the years. All they were interested in was the special top price for 100 out of 2000 seats, at only 10 out of 260 performances a year, when Domingo or Pavarotti was in the House. That price, which did not add to the artist's fee but brought in additional desperately needed revenue, was used to characterize the entire season, to denounce us as 'élitist', and to demonstrate, though the public filled it, that we ran the House as an exclusive, private club. Of course we got things wrong and more than once deserved a pasting. But, by and large, on the principle of give a dog a bad name, the Royal Opera House habitually got a less than fair press.

An opera or ballet critic is employed to write of what he or she sees and hears on the lyric stage. I have no quarrel with any honest critic, nor any complaint at their work. I never once disputed with anyone what he or she wrote in judging a performance, though I did once complain on a point of fact. A learned opera critic regretted that our *Peter Grimes* – Elijah Moshinsky's staging, effectively revived – contained not a hint of the sea. This, I thought, carried literalism too far. The production, which might have been designed at Aldeburgh, exhibited boats, sailors, nets, creels, the catch and the shingle; we could see the horizon. Surely even the dimmest imagination could detect a hint of the sea in that? Otherwise, I was all mildness, revelling in Clement Crisp's excoriating critiques of other companies' work in the *Financial Times*, rejoicing in his glowing praise of our rivals, in Paris or St Petersburg, laughing through the pain at his prickliest prose when he bared his fangs and tore into whatever of ours he vituperatively targeted. Clement Crisp lives to celebrate ballet, in whose history and practice down the years he is expert beyond compare. When Kenneth MacMillan died in the theatre I saw Clement, as I spoke on stage, rise from his seat at once, and leave first. At the funeral at St Paul's, Hammersmith, he spoke with an eloquence that elevated the day. Clement, though he has blind spots, and carries his patrician distaste for the vulgar too far, is nevertheless, and will always be for me, beyond reproach. Let one who writes so brilliantly stand for all: critics should write what they like.

But only, I would add, if they stick to criticism. As many nowadays will admit, that is precisely what they are not encouraged to do. Editors have rather gone off the straight review in recent years. You can follow the logic: why give space to a recital in the Wigmore Hall in front of a few hundred the day before yesterday, even if Anne Sofie von Otter or Yevgeny Kissin held the audience in the palm of their hand? Now a feature on Anne Sofie, with something about her home life, would be of much more interest to our readers. Spice it up a little, please. And, if you must review the opera, why not put in a paragraph or two on the latest Covent Garden imbroglio? But to combine criticism and tendentious feature writing in the same piece seems to me highly undesirable.

I do not see how a critic can honestly review what he has seen on stage if, in the same piece, he is slagging off the management. How Trevor Nunn directs *Oklahoma!* and how he runs the Royal National Theatre are distinct matters, as were Richard Eyre's dual roles. They deserve separate treatment. In reviewing the play, the critic must concentrate on the performance before him. To mix criticism with sermons on management, to my mind, muddles both. I do not say that the practice is all pervasive; I do say that it is more prevalent than it should be. Argumentative feature writing devalues criticism; yet it is true criticism that holds up to the public an image by which to judge, and to the artist a mirror in which to learn.

I have not forgotten the tearful telephone call I took on a Thursday from a newly prominent critic begging for help with a piece to be finished that evening for Sunday's paper. The answers this chap sought to factual questions ought either to have been familiar, or to have been carefully researched days before. When I corrected his assumptions, he wept. He met his deadline. The piece, in which my manner was described as 'bullying', appeared on Sunday. Later, reviewing Nederlandse Opera from Amsterdam, he praised their seat-pricing policy against that of Covent Garden, without troubling his readers with the fact that their subsidy was twice ours. When, finally, he described my last season as 'dross' compared to the Met's, though that contained Zeffirelli's notorious overblown *Carmen*, while ours, admittedly short on new productions, contained fine casts conducted by Ted Downes, John Eliot Gardiner, Christian Thielemann, Valery Gergiev, Georg Solti, Bernard Haitink and others, I had a colleague write to him privately to ask how he substantiated that view. With no attempt at justification, he wrote one querulous line: 'Why should I trust what anyone at the Royal Opera House says?' Is that the mind or habit of a critic? When Andrew Porter retired from the *Observer*, Nicholas Kenyon, wearing his Radio 3 hat, put on a concert for him at St John's, Smith Square – Stravinsky's *Soldier's Tale* – the first piece Andrew ever reviewed. There was a drink afterwards at which Andrew spoke, listing the critics he had learned from: Ernest Newman, Desmond Shawe-Taylor, Eric Blom, William Mann. Such critics, writing at length, gave the reader the context in which to respond to a review and the judgement it contains. Andrew Porter, happily still to be read in the *TLS*, is the last in a line. British newspapers, vying each to out-tabloid the other, have little room now for that sort of review. With space at a premium, something precious, Porter surmised, may be departing from our musical lives. There are still critics who are knowledgeable, sensitive, fair-minded – the editor of *Opera* and Porter's successor among them – critics I enjoy reading; long may they survive the winter of popcorn culture, and the frowns on foreheads villainous low.

One minor quarrel I picked with opera critics early on did me no good at all. Foolishly, I suggested that some were frustrated opera-company directors. I was piqued, if I remember, at critics who persisted in telling us who should have been singing or conducting, though we knew, and could have told them if asked, that he or she was not available. Howsoever, my unnecessarily offensive remark caused a stir. I apologized. But it was true. More than one reviewer, consulting me privately about a career move, bluntly asked to be considered for a managerial job. Bored, they wanted a change. I warm to several experienced practitioners, whose enthusiasm and zest appear undimmed. But I can understand that others begin to tire at the prospect of yet another *Tosca*. What is there left to say? How does one stay fresh, when so much is familiar? Critics should move about a bit, or retire early, or at least be allowed to take an occasional sabbatical.

It is even more trying for the ballet critic. There, repetitious repertory must, for those at least whose papers will not send them frequently abroad, engender staleness and tedium. One doyen told me that, dreading the annual Christmas overdose of *Nutcracker*, he fled once to Vienna where Nureyev would offer *Coppélia*, only to discover when he got there that *Coppélia* was cancelled: it would be *Nutcracker* after all. I do not know how keen minds can easily endure the same piece over and over, responding to it, like the young lady from Spain, who was frequently sick in the train, not once and again, but again and again, and again and again and again. Yet they do, gluttons for punishment all. Sometimes I would read a fiercely hostile review of the first night of a production with several changes of cast. Taking pity, I would suggest to the ballet press officer, Amanda Jones, that she enquire whether the critic really wanted to return to the show. If not, we could easily sell the tickets. Invariably the answer was 'Oh no, he wants to come again.' One loutish figure who wrote, minimally, on opera, once bellowed at me in the Ivy how unspeakably dreadful he thought our new *Ring* was. In that case, I said, you will not want tickets for the rest of it. 'No, no,' he cried, 'I do want them.' Surely such masochism is beyond the call of duty.

Members of the opera audience who had read a harsh critique of the production before coming to the theatre would frequently tell me that they did not recognize the piece. They were enjoying themselves; the critic's experience was not theirs. How, consistently, could this be so? One explanation, hazarded in talk to colleagues, and carrying some credibility, was that the first night had been a downer; that after a demanding rehearsal period and a full-out general rehearsal in front of an en-thusiastic audience, the singers had been tired and flat, or too edgy with nerves, to do themselves justice. Sometimes this was the case. Some great singers opposed the practice of having an audience at an open final rehearsal for just that reason. For an audience, they would give their all, and two nights later might sing below par as a result. But for the Friends of Covent Garden, and some Opera House staff, those rehearsals could be their only chance to see the show. We had to have the cast's and con-ductor's agreement to every one of them; but we could not give them up. The critic might not spot that, after a poor opener, the show could pick itself up and frequently does.

Another reason for the discrepancy was simple: the critic's sensibilities were far more finely tuned than the patron's or the punter's, ear and vision keener, standards higher, judgement sterner. That explained the gap. This is irrefutable. But, searching my own mind, I find a more routine cause behind the difference of opinion: the critic may respond to the production before him, the opera-lover to the piece itself. Coming late to dutiful attendance in the opera house, hearing and seeing, for the first time in my life, opera and ballet four or five times a week all year round, I still found myself responding principally to Beethoven and Tchaikovsky, to Petipa and Ashton, rather than to the version of their work then before me. However jaded I felt entering the theatre for *Swan Lake*, the first bars of Tchaikovsky's score were always enough to warm me into a readiness to enjoy myself. As for *Fidelio*, I am never not moved by it; the work itself gets to me every time, almost irrespective of the executants. Very many in the audience are going to enjoy the piece in itself, without comparison with other versions. The knowledge that this is so should surely be kept in mind.

The best critics I have come to know as friends. They try honestly to get it right; some qualify superlatives, shuffling shades of grey, rather than state everything in black and white; others enthusiastically award marks to what they review on a scale of 0 to 10, their verdicts falling mainly in the ranges 1 out of 10 or under, and 9 out of 10 or over, with very little in between. None of us ever cavilled at being awarded 10 out of 10 – 'Kill for a ticket' – though the audience may be bewildered if the show disappoints expectations. But awarding 0 out of 10 ignores the needs of the reader, with whom after all the critic is in dialogue, who may still respond to and enjoy the piece itself. Critics like Michael Kennedy and Rodney Milnes, Jann Parry and Judith Mackrell and others play an invaluable role in the ecology of the arts. But they write for readers, as we perform not for ourselves but for audiences.

I wish I thought more critics were read rigorously by their editors – by whoever is in charge of the page or the paper. My least favourite critic, now happily retired, more than once criticized in advance Anthony Dowell's intention to include a particular piece in the coming season. He hated, he announced, Baryshnikov's ABT version of *La Bayadère*; we should not be doing it. To commission a new ballet from Twyla Tharp would be a colossal waste of money; he dreaded its première. How, in conscience, he could then review either piece, I never understood. I meant to ask his editor to comment, but never got round to it. One editor who did intervene positively was Andreas Whittam Smith at the *Independent* in its pioneering early days. When we started the Garden Venture to give would-be opera composers their first chance, he enthusiastically supported it, inviting 1000 of his readers to subscribe £100 each to make it possible. They did.

'How I enjoyed your series! Marvellous! I watched every minute of it. I wish there were more.' Balm to the ears of a television producer. Was it *The World at War* they were congratulating me on, or *Ireland: a Television History*, or even, nowadays, *Cold War*? Alas, no. Land's End to John O'Groats, Perth to Sydney, New Haven to San Francisco, compliments have flowed in, recognition been accorded not for something I made but for something I appeared in. And since as gatekeeper it was I who allowed the cameras in, the attribution to myself may be ironic but is not wholly unjust. *The House*, a so-called fly-on-the-wall documentary, ran on BBC2 for six consecutive weeks on Tuesdays at 9.30pm in January and February 1996. It was seen in the UK by audiences of up to 4 million a week, very many of whom had never been inside an opera house in their lives. By the fascinating detail of its subject matter, and the skill and cunning of its construction, it proved compulsive viewing. It vividly conveyed the tensions which form the background to live performance. It offered a role before the cameras to everyone it purported to observe. With scarcely an exception, from cleaner to Board member, all seized that opportunity to star. Among the Board, only Deborah MacMillan made up her mind to say nothing while the cameras were in the room, and kept to it. *The House* conveyed a vivid impression of what working life in a frantically busy theatre was like, while seriously misrepresenting key aspects of it. It did considerable long-term good in 'demythologizing the arts and arts institutions'. It distorted by selection and left a legacy, in recycled quotation, that did long-term damage. It was held, universally, to be 'good television'. *The House* won every prize that was going. It was not documentary as I understood it, but, as I belatedly realized, 'docu-soap'. Were it not for me, it would never have happened. What was I thinking of?

Concerned about image nowadays, you can try to do something about it. I hoped that simply doing our job well, on stage and off, hitting artistic heights, balancing the books, would do the trick. Patently, it did not. Attempts at 'spinning' did not work either: one word from us, and journalists wrote what they liked. I suppose an assiduous, concerted, protracted campaign of argument and exposition might have had an effect, but with our genuine financial difficulties constantly threatening to provoke unhelpful news, and the controversial, hard-fought development generating a steady stream of critical comment – 'Arrogant ROH Rebuked'; 'Opera House Changes Mind Again' – we spent much time on our heels fire-fighting, and never were able properly to go over to the offensive. We lunched and lunched, but to no avail. I was mindful of what the PR guru Peter Gummer, a friend and supporter of the ROH, had once told me: 'Get the readers of the *Sun* on your side.' And I remembered a Conservative Minister for the Arts, in Alasdair McAlpine's house in Westminster, conspiratorially close to the House of Commons, saying to me, Richard Eyre and others, 'Of course I myself agree with everything you say; it is my backbenchers you have to persuade. If you could get the public on your side, and have them write in support of the arts to their Members of Parliament, why, I'd be able to help you in no time.'

Why should the Opera House not appeal over the heads of newspapers, direct to the public? If television showed us hard at work, without airs and graces, giving our all to entertain, might that not, unfiltered, unmediated, do the trick? In 1992 more than one TV company wrote enquiring if we would allow them access to make a documentary series. Not that year, I thought – 1992 would be rough; the following year might be easier. In the end, we agreed to allow Double Exposure, an independent production company based in Clerkenwell, to make six programmes for the BBC. Andrew Bethell, Double Exposure's leading light, and Edward Mirzoeff of the BBC would be executive producers. Michael Waldman would produce and direct. Keith Cooper, who doubled as Head of Marketing and PR at the Opera House, was party to the decision. He indeed conducted all the preliminary discussions. The staff were consulted, at least in some departments, both by us and by Double Exposure, and agreed. The Board approved. But my voice, with thirty years' experience in broadcasting behind it, was certainly decisive. I was for it, and my view prevailed.

In some ways we had little to lose. The House had at best an unflattering press, and wanted desperately to be more fully and accurately represented to the public. And we had much to be proud of; we did good work on the whole, and most people enjoyed doing it. With an application to the National Lottery coming up, it must be worth one more stab at winning over opinion to our side. Besides, although the BBC would expect access to pretty well everything – that was their presumption – we should, by formal agreement, have a right of veto in the making of it. If we declared a meeting private, the door would stay closed, the camera locked out. If we allowed coverage, and an unexpected embarrassment resulted, which violated the spirit of our understanding, then we must instantly disallow it. We had that right too. As to what was left on the record, we had the right to view the films before transmission and make representations against the inclusion of any item in them. Our voice at that stage would be listened to; however, it would not necessarily be heeded. The veto was then with them. This contract was not sufficiently in our favour. The real problem, though, was that having so much else to do, we were nothing like tough enough in enforcing a veto on what was filmed as we went along. The camera crew were on their own; we did not dog their footsteps.

Working in television all those years, as a journalist, I had often backed attempts to get cameras in when institutions wanted them kept out. My first employer, Granada's Sidney Bernstein, had pioneered live television coverage of elections and party conferences. I had wanted to show, so that people could see with their own eyes, what our slums and schools and hospitals were really like. I remember filming in hospitals with paint flaking off the walls. 'You should not be showing that,' the authorities objected. I disagreed. I was, by temperament and background, sympathetic to journalistic entry and disclosure. I was biased for openness, against concealment and secrecy.

Then again, going back a bit in memory, I had quite the wrong model in my mind of the programmes that would result. I had admired early examples of the fly-on-the-wall genre – famous films made by Roger Graef for Granada about British Steel and Hammersmith Council, scrupulously observed, detailed accounts, neutral in tone, of complex issues and proceedings, sometimes dull, often fascinating. And I remembered Graef's riveting series on the Thames Valley Police for BBC, when he had prised loose doors not previously opened. An enterprising, well-led police force had dared reveal more of itself than ever before – rape victims verbally abused by sceptical coppers – and benefited from the exposure. But Graef, who made his name with those films, is meticulous, almost legalistic, in defining in advance precisely what he proposes. He agrees an exact framework, and operates within it. He offers a clear account of what he will film and what omit; there is no room for misunderstanding afterwards. Roger Graef is a very different film-maker from Michael Waldman. Nothing Waldman did was dishonest; I allowed him too much rope.

I first met Michael when I was making *Ireland: a Television History* in 1980 with Robert Kee for the BBC and RTE. He worked as a researcher. It was, I think, his first job. He was bright, quick, willing. He got on. The first film he made himself, on undertakers, I liked enormously. He then made a fly-on-the-wall series on undergraduate life at Queen's College, Cambridge. It made, I gathered, pleasant viewing but caused little stir. When he and his colleagues, preparing to film, had been around Covent Garden for a while, I bumped into him in a corridor and we chatted. 'When you are ready, Michael,' I said, 'and know what themes you are considering pursuing, come and see me. I should like to hear of them, and talk them over with you.' 'Er, yes . . .' he said. But he never came. There were to be no themes, anyway none plotted in advance; randomness was all. That is the root of my disappointment with *The House*. I had hoped that, while exploiting access to every nook and cranny and filming every drama, minor or major, that he found, the series would still take a considered and measured view of the problems we faced and our relative success in overcoming them.

The cameras would be with us for over a year. I was sure one film would take advantage of the time allotted to show the slow, germinating process, both creative and managerial, that leads from concept and design, past planning, budgeting and casting, through rehearsal to performance. Every arm of the House would be involved; all would combine to produce the end result. If, as I also hoped, that result could itself be broadcast, *Die Meistersinger*, say, or *The Sleeping Beauty*, we should have offered viewers new insights, perhaps made converts, won new friends. I expected too, that one film of the six would show the annual agonizing process of inching our way to an agreed budget, and see the hope of operating within it realized at the year's end. I assumed the BBC, wanting to enlighten viewers, would want to do that. It did no such thing. You would never know from watching *The House* that after a struggle, of which we saw plenty, we achieved precisely that success, operating within budget during the year the cameras were with us. But that was the case.

I imagined that Michael Waldman, seduced by images of children involved in making opera or dance with wonder in their eyes, would use film to bring, at last, the work of our education departments into the limelight it deserved. Nothing could more effectively alter the image of an 'élitist' house than primary-school children from Brixton or Wandsworth taking their first tentative steps in classical dance, or showing us what they could invent themselves. *The House*, apart from one scene in a shopping centre – not the Education Department at all – and a cursory view of the audience at an unexplained Schools Matinée, showed nothing of our educational work. It was, we were told, too widely dispersed from Covent Garden to be covered. It is dispersed, that is the whole point; but you can cram a great deal, as I often found, into half a day's visit. An opportunity was missed.

What we did see was a skilfully mixed pot-pourri of incidents – funny, tense, contrasted, revelatory, but wholly unrelated to any intellectual overview. Entertaining yes, but the programmes were, to my mind, mindless. Richard Eyre thought them heartless. The technique was very simple: film anything interesting; as soon as it ceases to be interesting, stop; when assembling, at that point cut immediately to something quite different. The director was observant, the camera deft, and, in the cutting room, the editor was king. And what a cast they had: all of us played our roles with eagerness and aplomb. Fly-on-the-wall purports passively to observe; in fact, for the camera everyone present acts unnaturally. In this drama, we were all actively encouraged to perform.

Colleagues who would normally have sent me down a paper to study the day before a meeting would instead, worked on by Waldman, enter my office unheralded, the camera backing before them, to bring me an instalment of financial bad news, provoking a reaction for the world to note. Members of the chorus, never slow to grouch, took advantage of the chance to criticize a borrowed *Magic Flute* and Tim Albery's marvellous home-grown *Chérubin*. The Orchestra Committee were heard, *adagio maestoso*, complaining about one recent over-parted conductor, ignoring the star performers of the weeks before and after. No one put this, or anything else, in perspective. Nicholas Payne, on his way up to see me in the interval of a first night, remarked loudly and unnecessarily that he had no wish to meet these 'fucking rah-rahs'. Nicholas had been educated at Eton; the people I hoped to introduce him to certainly had not. Board members, before your very eyes, grew in stature and indignation as they pitched into me over overspends, in the end easily corrected, on *Káťa Kabanová* and *The Sleeping Beauty*. Angus Stirling struck a note of moral indignation worthy of Gladstone; Tessa Blackstone, after her intervention, could have had any schoolmistress's job in the country; James Spooner, on his shortest fuse, temporarily made an ass of himself by demanding to know 'why we put up with people like Trevor Nunn at all?' (Trevor, having to spend far more time repairing *Sunset Boulevard* in Los Angeles than he had expected, got behind in his briefing of Maria Bjornson on *Káťa Kabanová*. She in turn was late with costume designs for *The Sleeping Beauty*. Yes, it was rather a muddle, but theatres do not make widgets.) Terri-Jayne Gray, on whose petite shoulders many a singer cried and found comfort, was shown uncharacteristically boot-faced, refusing Denyse Graves, making her début as Carmen, a supper table for her family. Mike Morris, reaching agreement with the chorus over a trivial incident in which they were completely in the right and management in the wrong, played Gary Cooper in *High Noon*. His remark, in this context, that Thatcherism had never touched us, was inaccurate and unhelpful. The taxi-driver who accosted me on ticket prices was put up to it. This camera was never a mere observer.

Keith Cooper, who should have known better than any of us how to behave in front of the camera, seemed to enjoy his tantrums as Mr Nasty. He didn't need to curse and throw the telephone receiver down, but he did it with a will. He was totally in the wrong to let them film him firing a colleague. It was callous, and he should never have allowed it. Once he had it on film, Michael Waldman immediately anticipated our tardy objections by interviewing the victim: 'Tell us what you feel about it.' The sacked box-office manager expressed his indignation and sense of injustice. That was firmly lodged in the rough cut when, many months later, we first saw it, validating Cooper's scene. We all knew it was sickening, but I could not persuade Waldman, Bethell and Mirzoeff to remove the incident. Instead, maintaining that the victim had made no objection, they moved it up to the first episode in the series.

Everything these films sought to capture was exceptional; there was nothing of routine. The Hamlyn Week of specially funded performances – no ticket over £5 – in which 12,000 came to the House who had never been before – was represented by a glimpse of Princess Diana in the audience and one poor woman arriving late and being directed to the wrong part of the House. Twice, in 150 performances, we were shown the dash and drama that gets a replacement artist on to the operatic stage at the last possible moment. The second time, I played up to it for all I was worth, telling the audience for *Figaro* that we had lost Jeffrey Black as the Count, but had found, forty minutes before, just back from Los Angeles, Thomas Allen. I also put on a fine scene of sincere indignation at Arts Council parsimony, when I did manage to find the right words: 'The least-cost option means no art.'

Two episodes struck home with me. Anthony Dowell, quiet, cool, thoughtful, consulting with Merle Park to choose, from the Royal Ballet School, two young dancers for the lead role of Clara in *The Nutcracker*. That testing gaze, and the joy and terror of his choices, showed us the hard judgement needed at the heart of show business. And Michael Nunn, a Royal Ballet soloist, unwrapped the bleeding foot he brought off stage with him, and then we saw the operation that he must then undergo. Dance, this screamed at us, is made in pain. This last was the revelation of the series.

The House gave pleasure to millions and, in introducing us to them, did some good. In stressing shock horror rather than our solid achievements – performances of quality begun on time and ended on budget – *The House* did damage. It continues, in recycled quotation, to do damage. Maybe the managerial flaws and failings it pointed to deserved the spotlight, but so did our overall success. I would let cameras in again, but on different terms, and in a more sceptical frame of mind.

I asked Michael Jackson, when he was Controller of BBC2, if he would allow Jeremy Isaacs Productions to make a similar series within the BBC, publicly accountable as it proclaimed itself to be. 'You must be joking,' he replied.

15

TOUCH ME TOO

The ROH Annual Report was prefaced each year by a page of bullet points summing up performance, artistic and financial, listing revenues raised, itemizing achievement. One cluster dealt with education and outreach. For 1994/95 it read:

- 5.3 million saw two operas and two ballets on television
- 1.1 million heard 11 operas on radio
- 10,800 attended five Midland Bank Proms performances
- 12,900 attended six Paul Hamlyn Westminster Week performances
- 19,000 saw three Big Screen relays
- 9000 heard *Aida* at Kenwood
- 27,000 attended 16 Schools Matinées
- 38,000 children participated in education and outreach projects
- 5600 attended three Saturday Specials

Is this élitism, or its opposite?

In the foreword to his 1998 report on *The Future of Lyric Theatre in London*, Richard Eyre movingly argues for a Utopia which would, among much else, 'abolish the cultural apartheid which divides the country between those who go to galleries, theatres and opera houses, and those who feel excluded from them'. He knows, he says, 'how to bring this Utopia into being, and so does the Prime Minister: education, education, education'. Putting out of my mind the irreverent memory of hearing

Tony Blair utter this mantra – what I tell you three times is true – when he opened a new block at a university which has since been shown to be an academic disaster, I know they are both right. Only when the whole of society is imbued with a feeling for the arts, or at least when a wider cross-section senses their benefit as part of the natural order of things, will the arts be supported as they need to be. But that they are part of all our birthrights, and that we need to offer them to all, I have never doubted. Putting necessary information in palatable form before millions was what I worked at in television. I was, am and always will be adamant about raising up, not dumbing down. I once heard Colin Davis, at a lunch given for him at the Admiralty by a thoughtful Minister for the Arts, Richard Luce, say most movingly that 'Listening to Mozart would make anyone a better human being.' I cannot quite go along with that; Adolf Hitler enjoyed great music. But I do believe that theatre, painting, music can make us all more fulfilled, lift and enrich our spirits and aspirations. Not everyone will want to drink at the well; everyone should be invited to sip the water.

The loudest, the happiest noise heard in the Royal Opera House each year came from audiences at Schools Matinée performances. It was not so much the clapping and cheering that did it as the earsplitting whistles of approbation, adding to applause a treble we did not normally hear. Culled from a range of schools, some private and fee-paying, others very much in the public sector, briefed and prepared for what they were to hear and see, they sat in rapt silence throughout performances and raised the roof at the curtain's fall. They booed villains. Pinkerton in *Madama Butterfly*, having betrayed his Japanese wife and stolen away their child, was bound to hear a storm of noise raised against him. We took pains to warn the tenor. Perhaps sixth-formers should have been sophisticated enough to distinguish the character from the artist, but we preferred their honest response. These performances for schoolchildren were hard to fund, though no one attending them could ever doubt their worth. They were, in important ways, the high spots of our season, the culmination of efforts which went on through the year. Members of the opera and ballet companies performed for thousands of children, and encouraged them to active participation in dance and – let's make an opera – in song.

When the Secretary of State for the Arts concedes today that the Opera House deserves more funding, he stipulates that, as a prime condition, it must extend its educational and outreach activities. The impression is given that up to now we have done none of that, or very little. Delivering his Arts Council lecture, *An Arts Council for the Future*, on 14 October 1998, the new Chairman Gerry Robinson read from a text drafted by Phil Murphy, a spin-merchant in the marketing department. The Royal Opera House, he pronounced, must 'develop significantly its educational programmes if we are to carry through its rescue plan and consider awarding any extra grant'. In the same speech Mr Robinson asked:

> How many major performing arts companies can claim they success-fully and repeatedly reach out beyond the so-called traditional audience? There are some notable examples such as the Theatre Royal Stratford East, and the Nottingham and West Yorkshire Playhouses. Certainly not the Royal Opera House – yet!

This blatant falsehood, uncritically reported as fact by arts correspondents who should have known better, was compounded four paragraphs later:

> And remember too the Hamlyn Week at the South Bank. Chris Smith, who is here with us tonight, talks enthusiastically about the way in which tickets at £5 per head brought in less than reverential audiences to the theatres. These people charged up and down the aisles, shouted

across the auditorium before curtain up, only to fall into rapt entrance-
ment once the performance began. So don't tell me that we're foisting
the arts on reluctant newcomers.

There was indeed a Hamlyn Week at the South Bank. I went to it, and saw
Peter Pan (with Ian McKellen, who later fled to Yorkshire to escape, he
said, middle-class audiences). The week was a great success, but the only
reason it was held on the South Bank was because the Royal Opera House
was closed. There, over the previous twelve years, ten Hamlyn Weeks had
brought ballet and opera to 120,000 people who had never been to the
Royal Opera House before. Gerry Robinson's rhetorical own-goal was
pointed out by me in a letter to the *Daily Telegraph*. The facts were put to
him by the Hamlyn Foundation. Neither he, nor anyone at the Arts
Council, has publicly apologized for so misleading those who heard the
lecture, or read excerpts from it. This travesty of the truth must have
been particularly offensive to the Arts Council's new Director of
Education and Training, Pauline Tambling. She had been responsible for
opera education at the Opera House since 1983. Phil Murphy, who
worked on the speech, is now Head of Communications at New Labour.

The ROH was one of the first arts organizations in the UK to have an
Education Department. Even before the theatre opened officially on 20
February 1946, it hosted a Robert Mayer Concert for children. The first
Schools Matinée, of Purcell's *Fairy Queen*, was in 1947. From then on
matinées continued, both opera and ballet – over 120 of them up to 1997.
Casts at the opera performances were always of starry quality: Jon
Vickers in *Peter Grimes*, Kiri Te Kanawa in *Die Fledermaus*, Mirella Freni
in *Eugene Onegin*. Singers, particularly the most famous, readily agreed to
meet youngsters after a performance. One child told Jon Vickers that he
couldn't hear his words.

Covent Garden did education work, and had appointed an Education
Officer, well before the Arts Council began to require its clients to do so.
When I arrived in 1988, I found two fiercely able women dedicated to the
tasks of education: in opera, Pauline Tambling, and in ballet, Darryl
Jaffray. John Tooley had, in a sideways move, put over them and in overall charge an opera producer whose production duties – he was a dab hand
at revivals – were decreasing. Pauline and Darryl resented this overlord-
ship. I removed him. I also gave the department an increased budget; this
was far less than we would all have liked, but more than we could easily

afford. It funded their core activity, but not specific projects. For each of those, separate funding had to be raised; the core budget bought the time to develop projects to attract sponsors and within a couple of years, the eight members of staff were pulling in £200,000 a year. The matinées needed separate funding. In addition to their budget, the Education Department got help in kind from all areas of the House – wigs, costumes, props. Singers and dancers were detached from other commitments to go out on the road to schools. I added two dancers to the strength of the Royal Ballet and to the Sadler's Wells company, as it then was, to reduce the strain regular educational work placed on performance and rehearsal. We could not manage more. The post of Director of Education, at senior management level, we never were able to fill, and for the same reason: cost. The House's educational programme is now being extended and a Director, Darryl Jaffray, has at last been appointed. Meanwhile, ROH education achieved more, and more consistently, than many flashier, more ephemeral exemplars.

One strength of our programme on which Pauline Tambling placed particular emphasis was the work we did with teachers. The arts-funding system is only now talking about the importance of teachers, but it is through them, my colleagues realized long ago, that the best approach is made to children; get them on your side, show them what opera and ballet are about, and you are halfway there. We organized courses and weekend schools at Covent Garden to show teachers how an opera production was put together; we sent information packs in advance to stimulate their interest in the piece that their class was coming to see. The result: schoolchildren came to our matinée performances well prepared. I remember in my own schooldays seeing Donald Wolfit play *Lear* in Glasgow for an audience of schoolchildren. They talked throughout. Wolfit protested from the stage. The other day I read a report of similar ill manners at an RSC performance. Free tickets alone are not enough; keen, informed anticipation is all.

In the summers we opened the House to 16–21-year-olds for a week to help them get to know it – 'Behind the Scenes'. There were six-day courses at Easter for secondary teachers and numbers of smallish projects lasting two or three days in schools throughout the country, linked to particular operas. In 1985 the Opera Education Department linked up with the Metropolitan Opera Guild (New York) and trained twenty teachers each year from ten schools; we found that two colleagues, enthused with

Thankyou for a wonderful tour. We loved it!

The Education Department receives hundreds of letters from children who have been thrilled by visits to the House or other activities. This card from Bishops Down School, Tunbridge Wells, used surtitle technology to put its message across

From the 1988/89 Annual Report

the lyric-arts bug, did more effective work in schools than a singleton proselytizer. When the House won European funding for this work, we were able to bring teachers from eleven different EU countries to London to learn how to create music theatre for and with young children. In fact, we led the world.

Staple fare in our opera education was the touring workshop. Groups of singers led by company principals John Dobson and Roderick Earle visited, each year, sixty new schools – that is, schools not already applying for tickets for matinées. They took with them carefully devised, participatory workshops: 'Once Upon a Time' for primary school-children; 'Quarrels' and 'Family Relationships' for secondary students. To fit us in to their timetables, schools had to be willing to adjust. They made us welcome. We could not supply the demand we helped create. I saw 'Quarrels' in a school near me in Bermondsey, and watched the class, themselves playing guests at the ball at Madame Larina's, react to the row between Lensky and Onegin that leads to the fatal duel and Lensky's death. They were involved all right, and for 'Family Relationships' even more so. Opera is about life. You only have to go to the heart of it to connect.

'What did you do outside London?' MPs and others have asked. At first I urged Darryl and Pauline to confine themselves to London; long rail journeys seemed to me a poor use of their time. I liked the Egyptian fantasy some London schools combined to put on in the Bloomsbury Theatre, and a co-operative venture I saw in Harlow. But some of our best collaborations did take place well outside London. East Midlands Electricity's sponsorship took us each year to successive counties in their area – Leicestershire, Derbyshire, Nottinghamshire; then they bussed children down the M1 to matinées at Covent Garden. At Snape, in March 1992, six Suffolk schools combined with us and with the British Museum's Education Department to explore the legend of Beowulf and the loot of Sutton Hoo. 'Treasure and a Tale' was a 60-minute spectacular made, with a little help from us, by the children themselves. A composer we supplied obeyed *their* suggestions; a soprano and a few orchestra members took part. The children wrote the story, helped write the score, made the scenery and costumes, and played the piece. A large cast gave two packed performances at The Maltings one weekend, hugely success-fully. One teacher told me: 'Making this happen has enthused the whole school. It will do wonders for music, and for music teachers.' She left rejoicing.

If you asked a *Daily Mirror* reader to choose one image that meant ballet, it might well be a demure young girl in a dazzling white tutu, a ghost in *Giselle*, one of the shades in *La Bayadère*, a swan in *Swan Lake*. White captures the purity of delicate, spiritual femininity. And a line of evenly matched young girls, pointing, dipping, turning, stretching on pointe, in unison, comes to symbolize ballet itself, a blinding snowstorm of virginity. In our politically correct age, perhaps this will not do. They are all white. In a multicultural society, they ought not to be. Princess Margaret is supposed to have said once that she hoped never to see a black member of the *corps de ballet*, a black swan. Her hope will soon be dashed. For years, with the stunning example of Arthur Mitchell's Dance Theatre of Harlem Company before it, the Royal Ballet has sought black and Asian dancers to join the company. We have now had one or two. Evan Williams held his place in BRB with distinction for some years. Benazir Hussain, sister of the England cricket captain, was an admired soloist with the Royal Ballet; she now dances in Australia. But the difficulty in attracting black youngsters to train for classical ballet is only part of the problem of persuading others to take part. Ballet dancers begin young, when they are about eight. They need their parents' keen support. And there's another problem: girls want to be ballet dancers, boys want to be footballers. Each year the Royal Ballet School holds auditions all over the country to find the ballet dancers of tomorrow. Some will already be RBS associates who have been taking Saturday morning lessons with approved teachers for years. Very few make the grade.

'A Chance to Dance', which has been running now for nine years in London, gives young boys and girls of all shades the opportunity to learn basic positions and first steps in the physical language of classical ballet. It is a two-year scholarship course for seven-year-olds; the most talented are given the opportunity to stay on till eleven. It operates in Lambeth and Hammersmith, and draws children from a clutch of state schools in each borough. It works. To see a class, at first gawky, shy and stumbling, gradually, over a term, learn to carry themselves tall, place their feet just so, adapt their natural sense of tempo and rhythm, observe the disciplines of dance; to note the pride in their parents' faces as, coming to collect them, they peek into the gym to see how Emmeline and Joseph are getting on, is to know that someone is doing a good job. That someone, under Darryl Jaffray, was Brenda Garratt-Glassman, herself black, a skilled teacher with the deftness of a ballerina and the authority of a Guards sergeant-major. More than half the boys and girls in 'A Chance to Dance' are black or Asian; the selection process favours them. ROH opera education and outreach had a field day when we put on *Porgy and Bess*. 'A Chance to Dance', like 'Ol' Man River', just keeps on going, year after year. The generous bounty of our benefactress, Mrs Jean Sainsbury (no relation of the other Sainsbury), kept 'A Chance to Dance' going throughout the House's closure period, and beyond.

We did not adequately publicize or exploit our educational work. All participating took it for granted that what we were doing was right and worth doing; we did not think to boast. And we had no funds to spare for glossy brochures. With the help of the Goldsmiths' Company, we published, at three-year intervals, brief reports. In 1992, I wrote:

> To be at class in 'A Chance to Dance' in Lambeth or White City, or to watch a shoal of schools perform in 'Birmingham Dances' is to be inspired. Whether any of the children learning first steps will ever become a professional dancer or not is an irrelevance. If it happens, it will be a bonus. What most matters is that young energy is corralled and youthful talent tapped in the disciplines of dance. These children,

realizing some of their potential, will move differently, all their lives. This may sound to you way over the top. Perhaps it is. But it is my way of saying that nothing the Royal Opera House does is more important than our education work.

Paul Hamlyn, like his contemporary and dear friend Claus Moser, came to Britain just before the war, a refugee from the Nazis. A publisher of genius, his gift was to make the excellent popular and accessible. He sold good books in supermarkets. He invented the 'Music for Pleasure' recording label, expressing in those three words what the publicly funded arts could best achieve. When he sold his company Octopus to Reed for £100 million, he put half the proceeds into a charitable trust and set up the Hamlyn Foundation. Through that, he and his wife Helen do good, worldwide. In Mexico they fund literacy programmes; in India they build factories to make artificial limbs. In the United Kingdom they introduce the arts to people of all ages who would not otherwise know them. Since 1986, their principal project has been to bring people, always at under £5 a ticket, and many at only £1, to the Royal Opera House. The one precondition is that they should never have been there before. And Hamlyn has done this in style, taking the theatre for six or seven performances. The arrangement is straightforward enough: the Opera House sets aside a week which is denied to subscribers and patrons, calculates what the box-office take might have been, and charges that to the Hamlyn Foundation and its partner Westminster City Council. They undertake to sell the tickets at the low prices they stipulate, and pay the Opera House the difference. We would hang a banner outside over the Bow Street entrance, stock the bars up to sell beer instead of champagne, cups of tea rather than smoked salmon, and welcome everyone in. Camilla Whitworth-Jones found the audience. She canvassed social clubs, trades unions, community centres, from near and far, for 12,000 participants in a new experience. She never failed to fill the House – a marvellous feat. Over a decade, 120,000 have come to Hamlyn performances at Covent Garden.

Putting it into practice was not always simple. The Hamlyn Foundation was prepared to put up £100,000, say, to make the week possible. As our prices rose, this was not enough to bridge the gap between what the House might have earned at the box-office and the Hamlyn Week's much lower receipts. Westminster City Council, through its Art Sub-Committee, was also prepared to help; tickets were made available to Westminster residents. The Committee's Lead Member, Roger Bramble, a stalwart supporter, would bring his guests – they often included Princess Diana – on one or two nights of the week. Westminster's contribution, about half what the Hamlyns subscribed, helped make it happen.

But even the joint Hamlyn–Westminster subsidy might still leave the House out of pocket by £20,000 or so. Lower takings at the bars and buffets might mean another £10,000 lost. I would go back to Paul and ask him to increase the Foundation's contribution. He would not budge. Then let him at least charge £2 instead of £1, and £6 instead of £5. He still would not budge. Caught between a rock and a hard place, I would report to the Board that, happily, there would be another Hamlyn–Westminster Week next season, but that I had agreed with our Finance Director to make a provision of £30,000 against it. The House itself subsidised these performances. We could ill afford it, but could not refuse.

The Hamlyn Weeks were happy ones for those who came from Tower Hamlets, or by coach from Merthyr Tydfil. We made extra provision for the disabled in the stalls circle. It is strange and touching that the severely handicapped take such pleasure in the athletic grace of ballet. Yet, without envy, and without self-pity, they do. Sylvie Guillem and Darcey Bussell, still in costume, tiptoed among the wheelchairs afterwards, greeting Paul Hamlyn's guests.

For twenty-six years the Midland Bank sponsored a week of Promenade Performances at Covent Garden. The Bank took the Grand Tier for its own guests, and bought out the stalls. For Proms week, we ripped out all the stalls seats and stored them; quite a job – the maintenance crew enjoyed the overtime. On the floor's shiny surface we laid a red carpet. Students, and anyone else prepared to sit on their bums or stand, could hear the best singers in the world in Verdi, Mozart and Puccini. Some tickets were sold in advance; the rest to a queue that would form in Bow Street in the early afternoon. Simon Rattle opened our *Cunning Little Vixen* at a Midlands Bank Prom. The piece is moving; the reception was heartfelt. The audience, unable to believe its luck, raised the roof for Domingo as *Otello*, and for *The Flying Dutchman* conducted by von Dohnányi, with Julia Varady as Senta.

Companies who want publicity look out for novelties to sponsor; giving regular satisfaction is all very well, they mutter, but what public recognition will we get for it? There are no headlines in funding something that by annual persistence everyone takes for granted. Yet the Midland Bank stuck with their Proms at the Opera House, year after year, even after they were taken over by the Hongkong and Shanghai Banking Corporation. The new boss, Willy Purves, heroically endured the performances he paid for, though he did not enjoy opera one bit. The enthusiasts, crammed like sardines on the floor, heightened the enjoyment of the Bank's guests, with the Cabinet well represented in the Grand Tier. I would attend a dinner in the Crush Bar after one of the performances, thank the Bank warmly and, without pausing for breath, look forward to another year. On the way up to the twenty-fifth anniversary, there was little to fear. They were bound to want to mark that. But after? The twenty-sixth Midland Proms would occur during our last season in the House before closure. I was particularly nippy in hoping we should all meet again at that. Willy Purves saw exactly what I was up to, but cheerfully acquiesced. The Midland Bank marked the end of their great endeavour, one of the most remarkable examples of enlightened arts subsidy in Britain, by including in their offering a complete *Ring* cycle. We were able to mount three cycles instead of two, the third, thanks to the Midland, for a young audience, at prices they could afford. At the end of this third cycle, after *Götterdämmerung*, I was sucked in from Bow Street to the main foyer as the audience was leaving and, literally, mobbed – surrounded, embraced, jumped on by young enthusiasts thanking me for the glorious experience they had had. Joy in what they'd seen and heard expressed to me by members of the audience is my best memory of the Opera House. But, this time, they should have thanked the Midland Bank.

If Hamlyn Week stretched our budget, so too did Schools Matinées. Again, the financial calculation was simple. We needed to recoup from sponsorship what we lost by not being able to sell a performance to the public. Various trusts and foundations, companies and corporations, shouldered the burden of making up the difference over the years. Then sponsorship stopped. Companies knew they were doing good, but there were no opportunities to entertain their guests. Afternoon performances do not suit big business. In 1991 we had no one to pay for next year's Schools Matinées. Jeffrey Sterling flew by helicopter to Brighton and spoke to the late Octav Botnar, who had the Nissan franchise in the UK. Botnar, who had lost a daughter in a car crash, was willing to do something for British children; he agreed to stump up £250,000 a year, for three years. Much pleasure resulted. But when the three years were up, and we were anxiously seeking to renew, Mr Botnar had retreated to a redoubt in Switzerland where he was refusing to take urgent telephone calls from HM Customs and Excise to whom, they claimed, he owed £8 million in VAT. Gifts that result from whim, however generous, leave holes later. Those who believe that private money should play a greater part in funding the arts may reflect on this. Immediately after the Lottery award to the development, a minor public-relations débâcle ensued when a clumsily unco-ordinated press release revealed we would have to end Schools Matinées. This was unfortunate, but true: we did not then have the funds. We drastically trimmed the cost by using, as we never had before, untried second casts, found other generous donors, Blackburn Associates, at a lower rate, and soldiered on.

Hamlyn Week, the Midland Bank Proms, 'A Chance to Dance', Schools Matinées, expensive semi-sponsored live relays in the Piazza, with crowds sitting in the rain to hear Domingo in *Carmen* and waiting to greet him under an umbrella afterwards – all these reached out to new audiences. All tugged at the heart. Nothing for me surpassed a 'Once Upon a Time' opera workshop I went to at Belleville Road Primary School in Wandsworth.

Some weeks before we got there, the children, aged about seven, had learned to sing a simple melody from *The Magic Flute*; they had made, from paint and paper, the dragon Fafner from *Siegfried*. Thirty seven- and eight-year-olds sat on the floor in a circle. One of them, precocious or very well primed, told me that 'In an opera you tell a story by singing.' From the Opera House had come the tenor John Dobson, our Siegfried, baritone Roderick Earle, two new young women singers, and Elizabeth Sykora from the chorus. David Syrus, Head of Music at the Opera House, was at the piano. Roderick Earle opened a box of props and tricks and legends, and began 'Once upon a time . . .' We moved into a magic world.

The children, entranced as are the *Flute*'s jungle creatures, danced to Mozart's musical spell. They impersonated the dragon and helped Siegfried kill him. The class listened to a trio from Rossini's *Cinderella*, sung in Italian, and could easily tell, one told me, which were the Ugly Sisters by their expressions. And, at the end, they took part in the finale of Humperdinck's *Hansel and Gretel*. We provided Hansel and Gretel, and the Wicked Witch. The class played and sang the chorus of gingerbread children whom the Witch has baked into statues. They can be freed only if Hansel and Gretel, who have shut the Witch up in her own oven, will set them free: 'Touch me too, that I may see the world anew!' These words the gingerbread children sing are, I thought, the perfect metaphor for what the arts and education and arts-in-education do.

16

A WORD FOR THE SPONSOR

At the beginning of the Marx Brothers' *A Night at the Opera*, that low-key, understated documentary account of managing the lyric arts, Otis B. Driftwood is keeping his dinner guest waiting. Mrs Claypoole, an attractive woman of a certain age, is an opera-lover, and very rich. She would like to join New York high society. Driftwood is a scoundrel agent and would-be impresario, eager to take over opera and the opera house in New York. He would do anything to raise funds, including make love to Mrs Claypoole. The lady is susceptible. A new exciting opera season may now be said to be underwritten. A sponsor has been wooed, and won; the arts will flourish, and art-lovers rejoice.

Margaret Thatcher, determined to limit, if not cut, government expenditure, believed that her policies would create a climate of giving. The private sector, both individuals and corporations, taxed less than before, would join a partnership with government to fund the arts. Sponsorship would transform the scene. In the Thatcher years and after, sponsorship of the arts in Britain rose steeply; the Association for Business Sponsorship of the Arts (ABSA) came into being. The arts became more dependent on the private sector than ever before in the post-war world. Until the Second World War, there was no public funding of the arts; in previous centuries, the Church, the court, the landed aristocracy, then the merchant bourgeoisie patronized painters and musicians, architects and sculptors. The state itself had no role. The suggestion from 10 Downing Street that arts bodies should seek support from industry, the City and the rich was, in a way, a reversion to the style of previous ages. Government urged the Royal Opera House to let the market determine ticket prices; it also adjured the wealthy to pay up. By steeply reducing the top rate of tax on earned income, and cutting back corporation taxes on industry, Mrs Thatcher was saying, 'I am leaving you discretion to spend your own money. But spend it wisely, and remember you have social obligations to fulfil.' Ministers implied that this partnership would be genuine; the Treasury would not reduce its funding of the arts. But the Treasury did not increase it either. The annual grant to the Arts Council, with troughs and bounces on the way, decreased in real value year on year. The Arts Council's grants to arts bodies, whose number multiplied and whose appetites quickened annually, steadily decreased in worth also. The Royal Opera House had long been the Arts Council's biggest client; it had, after all, three companies to sustain, giving 450 performances a year. William Rees-Mogg's strategy document, *The Glory of the Garden*, in 1984, devolved resources both away from opera and out of London; the Opera House's lion's share of the annual spend fell from 12 per cent to 9 per cent. It could not survive unless, somehow, it replaced those funds; the paying customer at the box-office and sponsorship were the only identifiable sources.

Under Claus Moser and John Tooley, a successful push was begun to increase income from the private sector. Those efforts were boosted when John Sainsbury persuaded Alex Alexander to accept the chairmanship of the ROH Trust, and he increased the Trust's income, in just two years, from an already substantial £3 million to a heady £6.5 million. This is more than any other British arts body raises annually; indeed, it is more than all Britain's performing arts companies then raised in any one year, combined.

Any of this is unheard of on the continent. No European opera house, until very recently, depended on any private funding whatever. They sported no fundraisers; they pursued no Claypooles. Their approved budgets, as we have seen, were and are met by the state, or the province, or the city. Subsidy, in some cases, is so high that it reduces all incentive to earn other income, including at the box-office. In the summer of 1996 the Royal Opera was asked to take *Peter Grimes* to Palermo on its fiftieth anniversary. The management suggested ten performances; we compromised on eight, pushing Palermo's interest in Britten to the very limit. Our *Grimes* begins with the coroner's jury taking their places on stage –

no curtain. When cast and chorus entered at the Teatro Politeama-Garibaldi, they saw, on the first night, a virtually empty theatre. The Mayor of Palermo, marked out by the mafia, came. Very few others did. But the organization putting on the opera was unconcerned – it was the performances that counted, that is what the subsidy was for.

Carlo Fontana, Sovrintendente of La Scala, boasted to me that his house raised 37 per cent of its own income – unprecedented, he thought. I told him we raised 63 per cent. 'La Scala', Zeffirelli used to say, 'is an udder with a thousand teats,' every member of staff a pensioner on it. Recently La Scala has made overtures to the private sector, as the Italian state seeks reform, inviting sponsors and private investors to take a stake. Glyndebourne – pastoral, picnicking Glyndebourne, where the dinner intervals are sometimes nearly as long as the operas – is the shining exemplar of the private spirit in Britain's performing arts today. Its supporters paid for Michael Hopkins' elegant new theatre. Its patrons keep up the tone, and very relaxed, jolly and friendly it is – quite unlike the expensive vulgarity that has been associated with Salzburg.

At Covent Garden members of the Trust, who buy booking privileges by their subscription, and Premium seat-holders, who pay way over the odds for their tickets, take up 15 per cent of the seats, and nearly half the most expensive seats. This is said to affect for the worse the atmosphere of the House – rows of cottonwool in the audience, ignorance in the stalls. 'I say, this is by Mozart,' someone overheard a corporate guest saying at a performance of *Figaro*; the listener found the remark off-putting. Well, I see that it might be surprising, but I do not understand why it is acceptable for one of the thousands of newcomers that Paul Hamlyn brings to the House not to have heard of Puccini or Petipa, yet unacceptable for a corporation guest. Should we not reach out to them too? The argument is that these first-timers, whom we hope will catch the bug, are by their presence keeping out others who would enjoy the piece more. That may be true. If prices were lower, as they should be, more people who already love opera and ballet could certainly afford to come more often. In fact, only some of them would come more often. At the Opera House, seats are rationed not just by price but by scarcity; the passionate opera-lover or balletomane who comes ten times freezes out nine others. If Covent Garden prices are ever lowered drastically – it will take a hefty increase in funding to achieve it – the Sold Out and House Full signs will immediately go up.

Meanwhile why should taxpayers – particularly, as Gerald Kaufman, chairing his Select Committee, kept asking, 'my inner-city constituents' – subsidize the rich? Robustly, in her evidence to the Committee, Vivien Duffield put paid to that myth. 'The people paying these very, very high prices are not only paying for themselves, they are actually paying for other people. This is because if we did not have the corporates pay what they pay – and that is only 15 per cent of the seats – everybody else would have to pay twice as much. It is something which must be remembered. It never gets in the papers. If you are paying £50, they are paying £100 for exactly the same seat. The papers are always banging on about how the Domingo seats cost £150. Yes, they do, but the corporates are paying £300. If they were not, you would all be paying £200. That is the terrible problem we face.' In any case, Kaufman's constituent does not, through taxes, contribute more than 50p a year to subsidizing the Opera House. It is humbug to suggest otherwise.

Plcs, banks, corporations have been persuaded over the years not just to buy tickets for themselves and their guests, but to pay for productions too; perhaps as much as £250,000 for a new opera production or a three-act ballet; £25,000 to £50,000 to sponsor a revival; £10,000 for a special night at the Opera House. Without that sort of help, part of the work presented in my time would never have seen the light of day. What did sponsors want for their money? First of all a sense that they were doing good, putting back into society some of the resource their profits were, legitimately, siphoning out of it. Second, to put their name about, heighten their profile, call attention to themselves. Third, opportunities to entertain, and in uniquely attractive surroundings.

My colleagues and I would scan the repertory and mark out for the Trust the pieces we thought might attract sponsorship. But we never asked sponsors what they wanted and changed our repertory accordingly. My impression is that at the Met sponsors, rich individuals rather than corporations – US stockholders object to seeing their profits diverted to the arts – have more of a say in what is seen on stage; the millionairess who pays the piper expects to call the tune. Certainly hypothecated patronage has been behind some of the Met's most extravagant offerings of the last two decades.

Looking for a link, a connection, pointing out something that will particularly appeal to a sponsor, seems a promising tactic. We asked each of the German banks in 1996/97 if they would help with the *Ring*, or

Lohengrin, or *Salome*, or *Elektra*. No luck. Cable & Wireless, when David Young, Lord Young of Swaffham, was Chairman, backed *Meistersinger*. But David Young is a passionate Wagnerite; *Meistersinger* was the production of the year, and something to remember always. Nobly, Young went on to help us with Jones and Lowery's *Ring* cycle; Cable & Wireless sponsored *Das Rheingold*. Graham Vick's *Meistersinger* was a crowd-pleaser; Richard Jones's *Ring* a provoker. Lady Young hated *Rheingold* from the first sight of the blubbery Rhinemaidens. She thought it dreadful, and said so, rather loudly. I urged her to give it, and the rest of the cycle, more of a chance. She may have come round in the end.

Sponsors have either to be totally cavalier with their gift – here you are; do what you like with it – or else should satisfy themselves very precisely beforehand that their money will be put to use they will themselves enjoy. John and Anya Sainsbury's Linbury Trust, which has supported so much of the House's work, is not an undiscriminating source. John and Anya want to see the designer's models before they decide. If they don't like what they see, no Linbury sponsorship; they declined both *The Sleeping Beauty* and *Don Quixote*. Away from Covent Garden they provide bursaries to enable young theatre designers to get a start with professional companies. The scheme has been running for ten years. The Sainsburys take pride in seeing, not too many years later, those designers' names up in lights. I thought of them when admiring Anthony Ward's sets for the National Theatre's *Oklahoma!* He had been a finalist in the first year of their scheme.

Mrs Jean Sainsbury – no relation to the above – came into a sizeable inheritance lateish in life, and put half of it into a trust to fund the Opera House. She was keen to help with running repairs, as well as with productions; opera and ballet took year and year about with necessary improvements to the ladies' loos. Mrs Sainsbury had sponsored Andrei Serban's *Fidelio* in 1986, and was still getting over it. I would carefully point her to something I thought she would be sure to enjoy, and usually got it right – *La traviata* for one. We met twice a year to review her investment portfolio, and to decide what productions to back: pleasant, good-tempered gatherings.

It was expected of members of the ROH Trust, as it was not of Board members, that they should work to boost our finances either by contributing through their companies, or by pointing us in others' direction. David Plaistow of Inchcape, Jim Butler of KPMG and Rudi Mueller of

UBS saw to it that their companies did sponsor something, in UBS's case more than once. Jeffrey Sterling, Lord Sterling of Plaistow, provided invaluable help in kind: P&O shipped the Royal Ballet's scenery around the world at favourable rates, and minimal cost to us. Bob Gavron, late of St Ives plc, was an invaluable backstop through his personal charitable trust. When I was in real trouble, when all other avenues had been exhausted, and some lovely piece coming up had no sponsor, even in a season already under way, I would scribble a line to Bob, asking for £30,000 or £40,000. He rarely disappointed, and would say immediately, by return, whether he could help or not. The Robert Gavron Charitable Trust's name was attached to *Daphnis and Chloë* and to *The Midsummer Marriage*. Not bad gifts to your fellow citizens. Since the pieces were going to happen anyway, the money went straight to our bottom line.

The Mercers Company and the Esmée Fairbairn Charitable Trust were frequent contributors to our educational work. John Sacher, scion of Marks & Spencer, would help with small-scale ballet projects; David Cohen, a scholarly general practitioner, through the John S. Cohen Foundation, supported new music. David and Janice Blackburn helped us out of a hole with Schools Matinées. People put their money into what they believed was worthwhile. But for the dependent institution it is a hand-to-mouth existence. Begging is undignified and dispiriting after a time. The community of those who do help stands for something fine in our society.

There were nearly 20,000 Friends of Covent Garden, many retired folk with leisure to spare, all active, keen supporters. They paid about £45 a year to belong. The subscription brought them a magazine – at first called *About the House*, edited by Ken Davison; a cultural asset, it survives as *Opera House*. And Friends have an opportunity to attend, at a price, recitals, lectures and interviews – 'Lunch and Listen'. They crowd study days on work upcoming – very popular events – and ballot to attend, at a modest charge, general rehearsals of ballet and opera, opened for their benefit twenty or thirty times a year. For some Friends, these are the great attraction, though only 1000 of them will be allowed in the theatre. At 10am, they are clustered in Bow Street, waiting for the doors to open. A placard invites those without tickets to take their chance – 'Come and Risk It'. Inside, the Director, Phyllida Ritter, sternly reminds us that this is a rehearsal, not a performance; artists may not sing out, and may mark their parts, some technical work is unfinished. Nevertheless, she hopes we enjoy the morning. And we do.

The Friends run a prize draw, a pointe-shoe appeal, and they undertake other ingenious means of raising money. The result is a surplus available each year for disbursement. They used to have rather more than £500,000 a year to spend; this rose to £800,000 in 1996/97. The Friends Executive decide, on the Director's recommendation, how to spend it; the Director would have been got at by me. In this way work for which we have little chance of finding sponsorship elsewhere still gets supported on to the stage, and the decision is taken well in advance. For a new piece – *Un re in ascolto* or *Gawain* – this can be crucial. Conventional sponsors are leery of recent work. An exception, Amerada Hess, helped Scottish Opera bring Judith Weir's *Vanishing Bridegroom* to Covent Garden; they wanted to be seen to be innovative. For Harry Birtwistle's *Gawain*, I turned to the Friends. In that year, *Gawain*, MacMillan's *Winter Dreams* and Mozart's *Mitridate* were all sponsored by the Friends; all three won Olivier awards. Under the chairmanship of Angus Stirling, Bamber Gascoigne, Deborah MacMillan and now Carolyn Newbigging the list of lovely things the Friends have helped put on in London, and in Birmingham, is a long one. These are real friends indeed. They contributed between them, in several thousand small donations, nearly £1 million to the Development Appeal.

Bamber Gascoigne spotted that some Friends could afford to give more than the annual subscription. He started the Drogheda Circle, in memory of Garrett Drogheda, a distinguished former Chairman. Join that, and you were in, say, for £1000 over three years. The Drogheda Circle contributed modest but decisive amounts of money, and sponsored key works. After the performance of the piece they paid for, the Circle members would have supper with the cast. Most performers nowadays accept that as well as singing for their supper, they must sup too. Americans certainly do; British artists come to it more reluctantly, and would rather head for the nearest Italian restaurant. But for singers and dancers nowadays, being polite to the sponsor is almost a contractual requirement. For the General Director it is a regular duty.

In my time at Covent Garden, we solicited visits from Scottish Opera (*The Trojans*); Opera North (*Gloriana* and *Troilus and Cressida*); and Welsh National Opera, who gave a *Ring* cycle in John Tooley's day, and brought Peter Stein's productions of *Otello* and *Falstaff*, and later *Cav and Pag* and a rare Donizetti, *La favorita*. All treats. None of these imports from Wales would have been possible without the sponsor, Amoco, eagerly seizing the chance to bring their guests to Covent

Garden, rather than to the dowdy Dominion. Like so many others, I owe a lot to Amoco. But after one particular evening, I reckon they owe me one in return.

Sitting in the Grand Tier, I had become obsessed with noise leaking into the auditorium from the clatter of crockery in the Crush Bar. (I made up my mind then that in the new House, to ensure keeping extraneous noise out of the auditorium, all catering should be banished from the Crush Bar to other spaces.) The Crush Bar and Pit Lobby staff had to wash up between acts, or there would have been no clean glasses in the next interval. But ROH staff, given a reminder now and then, knew to keep quiet. Only the most expert of outside caterers could be trusted, silently, to lay tables during the last act for a post-performance supper; so occasionally they were laid after the curtain came down. One night, when Amoco's man in charge of the event seemed particularly keen to impress, we were kept waiting downstairs after the performance, while the tables were set, for nearly an hour. We sat down to supper at quarter to midnight. The delay was explained by the elaborate table settings – roses 5 feet high and fairy lights on each table. Four delicious and elaborate courses were served on blue glass platters. Our hosts could not have been friendlier. I like oil men. I was used to it, but the other guests wilted as the hour at which they would start work next morning drew nearer. Speeches began at well after 1am. I kept mine brief. Please, Mr Sponsor, if you must eat afterwards, let the food be simple and the service quick.

Support from the private sector for the Royal Opera House peaked and fell away. The Lottery award for the building led to the view that we were rich. We were not. Arts bodies, each seeking to raise funds to match Lottery grants, proliferated and competed with each other. The development, in our case, claimed donations that might otherwise have come to the revenue account. In my last two years I harried the Trust unremittingly and ungraciously to keep up the level of their contribution to the House's revenue budget. They could not manage it.

I suspect that, through the 1990s, the sparkle came off the sort of sponsorship that we were seeking. Not every prosperous plc wanted its Board to be seen entertaining at the opera. Some may even have come to the conclusion that sponsorship was bad for the share price. Mountleigh plc, which took such pride in the *L'elisir d'amore* gala, took a sharp turn for the worse not long afterwards. Mr Nelson Peltz, whose wife had worn the décolletage and the pear-shaped diamond, retreated to the United

Where shall we eat afterwards?

And a
Smoked
salmon...

Callas, of course...

Domingo...

2 bottles of champagne...

DARLINGS!

DARLING!

Dry White
wine...

Gin and TONIC please!
oh please!

Crush bar...

The Interval...

States. Asil Nadir's Polly Peck, whom Alex Alexander had persuaded to contribute to our coffers, also took a tumble. Other corporations experienced a dip in their fortunes after seeing their name on our programmes; I began to wonder whether there might not be, lurking in wait for those who came proudly to our aid, a curse which, shortly after, struck them down. This fate did not attend at all on the staidest and solidest of our friends in the City. But, especially in the heyday of the Lawson boomlet at the end of the 1980s, some businesses pushed the boat out, it seemed, because they knew fortune was ephemeral and wanted to make the most of it while it lasted.

Felicity Clark, of the ROH Trust, ascertained that the French oil conglomerate Elf Aquitaine was prepared to sponsor our new production of *Don Giovanni*. Wishing to impress with their determination to expand their market share in Britain, they did so in style. They put money into the production by Johannes Schaaf, with designs by Peter Pabst. At the première they gave each of their guests a handsome print of a costume design. The guest list was elaborate; protocol for the evening set out in detail. The word was that not only would the officers of Elf UK be present, but also the Chief Executive Officer himself. He came, a large, handsome man with the striking Breton name of Loik Le Floch-Prigent. A good time was had by all. Not too long later, Elf Aquitaine was in deep trouble; charges of corruption were being bandied about; a huge slush fund had been deployed; M. Le Floch-Prigent was behind bars, and remained there for some time. The scandal was sumptuous, with rich Gallic ingredients. Elf had engaged a sultry, sexy lady to make eyes at Roland Dumas, Mitterrand's Foreign Minister, to ensure that Elf did not lose out in foreign markets where the Minister could put in a word. Indicated, M. Dumas was in trouble too, at least politically. I found this interesting because I had been asked once to the French Embassy in London to see M. Dumas enrol into L'Ordre des Arts et des Lettres an old friend of his, José Carreras. What grand circles we move in, I then thought.

Barings was a sadder case, and closer to home. Andrew Tuckey, Deputy Chairman there, whom all liked, was on our Main Board and had for years served as Honorary Treasurer of the Friends of Covent Garden. He may well have put a word in for us with his colleagues so that they sponsored our new *La traviata* in the autumn of 1995. (Jean Sainsbury was Barings' co-sponsor.) This *Traviata* had many attractions, including Angela Gheorghiu, who sang Violetta and made herself a superstar overnight.

Barings, basking in the pleasure this popular masterpiece gave, entertained in the Crush Bar. The evening was relaxed, happy, informal. I rose to say a few words of thanks. Peter Baring, presiding, made a quiet gesture of acknowledgement. I felt very glad for them that they had given their guests and our public such enjoyment – but the curse of the sponsor was waiting to strike. Not long after, their employee Nick Leeson, trading illegally in Singapore in a bout of gambling fever – like Alfredo at Flora's party – built up a position, without his superiors in London realizing it, that would cost the bank £850 million.

Companies and corporations will queue up to be associated with the redeveloped Covent Garden; the splendid new House will need private supporters as never before. And the City of London will need the Opera House. Contending fiercely for Euro-business with Frankfurt, where the European Central Bank has its home, the City will need to point to every amenity it can to attract businessmen and women here. London boasts a great lyric theatre of international status. Government will not support it on its own. The City should consider extending its sponsorship of the arts from the Barbican, within the City Wall, to Covent Garden and to the South Bank. Perhaps companies will combine to endow work that asserts London's status as a great world city. Meanwhile, I have one word for our sponsors. Thanks.

17

CLOSURE

From the early summer of 1995, the pace at Covent Garden quick-ened. I had been there seven years, and had two to go. The most difficult task confronting me now was finding somewhere for the companies to go during closure, confirmed for July 1997.

Our National Lottery grant had been awarded in two tranches, subject each to a number of conditions. Until those were met, no funds for the development could be released. The most urgent was our need to show that we were solvent, and would remain so, that we had a viable business plan for the next couple of years. On this we were in reasonable shape; the House had now earned a surplus for three successive fiscal years and, thanks to the saintly Dr Stanley Ho, had sharply reduced its accumulated deficit. However, 1995/96 looked dicey. And we would have to demon-strate, before the second tranche of Arts Council funds was made available, that we had satisfactory plans for the closure period. We had not. Over that matter, a shadow lay.

Meanwhile, there were questions looming over the House's leadership, including mine. The previous summer I had made an error which upset the Board. A development document I ought to have tackled immediately lay unnoticed at the bottom of my heaped in-tray. It dealt with the terms on which some key consultants would work for us; we had thought their services were to be given *pro bono*; they insisted otherwise. I should have notified my colleagues immediately, but did not. They were taken aback at the claim, and wondered if I had too much on my plate. The development, they knew, added 50 per cent to my normal workload, and there was closure too. In the spring of 1995, the Board, of which I was a member, met without me to discuss a way forward. (I learned of the meeting after it took place.) They considered asking me to leave, but decided against it; they had nothing but praise for the House's artistic achievements and there was too much else that I was successfully driving forward. They confirmed that I would stay as General Director till September 1997, as planned, but they proposed that I should hand over closure – not the prior issue of where to go, but the planning of the work of the companies – to others. The Chairman invited me to make a new executive appointment. Should we go outside and recruit? This seemed unnecessary; we were scraping to balance the books and executive recruitment would not be quick or cheap. But, plainly, I was doing too much.

I asked Nicholas Payne to co-ordinate repertory plans for the closure period, and Clive Timms, Director of Finance, to oversee the whole. Mike Morris was tackling the renegotiation of union agreements; he would have his hands full with staffing levels and redundancies. John Seekings was working to me, alongside John Fairclough of Stanhope, in representing the House's interest in every detail of the development scheme. We were agreeing the specifications on which contracts would be let. Preliminary works were scheduled to start in earnest in January 1996. By the time the House closed in July 1997, every detail of the scheme would be drawn and costed and more than 90 per cent of contracts to build let, within budget, at fixed prices. By our work now, with our newly appointed project managers, Schal, getting into their stride, we could ensure we met those targets. The effort made then guaranteed success later. Seekings and I represented the client, day in, day out. It was right that I should have charge of the development, rather than the minutiae of closure, whose implementation I would not be around to oversee.

More change was looming. There were mutterings among the donors, and also at the Arts Council, about the Chairman, Sir Angus Stirling. Angus was carrying a peculiarly heavy workload at this critical time. He was the full-time executive Director General of the National Trust, now in its centenary year. When we chose him, I think none of us foresaw quite how fraught our own affairs might be, and how demanding the chairmanship. The conjunction of the Trust's centenary was unfortunate; the ceremonies that attended it were frequent and farflung. Some – very few – ROH meetings the Chairman would have to miss. Given the fax and the telephone, this did not seem to me to pose a problem; to some others it did. They began to question whether Angus, with his slightly other-worldly air, was quite the right person to stand beside Vivien Duffield, who would lead the Appeal and help pull the money in. Vivien herself was particularly twitchy. Angus had expected to go on as Chairman till the House closed, but by August 1996 he would have served his five-year term: would that be renewed? Perhaps we already needed a Chairman who would be there through closure and after re-opening. When this issue surfaced, it took several of us completely by surprise, which shows I think that the criticism of Angus was unfair; he was abreast of every decision that mattered. However, the doubts expressed behind his back were shared with Grey Gowrie, Chairman of the Arts Council. Gowrie did not demur.

As it happened, in and out of the Arts Council, there lurked someone who very much fancied the prospect of becoming Chairman of the ROH. Peter Gummer, member of the Council and Chairman of its Lottery Advisory Panel, had himself recommended the award of £78.5 million to the ROH for development and closure. He was Chairman and Chief Executive of the public-relations company Shandwick plc, and brother of the Secretary of State for the Environment, John Selwyn Gummer. Peter was also an adviser to the Conservative Party; he had been on the Executive Board of the National Health Service and was now on the Board of the Halifax Building Society. He was a busy wheeler-dealer, slim and fit despite eating up to three business breakfasts in a row each morning at the Connaught. In his office he wore pink cashmere slipovers and monogrammed velvet slippers. He was a frequent visitor to the House and an admirer of our work. At the same time as we first heard the suggestion that Angus Stirling should relinquish the chairmanship, we learned that Peter Gummer was a possible replacement. The issue would come to a head that autumn.

The question of closure overlay all, as it had always promised to do. There was no easy answer. It was not a problem that could have been resolved long in advance; there was no obviously suitable theatre, or any other venue, available, ready, waiting for our occupation. This was not flippant surmise, but the result of a thorough search. London has many theatres, but none whose auditorium, stage, scene-dock, dressing rooms and other facilities could easily accommodate one ROH company, let alone both of them. Our Technical Director John Harrison knew every theatre in London. Their exact specifications and detailed plans were on his desk. He visited any of which he had no first-hand knowledge. He revisited those he knew well. Often I accompanied him, over the several years of search. The Palladium was spoken for, and likely always to be booked. The Dominion, where Welsh National Opera had played its short London week of touring before being invited to Covent Garden – John Harrison was at that time WNO's Technical Director – had ample seating but a shallow, cramped and steeply raked stage. It would never have served well. The ballet company could not have danced there. And there was no scene-dock. Every changeover went straight out into the street, and the area was partly residential. We would not be permitted to inflict on local residents the disturbance our normal operations involved.

We looked at many others. Everyone had somewhere to suggest: Streatham, Golders Green, Hackney, Docklands. The Coliseum, occupied by ENO, was not for us. Sadler's Wells would not be redeveloped before 1998; that would be too late. We spent most time pursuing the Theatre Royal Drury Lane, which would have served best. Here Cameron Mackintosh's *Miss Saigon* was in occupation, but there were rumours that box-office was weakening. If *Miss Saigon* came off, our troubles might be over. The Theatre Royal had once been home to opera; the Royal Ballet had performed there; the seating was ample, the public spaces comfortable, the stage adequate, the scene-dock capable of conversion, the pit, at some expense, could be enlarged. If at any point in our search the Theatre Royal Drury Lane had been available to us, we should have seized with open arms the opportunity to book it. The theatre was owned by Stoll Moss whose Chairman, Robert Holmes à Court, I went to see in his office in Soho Square. Stoll Moss had been helpful recently to ENO, their tenants at the Coliseum. (ENO's lease was running out. Government found £11 million directly, which David Mellor personally wrung from the Treasury, to purchase the freehold for ENO; they were left to raise a mere £1 million themselves.) If Stoll Moss could help ENO, and thereby London's cultural life, perhaps they would help the ROH too. Holmes à Court was courtesy itself – but 'I cannot help you, Mr Isaacs,' he said. Stoll Moss had granted Cameron Mackintosh a lease on the Theatre Royal for *Miss Saigon* that only Mackintosh, at his sole discretion, could terminate. 'I will never allow any employee of mine', Holmes à Court told me, 'to enter into such a lease again.' As it was, he was powerless. Holmes à Court died suddenly; his wife Janet succeeded him. The company was run by Richard Johnston, whom we had known as director of the Birmingham Hippodrome. With him I kept in constant touch. How long would *Miss Saigon* remain at the Theatre Royal? Could we have it if they vacated? Of course we could, and welcome. But, contrary to rumour, there was no sign of *Miss Saigon*'s run ending. I saw Cameron too. He was singing from the same hymn sheet; he had written the hymn.

For millions of visitors to London, a West End musical is a must. Coaches bring parties to fill seats throughout the year. Air-buses do the same. The US tourist in London is hell-bent on seeing either the hit musical that will shortly open on Broadway, or the one that already has, provided it's a hit there too. What helps sell *Miss Saigon* in London's West End is the fact that it is a long-running hit on Broadway, or vice versa. And that will apply the more when touring versions reach Düsseldorf and Barcelona, Toronto and Chicago. It is vital, therefore, that, wherever it goes, the show never falters at the box-office, anywhere; closing *Miss Saigon* in Drury Lane means an end to profit and cashflow here and wherever else they are billing *Miss Saigon* as 'London's Longest Running Musical'. (I could wish the millions who have seen *Miss Saigon* would see *Madama Butterfly* as well. One is a commercial hit; the other a masterpiece of music theatre.)

Drury Lane was so much the answer to our prayer that for a year I allowed myself to be strung along by a sweet-talk proposition on these lines: *Miss Saigon* was no longer doing capacity business but was declining at perhaps 2 per cent a year. It would not close down; but it might switch theatres. *Miss Saigon*'s set at Drury Lane, helicopter and all, was too big for the venues it would occupy on any future British or Canadian tour. It would soon need replacing. Suppose, without interrupting the London run, Miss Saigon moved to another decent-sized but slightly smaller theatre, in a new touring-sized set, then the Opera House could occupy Drury Lane. There was just such another theatre close by – the Lyceum, derelict for years but now about to be refurbished by its owners, Apollo Leisure. This firm hoped for an Arts Council Lottery grant to help meet the cost of refurbishment. That would never be forthcoming for a purely commercial venture. But suppose it were to be refurbished to help meet the Opera House's needs, even indirectly? The deal that was mooted was this: *Miss Saigon* would move to the Lyceum; the ROH, at a commercial rent, would have Drury Lane for two years; the ROH would pay to improve Drury Lane; the ROH would support Apollo Leisure's application for Lottery funds to help refurbish the Lyceum. But Cameron Mackintosh then added the straw that would break this camel's back: the ROH would also have to compensate his investors for the loss of income they would suffer from lower takings at the Lyceum rather than Drury Lane. At the end of a year's talk, mega-bucks prevailed. There was not a glimmer of willingness to temper the wind to the shorn, grant-aided lamb. *Miss Saigon*, still aiming to break records, stayed at Drury Lane. We had wasted a year. There was still, however, the Lyceum.

After the Theatre Royal, the Lyceum appeared the obvious place for the ROH to go during its brief exile from Covent Garden; it was just 300 yards down the road. None of our patrons would have any difficulty in finding it. The refurbished Lyceum would have 1800 seats; the stage could be enlarged a little, but not much – the back wall abutted hard on to Burghley Street behind. But it would be adequate. Apollo Leisure were very keen to have us there. They wanted a rental from us of £3.5 million a year, and they wanted to know now. We had to look at this most obvious of options very carefully indeed. When we did, it did not look so obvious. John Harrison went over the plans repeatedly; Clive Timms sat down with Apollo's directors again and again. However hard we looked at it, the sums did not add up.

The Lyceum's stage is not very deep; not a single opera production we possessed could play there. Nor, without being cut down, could any major ballet. This was true even if the stage was enlarged to the last millimetre that its shell, bounded by Exeter Street and Burghley Street, permitted. We could never play in repertory there, only one show at a time – ten performances in a fortnight, say, of a new *Bohème*; in the next, ten of a new *Coppélia*. We could manage, we thought, 180 performances a year in all, eighty fewer than at Covent Garden. That alone would cost us at least £4 million a year in lost revenue. There might just be sufficient dressing rooms and lavatories for cast, orchestra and chorus, or for the ballet company, but only if every inch of space available on the site high on the north side of the theatre were expensively developed. The auditorium, to be handsomely refurbished, was not ideal for opera – because of the overhang of the balconies, one over the stalls, the other over the grand circle – the acoustic in the dozen or so rows underneath the balconies would be poor. The key factor, though, was financial: the Lyceum would cost us, over two years, at least £7 million we neither possessed nor could find;

and that was after planning to make redundant over 300 staff who would not be needed and would have to be dispensed with if we put our eggs in that basket. The Board instructed us, throughout 1994 and 1995, to see what could be done to negotiate down the rental Apollo Leisure proposed to charge. Seeking to recoup their own considerable costs, and aware of our desperate need, they consistently refused. Apollo, however, were insistent on an early response from us. For the Board, and for the Arts Council, this £7 million projected deficit was the stumbling block, and this figure gravely underestimated the eventual loss of box-office and sponsorship income out of the ROH. Finding a way forward without incurring a deficit was imperative. Was any other recourse open to us?

For years the Royal Ballet had performed successfully in the summer in a big tent at Battersea Park. Could we do the same, year round? We investigated. Tents are better suited to summer than winter, and their acoustic better suited to ballet than to opera. Inviting a bright young business school graduate, Matt Ringel, to help assess our options, we looked at a variety of central London sites on which we might put a temporary structure. I was keen on Hyde Park itself, where the Crystal Palace had been erected for the Great Exhibition of 1851. If then, why not now? The north-east corner, at Marble Arch near the underground car park, looked promising. The Commissioner for Royal Parks, who had once planted 5 million roses in Aberdeen, did not agree. Instead, we looked hard again at Battersea. Public transport was a problem – no tube. We investigated a site, a coach park, next to a car-pound on the south-west corner of Vauxhall Bridge, opposite the new MI6 building; the deeds and the owners were in the Cayman Islands and hard to trace. And we inspected a marvellously attractive site, bare open space, lightly landscaped, on Potter's Field, at the south-west corner of Tower Bridge. This was seven or eight minutes from London Bridge station, and the same from Tower Hill underground. It was a short walk along the riverbank from Terence Conran's restaurant Le Pont de la Tour in Butler's Wharf. It had a stunning view up to Tower Bridge, and across to the Tower. This was interesting. Southwark Council was eager to see the site developed, and warmly welcomed the idea of a theatre on it.

The Secretary of State for the Environment, John Gummer, brother of Peter, had spoken about development on just this stretch of the riverbank, in time for the Millennium. Shakespeare's Globe was open; the new Tate at Bankside soon would be; the South Bank perhaps would be redeveloped in time. His vision for London, he said, was to see fine new buildings cast like a 'string of pearls' all the way down to Greenwich and the Millennium Dome. Could we help fill the gap that lay, like a bad tooth in the mouth, between Tower Bridge to the east and an incomplete office project, London Bridge City, to the west? The developers of that were naturally keen to see the site come alive and were prepared to help; the Pool of London people, the City of London, the Government Office for London, London First, all expressed enthusiasm for the idea. We could put it to them in tangible form because a splendid architect, Ian Ritchie, had come to us with a bold scheme for an inexpensive temporary theatre; he used glass and steel, and cavity walls filled with pebble, and proposed to place his structure on the ground, rather than dig it deep in. Ritchie had tried the technique in France, where the building had worked; he could show us what he meant. He was certain the simple structure he drew could be built in time. The theatre would seat 2500; there would be side-stages and a rear-stage as well as the main stage; the acoustic would be aircraft-proof; there would be rehearsal spaces, and we hoped also to cannibalize an under-used further-education college on the southern edge of the site. We would have to show people the way to Tower Bridge, no doubt: it was not where they would expect to find a theatre. But, if we could do that, we would be responding to the Arts Council's endless pleas to go out and find new audiences – which we never would at the Lyceum. And we would have a theatre seating larger numbers than we played to at Covent Garden. We could, therefore, put on as many performances as we usually did – 270 or even 300 – at lower ticket prices. Every production we owned would fit the stage, though there would be no stage elevators. We could also keep gainfully employed a great proportion of our staff, whom we would hope to take back with us to Covent Garden when the Opera House re-opened. There would be no wasteful expenditure on forced redundancies.

Could we afford it? The figures looked promising. We would not own the theatre, but the hefty rent we guaranteed to pay, against expectation of much higher box-office income than at the Lyceum, would go far to get the theatre built. Other investors were needed; they were not hard to find. Harrison and Timms found plenty of interest in the City and in the theatre world. Stoll Moss and The Really Useful Group, Andrew Lloyd Webber's company, had no interest in seeing the theatre built – it would be a rival – but other theatrical groups, in the US and Canada, keen to get into a brand-new 2500-seater London theatre, were willing to put their money where their business instinct pointed. The attractions to the investor increased when it became apparent that, for modest extra cost, the theatre, although intended at first as merely temporary, could be constructed to last for fifty years. If these partners came forward, and if we took a sanguine view of likely box-office, the figures for the closure period showed an outcome far the most satisfactory of any option we considered. The Board, by now extremely anxious over where we should rest, were bound to give this possibility serious consideration.

Were there any other options? We could close down both companies, and all activity. George Christie, down at Glyndebourne, was heard to recommend this drastic course; it was what he had done there. Our total absence from the scene would certainly not have done Glyndebourne's current attractions any harm, and it was, of course, the 'least-cost' option beloved of the Arts Council. But, unlike Glyndebourne, we had a large permanent staff, and the ROH Board preferred to keep the performing companies alive and active. So did the Arts Council. It was particularly important that the ballet keep performing; if they stopped the company would die. Clive Timms worked out a variant of total close-down: we would fire everybody else and keep the companies; but they would not perform at all, unless the performances planned were self-financing. He called this 'suspended animation'. This too was financially attractive. It depended, however, on the Arts Council's maintaining its core grant to us for two years. Why they should do that, to pay only for redundancy and inactivity, was hard to fathom. There were only two other possibilities: the Lyceum, on Apollo Leisure's terms, or, if we could get it built in time, the theatre on the Tower Bridge site, on ours.

Ian Ritchie's striking design won many friends; but would it get speedy planning permission on so prominent a space, opposite the Tower of London, a World Heritage site? I went to see the Secretary of State for National Heritage, Virginia Bottomley, in her palace in Cockspur Street. (Taking her seat in the theatre once, she said to me, 'I hate what I keep reading about the ROH in the papers, then I come here for a performance, and it's so wonderful, and I'm so happy.' 'Come more often,' I said.) She listened carefully, looking beautiful and boot-faced, while I explained why I wanted us to go to Tower Bridge, its advantages to us over the Lyceum. I hoped she would agree, and say so to her colleague at the Department of Environment. She offered no encouragement. I went to see John

Gummer, he of 'the string of pearls'. He too listened, non-committally. I knew that certain of his key advisers were in favour of our and Southwark's scheme. He must, he spelled out to me, reserve his view of the building. He might need to express it in a quasi-judicial capacity. As Secretary of State, he had the right, and perhaps on such a site the duty, if the scheme secured local planning permission, to call it in for his consideration. He could then set up, if he chose, a public inquiry, and consider its recommendations before deciding. He could also, however, take the decision himself without an inquiry. I spelled out to him our timetable and our urgent need. I never asked his brother Peter to speak to him on our behalf, and do not know whether they ever discussed it.

I showed Mary Allen, Secretary-General of the Arts Council, over the site. We got on well as colleagues. Mary was open and straightforward in her dealings. She admired it, but seemed a little unsure what she was doing there. I waxed enthusiastic; she said little. I am constantly told that the Arts Council gave us clear guidance: do not go to Tower Bridge, do go to the Lyceum. If they did, I am not aware of it. Neither Mary Allen nor Grey Gowrie, verbally or in writing to me, ever delivered any clear directive to that effect. Their attitude appeared to be simply that it was a matter for us; that it was not their role to second guess our Board's decision. There was rumour; there was tittle-tattle. There may have been hints I did not take. Decisive intervention there was none. The signal I received was that it was for us to make up our minds and that, whatever we did, we must present viable closure plans *within* the cash envelope available to us, part-funded by them.

As accounting officer for Arts Council monies, which Mary kept stressing was her principal role, she could not authorize releasing money to us without confidence in our plan. That was all she said. Nothing I know of Grey Gowrie's actions that autumn suggests that he was any more positive. They could have said: 'If you go to the Lyceum, we will urge or assist Apollo Leisure to reduce the rental to you. Once your Board can see its way past that £7 million deficit, we are sure they will go for the safer option.' Or they could have said: 'With that huge development scheme on your hands, you are mad to contemplate building another theatre. Forget it, and we'll help make the Lyceum work.' They did not say that to me, or to Angus Stirling. Later on, in another scenario, they did try to broker a deal for ROH companies to play at the new Sadler's Wells in 1998, without pleasing either party.

Our own Board looked at the issue long and hard and often. On more than one occasion, Angus Stirling went round the room asking each member's opinion, collecting every voice before summing up. Tessa Blackstone was the most sceptical, believing we were taking on too much. Vivien Duffield was also doubtful, wondering how many Trust members, though it was closer to the City, would find their way there. But no one knew what to do about the projected £7 million deficit at the Lyceum. The September Board would have to take the crucial decision. Senior management met first to prepare the executive's recommendation.

We sat round the old Boardroom table in what had been my office, and before that John Tooley's and David Webster's. The Boardroom below was now rented out to an optician, and below my office was a clothes shop called Way Out West; western music pounded upwards into the room in which I worked. These lets in Long Acre brought in nearly £250,000 a year. (This was the London which, according to the Prime Minister, was the arts capital of Europe, the envy of the world!) The senior management group was precisely that – the executives who ran the house: Technical Director John Harrison; his deputy, and Development Project Manager John Seekings; Nicholas Payne, Opera Director; Anthony Russell-Roberts, Royal Ballet Administrative Director; Malcolm Warne-Holland, who had replaced Bram Gay as Orchestra Director; Keith Cooper, Corporate Affairs; Mike Morris, Personnel; Clive Timms, Finance Director; Felicity Clark, ROH Trust; Christopher Nourse, my assistant and Chair of the Planning Committee; and me. We had the papers in front of us; they showed we had a reasonable chance of keeping up our principal source of revenue, box-office not grant-in-aid, at Tower Bridge; we could give the same number of performances as at Covent Garden; we could avoid 300 redundancies. Catering would suffer redundancies wherever we went, and so, to an extent, would cleaning, maintenance and security. But 280 performances meant we would be able to keep the stage, the companies and the orchestra at virtually full strength.

The spread-sheets on the Lyceum showed eighty fewer performances a year than at Covent Garden, with a consequent steep drop in income. None of our productions would fit there; service facilities would be skimpy; some vital functions – props, wardrobe, construction – would need to be maintained elsewhere. We would have to reduce the size of the performing companies and make at least 300 staff members redundant.

But the Lyceum was waiting, if only we could afford the £7 million. The Tower Bridge theatre was only a design, for which planning permission had not been obtained.

We talked it over, again, for an hour. I went round the room asking for a view from each. Nicholas Payne suspected the audience projections for Tower Bridge were over-optimistic; he had helped prepare them, and had already reduced them once. He preferred the Lyceum, plus, he thought, performances in other venues – the Royal Festival Hall perhaps, or the Royal Albert Hall. He did not say how they could be funded. He was firmly against Tower Bridge, the only one. I looked hard at Mike Morris as he answered. He would have charge of implementing a redundancy programme wherever we played – some service facilities at the House would simply not be needed in someone else's theatre – and of maintaining staff morale generally; he would be renegotiating all our union agreements to fit the new House at the same time. He thought for a moment, and came down for Tower Bridge.

I summed up the clear sense of the meeting, but I knew that I was giving more than the casting vote. My colleagues were giving me their opinions, not telling me what to do. If I had gone against them and taken that to the Board and prevailed there, they would have accepted the decision loyally, and backed it. A key factor for the Board was the £7 million deficit predicted at the Lyceum. They could not opt for that. A principal concern in my mind was the staff; for years they had worked very hard for me, and for my predecessors, to get the curtain up nightly, in cramped and decrepit circumstances, to serve the public, to keep our standards high. Could we now decide to send several hundred of them away jobless? Could we, above all, take that decision before every avenue that might keep more of them with us had been fully explored? How could we justify not going the last mile to try to achieve that at Tower Bridge? And if we opted for safety at the Lyceum, and told the staff now, two years in advance, that 300 of them would lose their jobs, how would we manage for those next two years to perform the demanding programme to which, to close the House in style, we were committed? Would there, through low morale, industrial action or perhaps even sabotage, be lost performances? Could we bravely launch a public appeal for the future in that atmosphere? I paused a beat or so – I have played the scene through in my head a hundred times since – and said I was for Tower Bridge. That was it; the meeting ended. The Board had still to pronounce, but the die was cast. We had crossed the Rubicon.

The Board decided to pursue Tower Bridge, unanimously. Vivien Duffield, socially, picked up most vibes against it: we were taking on too much. But she did not register formal dissent. In any case, at this stage, the Board may have thought, we were still only investigating the possibility of a new theatre. Southwark would shortly receive our application for planning permission, but they might refuse it, which would end the matter. Or, if they granted it, the partners we would need to help finance the build might not come forward. And there was still, just, the Lyceum;

Sir Robert Scott, who had led Manchester's bid for the 2000 Olympics, was now leading Apollo Leisure's campaign to take us there. They were importunate, but could wait some weeks longer. If we said yes, they would crack on with refurbishment tailored to meet our needs, let the theatre for six months from January 1997, and be ready to receive us for two years from September. The final deadline loomed.

Angus Stirling meanwhile reiterated, at every opportunity, that whatever course we chose, we must have a fall-back. Neither I, nor he, nor anyone else, has ever identified a satisfactory one. It was becoming clearer that, if we lost the Lyceum and did not get to Tower Bridge, we should have to perform, let by let, in a variety of venues, suited alternately to opera and ballet, concert and stage, small-scale and large-scale work. We would be itinerant, at least in 1997/98. In autumn 1998 the new Sadler's Wells would be receiving; perhaps, for some weeks at least, we could go there.

In this enforced and tantalizing limbo, Apollo Leisure renewed their attempt to secure our commitment to them. They, of course, had to recoup their investment in reviving the Lyceum as soon as they could. If they had been able to wait three months, they could have had us signing up, gratefully. But they would not wait, and when the pistol was again put to our head, we preferred to see what Southwark and the Secretary of State would do. The Lyceum now committed to Andrew Lloyd Webber and a revival of *Jesus Christ Superstar* instead.

Southwark, whose officers were supportive throughout, received our application on 16 October 1995 and granted it six weeks later. They saw the theatre as contributing markedly to the riverside regeneration of the borough. One local political figure, ex-GLC, had opposed it; he wanted to see social housing provided on the site. Southwark knew they could not afford that. There were no other objections to the proposal; we had undertaken to house a reading room for residents within the building. The formal advisory bodies who must statutorily be consulted (English Heritage; the Royal Fine Art Commission) raised no objection to Ian Ritchie's handsome design. All the bodies with a particular interest in the Thames and this part of London were in favour. The first crucial hurdle was cleared; now it was up to the Secretary of State. This was a riverside site and a culturally important one. He called the scheme in for his personal ministerial consideration. If he was quick, and approved, there would still be time to build the theatre and see it open in September 1997.

John Gummer said nothing in December. January ticked away, and our hopes with it.

On 31 January 1996 the Secretary of State decided, though there were no representations to him that he should do so, to hold a public inquiry. Some thought he was obliged to because his brother was now the ROH's Chairman Designate. This was the absolutely decisive moment. We had by then given up hope, but if on that date Gummer had said what he said later: 'This is a fine project, build it,' we would still have been in business. Instead, he set up an inquiry. The Inspector, P. J. McDonald, sat in a room at Southwark Crown Court. The inquiry adjourned; the Inspector had suffered a bereavement. He completed and closed the hearings, and laid his report before the Secretary of State. On 30 October 1996 the Secretary of State accepted the recommendation it contained: the ROH could have its fine new theatre on Potter's Field. But it was too late. By then the auditorium we needed for September 1997 could not be ready till September 1998. Embroiled in new financial difficulties, current and for the closure period, we were all far too wearied to force the building up when it would not be ready in time. The 'string of pearls' along Thameside will show a drab, neglected space beside Tower Bridge as Britain and its visitors celebrate the Millennium. Ironically, it is now proposed that the site just next to 'ours' will eventually house Norman Foster's glittering council chamber for London's new government.

We were homeless. The choice on closure was the crucial decision of my last years in post at Covent Garden. I do not regret attaching importance to the staff's interest in the course we adopted, though I know that marks me as a soft touch in a hard world. But, in aiming for the best, I rejected what might have been tolerable. The Lyceum could have been no worse than what we ended up with.

Many will have good memories of performances during the ROH's two and a half years of closure: *Paul Bunyan* at the Shaftesbury Theatre and *The Turn of the Screw* at the Barbican; *Der Freischütz*, *Mefistofele*, *Parsifal*, *Die Ägyptische Helena* in concert; *Der Ring des Nibelungen* at the Albert Hall. Even at Labatt's Apollo in Hammersmith, the Royal Ballet, though it lost against budget, played to audiences of 50,000 – twenty-five Royal Opera Houses full. And it adapted itself to the Barbican and the Royal Festival Hall and Sadler's Wells. Both companies toured and triumphed, in the USA, in Japan, in Germany, Finland and at the Edinburgh Festival. Actively, they put themselves about. Performances of quality meant that closure was far from the total shambles it was represented as being. The Royal Opera carried off the Evening Standard Awards, both years. All the same, some will think we took the wrong decision; it was the Board's, and mine.

Mike Morris, when I raised the issue in a retrospective chat, put two points to me. First, that the figures we were looking at were convincing enough, but that we had commissioned no risk analysis of Tower Bridge. That would have shown how timing could very easily defeat us. And he thought, in the light of later experience, that had we somehow squeezed out that £7 million and opted for the Lyceum, the staff would have worn it. Given harsh clarity and level dealing, consulted immediately in every detail of what we were up against, understanding why we were acting as we believed we had to, they might have taken the prospect of all the redundancies on the chin and, still working cheerfully, given us two years of fine performance and a grand Covent Garden send-off. He may be right; we shall never know. The Board in any case would not have agreed to our going to the Lyceum without believing we could afford it. For want of an estimated £7 million, we refused to go there. Closure cost not that extra £7 million, but an additional £17 million in the end.

18

PUSH COMES TO SHOVE

1995-1997

In the summer of 1995 the Royal Opera House, to all appearance, stood high and dry above the tide of problems that ever threatened to beset us. For three successive years, by whatever privation, we had earned a surplus; eight out of eight nominations for excellence in opera had come our way; the Royal Ballet too had won awards for its achievements; the National Lottery had awarded us the sum we had stipulated to redevelop the theatre and its surrounds; Westminster City Council would shortly grant permission for the scheme in a revised and all but final form. Plain sailing? In fact, the House was again in difficulty. We were like a juggler, keeping several balls in the air at once: one slip, and they could all come down. The stage was getting more slippery.

Artistically we were on something of a run. In the 1995/96 season, while cramming in extra performances to help the budget – fourteen *Figaros* – Nicholas Payne had given the opera season heart and shape and purpose. He placed Wagner at the front; with *Götterdämmerung* we reached the end of the Richard Jones *Ring* cycle. Brünnhilde's return to the Hall of the Gibichungs in Act Two, humiliated and betrayed, a paper bag over her head, walking the breadth of the stage, twice, on a trestle table as Hagen's men brutally banged on it, was devastating – the shattering high point of the cycle. In the middle we had a trio of twentieth-century works: the first-ever company production in Britain of Hindemith's *Mathis der Maler*; in his blessed presence in his eighty-sixth year – we just missed his eighty-fifth – we gave as we had promised

Michael Tippett's *Midsummer Marriage* (the chorus sang their hearts out; at the general rehearsal, Chorus Director Terry Edwards, no wimp at 6 foot 9 inches tall, was in tears because, he told me, 'It was so beautiful!'); and we put on a work that had special meaning for me, Sandy Goehr's re-invention of Monteverdi's lost *Arianna*, of which only the great lament 'Lasciatemi morire' remains. Susan Graham excelled in this fine piece. It had been Sandy, departing the Board as I took over, who warned me I should achieve nothing at the Opera House. He inscribed a score of *Arianna* to me, acknowledging he had been wrong. The twentieth-century triptych was made possible by a grant Nicholas Payne obtained from the Foundation for Sport and the Arts, topped up by the Arts Council. Dame Janet Baker, on our Opera Board and on the Foundation's, spoke up effectively for that, I guessed.

At the season's end, that year's Verdi Festival proper kicked off with *Don Carlos*, a new production, at last challenging Visconti's masterwork of 1958. This was shared with the Châtelet, Paris, where it was given first. Nicholas Payne provoked the Board by closing the House for a week to rehearse it; routine on the continent, unheard of here, except for the *Ring*. He was right to do so. Luc Bondy's production was thought cold by some, handsome by others. The appearance of the Court in the snowy forest, white on white, was dazzling and wonderful. *Don Carlos* is the Verdi opera that brings out the best in Bernard Haitink. The singing, as each lead character in turn holds our interest and the stage, was pretty marvellous. Roberto Alagna, saving himself for *La traviata* with Angela Gheorghiu, missed two performances, but Julian Gavin took over to good effect. One patron, an old friend Brian Wenham, now alas departed, wrote to me in indignation at Alagna's withdrawal. But the cast, I pointed out, contained five other stars; of them, Thomas Hampson as Posa gave I thought the performance of his life, and Karita Mattila as Elisabeth, tall and blonde and beautiful, riding the white horse in the white forest, sang high and true and with feeling, in that form the greatest female singer in the world. These performances were indisputably world class, a high point of my time.

In Birmingham that season, David Bintley made his mark again with a strong new narrative full-length ballet, *Far from the Madding Crowd*. The Royal Ballet's offerings included work new to us by William Forsythe and, promisingly, by Ashley Page. Tetsuya 'Teddy' Kumakawa, our Japanese virtuoso, thrilled everyone in a new *Rhapsody* and in a re-created *Les Patineurs*, spinning still as the end curtain closes and re-opens, as

The auditorium, handsomest in London; regilded, it will continue to delight.
Air-conditioning, too.

Before redevelopment. All paint frames are messy, but this is ridiculous.

Behind the scenes, order; tutus . . .

shoes . . .

. . . and wigs.

Early birds, 4 January 1995. Today's stars, and tomorrow's, deliver the Lottery application. We got the worm.

21 July 1995. Lottery winners; with Chairman Angus Stirling in the Floral Hall.

Vivien Duffield, CBE. You would want her on your side.

Client in a hard-hat, as development gets underway; the eagle is unimpressed.

The Floral Hall, barrel-vault roof restored, as part of Dixon's and Jones's design. Already this is London's most-in-demand venue.

Nothing is more important than education. Children listen patiently as I make the point.

Let's make an opera. St Clement Danes Primary School.

A Chance to Dance for schoolchildren in Brixton and Notting Hill; taking part matters.

Not every General Director gets to be cricket captain. We challenged ENO, and beat them three years running.

Midnight, 14 July 1997, with Gillian after the Closing Gala. Home.

Ashton provided. Lynn Seymour and Anya Linden tenderly helped revive MacMillan's *The Invitation*.

The main new piece was a full-length ballet by Twyla Tharp, *Mr Worldly Wise*, created on the company and showing it off to effect. There were fluent, pastel sets by Dave Rogers, and testing parts for Irek Mukhamedov, Darcey Bussell and Teddy Kumakawa. Did it quite hang together? I loved it. The music was a pot-pourri by Rossini, including the Overture to *William Tell* – try going faster than that – and some very simple piano pieces, played deftly as ever by Philip Gammon. Alfred Brendel, in the theatre, said to me, 'I like the way he doesn't try to make anything of that piece.' Kumakawa dazzled. When I saw him last, at Ninette de Valois's 100th birthday at White Lodge, Richmond Park, acknowledging my return to television, he said: 'Why you no make me great star?' Six months later he went back to Japan to seek a fortune in yen. He is a superstar there – young girls queue after every performance to offer him bowls of perfect cherries. He took half a dozen of his fellow male dancers with him. Even in a recession, the Japanese acquire our art.

Back in March 1995, the Board had approved a budget for the fiscal year 1995/96, beginning in April, with misgivings. An exchange of letters between the Chairman and myself throws light on a grim picture.

PRIVATE AND CONFIDENTIAL
Letter from the Chairman dated 30 March 1995

The Budget 1995/96

We have spoken about the budget since the Board meeting, and I must begin by saying that I am extremely sympathetic to the continuing difficulties you, Clive and your colleagues are faced with. Your efforts to balance the budget, given the gap we started with, are heroic. I will do all I can to help cajole the Trust into agreeing to increase their target; and to help raise funds from other sources.

It would, however, be a dereliction of duty if I failed to make it clear that I do not consider that, at this stage, we have a viable budget. Allowing for the fact that any theatre company's budget contains un-certainty, the one presented to the Board carries too many risky assumptions to be reliable. No Board member I have spoken to has confidence in it . . .

I would like the Finance and Audit Committee to review the Budget again before the next Board meeting. I should like to ask that consideration be given to building in provision for a realistic pay award – realistic, that is, to support the strategy Mike Morris is trying to pursue, and that in addition a specific contingency is created to underwrite shortfalls which may occur in some or all of the income-generation assumptions during the year.

In the meantime, we must certainly make a further approach to Dr Ho, and revitalise the Trust.

I am copying this letter to James Spooner and the members of the Finance and Audit Committee, and to Clive.

Yours

Angus Stirling

PRIVATE AND CONFIDENTIAL
Reply from Jeremy Isaacs dated 6 April 1995

The Budget 1995/96

I have your letter of 30 March. Thank you.

I will do my best to bring about the resolution you require, but it is not easy, and, in the fullest sense, impossible of attainment.

In no year that I can remember, since I became General Director, has it been possible to provide in our budget both for a wage increase and a contingency beyond that. We do not, even in what you might call an ordinary year, have the resource or the reserve to fund both. It is our habit to identify a contingency, and earmark it for a wage award if it seems desirable or practicable to make one. What you suggest is the right course in an ideal world. But our circumstance is different . . .

I maintain, therefore, that, though we continue urgently to seek economies, the solution lies in inviting the Trust to bring more money in somehow, and I shall welcome your support in that.

I also propose that one contingency serve to fund a possible wage award. But if, which I think unlikely, the bottom falls out of box-office this summer, we should have to forgo it.

This reveals yet again, I fear, the serious, structural underfunding of activity from which we suffer. Let us hope that new sources of revenue

will underpin the work of the redeveloped Royal Opera House.
Yours

Jeremy Isaacs

By high summer, the picture was grimmer still. After three years of trading in surplus, we were facing a substantial deficit again. The principal cause, already starkly evident, would be reported at the year's end. In 1994/95 we had secured, in funding raised by the Royal Opera House Trust, £7.2 million. In 1995/96 we would receive only £4.8 million, not for want of trying. The well was dry. The sum lost, over £2 million, could not conceivably be replaced at the box-office, or by the sale of suppers, programmes and ice-creams; yet it was crucial to our budget-making. Costs were tightly under control but, as the Chairman noted later in his Report on the year: 'a steep decline in sponsorship, disappointing box-office returns during the hot summer of 1995, and a standstill Arts Council grant have, I regret to say, taken us into the red.'

For years I argued that the Appeal for capital would have to be conducted alongside, and not instead of, the ongoing annual effort to raise private revenue. Tell donors, I would urge, that if in the redeveloped theatre they want the privileges they have purchased in the present one, they must donate to the development *and* help keep the House afloat meantime, before and during the closure period. This was easy enough to demand; very hard to fulfil. So long as we kept up an attractive programme of work in the House, supporters would continue their Trust membership and purchase seats at a premium. But they would not splash out to help with productions. Offered opportunities to contribute in new modes – use of the Royal Box at a temptingly low price – they were slow to respond. Worse, looking ahead to closure, companies would support us during that period only if they knew what they would get for their money; we were in no position to tell them.

I believed and argued, and still believe and would still argue, that whatever happened, we had to fight our way forward to the point where the development, funding guaranteed, was begun. Once that was under way, and the funds committed, it could not be stopped, since only fools would call it off half completed, at reckless waste of public money. Once that was built, the House had a future, and a bright one; without it, we had none. Indeed, without redevelopment, the House, unserviceable, must close within two years at the most, and without £25 million spent on running repairs would never re-open. (ENO will be in the same fix shortly, unless something is done about the Coliseum.) Getting the development started, and work begun on the site, meant not just detailed planning permission, not just drawing and costing every inch of the plan, not just keeping the Board together, and rallying behind Vivien Duffield as she launched the Appeal; it meant keeping on-side the Arts Council, and the Department of National Heritage, and behind them, somewhere, the Treasury and the Prime Minister himself. To do that, we had to be, and be seen to be, a going concern.

Drastic action needed to be taken to limit a deficit in 1995/96 and, if we could, to prevent one in 1996/97, while still maintaining a handsome stage presence. Repertory budgets were already trimmed to the bone; we would have to make savings on the wages bill. From early in 1996, we decided to lose up to 100 posts, partly encouraging early retirement among those who would have gone anyway in 1997, partly enforcing redundancies, as necessary. When the Queen came to *The Sleeping Beauty* on 20 February 1996, to mark the fiftieth anniversary of the re-opening of the Royal Opera House after the Second World War, she was met by a small, vocal band of protesters – ROH staff from every department except the companies, demonstrating against losing their jobs. They were there, in force, waving banners, handing out leaflets. They made no attempt to disrupt the royal arrival. Inside, all was glory, and nostalgia. Twenty-eight members of the company who had danced *The Sleeping Beauty* there on 20 February 1946 processed, one by one, on to the stage to curtsey and take a bow. Ninette de Valois, Madam, came last, indomitable, dominating.

Two problems, current financial viability and the lack of firm closure plans, were bad enough in themselves, but they bore also on the development, now raring to get under way but needing funds to do so. We were due to start preliminary works on part of the site, Russell Street, in January 1996. But Westminster would grant that permission, to start demolishing houses in Russell Street and begin pile-driving, only if we could demonstrate that we had all the necessary funds in place. Of those, £58.5 million towards construction were due to come from the Arts Council and now, nearly six months after the announcement of the award, not a penny had been advanced – nor would be until we had satisfied the conditions they had set. One of those, relating to plans for the closure period, would dog us for months yet. Others called for immediate answers: we were asked to strengthen the Board to enable us, to the Arts Council's satisfaction, effectively to manage the development.

When this last requirement was first published in July, we found it hard to understand what the Arts Council had in mind. The Lottery application had spelled out how the scheme was managed. I had made changes on ROH's executive client team, putting John Seekings, reporting to me, in charge. He would do a quite excellent job. We appointed Schal project managers. But the Board? Angus Stirling chaired a strong Development Steering Committee, reporting to the Main Board, with top-class professional advisers. Already we had strengthened those; we had taken on Stanhope plc, and Stanhope's chairman, Stuart Lipton. At their prompting, we had reshaped the scheme; the architects had leapt at the chance to lose the hated office block, to simplify the roofscape, to introduce, beside the reconstituted Floral Hall, an elegantly functional elevator linking it to the amphitheatre loggia bar. If the Arts Council wanted someone on the Board itself in charge of the development, Stuart

Lipton was the obvious candidate. But Stanhope were on the payroll. We could not put Lipton on the Board to take charge of his operation on our behalf; conflict of interest immediately arose. Lipton saw the point. (Later, at the end of 1997, he did join the Board.) But if Lipton advised us, what was the point of putting on the Board another senior property figure, John Ritblat perhaps, to second guess him? No one would benefit from a clash of egos, and of wills. As the weeks passed, it became clear that the Arts Council had something else in mind.

In August 1996, Angus Stirling would come to the end of his five-year term as ROH Chairman. He would by then have served on the ROH Board for seventeen consecutive years. In September 1995 he told us he would not wish to renew his term as Chairman. Wounded as he must have been by the muttered criticisms, he behaved with impeccable dignity.

James Spooner had been acting as messenger. The suggestion was now put: since Peter Gummer knew the House well, since he had fabled PR skills, since he wanted the chairmanship, should we not at once offer it to him? Some Board members favoured this direct approach. Others resisted. Clear of mind, courageous in debate, Tessa Blackstone insisted on due process; we must consider other candidates, she said, before arriving at a decision. In October the Board agreed to set up a committee to conduct a search and to make a recommendation by December; if not, then if humanly possible, by January. This was fast going. But there was real urgency: if choosing a new Chairman satisfied a condition precedent to our drawing down instalments of the Lottery cash, then we had only until January to do so and still keep the development on track. To hold it up from then on would cost £150,000 a week; without a cash inflow, after a very few weeks, the design team would have to be dispersed and all would grind, disastrously, to a halt.

There was another reason for haste: the coming search for a new General Director. It had been agreed that I would be in post until September 1997, when I should reach my sixty-fifth birthday. But the Board wanted to start its search in earnest early in 1996, hoping to have a General Director Designate appointed before the start of the 1996/97 season. This protracted lead-time to a changeover has long been the custom in opera. Nowadays it seems far too long. But that autumn an advertisement was inserted in the press; applications were invited by mid-January. The paragon appointed would need to combine outstanding artistic leadership with management wizardry and sure financial control. If the Board's timetable was to be adhered to, interviews would start early in the New Year; and the Chairman Designate ought certainly to be involved. In December, days before a crucial series of meetings with the Arts Council, the Board resolved to accept its Search Committee's recommendation that Peter Gummer be invited to join the Board shortly as Chairman Designate, taking over from Angus Stirling in September 1996. This fateful decision was conveyed to the Chairman of the Arts Council and to the Secretary of State for National Heritage. It was a genuine choice; Gummer was knowledgeable, enthusiastic, available. Telling the Secretary of State was one thing, winning her approval another. For weeks that was not forthcoming. Embarrassed at Gummer's close links with the Tory Party and government, Virginia Bottomley, backed by Grey Gowrie at the Arts Council, tried to insist that two known Labour supporters be appointed to the Board at the same time, making a total mockery of the idea that a genuine interest in opera and ballet was a prerequisite of membership. Angus Stirling and the Board dug their heels in; Virginia's proposal went away.

December 1995 was the darkest month I knew at Covent Garden. Senior management met virtually every day for a fortnight, struggling to pull finances for the current year into line and to arrive at a balanced budget for 1996/97. To achieve that we would seek 100 redundancies and take the charge in the current year's accounts. I saw each manager separately to learn what economies they could proffer, whom they would 'let go' and do without. Devoting December to pruning, slashing or tweaking to balance next year's budget was a familiar process. What we had never had to do before was submit detailed forecasts for a five-year period, based on standstill or reduced Arts Council grants and covering two separate, imponderable unknowns: a closure lasting two years and a bit; life in a new House of which not a stone was in place. For closure we had lots of good ideas, but not one theatre booked. This was unsurprising, given how the West End works. Closure was nearly two years off; who knew what theatres would be vacant in September 1997? The Arts Council did not yet require detailed plans for closure; we had a few months' grace. But it did want to know our general intention, and most important, that we could carry out all we had in hand, including the development, within the total cash limits available to us and on a cashflow that we could manage. We could: the Lottery grant, the proceeds of the

Appeal, the sale of property would see us through. But they would not take our figurings alone for an answer.

I can remember virtually nothing of the meeting we had with the Arts Council on 21 December 1995; it was so horrible that I have suppressed the memory, having only a dim recollection of abuse and recrimination, of men and women behaving badly. The strain was evident on either side. They probably wanted to be helpful if they could, but would yield not a jot or tittle on our fulfilling paper requirements that would satisfy their criteria, and so cover their backs if it all ended in disaster. We were certain we could get by on the current account until summer 1997, and would manage closure somehow. Above all we knew that if the development could only get going on time, it would complete within budget. This last lent a strenuous urgency to both sides. They knew too that if they prevaricated unnecessarily, they risked bringing us down and the new House into the bargain. They had paperwork in front of them which they thought less than complete. Could we be certain we had costed every possible eventuality during closure, and for the development? Had we modelled the future? They would trust neither their own judgement nor ours. At this winter solstice, on St Lucy's Day, the shortest day of the year, we were instructed to hand the facts and figures over to a firm of consultants – we nominated Peat Marwick Mitchell, KPMG – and have them pass them through a computerized model, showing how they were affected by every variation and sensitivity of wage inflation, grant erosion, supply and demand in goods and services, that intelligence could devise. If they had asked us to take account of the weather, I would not have been surprised. And when this exercise was completed, and KPMG had done their job, would the Arts Council look at the result and pronounce yea or nay? No. KPMG must pass their findings to consultants they would retain. Only if they were satisfied also, and the figures ran evenly on two computers, would the Arts Council, late in January, deign to decide. The accountants, at any rate, were happy; we have a cure for this disease, they murmured as they took their fees.

Perhaps the Arts Council wanted to be sure they were not missing out on some surprising, inexpensive solution. They did not really want, any more than we did, to close the House and its companies down totally and thus risk destroying the ballet company. But neither did they assure us that, in whatever circumstance, they would continue core funding. I had asked Mary Allen's strategically minded predecessor Anthony Everitt, several years before, to state what minimum level of activity by the companies during closure would ensure the continuance of core funding. Answer came there none. In January 1996 they confirmed they would continue core funding, but not for minimal activity. The officers responsible for opera and ballet began marking our cards. Could we, they urged, keep up the proportion of new work in what we proposed, and sustain our commitment to access, outreach and provision for the disabled? The green-light signal, when it came, was confusing. It strobed.

Christmas and New Year passed; the consultants worked on. Before the end of January 1996 the Arts Council told us that we would be able to draw down on last summer's Lottery award. But we got the money only in March. A Handel opera clinched it.

The début of the operatic year was the American soprano Ruth-Ann Swenson's, in John Copley's lovely old production of *Semele*, conducted by Charles Mackerras. This was the best coloratura of my time, more joyful than any other. Semele sings aria after gorgeous aria. I was most taken by William Congreve's lines for Athaenas: 'Invent no new delay/On this auspicious day'. I faxed them to Mary Allen at the Arts Council. They did the trick: she released the funds. Good old Handel!

But the delay had cost us time, and that was expensive. Work that should have started in January had to be put back; so, inevitably, was completion. The House, all still being well, would now re-open in December 1999. The estimate of £20 million of additional funds needed to carry us through the closure period would have to cover at least twenty-seven months, not twenty-four. The period from summer 1999 to the actual re-opening of the new House had always been the most problematic, and the hardest for which to forecast cost and revenue. In May 1996, this helped provoke a new crisis.

At the end of the 1995/96 financial year, we had incurred an operating deficit of £3.1 million, which included non-recurring expenditure of £1.7 million. A chunk of that covered redundancy payments brought forward into the year's accounts. We were now working on plans to get through 1996/97, if we could, in the black; predictably we were having difficulty. All the same, the prospects for closure re-examined in May caused upset. On 24 May 1996 I wrote to the Board:

CLOSURE

I very much regret the shock and surprise caused Members of the Board by our report that closure plans for the two companies, as currently envisaged, cannot be confined within a cost envelope of core ACE grant, £20m supplementary grant, reduced Trust subvention, and nomadic box-office revenue. For that I apologise.

However the difficulties of squaring that circle are readily apparent, as my note attached to this shows. We are doing all we can to present acceptable figures to the Board on 29 May. But we do want, somehow, to keep the companies in being, and active.

Jeremy Isaacs

We were now looking at a closure period which in programming terms began to seem exciting. The companies would have no permanent base, but would perform in various venues, reaching out to new audiences, as we had often been urged, in new locations. A further 200 redundancies were envisaged, but the companies would keep performing. Their core cost would be reduced but not eliminated. Box-office forecasts, however, and estimates for private-revenue funding, were now markedly lower than those we had submitted as part of our Lottery application to the Arts Council in December 1994. Clive Timms, Director of Finance and Resources, showed the strain of the burden he carried. Briefing the Chairman that he was having difficulty forcing a reduction of ambitious closure plans, Timms gave his own frightening forecast: additional closure costs of £34 million instead of the £20 million we were getting from the Lottery. By the Finance and Audit Committee meeting on 20 May this figure had been reduced to £27 million. It still caused outrage. There was an explosion. One Board Member, Bob Gavron, blew up, and stated that the Finance Director should resign. They were shooting the messenger. Clive Timms, acknowledging that the Board had lost confidence in him, offered me his resignation. I lost a capable colleague, though he was not and could not be the miracle-worker the Board appeared to expect.

The reasons for this gaping discrepancy were clear: at Covent Garden box-office had run at £19 million annually, and private support had reached £7 million. During closure we now knew we should be shy of at least £10 million a year in house receipts; private funding would be £5 million a year less. And there were theatre rentals to pay. An extra

£30 million might have closed the gap over twenty-seven months, but £20 million could not. The Board, when it met, could not agree even to consider the figure of £27 million. I was instructed to eliminate £7 millon. Revisiting the figures with colleagues' help, I got the total down to £23.5 million, adducing the extra three months in the twenty-seven-month closure period as justification for £2.5 million of that, and the other £1 million just to help close the gap. The Board agreed to proceed on that basis. The additional £3.5 million would have to come from a surplus on the Appeal, or from property. This was understood, but not nailed down.

The costings of the development showed, for construction and for closure, a total bill of £214 million. This would be met by the £78.5 million Lottery award, £70 million by realization of property values on the site, and £70 million from the Appeal. But we were going to appeal for £100 million, and had some expectation of getting £90 million. Already approaches to supporters abroad had resulted in a substantial sum for the development, lodged in the Floral Trust, of which I was a Trustee. And we had other hefty, long-standing pledges of generous support, particularly from John Sainsbury and Vivien Duffield. If the Appeal did succeed up to our highest expectations and raised a surplus, the plan was that it should form the beginning of an endowment, which would help meet the future revenue needs of the House, and enable us to reduce selected seat prices. Vivien Duffield was adamant that money she raised for the Appeal should not then be used for revenue purposes; donors would be betrayed by that, she said. She would not be party to it. I understood her point but could not entirely follow the logic: if a surplus on the Appeal led to an endowment that would supplement future revenue when the House re-opened, why could it not also eke out revenue at the most critical moment of our fortunes, during closure? And if not from the Appeal, perhaps funds raised from property sales could be applied? In any case, we had to keep the House's head above water while we were appealing for capital funds; if confidence went, so might our funding. Everyone saw the point of that. What I argued then, I still argue now: if the House, instead of keeping its funds separate in watertight compartments, would resolve to make use of all the resource expected to be available to it, it would get through closure somehow and complete the development. When we look back from the year 2001, and the whole picture is clear, we shall find this to have been the case. Meanwhile, in the summer, Clive Timms packed his bags and departed. The House was now without a Finance Director. It was also awaiting the appointment of a new General Director.

The Board's advertisement had not produced a rich trawl. For six months others were headhunted, or prodded into applying. I had regretted my inability to influence the choice of my successor at Channel 4. I thought on this occasion I would make my view known. I wrote to the Search Committee putting forward Nicholas Payne's claims. It was quite clear to me, from my first sight of him in action, that Nicholas, though he was a private and could be a prickly fellow, has just the combination of imaginative artistic judgement and management skill, including hard-headed financial acumen, that the post of General Director requires. He had demonstrated all that at Opera North, and proved it also while leading the Royal Opera. I have no doubt he will exhibit it in full in charge of ENO.

But, apart, at first, from Angus Stirling, the Board was not having any. They thought perhaps Nicholas played his cards too close to his chest, or they did not care for his sometimes brusque manner, or they thought he had quite enough to do running opera without having to oversee ballet too. But, as his Opera North collaboration with Adventures in Motion Pictures, Matthew Bourne's marvellous dance company, showed, he had shots in his locker for that. And he is as tough as army boots. Had the Board taken him, he would still be in post today. But they wanted a new broom. My letter commending him did nothing for his chances.

Gerard Mortier, the combative modernist who had triumphed at La Monnaie and was now artistic director of the Salzburg Festival, was the biggest fish to surface from the net. He would have been a world-class appointment to a House that aspires to the highest international status. But Gerard Mortier does not take kindly to close supervision; he has to be trusted. In any case, it was impossible to see how he could be given assurances that funding would be adequate. I should like to have seen a British Minister explaining to Gerard that the grant the Opera House receives, or may expect to receive in any foreseeable dispensation, is sufficient to sustain consistent excellence. Mortier withdrew his candidacy, much to the relief of the Arts Council's assessor on the selection panel, Mary Allen, who certainly did not fancy disputing the annual level of grant with him. Walking after lunch near her home in Suffolk one day, in the grounds of Helmingham – we were country neighbours – Mary mentioned to Gillian that the incoming Chairman, Peter Gummer, leading the search with Angus Stirling for my successor, owed her one. 'I delivered to him,' she said, 'now Peter must deliver to me.' We took this to mean that she had promoted Gummer's cause as ROH Chairman, so the executive selected to take charge of the ROH must be someone she could work with. (She did not mention that she had been sounded out as a candidate herself.) Naïvely under the impression that experience of running a lyric theatre was an actual advantage, I was still Nicholas's advocate, but his cause was already a dead letter.

There was by now another interesting candidate: Genista McIntosh, Executive Director at the National Theatre since 1990. I knew about Genista McIntosh's candidacy because Richard Eyre had rung me up and put the thought to me. Seeing Genista (Jenny) frequently in the House, knowing nothing but good of her, supposing Richard was keenly her advocate rather than simply tossing a name into the ring, I instantly said, 'What a good idea.' I passed the suggestion to Angus Stirling. Richard, on the Court of King's College, London, of which James Spooner was Chairman, put it to him directly.

Peter Gummer, soon to be Lord Chadlington, ennobled by John Major for services to the Conservative Party at elections, was not so keen, as later became very evident. Jenny's left-leaning views on class and ticket prices may have been a bit pronounced for him. At any rate, he took his time to agree that she was right for the job, and had more than one searching conversation with her before falling into line. The announcement, on 4 July, was of a unanimous selection, and won warm approbation on all sides. But it was qualified. Genista McIntosh would not be General Director; her title was Chief Executive.

Everyone looked forward to Jenny's arrrival, none more eagerly than I. 'The order of release,' Robert Armstrong used to mutter wistfully, as escaping the Cabinet Office he slipped into his seat at our Board table to take the minute. For Robert, for some considerable time, escape from Margaret Thatcher's thrall could not come soon enough. I was ambivalent. I was keen to see my time out, and close the theatre. The repertory for 1996/97 was fixed. The Royal Ballet, on the last but one evening, would perform my favourite, Balanchine's *Symphony in C*. And the Royal Opera would bring the House's curtain down with a great company piece, *Die Meistersinger von Nürnberg*. We were reviving *Meistersinger* because I had asked for it. I wanted to be there, and as General Director.

But there were compelling reasons why Jenny McIntosh could not arrive a day too soon. We were desperately pressed by the heaviest imaginable workload; she would bring fresh energies, a clear mind, new solutions. She and I talked, but she had little to say. I had hoped and expected she would be with us in October, or November at the latest. I wanted there to be a proper handover between us. But that apparently depended on her being allowed to leave the National Theatre, and Christopher Hogg, Chairman there, would not release her early from her period of notice before a successor was named. She would arrive in January. Angus Stirling now told me that the Board, and particularly the new Chairman, Peter Chadlington, wanted me to hand over to her at the end of 1996; they would pay out my contract. I could not argue with this; the House's needs were paramount. And, as it happened, I could return to television; *Cold War*, a 24-part series which Ted Turner had asked me to oversee, was waiting. I did stipulate, though, to keep the title General Director printed in the programme until the end of the season. Since Jenny had taken a different title, Chief Executive, this was possible. Assured that I would abandon executive responsibility and keep well out of Jenny's way, Peter Chadlington conceded. I asked that all official farewells be postponed till the summer. I remained a Board member.

On 21 December I entertained colleagues to Christmas lunch at my home in Bermondsey; this was a particularly boozy and sentimental one. I was sorry to leave them. On 31 December 1996 I left Covent Garden. On 6 January Jenny McIntosh arrived. Gillian and I had already set off for India. When we arrived at our first hotel, near the vast ninth-century carvings of Mahaballipuram, the first person we saw was a member of the Royal Opera House Board.

The House I had handed over was in a pretty parlous financial condition, as it would have been, beneath the surface, at almost any point in its history. When Jenny failed to turn up earlier, I had myself to take the series of budget meetings which would attempt to reduce the threatened revenue deficit in 1997/98, the first year of closure. It is recorded that Jenny McIntosh found it at the £3 million mark when she arrived. A note to me from Lisa Burger, our able acting Head of Finance, dated 12 December, shows that by then we had already identified £2 million of necessary savings. What is certain is that Jenny consolidated those, and had the cutting-edge skill to find the last £1 million needed to balance the books in a budget for 1997/98. But both of us were later shown to be hopelessly optimistic.

The development was well under way; the archaeological dig on the site had uncovered the remains of Saxon Lundenwic. It yielded information on their diet – oysters were favourite – but revealed no inviolable ruins to delay us. Building had begun. The shops in James Street were thriving. More than 60 per cent of the contracts to build had been let, at fixed prices, within budget; 90 per cent would be let by July. And we had adequate contingencies in place.

Of 1996/97, my last season, I really saw only part. Opera, with its roster of fine conductors, pleased the ear – Downes, Gatti, Gardiner, Gergiev, von Dohnányi. Myung Whun Chung gave *Otello*, which Luciano Pavarotti swore he would sing on our stage, but knew he could not, and would not, and did not. Mark Elder, Solti and Haitink completed the list. And Thielemann. We attempted only two new productions. Pfitzner's *Palestrina* had never been given in Britain; with it, we marked the fiftieth anniversary of the Royal Opera. Nikolaus Lehnhoff's production, Christian Thielemann's masterly conducting and a rich cast brought the piece vividly to life. *Palestrina* was the season's only extravagance. Doing without it would have saved at least £400,000. Immediately after we closed, the company took it to New York as the centrepiece of the Lincoln Center Summer Festival. In June, after a *Simon Boccanegra* – the usual, revised, version – I went on stage to embrace Georg Solti and thank him for all he had done for us. I never saw him again. He died later that summer.

At the season's end, Nicholas Payne over-reached for once and blotted his copybook, expensively, by attempting a *Macbeth* that our stage facilities, reduced by preparations for closure, could not begin to handle. The only other new production we succeeded in giving was of the early 1857 *Simon Boccanegra*, in which Plácido, having cancelled *I Masnadieri*, agreed to sing Adorno. He stayed on for the Closing Gala.

For me, the year was made memorable by performances of the operas of Richard Wagner, the master whose work I knew least well when I took charge. (Giving a toast at a supper party after one performance, instead of just 'To Wagner', I proposed the composer's health. The stalwart Gwynne Howell commented drily: 'I did not know he was ill.') The three *Ring* cycles at the start of the season realized my highest hopes: powerful innovatory work on stage, fine singing, chorus and orchestra excelling,

Front-cloths by Nigel Lowery for *Die Walküre*.

Haitink's mastery in the pit. Jenny McIntosh wrote to say how much she envied me for it. Apart from anything else, it is the privilege of a lifetime to work with singers as dedicated as that cast. Deborah Polaski, who once gave up opera to find God, came to my office to tell me how warm and supportive a house Covent Garden was to sing in. She seized every opportunity Richard Jones's production offered to electrify us. Graham Clark, Mime, had had a heart attack rehearsing in *Siegfried* in Turin. Recovered, picking up the role again, he came to the passage in which he had nearly died, and went on with it. That autumn he enlivened the Covent Garden stage by his voice and presence, and an unparalleled athleticism. When I think of opera singers, I think of a few British friends – Anne Evans, Felicity Lott, Ann Murray, Philip Langridge, Tom Allen, Robert Lloyd – who always give their all, who have power to move us always, who never give themselves airs. Anne Evans's Isolde and Brünnhilde, never the loudest but the purest; Ann Murray's Mozart and Handel; Philip Langridge's Grimes and Aschenbach; Tom Allen's Don Giovanni, Count Almaviva and Don Alfonso, his Forester in *The Cunning Little Vixen* and, above all perhaps, his miraculous new-minted Beckmesser, will stay with me all my life.

And John Tomlinson; his Wotan and Sachs have been among the wonders of the age. During the 1993 run of *Meistersinger*, the Staatsoper, Unter den Linden, rang. Would John, the day after his last Sachs, fly to Berlin and sing Gurnemanz in *Parsifal*? Could he? He said he would but promised not to hold back as Sachs. We gave permission. He sang out for us, and went and sang for them. Gratefully, the Staatsoper reported back: every Gurnemanz should sing Sachs the night before. Some critics carp at his robust vocal delivery, suggesting it could be more legato. But 'John Tom' sings for the stage, not the CD. I never in my life knew anyone so dedicated, so unfussy, so completely at the service of his art, a true master of song. One Saturday we skipped a performance of *Die Walküre* and drove to Suffolk; the performance was broadcast live on Radio 3. We were listening as we arrived at Market Weston. The stars were out above us and John Tomlinson was singing Wotan's Farewell. We could not get out of the car, but gazed heavenwards, entranced.

On Friday 11 July 1997, I attended my last ballet performance as titular General Director at the Royal Opera House – supper with the dancers after, Sylvie Guillem dropping by to say farewell – and on Saturday, 12 July, my last opera, *Meistersinger*. The programmes listed the new

In the props room.

productions of my time. The atmosphere at *Meistersinger* was overwhelming; the performance vindicated the occasion. At the end I went on to say a few words: 'We have given the piece because it showed off our chorus and our orchestra and the inspirational figure who has done more than anyone else to set our standards and hold the House together, Bernard Haitink. And because we too honour the masters, and their art.' Storms of applause. 'The curtain will fall now, but will rise again. Whatever the political circumstance,' I said, 'opera has a future here so long as two forces unite to defend it: the dedication of those on stage and behind who give it, and the passion of the audience – your passion – to enjoy it.' All knew that was true. The curtain fell. Backstage someone came up to grip my hand and tell me I had destroyed the place, as if closing the House was not right, necessary and inevitable. Upstairs, speeches and presentations.

Next day, Sunday, in the Wigmore Hall, the soloists of the Royal Opera House orchestra, led by Vasko Vassilev, honoured me by giving a concert for my friends. They played Mozart, Strauss, Schubert. I read Dryden's 'Ode to St Cecilia'. Together, we drained the last celebratory drop from the bowl.

Monday's Closing Gala, in the presence of the Prince of Wales, the stalls and Grand Tier crammed with bigwigs, came, to me, as an anti-climax. Lord Chadlington spoke confidently from the stage. Amazingly, the Chief Executive who had displaced me six amicable months earlier, Genista McIntosh, had already departed, and been replaced by the Arts Council's Secretary-General, Mary Allen. The first hearings of Gerald Kaufman's Parliamentary Select Committee on the affairs of the Royal Opera House were only a fortnight away.

19

APRÈS MOI

1997–1999

In the forty-two years before me, the Royal Opera House had two General Directors. I lasted nine years. In the two years since my leaving, there have been four, though they were titled Chief Executive, or Executive Director. The last of these, Michael Kaiser, has made himself at home.

Is it something in the water? In all the years I was associated with it, and in those before me, the Opera House kept itself together through thick and thin, cherishing its achievement, chafing and grumbling at financial constraint but determinedly, with commitment and dedication, getting on with the job. Screaming from the house tops was discouraged; chucking in the towel never seriously contemplated. Then things came to a different pass. From the summer of 1997 I was an outsider looking on. Emotionally tied still to the House I loved, and conscious of my part in decisions that helped shape the events we now lived through, I was no longer privy to the thinking that took the House forward. I only knew what appeared in public. That was enough to be going on with.

In January 1997 Jenny McIntosh, to all appearances, was settling in well. She made an immediate good impression on the staff; I have met no one who did not like her. And she tackled the problems she was facing with a will, trimming the next year's budget, sensibly reshaping activity. Plans for the first year of closure, finalized and commended as excellent and affordable by Chadlington and by her, were published with appropriate fanfares. But within five months she was gone. In that brief time there was little visible sign of the drama ahead. At the Board meetings I attended, she seemed coolly, though not exuberantly, in charge. A little pinched and drawn perhaps; or is that the imagining of hindsight? I cried off part of a Board awayday at Magdalen College, Oxford, and, I suppose to enable her to utter freely out of my shadow, was warned off the rest. The minute noted curtly that she had raised some key issues in a way that had provoked controversy, and that these had not been resolved. But so what? That is what awaydays are for. But personalities clashed. When his appointment took effect, Chadlington had immediately installed himself and a secretary in an office next to mine. No Chairman had done so before. The Board counselled him not to act as an Executive Chairman. When he told us he would, for an initial period only, chair Jenny's executive management meeting, I put it to him directly at the Board that he should not attempt to run the House himself. He said he understood. He would not do it for long. But there were accounts of an important House meeting at which Chadlington had stood beside Jenny McIntosh, interrupting what she had to say with observations of his own. There were similar reports of a press conference. It is not easy for a new Chief Executive to impose herself beside so active a Chairman. The Chairman's pre-eminence was further emphasized by the fact that he had not found a successor to Clive Timms as Finance Director. After an advertisement and a head-hunt, an able candidate accepted the job, but changed his mind at the last minute. It took another six months to find another executive willing to take it on. Lisa Burger held the fort.

A tough task faces any ROH Chief Executive. Jenny, with closure and all its unknowns hard upon her, had to endure a baptism of fire far fiercer than any of her predecessors. She may have found some of her colleagues – Nicholas Payne and the two Anthonys, Dowell and Russell-Roberts – hard to bend to her view; the companies after all were supposed to act as independent cost-centres. She will certainly have found Vivien Duffield, chairing the Trust and leading the Appeal, a formidable figure, with a mind very much her own, and never afraid to shout it. But it all goes with the job; Vivien was indispensable, the Artistic Directors knew their stuff. At the Board meeting on 28 April 1997 there was no sign of anything untoward. Jenny kept her head and her countenance. Chadlington was all decisiveness and smiles. Behind the scenes, it was quite otherwise.

In early May, leaving behind the post-election euphoria of New Labour's new Britain, I was on the campus at Athens, Ohio, at a

conference of Cold War historians. Chadlington tried to reach me by telephone from London on Saturday the 10th and missed me. Asked if he
would like a message relayed to me, he said, 'No, it's not important.' I
rang back on Sunday the 11th, and missed him. I tried him at the
Connaught before the recital Luciano Pavarotti gave that Sunday as his
farewell to the Garden – I was missing that too. Early on Monday the
12th, from New York, I called him again. He took the call. Jenny
McIntosh, he told me, had resigned. For weeks she had been in tears in
his office saying she could not do the job. Mary Allen was her successor,
and had been confirmed in the post by a Board meeting, for which he had
vainly sought my views. The meeting had just that moment finished. He
had seen the new Secretary of State, Chris Smith (in office for just four
days), on the Wednesday of the previous week; he had not gone alone but
had taken with him Board member Bob Gavron, who had given £500,000
to New Labour's election fund. According to Chadlington, Smith had
expressed his approval. Chadlington had then telephoned individually
every member of the Board and got each one to agree. This was a crisis.
Jenny, for her health's sake, he said, had to go immediately. It was futile
and dangerous, he had argued, to embark on a due but lengthy search
process. Mary Allen, though not formally a candidate, had been the best
of the bunch they had considered last time round (and, it now appears,
Chadlington's favoured choice). He had asked every Board member to
agree that she should immediately be appointed. On the telephone from
New York, I was presented – I attribute no bad faith – with a *fait accompli*,
signed, sealed and delivered.

I had never been so taken aback in my life. I told him immediately that,
if he had reached me earlier, I would have been in favour of asking
Nicholas Payne and Mike Morris together to hold the fort for a month or
so, but that I supposed no such interim solution would have satisfied him.
Now, I said Mary Allen was a good choice and he had my approval. Later,
thinking it over, I remembered the BBC had taken only a month to
replace Alasdair Milne, by advertisement and due process. I reflected how
easy it is to win assent from individuals picked off on the telephone one
by one – everyone else to whom I have spoken agrees – and how differently
we may behave in collegiate groups when one member's hesitation
strengthens another's. Given an opportunity to consider the issue from
scratch that Monday, rather than ratify a done thing, the Board might
have thought it right to pause and wait a few weeks. In that time, who

knows, Nicholas Snowman at the South Bank, Nicholas Kenyon at Radio 3, even Nicholas Payne, might have come in for reconsideration. John Tusa, at the Barbican, might have shown interest. The supposed urgency, the need for an immediate replacement, created its own momentum. Only after the event did it become clear that this was not so simple. Mary Allen would not be an immediate replacement. There might be impropriety, or the suspicion of it, if she moved at once to the Opera House. She would go into purdah, therefore, and not arrive in post at Covent Garden till September. This delay, at such a critical moment, had not been mentioned to the Secretary of State, though a similar delay had been observed only a year earlier by Chadlington himself. Now, from May till September, Peter Chadlington would be Executive Chairman, if not in name then in fact.

The result of these goings-on was the last thing the Opera House needed: another outcry. The press had a field day: this was the juiciest arts story for years. Vultures were hovering. After a tussle lasting some weeks, Gerald Kaufman had been confirmed in his wish to continue in the new Parliament as Chair of the House of Commons Select Committee on the National Heritage, later to change its name to Culture, Media and Sport. It did not follow automatically that he should. Gerald was a Privy Councillor of some seniority, but the post might have gone to a member of the Opposition. However, Kaufman, a New Labour supporter who was not offered office, was determined to have something that would keep him busy and in the limelight. This was to be it. He has a keen mind, a sharp tongue and pen. I had known him since Oxford, when he combined the Labour Club and the Union, as I did, with a liking for music and a passion for musical cinema. I remember his enthusiasm for *The Band Wagon*. And for ice-cream. 'Banana is the flavour of the month next month,' he told me, on the street outside the cinema. Bumping into him recently, I had hoped he would secure the appointment, and that he would, as I had discussed with him before, investigate the Opera House's affairs. Naïvely I imagined that, since there was no joy to be had on the funding issue from Arts Council or government, his Committee, taking a long hard look, might be helpful. I was encouraged in this hope by a serious Select Committee man, Robert Sheldon MP, who chaired the Public Accounts Committee during the Thatcher and Major governments. The National Audit Office, reporting to him, had once investigated Arts Council disbursements to the Opera House and others, and found all in order. Robert Sheldon came with a Parliamentary delegation to see over the House one day. I spoke briefly. He was briefer: 'You are underfunded,' he said. Gerald Kaufman would hold hearings on the Opera House, he told me, when he had finished with the BBC, on which he holds and expresses strong views. Chadlington had already drawn attention to himself by taking the ROH chair after recommending an Arts Council grant to us of £78.5 million. That he should now snatch the Arts Council's Secretary-General to work with him provided a heavensent opportunity for Kaufman to get the Committee hearings off to a sensational start. Once the lid was off the pot, who knew what else the Committee might find?

In the McIntosh–Chadlington–Allen *bouleversement* of May 1997, there were many good questions wanting answers. Why exactly did Jenny McIntosh leave the Opera House? The press statement said she was ill. No one believed it; she was seen running an audit rule over the Nottingham Playhouse the day before. She must, Chadlington said, since her health was his first concern, leave at once. Later she confirmed that she was concerned about her health, but appeared surprised at the urgency. Might she have been willing to stay a bit, till a successor arrived? Did he push her out? The Secretary of State could not have given a formal consent to the engaging of Mary Allen without a due selection process; he had no *locus standi* in the matter. But was he happy? Or happy only in the circumstances? Or unhappy? Did it not occur to him, in-adequately supported at the meeting on his fourth day in office, to counsel caution and insist on delay? When did Lord Gowrie know of this possible move? Was it true that Mary Allen advised Chadlington not to clear his proposal with her Chairman at the Arts Council, but with the Department of National Heritage instead? If so, why? What did the Arts Council think of these goings-on? Not much, it transpired. And when did Chadlington first realize that Jenny McIntosh wanted to leave, and would have to be allowed to go? When did he first approach Mary Allen and dis-cuss the job with her? If it was before 28 April, when the ROH Main Board met – and it turned out it was – why did he not, by a hint, by a flicker of expression, or by going into private session and speaking to us frankly, convey to the Board that so grave an upheaval was impending? Bar oral sex in the Cabinet Office, a Commons Committee could scarcely be offered a more tempting target. No other event in my experience of the Opera House called so much attention to itself as Peter Chadlington's peremptory dispatch of Jenny McIntosh and recruitment of Mary Allen.

The Select Committee met first on 24 July 1997. Grey Gowrie, Jenny McIntosh and I gave evidence. The Chairman of the Arts Council had to deal with methods of appointment to the Board of the Royal Opera House; should not government, the Committee wanted to know, be more involved? Since 1993, he was able to point out, the Secretary of State had approved names from lists submitted to him. Gowrie was asked to explain what he knew of the circumstance of Mary Allen's appointment. When told by her that it had been offered, and approved by the Secretary of State, he was 'gob-smacked'. Gowrie said he took a dim and critical view of my handling of closure, while praising me as a 'visionary' in other respects. On funding he was, at last, realistic: the Opera House was at a plain disadvantage compared to any European house. The relationship between Arts Council and Opera House could, of course, be improved.

Jenny McIntosh took her place in front of the Committee. From her first words, praising her colleagues at Covent Garden and the quality of their work, she impressed all who heard her in that crowded room with her clarity of thought and honesty of mind. She was reluctant to be drawn on precise reasons for her leaving; she had been not ill but unhappy, and that unhappiness in her work, she felt, would make her ill. She had been made welcome at the Opera House, but was still un-comfortable there. She found management structures at the Opera House diffuse and fragmented; there was perhaps a mismatch between herself and the organization. Pressed by Gerald Kaufman in the chair to agree about the ROH's 'clubbiness', she replied that was his word, not hers. Invited to say that she was made 'to feel an intruder', she answered: 'Let us say that is not entirely unfair, Chairman.'

Through everything Jenny said there shone a concern for the work of the House, and its potential audience. She discounted personalities, but it was obvious she found dealing with two companies, and with the Royal Opera House Trust, difficult. And, perhaps, with the Chairman. I sensed that she felt that her aspiration to make the House accessible, as she put it, to a new audience would be impossible to achieve in any foreseeable funding dispensation. I did not share her view of the intractability of ROH management structures; that apart, I could hardly disagree with a syllable she uttered. The Committee, at the end of her evidence, still could not quite understand why she had gone, or, having decided to leave, gone so quickly. They could not understand at all why anyone at the

Opera House should wish her to do so, or let her go.

I was next, still confident and optimistic. The House, I said, was in reasonably good shape. I described our work, our subsidy, our deficit, our ticket prices, our closure plans, our progress on the development. There had been a call for a People's Opera from the Secretary of State. 'You cannot have a People's Opera unless the people are prepared to pay for it,' I said. I mentioned our educational work, my enthusiasm for it, my wish to expand it. Closure had only just begun; I was content, I said, to be judged at the end of the day on what was achieved. Our work would be more varied, more lively, more interesting than if we had – supposing we could have afforded it – chosen the simpler, safer option of going 300 yards down the road to the Lyceum. Audiences enjoying what we put on in the venues we played in would not understand what it meant to describe those plans as 'a shambles' as Grey Gowrie had done. (The Committee, when it reported in November, refused to accept this from me.)

A Committee member, Mr Fearn, wanted to know 'how I justified the £120,000 I was now going to receive for doing nothing'. The figure was exaggerated, but the thrust was clear. I answered that the Board had asked me to go at the end of December to give Jenny McIntosh a clear run; my contract ran till the end of September 'when, please God, I shall be sixty-five. What in effect they did was to pay out my contract.' Mrs Golding wanted to know about the relationship between my management role and my Board membership. I explained that, peculiarly, having been first a Board member, I had combined the roles. 'Should there not be a proper division between the management of the Royal Opera House and the Board?' I said yes there should; but the Board had given me, I thought, just as hard a time as they would have given anyone else. Mrs Golding pursed her lips: 'That is as may be.' But I sensed no virulent hostility towards me. The Committee had fresher fish to fry.

A week later it was Peter Chadlington's turn. He took Keith Cooper, still in charge of Corporate Affairs, and a new Finance Director, Richard Hall, with him. At once, in his prepared statement, Chadlington heightened the drama: the auditors had advised the Board at the end of June that 'without an urgent injection of a significant cash sum, the Royal Opera House faced insolvency'. Whatever deep concerns were expressed, in private, at the Audit Committee, round the Board table, to the Arts Council even – and those were often real enough – no previous Chairman would have shouted insolvency in a public arena. No sooner mentioned, and alarm bells ringing, than the public-relations wizard sought to calm the concern he had raised. 'It is only an eleventh-hour intervention at the end of last week, by private trusts with a £2 million facility, which has enabled us to go on trading.' There – that should make a headline or two. It did. What it did not do, however, was deflect the Committee from the line of questioning on which it was bent: who said what to whom and where and when and why, as Jenny McIntosh resigned and Mary Allen was hired in her place. In the evidence Chadlington now gave, in Mary Allen's, given when she came in October, in the Secretary of State, Chris Smith's, and in the separate re-examinations of Grey Gowrie and Peter Chadlington just days before the Committee sat down to write its report, this limited but fascinating topic took up many more broad column-inches than any other. And the Committee was not pleased with what it elicited.

Mary Allen, on 30 October, poured oil on the flames. 'Genista McIntosh', she reminded the hearing, 'used the word "diffused" and "fragmented" to describe the management structures. I think she was slightly understating it. There are very few management processes at all at the Royal Opera House . . .' This, when I read it, was news to me and also, I imagine, to the colleagues who strove with me to produce top-class work while balancing the books in five out of nine years of my tenure, all of which had been under the Arts Council's close supervision. But Mary was grappling with the novel hazards of closure, and with the loss of the cashflow benefit that normally accrued in June and July from advance box-office for the autumn. And she had to explain her own actions in the April/May revolving-door shenanigans. But she did not need to say quite what she did, unless she meant that beneath the Executive Chairman in sole charge from May to September, there had been a vacuum. If you consult the diary Mary published of her days at the Opera House – *A House Divided* – the stress she says she was under makes it extraordinary that she managed to say anything coherent at all.

Suddenly, Chris Smith leapt into action on 3 November 1997, the day before he was due to appear before the Committee to answer questions on his own role in the revolving-door affair. Smith had had a bright idea, and briefed the press. He had invited Sir Richard Eyre to consider a proposal on the problems of lyric theatre in London, and the difficulty of funding two separate opera houses, the Coliseum and the Royal Opera House; this

UpROHr
Summer 1997

The Royal Opera House Magic Show

was that three companies, the Royal Opera, the Royal Ballet and English National Opera should crowd in under one roof at Covent Garden, share that House, and that single stage. The Coliseum might be sold off to pay the bills. This was an extraordinary proposal by any standards. It bore every sign of over-hasty preparation. It denied, in effect, individual identity to two distinctive opera companies, reneged on pledges made in the application to the Lottery and to private donors on future usage of the ROH and – particularly oddly from the minister who advocated a People's Opera – smacked down ENO's aspirations, devalued the user-friendly Coliseum and insulted its loyal audiences. What it would achieve, were it ever to be implemented, would be to let government off the hook, one day, of authorizing capital expenditure through the Lottery to renovate the Coliseum, nearing, perhaps within a decade, the end of its useful life.

Oddest of all was the way Smith's 'idea' was presented, more as a firm intention than as a kite flown at random, as was clear to every newspaper next day. Would Richard Eyre conceivably rubber-stamp that? On the previous Saturday evening, at a birthday party thrown by John Sainsbury in the National Gallery, I had talked to Richard, who seemed uncharacteristically ill at ease. He said, very oddly, to Gillian, that no one went to the Coliseum. Now I knew why. But I also knew he was no one's patsy. I was rung at 7am on Tuesday, 4 November by the *Today* programme. This was the news – would I comment? I swallowed, and said yes. At 8.20am James Naughtie put it to me: 'Well then?' 'This pig', I said, 'won't fly.' I explained why. Someone had to say it. ROH was much more politic, welcoming the inquiry. ENO was immediately up in arms; Paul Daniel led a brave stand against the move, with the enthusiastic backing of the ENO audience. George Harewood, ENO's father-figure, and I went on Channel 4 News and, given an easy ride by Jon Snow, pooh-poohed the notion: George suggested that only £2.5 million more a year for each House would solve most problems. (For the Opera House £10 million might have been nearer the mark.) The Secretary of State, in front of the Select Committee that morning, insisted his was only a proposal not a diktat; Richard Eyre was free to reject it. The Committee had from the newspapers received the other impression: 'Whilst you have set up the review, you have also announced its conclusion.' And later, when this was repudiated: 'Perhaps we have witnessed a very small U-turn in this Committee by the Secretary of State, I do not know . . .'

I went on *Newsnight*. Mark Fisher, Minister for the Arts, was in the studio. I watched in admiration as Kirsty Wark skilfully coped with a shuffled running-order that pushed us back and back to the end of the show. Mark Fisher put emphasis on the companies' touring, to ease the likely congestion at Covent Garden. I slammed into that on cost grounds alone. Later Tessa Blackstone told me I had been too hard on him. Then, with a minute to go, I asked if we could have an assurance that Richard Eyre would have a free hand. Could he, if he chose, reject rather than endorse the Secretary of State's proposal? Kirsty Wark relayed the question. 'Let us see what he comes up with,' said Mark Fisher, 'but we are convinced he supports our plan, and will make it work.' I could not believe my ears. Leaving the studio, I told Mark Fisher so. He claimed not to see the point. Next day Richard Eyre forced a repudiation, and not much later Mark Fisher, a pleasant, honest man, lost his job.

Grey Gowrie, next up to the Committee, added little, though he did mention, as the sort of expedient that might be turned to, the 'stabilization' grant of £4.5 million awarded to ENO to help it out of a hole. (ENO received £9 million for stabilization in all. None was available for ROH.) Gowrie was certain the Arts Council must not 'shadow-manage', must leave arts bodies to manage themselves; though the previous management of ROH did some outstanding things, they made a mess of the closure plans. But the last government had been taking cash out of the arts, and the new regime 'very regrettably has decided to stick to the previous government's planning totals, and the management of these organizations at international level on a continuously diminishing revenue cashflow is a nightmare and I do not know who can do it'. The Committee's Chairman established, to his satisfaction, that cash shortage was no alibi for failing to make sound closure plans.

Last that afternoon came Peter Chadlington, with a fresh canister of fuel to pour on the flames; with the summer's alarms behind him, it was insolvency time again. 'If we cannot get funds into the Opera House in the very short term, then the probability is that the House will become insolvent.' We knew this now, he said, because at last we had financial information. For twelve months there had been no Finance Director. (Whose fault was that? the Committee would want to know.) 'The figures were like catching a falling sword, and they changed every month in the most alarming way. So the answer is that unless we can find a solution on our own, then the House will become insolvent.' Gerald Kaufman, after these further alarms, was obviously aware that a solution could be imminent because he promised not to press Chadlington on its source. Sure enough, a moment later: 'I believe that there is a way through. It is going to be extremely difficult this week, and maybe over the next ten days, to get ourselves through it, but I think we have a small opportunity to get through it.' 'Are you able to expand on that? If you are not, I shall not press you.' 'Chairman, I would be grateful if you did not press me at this time.' This discourse seems to me an object lesson in how to get the worst of all possible worlds. Why mention insolvency if there is a possible way through? A way through was found. Whatever Chadlington's rationale for it, running the insolvency hare did not serve to deflect attention from the revolving door. The Committee worried away at its favourite bone: what had Chadlington told the Secretary of State about Mary Allen's arrival? Had he made clear that she would not be at the Opera House before September? There was just time for another reference to finance: 'I no longer feel that we are going to have some huge disaster falling out of the tree as far as the numbers are concerned, which was happening every day.' The session adjourned.

The questioning had been tough. The Report would be much tougher. No one could be in any doubt what to expect: Gerald Kaufman had made clear from the outset, in the Committee room and outside it, his feelings about the Royal Opera House. You might suppose he was duty bound to inquire with an open mind, or at least to encourage his colleagues to do so. But Gerald, with what *Private Eye* memorably called 'toxic conceitedness', put his own view, from the chair, first.

To Jenny McIntosh: 'When I go to the Royal Opera House . . . I feel as though I am intruding into a private club which is tolerating my presence with difficulty – maybe that is just me, of course.' To Mary Allen, first question: 'It is a shambles, is it not? It really is a shambles.' At Labatt's Apollo: 'Dancers', he told Mary Allen he had read in the paper, 'were falling over and injuring themselves.' Was this last sort of detail really matter for a Select Committee, or ought it to have concentrated on a bigger picture? Gerald also wrote an article in the *Spectator* on 'The Opera House and Me'. Public expressions of his personal view by the Chairman of a House of Commons Committee, some offered before evidence was taken, raised eyebrows. It was hard to see how to take the Committee's procedures seriously if the Chairman pronounced his verdict in advance.

The verdict, when it came on 3 December 1997, was cruel and

unforgiving. Angus Stirling and the Board and I were castigated for our closure planning, or lack of it, and for, somehow, proceeding for years without adequate financial information. The Arts Council had failed in letting us get away with it. Lord Chadlington should have appointed a new Finance Director with greater urgency. Mary Allen's convoluted explanation of her actions in May was entirely unconvincing; her conduct fell seriously below the standards to be expected of the principal officer of a public body. The Secretary of State should have paused and taken advice before waving through her appointment, in which officially he had no say. The current Board should dissolve itself, and the Chief Executive should resign, with immediate effect. The Secretary of State should appoint an administrator to take the place of the Board and the Chief Executive throughout closure. Should the Board and the Chief Executive decline to accept the Committee's recommendation that they resign, the Secretary of State should tell the Arts Council to cease payments of grant-in-aid. No one, surprisingly, was to be hanged, drawn and quartered. The language was so intemperate as to offend. John Major wrote to *The Times* and went on the *Today* programme to defend the Opera House. The Select Committee's first duty was to be fair; in his view, they had not been. The Committee charged that the lack of financial information of which Chadlington complained had been a feature of my time also. This was untrue. I wrote to *The Times* to point out that it was also defamatory of successive Chairmen and Boards above me, of Finance Directors under me, of their staff, of the Arts Council, and of the auditors.

Smarting under the lash, I was still disappointed that the Report said nothing about the fundamental problem: funding. At the end of a brief supplementary note of evidence I had submitted to the Committee in November, I had put this:

10. FUNDING

Finally, I urge the Committee not to pass over the funding question. Government will presently allow no increase. But the Committee, surely, can ask itself for how long the issue can be set aside.

Comparisons with Europe and with the USA are instructive. What the Royal Opera House is asked to do is emulate in quality several Continental houses, with high state subsidy, and New York, where the Met has an endowment of $150 million. The strain shows.

The UK scene is instructive too. It is no coincidence that, in the last decade, Welsh National Opera, Opera North, Scottish Opera and English National Opera have all, more than once, been in financial crisis, and have had to be rescued.

ROH is not alone.

The root cause is not management, but funding. The Committee could note that, and recommend that attention be paid to it.

The Committee paid no attention, stating at the outset: 'This has not been an inquiry into arts funding, and its justification: these matters were considered in 1996 by the National Heritage Committee. The Committee endorsed wholeheartedly state funding of the arts, which should be maintained at least at present levels in real terms.' Now the Committee did not consider whether that level was in any way adequate. It did, however, recommend lower ticket prices, as if those could be afforded without increased funds.

On the two charges levelled at my account, I am pretty clear that the financial governance of the House in my time was as good as could be managed, at least if we aimed at artistic excellence. If we had aimed much lower, we might of course have enjoyed a smoother financial ride. Management of an opera house, in any case, is to be tested both financially and artistically. On closure, I know of no better scheme available to us. The Committee proposed a false dichotomy: an expensive nomadic existence, against economy in a fixed base. But a principal reason we rejected the Lyceum as that base is that it would have cost us £7 million we could not find. Had we attempted to cut back further to save that sum, the level of activity we offered would not have deserved Arts Council core subsidy.

What *is* true is that at every stage my colleagues and I underestimated the real costs of closure. In 1994 we did not foresee how much we would lose in annual private revenue, given the counter-pull of the Development Appeal. And we seriously underestimated the fall-off in box-office outside the ROH. If we had asked for and got not £20 million but £30 million to help us through closure, our worst difficulties may have been averted. But there was then no chance of getting £30 million. The Committee's strictures on the closure plans, like Gowrie's, were unhelpful. They were aimed, with justice, at how those plans were formed; they were taken to describe the artistic results. But *Paul Bunyan* at Snape, *Turn of the Screw* at the Barbican, *Otello* and the *Ring* at the Royal Albert Hall, and *Der Freischütz, Mefistofele, Die Ägyptische Helena* and *Parsifal* were triumphs for those who saw or heard them. The ROH orchestra won every award for outstanding achievement in opera in 1998. Some shambles! Clement Crisp's praise, as the year ended, of Darcey Bussell's *Cinderella*, and others' appreciation of Sarah Wildor in *La fille mal gardée*, persuade me that the Royal Ballet, in spite of all vicissitudes, remains in good heart.

The Committee urged the Board of the Royal Opera House to resign. It did. Peter Chadlington was the first to fall, reluctantly, on his sword. He believed himself the victim, he wrote to sympathizers, of a monstrous practical joke played on him by life. The others gratefully, eagerly I would guess, also submitted their resignations, but agreed to stay on till a new Chairman was appointed and a new Board could be in place. Small thanks they got for long hours of dedicated labour and for all they had achieved together. Vivien Duffield, chairing the Appeal, and the composer Michael Berkeley stayed on, with the Secretary of State's blessing. So did Carolyn Newbigging, representing 15,000 Friends. The others prepared to depart. They had contemplated abdication all too often before.

Mary Allen, with her colleagues' and the Board's support, dug in her heels, though wounded. Part of a rescue package devised to help the Opera House come through imposed on her a quasi-administrator, Pelham Allen from Coopers & Lybrand. (This was put forward by the Floral Trust, of which I am a Trustee.) He was to work with her and to her, but was nevertheless empowered to insist on measures she might not contemplate herself. She found this extremely hard to stomach, as anyone would. But reluctantly, by the New Year she had come round. Chris Smith appointed – technically, he suggested and the rump of the old Board appointed – a new Chairman, Sir Colin Southgate of EMI. He got off to a wonderful start by telling the press that 'he did not want to sit next to someone in smelly trainers at the Royal Opera House'. But his fresh, big-business, realistic analysis of the House's finances would carry real weight.

Colin Southgate, we gather from her book, told Mary Allen that he was not sure whether he wanted to keep her on or not. Mary, who had been sunk in misery and gloom, now perked up. She decided to fire three key senior managers: Richard Hall, her new Finance Director; and my two henchmen, John Harrison, Technical Director, and Keith Cooper, Corporate Affairs Director. In her published diary for 25 February 1998, she wrote:

After the Board meeting Colin [Southgate] came into my office and we went through the press release about Richard and Keith. Mike [Morris], Judy [Grahame, new Head of PR] and Pelham [previously hated administrator, now putative Finance Director] were in my office, and once Colin had gone we all started planning for the next few weeks. It was the first time at the Royal Opera House I felt the sense of there being a proper team that could really achieve something.

The thought of herself and a new tight 'battle-team' managing the Royal Opera House was 'tremendously exciting'. Next day she arrived at the office at 6am and prepared to despatch her three victims. Letters of dismissal were ready; her new team stood in the wings. At 9.25am, with her first victim due, she started to sweat.

Richard Hall came in, sat down and was told he was out. 'We started to talk about it but he then decided he didn't wish to continue the discussion. He took the letter and left.'

John Harrison, when found, 'went white and suddenly his skin looked as though it was stretched over his skull much more tightly than it had been before. He picked up his letter and said, "Well, that's it, then, isn't it," and walked out.'

'Mike [Morris] and I', the Lady Macbeth of Floral Street continues, 'relaxed and waited, and waited some more, and then at 10.30 Keith came in, and I said the same thing to Keith as I had said to Richard . . . and he could barely speak and took the letter and left the room. Mike said, "He was very, very angry".'

After lunch she tried to tell Bernard Haitink what she'd done. ' "Bernard, can I have a quick word" and he said, "No, no, no. I am about to rehearse", so I said, "Look, Keith Cooper's going and Richard Hall is going – don't forget you heard it first from me, and not from the press."'

John Harrison did not go. He stood his ground, appealed to the Chairman, and is now Commercial Director.

In the course of agreeing what the Royal Opera House would submit as evidence to Richard Eyre's review, the new Chairman had by now decided on further change. He wanted, he thought then, a leading artistic figure in charge of the ROH, as intendant. After a Board meeting on 25 March, Mary Allen herself had to go, leaving Pelham Allen in charge, the third Chief Executive, albeit a stop-gap, in fifteen months.

Southgate spent the spring and summer getting to grips with his problems. The wait for Richard Eyre's Report stopped the Appeal short and delayed forward planning. When it came, though, on 30 June 1998, the Eyre Report expressed a profound distaste for the ethos of the Royal Opera House I managed, but it effectively kyboshed the three-in-a-bed option which the Secretary of State had proposed. And, after severe strictures on Board attitudes to fiscal responsibility, Eyre recommended – surprise, surprise – increased funding 'if government truly wanted to sustain the lyric arts at international standard'. The Secretary of State's proposal that ENO, the Royal Ballet and the Royal Opera share the new Covent Garden theatre, which had called the entire future into question, was dead in the water.

I summarize the events that followed. Colin Southgate looked at the accounts, and at the future. Pledging drastic change, he wrote to the Secretary of State saying he calculated that the ROH needed an extra £15 million a year to function in the new House. Someone at the ROH leaked the letter. Chris Smith was not amused. But a deal was impending: if the ROH took drastic measures to cut costs, and pledged to charge lower prices and increase outreach activity, increased funds *would* be forthcoming. A series of press releases from the Opera House now announced that change was on the way; indeed, if it were not forthcoming, the Opera House would close completely in its present form in January 1999: 'BOARD DECIDES TO CLOSE AND START AGAIN', it announced on 9 September 1998. Mike Morris, against the deadline of 26 October, started urgent union negotiations. The threat of complete shut-down was used to force agreement on more flexible working arrangements, and much tougher terms of employment. The intention was part cosmetic; these changes would serve as an excuse for government to find increased funds. The orchestra was not exempt from change. Bernard Haitink offered his resignation. After *Götterdämmerung* at the Albert Hall, he invited the audience to tell government to do something. A further press release, before October's end, proclaimed success: 'ROYAL OPERA HOUSE ACHIEVES FIRST STEP IN THREE-PART SURVIVAL PLAN'. The Board had insisted on employing chorus, orchestra, stage crew for nine months of the year only, not twelve. It sought the same reduced activity for the dancers, but reneged when it realized that would kill the company.

On 16 September 1998, the Opera House had announced the appointment of an American, Michael Kaiser, as Executive Director. An expert at fundraising, he had successfully 'turned round' the fortunes of

American Ballet Theater, and advised other companies. On 17 December the Arts Council, grudging every penny, and under fierce pressure from the Secretary of State and donors to the Appeal, announced new funding for the ROH: £1 million more in April 1999, a further £4 million more in April 2000, and not less than that in April 2001. Not the additional £15 million thought necessary by Southgate, but enough to tempt a new management to keep going.

On 21 December 1998 came this: 'THE ROYAL OPERA HOUSE MOVES FORWARD'. Bernard Haitink, who in these matters makes the Grand Old Duke of York look resolute, had rescinded his resignation. (But he had won his point.) He would remain as Music Director till 2002. New agreements had been reached with ROH unions. The ROH Development Appeal – the building itself kept rising; only the Appeal had ground to a halt – would resume, with the committed support of the existing major donors. And the Royal Opera, which had cancelled its bookings at Sadler's Wells and was not going to perform at all from January till December 1999, would now repeat *Paul Bunyan* and give some Verdi concerts, in lieu of a proper Festival, in 1999.

The nub of this settlement was that government, after years of refusing to admit that the funding issue was serious, was granting a 33 per cent increase, and exacting a price. This was part cosmetic, part substance. The staff would receive twelve months' salary for their nine months' engagements. So they were not out of pocket. But they had all agreed more flexible and productive contracts, and would receive no overtime. In addition, for the future, all agreed to provide rights in the UK television transmission of any performance, opera or ballet, without additional fees. (However, to what extent this will increase TV coverage will be up to the broadcasters.) All this represents an important breakthrough by Mike Morris, armed with the nuclear weapon of threatened close-down.

Executive Director Michael Kaiser has made an excellent impression, avoiding recrimination and retrospection, focusing positively on the attractions of the new House, now filling out and taking internal shape as it nears completion, on time and within budget. 'The more I see', Kaiser has stated, 'of the Covent Garden development, the more I am aware that this building, as well as the artists it houses, will provide the most tremendous asset for the whole country.' It will, too. On 16 February 1999, the topping-out ceremony filled the Floral Hall with happy anticipation. I was proud to be there. Kaiser and the Board have appointed

Antonio Pappano as Music Director to succeed Bernard Haitink in 2002. Pappano is a live-wire bundle of energy, a fine conductor who will be a positive force for good. Financially, too, things are looking up. The Royal Opera House's accumulated deficit has been cleared, as I forecast it might, by utilizing the excess proceeds of buoyant property sales. Astonishingly, the Arts Council in 1999 provided the ROH core grant against minimal operatic activity. That core grant, from 2000, is substantially increased.

At whatever cost, we kept up artistic standards through the 1990s, carrying forward a deficit if we had to. We performed always to our uttermost. We imposed privation on the staff. We plunged into the quagmire of closure without a full measure of the financial depths to which we might sink. We suffered the sting of the Select Committee's invective. The end result is that the companies, better funded, survive to perform in a great new House which accommodates the ballet company, has modernized the stage, adds a second auditorium, will welcome audiences to handsome spaces and will enliven the Covent Garden cityscape. The agony will have been worthwhile. At several points on that decade's odyssey the House could have declared itself bankrupt, as Chairman Chadlington came perilously close to doing. What would that have achieved? Disaster for the companies, for the development, for the public. As it is, we have something wonderful to look forward to. By calling on all available resource – that is what it comes to – the House has found a way through to a new future.

THEATRE ROYAL,

Covent-Garden.

SATURDAY, NOVEMBER 29, 1828.

IT being the determination of the Managers of this Theatre, not to have it Re-Opened until the most satisfactory Report has been made from the Persons employed to remove the Gasometers, and such Report not having yet been offered ----It is most respectfully announced to the Public, *that NO PLAY will be acted on Monday,*---but on that day it will be positively stated on which night the Theatre will RE-OPEN.

Printed by W. Reynolds, 9, Denmark-Court, Strand.

20

CODA

At the memorial service at Westminster Abbey for Sir Geraint Evans, the great Welsh baritone, every major Welsh operatic talent took part. Dame Gwyneth Jones sang twice. One performance stood out. Bryn Terfel, a mere twenty-six years old, cheekily sang Falstaff's monologue. He was telling us that what Geraint could do, he could do better, and that opera's future was bright. Bryn Terfel has accepted to sing the lead role in Verdi's *Falstaff* when the Royal Opera House, reborn, re-opens.

The old Victorian auditorium gleams and sparkles in its new gilded coat; sight-lines have been improved; leg-room has eased; wonder of wonders, air-conditioning has been installed. At the push of a button scenery will move from side-stage to main stage. The higher fly-tower will hang the cloths, if necessary, for two complete productions; two performances on Saturdays and matinées on Sundays will one day be routine. Audiences will no longer be segregated; an escalator links the loggia bar, with views west across the London roofscape, to a new welcoming space, the Floral Hall.

The Royal Ballet will, at last, come into its own at Covent Garden. One ballet studio will seat audiences of 200, for workshops, open rehearsals, minimalist performance. The House will boast a fully equipped second auditorium, seating 400. In this, when funds allow, there will be fully staged small-scale work.

The building is entered both from Bow Street and from the Piazza. The porticoed colonnades of Dixon's and Jones's scheme adorn the cityscape. This is not a self-regarding marvel of modern design, but an elegant and appropriate link between past and present. (There will be no car parking for anyone, neither staff nor patrons. Something will have to be done about that.)

The Royal Opera House's financial fix will continue much as before. The House is committed, as part of its settlement with government – the Arts Council squeezed into insignificance in the middle – to reducing seat prices. The top, 'standard', ticket for opera will, we are told, be £100, bringing the average down with it. Audiences will be duly grateful; every seat will be sold, and queue rationing reinstated. But the House will lose income, which will have to be made up somehow.

The Secretary of State for Culture, Media and Sport, Chris Smith, announced in 1998 the biggest ever increase in funding for the arts in Britain. This language flatters to deceive. The sum secured from the Chancellor was helpful, but unremarkable: £290 million of new funds spread over three years, and covering galleries and museums as well as the performing arts, will take arts funding overall back to the level enjoyed in 1992, when every arts institution struggled. The ROH Board would like to think that funding will rise by a further £5 million in 2001. The reality may be that funding for 2001/2002 will be at a standstill. If it is, public subsidy to the two ROH companies will represent under 40 per cent of the House's total income, about half the proportion found in Vienna or Paris. This is where we came in.

No Arts Minister is likely to secure Treasury backing to assess each arts body deemed crucial to Britain's cultural well-being, agree its budget and meet its need. The Royal Opera House will depend, in the future as in the past, on a spread of funding sources. But half the Opera House's revenue should be provided as government grant-in-aid. That is a feasible target; we should press government towards it. It is more than is presently on offer; less than obtained twenty years ago. Peter Palumbo, when he left the Arts Council's chairmanship, told me he thought the Opera House should get 75 per cent of its funding from the state. 'Peter,' I said, 'I will settle for 65 per cent.' My successors will have to settle for far less.

Is there a chance of anything better? If government were serious about low ticket prices, there would have to be. So long as the Opera House earns £20 million at the box-office, it will cost £10 million a year more to slash ticket prices by half.

How much importance we attach to making opera and ballet accessible to all depends on what sort of society we believe ourselves to be. For decades Britain's spend on the arts, as a proportion of public expenditure, has been the lowest in Europe – 0.24 per cent, less than a farthing in the pound. France's and Germany's were nearer 0.75 per cent. Lottery funds, so far for capital projects only, alter the picture. If government could keep its sticky fingers off Lottery arts funding, and not winkle it away to spend on health and education, that would make lasting improvement possible. The arts' share of Lottery proceeds will reduce from one-fifth to one-sixth; the proportion is fixed for ten years.

London has the potential to excel. That potential is unfulfilled: the V&A has galleries closed; London's orchestras struggle to survive; the Royal Shakespeare Company is in deep trouble; the National Theatre is constrained in its repertory; even the superbly run National Gallery cannot keep open all the hours it would wish, or expand its educational work. The arts in Britain under-perform; arts administration is a survival course, with casualties. It could all be different if we were to commit to spend just 1 per cent of public expenditure, one penny in the pound, on the arts.

Britpop can take care of itself – pop and rock and blockbuster musicals easily reach mass audiences. But Britain can do better for its citizens. We should use every resource we can to foster art which enriches our lives. The best news of early 1999 was that government would act to restore the cuts in music-teaching provision in schools that we suffered during the Thatcher years. If more children make music, more will come to love it. I once heard, at Fairfield Hall, Croydon, a concert by the Leicestershire Schools Symphony Orchestra; they played a new work by Michael Tippett, in his presence. The standard was exemplary, the result enthralling. Leicestershire then had Directors of Music and of Education who aimed high. More should follow where they led.

Gaudy, high-street satisfactions, conspicuously consumed, obscure important facts: more people go to arts events each year than to football matches. As the population ages, men and women will demand more fulfilled leisure lives. Meeting their needs is a proper priority for any would-be centrist party.

To urge this goal is to affirm certain values. I affirm them: Keats *is* a better poet than Bob Dylan; so are Wordsworth and Auden and Seamus Heaney. Schubert's songs and song-cycles, which move us profoundly, deserve to last longer than the Beatles, and will. Britain's full well-being in the next century depends on all of us being able to exercise a variety of choices, enjoying opera and ballet among them. By exacting effort over three decades, the new Royal Opera House has, deviously and deter-minedly, been brought into being for our delight. Petipa and Fokine, Balanchine and Robbins, Ashton and MacMillan will flourish there. So will Mozart and Rossini, Wagner and Verdi, Britten and Janáček, Berg and Birtwistle, Weir, Turnage and Adès. The best is yet to come.

The moon rises over the Herne Oak in Windsor Forest. Falstaff fails to persuade Alice to get her knickers down. At the end of Verdi's master-piece Sir John, mocked and harried, dowsed in the Thames, pinched, pricked and tormented in the great wood at midnight, accepts his fate and leads the cast in a round; honour is dented, dignity cast down, but life goes on. 'Tutto nel mondo è burla': all the world's a joke, we are only here to be laughed at. The Royal Opera House too, a source of wit in others, brought, we are told, to its knees, has risen again, and opens its doors to us.

APPENDIX: PERFORMANCES
1988 TO 1997

Listed here are the pieces performed by the three Royal Opera House companies during the nine seasons from September 1988 to July 1997. New productions are shown in bold. Performances by the Royal Opera and the Royal Ballet on tour are not listed, nor are those by visiting companies.

1988/89 SEASON

The Royal Opera

Turandot
Die Entführung aus dem Serail
Das Rheingold
Madama Butterfly
Manon
Rigoletto
Semele
Die Fledermaus
Un re in ascolto
Così fan tutte

Don Carlo
La clemenza di Tito
Albert Herring
Il trovatore
Der Rosenkavalier
Le nozze di Figaro
Cavalleria Rusticana/I Pagliacci
L'italiana in Algeri
Die Zauberflöte

The Royal Ballet

Ondine
Rhapsody/**The Trial of**
   Prometheus/'Still Life' at the
   Penguin Café
The Sleeping Beauty
Apollo/Don Quixote pas de deux/
   The Spirit of Fugue/A Month in
   the Country

Cinderella
Romeo and Juliet
Capriccio for Piano and
   Orchestra/Enigma
   Variations/Rhapsody
Swan Lake
La Bayadère

Sadler's Wells Royal Ballet

Les Sylphides
Petrushka
Theme and Variations
Concerto barocco
The Edge of Silence
Pineapple Poll
Giselle
Bastet
The Snow Queen

Choros
Hobson's Choice
The Sleeping Beauty
La fille mal gardée
Lazarus
Aurus
Those Unheard
The Two Pigeons
Swan Lake

1989/90 SEASON

The Royal Opera

Rigoletto
Die Walküre
Peter Grimes
Medée
Idomeneo
Der Freischütz
Otello
Prince Igor
Don Pasquale

Elektra
L'elisir d'amore
Die Meistersinger von Nürnberg
La Cenerentola
Il trovatore
The Cunning Little Vixen
La bohème
Guillaume Tell
Arabella

The Royal Ballet

La Bayadère
Rubies (Capriccio for Piano and
 Orchestra)/Other
 Dances/Piano/Requiem
Rubies/Grand pas
 classique/Piano/Requiem
Swan Lake
A Wedding Bouquet/My Brother,
 My Sisters/Frankenstein,
 The Modern Prometheus
The Prince of the Pagodas
Cinderella

Laurentia/La Fille mal gardée
Giselle
Galanteries/Other
 Dances/Pursuit/Gloria
A Month in the Country/Song of the
 Earth
Romeo and Juliet
**The Planets/Enclosure/Farewell
 pas de deux from Winter
 Dreams/'Still Life'**
 at the Penguin Café

Sadler's Wells Royal Ballet

Hobson's Choice
Swan Lake
Divertimento No. 15
The Dream
Solitaire
Danses concertantes
Auras
Those Unheard
Façade
Les Sylphides

The Two Pigeons
Allegri diversi
Tchaikovsky pas de deux
Meridian of Youth
Elite Syncopations
La fille mal gardée
Paramour
Flowers of the Forest
Inscape

1990/91 SEASON

The Royal Opera

Turandot
Siegfried
Attila
Il barbiere di Siviglia
Fidelio
Die Fledermaus
Capriccio
Götterdämmerung
Samson et Dalila

Die Zauberflöte
Boris Godunov
Carmen
Tosca
Gawain
Les contes d'Hoffmann
La Cenerentola
Orfeo ed Euridice
La fanciulla del West

The Royal Ballet

The Prince of the Pagodas
The Planets/Enclosure/Elite
　Syncopations
La Bayadère
Stravinsky Violin Concerto/
　Bloodlines/Raymonda Act III
The Nutcracker
Manon

Danses concertantes/**Winter**
　Dreams/Raymonda Act III
Agon/A Month in the
　Country/Requiem
Cyrano
Les Biches/Scènes de ballet/Les Noces
Raymonda Act III/A Month in the
　Country/Elite Syncopations

Birmingham Royal Ballet

Theme and Variations
Brahms Handel Variations
Jazz Calendar
The Sleeping Beauty
La Fin du jour
Symphony in Three Movements
Elite Syncopations
The Nutcracker
Swan Lake
Façade
Hobson's Choice

Airs
Sacred Symphony
Valses nobles et sentimentales
Les Rendezvous
Pavane pas de deux
License My Roving Hands
Paquita
La fille mal gardée
Inscape
Jazz Calendar

1991/92 SEASON

The Royal Opera

Rigoletto
Das Rheingold
Die Walküre
Siegfried
Götterdämmerung
Les Huguenots
Simon Boccanegra
Mitridate, re di Ponto
Le nozze di Figaro
Così fan tutte
Don Giovanni
Les contes d'Hoffmann

Death in Venice
William Tell
The Fiery Angel
L'elisir d'amore
I Puritani
La bohème
Salome
Der fliegende Holländer
Samson et Dalila
Don Pasquale
Il viaggio a Rheims

Wembley Arena: Turandot

The Royal Ballet

Cyrano
Les Sylphides/**La Luna**/Thaïs pas de
    deux/Tchaikovsky pas de
    deux/Winter Dreams
Agon/**Stoics quartet/Present
    Histories/Symphony in C**
La Fille mal gardée
The Nutcracker
Giselle

Scenès de ballet/Monotones/**In the
    Middle, Somewhat Elevated**
Manon
Stravinsky Violin Concerto/**The Judas
    Tree**/Symphony in C
Les Sylphides/A Month in the
    Country/Elite Syncopations
Romeo and Juliet

Birmingham Royal Ballet

Hobson's Choice
Divertimento No. 15
Petrushka
Choreartium
Les Sylphides
The Burrow
Le Corsaire grand pas de deux
Five Tangos
Pavane pas de deux

Swan Lake
The Nutcracker
Giselle
Galanteries
Card Game
Dark Horizons
Elite Syncopations
Romeo and Juliet

1992/93 SEASON

The Royal Opera

Tosca	Turandot
I Capuleti e i Montecchi	**La damnation de Faust**
Fidelio	**Pelléas et Mélisande**
Porgy and Bess	Jenufa
Otello	La bohème
Die Frau ohne Schatten	Attila
Madama Butterfly	The Cunning Little Vixen
Alcina	Don Giovanni
Stiffelio	**Eugene Onegin**
Il barbiere di Siviglia	

The Royal Ballet

Swan Lake	The Firebird/Tombeaux/In the Middle,
Mayerling	Somewhat Elevated
The Dream/Tales of Beatrix Potter	**Don Quixote**
Cinderella	Ballet imperial/'Still Life' at the
Apollo/The Judas Tree/Symphony in C	Penguin Café/Gloria
The Sleeping Beauty	Prodigal Son/**La Ronde**/Checkmate

Birmingham Royal Ballet

Flowers of the Forest	Twilight
Symphonic Variations	Pavane pas de deux
The Green Table	Façade
The Snow Queen	The Sleeping Beauty
Romeo and Juliet	**Street**
The Nutcracker	**Choreartium**
Paramour	Hobson's Choice

1993/94 SEASON

The Royal Opera

Madama Butterfly
L'italiana in Algeri
Die Meistersinger von Nürnberg
Mitridate, rè di Ponto
Eugene Onegin
Die Zauberflöte
Tosca
Carmen
Elektra
Chérubin

Rigoletto
Kát̓a Kabanová
Un ballo in maschera
Gawain
Le nozze di Figaro
Fedora
Mosè in Egitto
Aida
Manon
La fanciulla del West

The Royal Ballet

Fanfare/If This is Still a Problem/
    Herman Schmerman/Different
    Drummer
Romeo and Juliet
Ballet imperial/Tales of Beatrix Potter
The Nutcracker
Mayerling
Dream/Tombeaux/A Month in the
    Country

The Sleeping Beauty – World
    Premiere in USA
Don Quixote
Danses concertantes/Winter
    Dreams/Fearful Symmetries
Tombeaux/A Month in the
    Country/Renard

Birmingham Royal Ballet

Sylvia
The Sleeping Beauty
Street
The Dream
Elite Syncopations
The Nutcracker
Serenade
Job

The Green Table
La fille mal gardée
Fall River Legend
Swan Lake
Brahms Handel Variations
Prodigal Son
Symphony in Three Movements

1994/95 SEASON

The Royal Opera

Turandot
La Cenerentola
Das Rheingold
Die Walküre
Roméo et Juliette
La traviata
Otello
Così fan tutte
Der Rosenkavalier
La bohème
Salome

Siegfried
Peter Grimes
Un ballo in maschera
King Arthur
Billy Budd
Stiffelio
I due Foscari
Simon Boccanegra
Simon Boccanegra 1857 - Concert
    Performance
Aroldo - Concert Performance

The Royal Ballet

The Sleeping Beauty
La Valse/Birthday
    Offering/Sylvia/Symphonic
    Variations/**Daphnis and Chloë**
Fearful Symmetries/Symphony in C/
    Herman Schmerman
Dream/Air/La Chatte/Thaïs pas de
    deux/Raymonda/Façade
Cinderella

Swan Lake
Giselle
Romeo and Juliet
Danses concertantes/Ebony
    Concerto/Duo concertant/Petrushka
Firstext/**Steptext**/La Ronde/
    Rhapsody
La Valse/Thaïs pas de deux/
    Rhapsody/Daphnis and Chloë

Birmingham Royal Ballet

Galanteries
Enigma Variations
Le Tricorne
Romeo and Juliet
La fille mal gardée
The Nutcracker
Street
Prodigal Son
Pineapple Poll

Coppélia
Theme and Variations
Pillar of Fire
Libramenta
Choreartium
Swan Lake
Serenade
The Nutcracker
Las Hermanas

1995/96 SEASON

The Royal Opera

Le nozze di Figaro
Arianna
Tosca
Götterdämmerung
Mathis der Maler
Fedora
Aida
The Midsummer Marriage

Samson et Dalila
Semele
La traviata
Arabella
Nabucco
Die Entführung aus dem Serail
Don Carlos
Giovanna d'Arco

The Royal Ballet

Swan Lake
Manon
Apollo/Sideshow pas de deux/Duo
  concertant/Fearful Symmetries
Mr Worldly Wise
Les Patineurs/Tales of Beatrix Potter
Peter and the Wolf/Tales of Beatrix
  Potter
The Sleeping Beauty
Rhapsody/**Dances with Death**/

Now Languorous, Now Wild/
  The Invitation
Giselle
Illuminations/Symphonic
  Variations/The Dream
Anastasia
Rhapsody/Le Corsaire-Grand Pas
  Classique-Tchaikovsky pas de
  deux-Farewell pas de deux/
  Herman Schmerman

Birmingham Royal Ballet

Hobson's Choice
Birthday Offering
Carmina Burana
The Nutcracker
Agon
The Cage

Far from the Madding Crowd
Mozartiana
Mozart Mass in C minor
'Still Life' at the Penguin Café
Theme and Variations
La fille mal gardée

1996/97 SEASON

The Royal Opera

La bohème
Das Rheingold
Die Walküre
Siegfried
Götterdämmerung
Don Giovanni
Tosca
Turandot
Chérubin
Palestrina
Lohengrin
Così fan tutte

Die Meistersinger von Nürnberg
Salome
Otello
L'elisir d'amore
Elektra
Káťa Kabanová
Simon Boccanegra 1881
Simon Boccanegra 1857
Rigoletto
Macbeth – Concert Performance
Oberto – Concert Performance

The Royal Ballet

La Valse/Pavane/La Fin du
  jour/Daphnis and Chloë
Romeo and Juliet
Prince of the Pagodas
Steptext/**Two-Part Invention/**
  Winter Dreams
Cinderella
Swan Lake
The Sleeping Beauty

Consort Lessons/**Push Comes to
  Shove**/Judas Tree
La Bayadère
Anastasia
Judas Tree/**Amores**/Symphony in C
Don Quixote
Push Comes to Shove/**The Talisman**
  pas de deux/Symphony in C

Birmingham Royal Ballet

Agon
Carmina Burana
Swan Lake
Les patineurs
Le baiser de la fée
The Nutcracker Sweeties

The Nutcracker
The Sleeping Beauty
The Dream/Songs of the Earth
Bright Young Things
Tombeaux/Sanctum/Nutcracker
  Sweeties

INDEX